NELSON
MANDELA

IN HIS OWN WORDS

NELSON MANDELA

IN HIS OWN WORDS
From Freedom to the Future

Tributes and speeches

Edited by
Kader Asmal
David Chidester
Wilmot James

LITTLE, BROWN

A *Little, Brown* Book

Published in Great Britain in 2003
by Little, Brown

First published in South Africa in 2003
by Jonathan Ball Publishers (Pty) Ltd

A CIP catalogue record for this book
is available from the British Library

ISBN 0 316 72738 5

Printed and bound in Great Britain by
Clays Ltd, St Ives plc

Little, Brown
An imprint of
Time Warner Books UK
Brettenham House
Lancaster Place
London WC2E 7EN

www.TimeWarnerBooks.co.uk

CONTENTS

11. HEROES   441

A Self-Effacing Hero, *by Ahmed Kathrada*   443

12. PEACE   497

Promoting Peace and Practising Diplomacy,
by James A. Joseph   499

CONTRIBUTORS   547

INDEX   549

ACKNOWLEDGEMENTS

First and foremost, we pay tribute to Mr Nelson Mandela, the heart and soul of this book, for providing its substantial content, the record of speeches he delivered from the mid-twentieth century to the beginning of the twenty-first. For granting permission to edit these speeches, we thank the Nelson Mandela Foundation, with special appreciation for the help provided by Jakes Gerwel and John Samuel. Proceeds from this book will go towards supporting the work of the Nelson Mandela Foundation.

For deepening our understanding of the lasting legacy of Nelson Mandela, we are grateful to all of the contributors who generously shared their insights by writing introductions to the chapters. The list of contributors is truly extraordinary: Bill Cosby, Jakes Gerwel, James A Joseph, Ahmed Kathrada, Graça Machel, Miriam Makeba, Cyril Ramaphosa, Mamphela Ramphele, Albie Sachs, Olive Shisana, F van Zyl Slabbert, and Desmond Tutu. We thank them all, as we also thank Adrian Hadland for his biographical essay on Nelson Mandela, Fintan O'Toole for offering us his remarkable reflections on Nelson Mandela's release from prison, and UN Secretary-General Kofi A Annan and William J Clinton, 42nd President of the United States, for providing forewords for this book.

In turning this book from an idea into a reality, we are grateful to Jonathan Ball, our publisher, who clearly captured the vision we had for this book. We extend special thanks to our editor, Barry Streek, who was an active collaborator on this project from beginning to end. Supporting our editorial work, an informal editorial committee of Pam Barron, Adrian Hadland, Bronwen Levy and Michael Morris offered valuable advice, counsel and words of encouragement. We thank Rodica Mischiu of the office of Susan Berresford of the Ford Foundation for assistance. During the production of the manuscript, our base of operations was the Social Cohesion and Integration

Research Programme of the Human Sciences Research Council (HSRC). We thank the HSRC for creating such an enabling environment.

Kader Asmal
David Chidester
Wilmot James
Cape Town, July 2003

FOREWORD

KOFI A ANNAN

Secretary-General of the United Nations

People often ask me what difference one person can make in the face of injustice, conflict, human rights violations, mass poverty and disease. I answer by citing the courage, tenacity, dignity and magnanimity of Nelson Mandela.

I cite his lifelong struggle against apartheid, and his steadfast refusal to compromise his beliefs during long years of incarceration. I cite his inspired leadership, upon his release, in the peaceful transition to a genuine, multiracial, multi-party democracy firmly founded on a Constitution protecting fundamental human rights. I cite his efforts, as President of the Republic of South Africa, to create the political, economic and social conditions needed to bring Africa the peace and prosperity it needs and deserves.

Above all, I cite his ready willingness to embrace and reconcile with those who persecuted him the most, and the grace with which he stuck to his promise to serve only one presidential term of office.

His contribution did not end there. To this day, Madiba remains probably the single most admired, most respected international figure in the entire world. He continues to inspire millions of people and several generations throughout the globe, by continuing to fight for reconciliation before recrimination, healing before bitterness, peace before conflict; by fighting for health, for education, for the right of every child to have a better start in life; by spelling out the right and duty of not only South Africa, but of *all* Africa, to take charge of its own future and fate. As he said in one of the many eloquent speeches included in this book, 'Africa has long traversed past a mind-set that seeks to heap all blame on the past and on others.'

This book is a fitting tribute to Madiba on his 85th birthday. But the only adequate way in which we can truly express our gratitude for his lifetime's contribution is for every one of us to work every day to seek to follow his example. If just one small part of what he has sought to achieve for his fellow human beings is translated into reality, if we live up to just one fraction of the standards he has set for himself, then Africa, and the world, will be a far, far better place.

FOREWORD

WILLIAM J CLINTON

42nd President of the United States

I love and respect President Mandela very much, not least for his unfailing kindness and generosity to Hillary, Chelsea and me.

He has taught us so much about so many things. Perhaps the greatest lesson, especially for young people, is that, while bad things do happen to good people, we still have the freedom and the responsibility to decide how to respond to injustice, cruelty and violence and how they will affect our spirits, hearts and minds.

In his 27 years of imprisonment, Mandela endured physical and emotional abuse, isolation and degradation. Somehow, his trials purified his spirit and clarified his vision, giving him the strength to be a free man even behind bars, and to remain free of anger and hatred when he was at last released.

That freedom is reflected in the way he governed as President, bringing those who had oppressed him into his administration and doing everything he could to bring people together across racial, economic and political lines, and trying to get all South Africans to make the same 'long walk to freedom' that has made his own life so extraordinary.

The best gift we can give him on this special occasion is to persist in our own struggle to forgive those who have trespassed against us and to work, every day, to tear down the barriers that divide us.

At 85, President Mandela is still building bridges, especially those that unite us in the battle against HIV/Aids, which he calls an 'even heavier and greater fight' than the struggle against apartheid.

Through times darker than most people ever will endure in their own lives, President Mandela saw a better and brighter future for himself and for his country. Now, he gives us hope that our work to eradicate HIV/Aids from the world is not in vain, and that one day, this awful scourge will exist alongside apartheid only in the history books.

Mandela's enduring legacy is that, under a crushing burden of oppression he saw through differences, discrimination and destruction to embrace our common humanity. Thanks to his life and work, the rest of us are closer to embracing it too.

INTRODUCTION

KADER ASMAL, DAVID CHIDESTER AND WILMOT JAMES

On 18 July 2003, Mr Nelson Mandela is 85 years old – or 85 years young – and still with us, still going strong. As a tribute to Madiba, and as a testimony to his lasting legacy, we are presenting him with this book as a birthday gift. To the readers of this book, who share in that legacy, we want to welcome you to the celebration.

Our book honours an individual imbued with great ideals of reason, imagination, justice, and freedom, with the depth of moral character formed by the toughest of circumstances, able yet, as the philosopher Immanuel Kant once had it, to 'treat humanity, whether in thine own person or in that of any other, in every case as an end withal, never as means only'.

Based on selections from Nelson Mandela's speeches, this book provides a lively, memorable profile of his enduring commitment to freedom and reconciliation, democracy and development, culture and diversity, and the flourishing of all the people of South Africa, Africa, and the world. The book highlights Madiba's ongoing concerns for children, education, and health; it features his own tributes to South African heroes, such as Steve Biko, Oliver Tambo, and Walter Sisulu; and it concludes with his significant contributions to international peace building. In this book, we will be able to recall and reaffirm the solid foundation that Nelson Mandela established for building a sustainable future.

The chapters are introduced by leading national and international figures in the fields of politics, diplomacy, development, education, health, religion, culture, and the creative and performing arts. In these introductory essays, authors pay tribute to Nelson Mandela's achievements, animating their accounts with personal memories, stories, and reflections, but they also creatively engage the principles at stake in each of these areas. In the light of the legacy of Nelson Mandela, they identify the building blocks for a South African future.

We are well aware that the praises of Nelson Mandela have often been sung. He has been honoured, awarded, feted, and revered all over the world, by international political leaders and ordinary people, in an unprecedented, sustained chorus of love and respect. Enraptured by all this praise singing, we might sometimes forget the long struggle and the dark days, the painful losses and the hard negotiations, which made this joyful music possible.

Also, we might find ourselves taking for granted the truly remarkable consensus, across every conceivable divide, that has greeted the achievements of Nelson Mandela. As we saw in the 1990s, the presidents of the United States and Cuba, who were politically divided on many matters, nevertheless agreed on singing Madiba's praises. Here is the former US President Bill Clinton:

> For a long time the name Nelson Mandela has stood for the quest for freedom. His spirit never bent before the injustice of his 27 years of imprisonment. Apartheid could not silence him. . . . After his long struggle, Nelson Mandela found in himself the strength to reach out to others; to build up instead of tear down. He led his country forward, always choosing reconciliation over division. This is the miracle of the new South Africa. Time and again, President Mandela showed real wisdom and rose above bitterness. President Mandela and the South African people, both black and white, have inspired others around the world.[1]

Recognising Nelson Mandela as 'the symbol of freedom for the world', President Clinton sang his praises, identifying personal qualities of strength, determination, and wisdom that bore profound political significance. In similar terms, the President of the Republic of Cuba, Fidel Castro, addressing the South African Parliament in 1998, began his speech by singing the praises of Nelson Mandela. Here is President Fidel Castro:

> Nelson Mandela will not go down in history for the 27 consecutive years that he lived imprisoned without ever renouncing his ideas. He will go down in history because he was able to draw from his soul all the poison accumulated by such an unjust punishment. He will be remembered for his generosity and for his wisdom at the time of an already uncontainable victory, when he knew how to lead so brilliantly his self-sacrificing and heroic people, aware that the new South Africa would never be built on foundations of hatred and revenge.[2]

So, here is a mystery: We hear similar praises coming from different positions along the global political spectrum. In both cases, however, Nelson Mandela is recognised for his distinctive merger of the personal and the political. Political transformation in South Africa was enabled by Nelson Mandela's personal capacity to purge any poison of hatred or revenge from his soul, to rise above bitterness, to demonstrate a generosity of spirit, and to reach out to others, all the while remaining true, even under the harshest conditions of injustice, imprisonment, and oppression, to his political principles.

Those principles, Nelson Mandela would argue, were not his alone. They were the shared achievement of a political movement, the African National Congress. As his favourite self-description, he often has explained that he is first and foremost a loyal member of the ANC. Still, as Presidents Clinton and Castro recognised, the political assumed a distinctively personal quality in Nelson Mandela. He proved, as Secretary-General of the United Nations Kofi Annan observes, in his Foreword to this book, that one individual, with such courage and tenacity, with such dignity and magnanimity, can actually make a difference in political struggles.

These praise singers, you might say, are just politicians, engaging in political rhetoric. But real singers, real artists, poets, and musicians, have also sung the praises of Nelson Mandela. Here is the poet laureate of Great Britain, the poet Andrew Motion:

> That straight walk from the
> prison to the gate –
> that walk the world saw, and
> which changed the world –
> it led you through to life from
> life withheld,
> from broken stones with your
> unbroken heart.
>
> To life which you imagined
> and then lived,
> which once we shared in your
> imagining
> but soon shared in the
> present that you shaped:
> the life which gave each

> human hope its chance
> of turning into truth and
> staying true;
> the life which understood
> what changing takes;
> the life which showed us we
> become ourselves
> in part by watching you
> becoming you.[3]

As both dramatic art and political rhetoric, praise singing enables a special kind of identification between singer, community, and the focus of praise. In Andrew Motion's evocative formulation, we, the new South Africa, but also we, the human community, become ourselves by forming a sense of belonging to a shared, collective identity, by watching Nelson Mandela become himself.

In his commitment to truth, as Andrew Motion proposed, Nelson Mandela created a space of hope in which people could find their own dreams and aspirations taking shape and finding a place. By providing a focal point for a sense of human solidarity, shared in the present, Nelson Mandela changed the way people experienced the space of South Africa and the larger world. That shared space of human solidarity, mutuality, and recognition, however, was shaped by Nelson Mandela during a time of dramatic historical transformation. Praise singers must also link the space of the present with its historical genealogy, locating our current place in the flow of time. Space and time, geography and history, are both mediated by the traditional poet's praises. In the chorus for the epic poem, *The Cure of Troy*, composed by the Nobel Laureate for Literature, Seamus Heaney, a chorus inspired by Nelson Mandela's return from prison, the poet reflects upon the world-historical significance of such a rare merger of hope and history. Here is Seamus Heaney:

> Human beings suffer.
> They torture one another.
> They get hurt and get hard.
> No poem or play or song
> Can fully right a wrong
> Inflicted and endured.

History says, Don't hope
On this side of the grave,
But then, once in a lifetime
The longed-for tidal wave
Of justice can rise up
And hope and history rhyme.

So hope for a great sea-change
On the far side of revenge.
Believe that a farther shore
Is reachable from here.
Believe in miracles
And cures and healing wells.

If there's fire on the mountain
And lightning and storm
And a god speaks from the sky
That means someone is hearing
The outcry and the birth-cry
Of new life at its term.

It means once in a lifetime
That justice can rise up
And hope and history rhyme.[4]

Although inspired by Nelson Mandela's freedom, and the freedom mobilised in South Africa in large measure by his ability to merge hope with history, this chorus resonates with other historical struggles, from ancient Greece to colonial Africa, from the past to the present, wherever human beings suffer and unexpectedly, remarkably, discover that their hopes are justified by being borne out in history. Rarely, as the chorus sings, have we seen such a birth. Emerging from confinement, Nelson Mandela's release from prison was the 'outcry and the birth-cry of new life'. In the chorus of Seamus Heaney, the life of Nelson Mandela, animated by the uprising of justice, has given birth to a new harmony of hope and history in South Africa.

So, as we see, poets sing his praises. All the world celebrates. Nelson Mandela belongs to the world. However, South Africans can say, with justification, that he belongs, in the first instance, to us, with us, as an integral part of our struggles, accomplishments, and hopes for the future. The chapters of this book document that South African story, tracing the basic themes of Nelson Mandela's political vision, not only to recall the past, but also to identify enduring foundations for the future.

Helping us to understand the enduring legacy of Nelson Mandela, the authors of the introductions to each chapter of this book, who are leaders, in their own right, in many fields of endeavour, reflect upon the personal and political ingredients for building a South African future. Their thoughtful, vivid, and revealing commentaries, we will find, cast new light on our path.

At the same time, the speeches of Nelson Mandela, as they are gathered in this volume, have their own clarity. Let us reflect, briefly, on the illuminating story that unfolds through this review of the speeches of Nelson Mandela.

In the first chapter, *Struggle*, we collect classic speeches, from 1951 through the 1980s, in which Nelson Mandela enunciated the principles for mobilising resistance to oppression. As early as 1951, he announced that Africans were struggling to become agents of their own destiny against opposition mounted by both apartheid and global forces. With the entrenchment of oppression in South Africa under the apartheid regime, Nelson Mandela maintained the integrity of those principles in the face of persecution, trials, and imprisonment. This history is captured in the powerful record of his testimony, spoken before judges who sought his death, about the principles for which he lived and for which he was ultimately prepared to die. In the last speech of this chapter, delivered by his daughter Zindzi in 1985, Nelson Mandela reaffirmed that he would rather remain in prison than sacrifice the birthright of freedom that would be the inheritance of all the people of South Africa. During those dark days of apartheid, Nelson Mandela's promise, defying his life-sentence in prison, seemed impossible: 'I will return.'

The second chapter, *Freedom*, recalls the surprising, exhilarating realisation of that promise. Beginning with Nelson Mandela's first speech after being released from prison in 1990, this chapter collects the speeches he delivered upon his election and inauguration in 1994 as the first president of a democratic South Africa. Giving a sense of his continuing, deepening understanding of freedom, the chapter features Nelson Mandela's annual addresses on the new national holiday of Freedom Day, every 27 April, during the term of his presidency.

In the third chapter, *Reconciliation*, we are reminded that freedom was achieved through difficult processes of negotiation. Although the release of political prisoners and the unbanning of political organisations introduced a new era of hope, the negotiations that followed were constantly threatened. Giving a sense of the hard work of negotiation, the speeches in this chapter also demonstrate Nelson Mandela's commitment to reconciling conflicting interests, not for the sake of reconciliation at any cost, but for the practical realisation of democratic goals. The Truth and Reconciliation Commission (TRC) was part of this process, as reflected in Nelson Mandela's speeches at commissioning and receiving the report of the TRC. Like Freedom Day, Reconciliation Day, 16 December, has also become a national holiday in South Africa, transforming a day associated with specific nationalist interests – the apartheid regime's Day of the Covenant, the ANC's Heroes Day – into a commemoration of the broader interests of reconciliation that are at work in building a new nation.

Nation building, the focus of the fourth chapter, collects speeches in which Nelson Mandela reflects on the transition from resistance to governance, from the principled opposition to nationalist oppression to the principled creation of a new national identity. As these speeches recall, the language of building, evident in the programmatic slogan, *Masakhane*, 'Building together', infused all of these efforts to mobilise support for a new national project. Nation building, as reflected in Nelson Mandela's speeches, was underwritten by a 'new patriotism', but it also had to be true to the principles of the struggle for liberation. In the process of 'building the country of our dreams', he insisted, the long walk to freedom continued.

Building together, as the fifth chapter, *Development*, shows, required critical and creative interventions in the South African economy. To address the legacy of apartheid, with its widespread, endemic impoverishment of South Africa's people, required a political programme that was also an economic programme. Reconstruction and development, at the beginning of Nelson Mandela's presidency, laid the basis for this programme. As the speeches in this chapter recall, President Mandela was actively involved in advancing this through development projects, urban and rural, but also through participating in ongoing negotiations, facilitating a new social dialogue, among government, business, labour, and community organisations. In the speeches of this chapter, we also see Nelson Mandela's abiding concern for sustainable development that merges human needs with conservation, environmentalism, and ecology in ways that are good for humanity and the planet.

Beginning with the sixth chapter, *Education*, we highlight Nelson Mandela's commitments to the broad range of human formation, including his concerns with teaching and learning, culture, religion, health, and the wellbeing of children. All of these issues, of course, are directly related to his political vision. Education, for example, was central to the political struggle against apartheid. The student uprising of 16 June 1976, now commemorated annually by the national holiday, Youth Day, was a watershed in the political role of students. As the speeches in this chapter illustrate, Nelson Mandela was, and still is, actively involved in education, not only receiving honorary degrees, but in opening schools, initiating school projects, encouraging transformation, and reflecting on the importance of education, at every level, for the future of a democratic South Africa.

Culture, as the seventh chapter documents, means more than merely entertainment, recreation, or leisure pursuits. Cultural resources, according to Nelson Mandela, have a power, an efficacy, in politics. As we recall, singers, poets, and artists, who were active in demanding his release from prison in the 1980s, were celebrating his leadership of a new South Africa in the 1990s. In the speeches collected in this chapter, we recall how music, dance, and poetry, sports and athletics, and a free media are all potentially liberating forces of culture in a democratic society. At the same time, as the speeches in this chapter recount, Nelson Mandela has been attentive to cultural diversity, encouraging, by example, respect and understanding for all of the many cultural formations of South Africa.

Focusing on an important aspect of culture, *Religion*, the eighth chapter recalls Nelson Mandela's efforts to address specific religious concerns while promoting tolerance, respect, and understanding among all of the different religious communities of South Africa. In the speeches collected in this chapter, we find Nelson Mandela speaking with Christians, Muslims, Hindus, and Jews, valuing them as human beings, while acknowledging the importance of religion in the struggle against apartheid and the building of a new nation. Religious diversity, as Nelson Mandela proposes, is not an obstacle to national unity but a vital resource for a nation based on a commitment to unity in diversity.

Nelson Mandela's concern for the wellbeing of people, as reflected in the ninth chapter, *Health*, is evident in his ongoing commitment to advancing health care as a basic human right. During his presidency, as the speeches collected in this chapter show, the ANC government demonstrated a commitment to advancing public health and community health. This concern for health was demonstrated through the building of clinics such as the one in the village of Nobody. This village derived its name, according to legend, from white settlers in the region who insisted 'nobody but whites can live here', though in fact the vast majority of its residents were African when its clinic, the 350th health clinic opened under Nelson Mandela's administration, was established in 1997. In response to the crisis of HIV/Aids, Nelson Mandela engaged in an ongoing effort, as demonstrated by the speeches in this chapter, to break the silence, move from rhetoric to action, and take on Aids as the 'new struggle' in Africa.

The Nelson Mandela Children's Fund, which has emerged as an important focus for his political activity after his presidency, sustains Nelson Mandela's concerns for the wellbeing of children that are reviewed in the tenth chapter, *Children*. Weaving children into a social fabric of care, these speeches call for a programme of action on behalf of children, both locally, within South Africa, and globally, which will advance children's rights as human rights.

During the early 1940s, one of the founding members of the ANC Youth League, Anton Lembede – who was, in some respects, its intellectual catalyst, a colleague in those days of such youthful activists as Oliver Tambo, Walter Sisulu, and Nelson Mandela – argued that forging a future required remembering the past. 'One who wants to create the future,' Lembede observed, 'must not forget the past.' In the eleventh chapter, *Heroes*, we collect speeches by Nelson Mandela that pay tribute to great leaders of South Africa's recent past. In these powerful tributes, which often bear the sorrow of loss, we recall Nelson Mandela's heroic efforts in the ongoing struggle, as the novelist Milan Kundera put it, of memory against forgetting.

Looking towards a sustainable future, Nelson Mandela has been active, since his presidency, in international peace building. The twelfth chapter, *Peace*, collects speeches that demonstrate the depths of Nelson Mandela's commitment to sustainable peace in the global arena. Beginning with his address for the ceremony marking his Nobel Peace Prize, the chapter contains his speeches before the United Nations, during his presidency, as he sought to apply the lessons learned in the South African transition to international relations. Subsequently, as Kofi Annan observed, Nelson Mandela's ongoing commitment to international peace building has continued to inspire people all over the world.

The speeches of this book, which range over 50 years from the middle of the twentieth century to the beginning of the twenty-first, show how the world was changing while Nelson Mandela was changing the world.

Unfortunately, some things do not seem to have changed. The first speech of this collection, delivered in 1951, could have been delivered today. Speaking to a meeting of the ANC in the Transvaal, now Gauteng Province, Nelson Mandela warned of forces in the world, waging military and psychological warfare, which was designed to incapacitate people, through fear, so they could not think. Those global forces, he observed, were 'determined to perpetuate a permanent atmosphere of crisis and fear in the world. Knowing that a frightened world cannot think clearly, these groups attempt to create conditions under which the common men might be inveigled into supporting the building of more and more atomic bombs, bacteriological weapons, and other instruments of mass destruction.' However, the common people, he argued, were struggling to make history under these conditions, but on their own terms, by defying global forces of oppression in their determination for sustainable peace.

Over 50 years later, in 2003, Nelson Mandela issued a similar warning, in this case advising US President George W Bush against adopting a military policy that created a climate of fear, undermined the United Nations, and threatened to lead the world into a 'holocaust'.

Let us say that throughout all of these engagements Nelson Mandela has been irrepressible. Consistently, as the speeches in this book demonstrate, he has been irrepressibly committed to liberation from all forms of repression, locally and globally, which wage war against the inalienable human right, and human impetus, to be free.

On the long walk to freedom, we have all been privileged to walk alongside Nelson Mandela.

NOTES

1 Selection from US President Bill Clinton's Weekly Radio Broadcast, 8 October 1994.

2 Selection from Address by Dr Fidel Castro Ruz, President of the

Republic of Cuba, to the South African Parliament, 14 September 1998.

3 Andrew Motion, 'To Nelson Mandela: A Tribute', *The Guardian*, 7 April 2000.
4 Seamus Heaney, 'Chorus', *The Cure of Troy: A Version of Sophocles' Philoctetes,* Noonday Press, 1991.

NELSON MANDELA: A LIFE

ADRIAN HADLAND

Few politicians in the history of the world have attracted such widespread veneration as is now bestowed on the figure of Nelson Rolihlahla Mandela. This is all the more remarkable in an age when technology and the ubiquitous media ensure hardly a breath is taken by an international figure that is not instantly captured and critiqued. But, in spite of the attention of the world in the 13 years since he walked free from prison and the rigours of accepting the presidency of what was one of the globe's most divided nations, Mandela's reputation remains as impressive as it is unsullied.

Mandela has become synonymous with the triumph of the human spirit. His name will forever speak of his capacity for suffering, of victory over adversity, of patience, forgiveness and a steadfast, iron-clad conviction that principles will always endure. The qualities of character, courage, humility and compassion that are personified in Mandela have granted him an authentic, contemporary moral authority. He is, in the words of his official biographer Anthony Sampson, 'a universal hero'.

Like so many heroes, Mandela's origins are to be found in the humblest of circumstances. On the day of his birth, 18 July 1918, his home in the village of Mvezo in what is now South Africa's Eastern Cape province consisted of three mud huts: one for sleeping, one for cooking and one for storing food. Each of the huts had been crafted by the hands of his mother, Nosekeni Fanny, from earth moulded into bricks. In the living hut, which Mandela shared with his two sisters, chairs and cupboards were made from earth. There were no beds or tables. The family slept on mats. The roof was made of bundles of dried grass tied together with rope.

Mandela's father, Hendry, had four wives of whom Nosekeni was the third. He was a strict, stubborn, illiterate man who was both tall and proud. Royal blood from the Thembu tribe, an important people in South Africa, ran through his veins. The year after Mandela was born, Hendry was stripped of his chieftainship after a quarrel with the local white magistrate over an ox. Hendry refused to budge from his stance and consequently lost most of his cattle, land and income. No longer able to provide for his four wives and 13 children, Hendry was forced to break up the family. He sent Nosekeni to live in the village of Qunu. It was here that Mandela, whose given name at birth was Rolihlahla (which means 'pulling the branch of a tree' or troublemaker) spent most of his childhood.

Mandela recalls his years at Qunu with nostalgic pleasure. His memories of swimming in rocky pools, of drinking warm milk straight from the udder, of the traditional stick fights with his peers and of the overwhelming beauty of the gently undulating, verdant countryside were to keep his spirits high during some of his bleakest moments. For Mandela, home will always be Qunu. It was at school in Qunu, that he was given the name of Nelson. It was a common practice for children educated in mission schools at that time to be given the name of a British imperial hero.

On the premature death of his father, nine-year-old Mandela was adopted by his uncle, Jongintaba, who was Regent of the Thembu. It was a position Jongintaba had secured in part with the backing of Hendry Mandela, a royal counsellor. Jongintaba lived in relative splendour at the seat of the Thembu royal family called Mqhekezweni, the Great Place. It was here that Mandela was introduced to many things that were to have a profound impact on him. It was in Mqhekezweni that he sat round the fire listening to the tribal elders tell stories of great African kings and warriors. It was here he secretly (at first) sat in on the tribal council meetings of the Thembu. People travelled many miles to attend such meetings and each person was given an opportunity to speak. Decisions were only reached by consensus or were delayed until a future meeting. It was in Mqhekezweni, where he shared a hut with Jongintaba's son Justice, that Mandela blossomed as a student and where he underwent circumcision.

As Mandela's father had been a royal councillor, so it was planned that Mandela would be trained to fulfil a similar function for the young Thembu King, Sabata. Consequently, he was sent, together with Justice, to the renowned Methodist institution of Clarkebury and then on to the even more highly regarded Healdtown. It was here, at Healdtown, in about 1938, that Mandela first heard of an organisation called the African National Congress (ANC). Mandela graduated from Healdtown and went on to study court interpreting at the South African Native College of Fort Hare in 1939. Being a court interpreter was considered a highly prestigious post at that time, especially in the rural areas.

Mandela enjoyed cross-country running and was a fine boxer. He joined Fort Hare's ballroom dancing fraternity and signed up for the drama society. He was not especially interested in politics in those days but was certainly becoming aware of developments in South Africa and in the world at large. Before he could graduate from Fort Hare, however, Mandela became caught up in student activism. It still wasn't political activism, though. He was expelled for leading a protest against bad food.

At about this time, the Regent informed Mandela – and Justice – that he was dying. Before he died, he told them, he wanted to see the two young men married and settled down. Wives had been selected for both of them. But neither Justice nor Mandela approved of the choices, nor of the manner in which their prospective brides had been selected. They were modern young men who wanted to make their own decisions in this regard. To avoid the pending finalisation of their marriages, Justice and Mandela ran away from home and found themselves hundreds of miles away in Johannesburg, the city of gold, looking for work.

After taking up a post as a policeman on the mines, Mandela fortuitously met a young, urbane estate agent by the name of Walter Sisulu. They immediately liked each other and Sisulu, on hearing Mandela's wish to be a lawyer, had soon arranged for him to begin his articles at the offices of local firm Witkin, Sidelsky and Eidelman. 'Stay out of politics' were Lazar Sidelsky's famous words of warning when Mandela first started out at the law firm.

Mandela worked for the firm during the day, studied at night and lived in a backroom in the noisy, dirty slum of Alexandra. According to Mandela this was the most difficult period in his life. Hungry, poor, hardworking and dressed in a threadbare hand-me-down suit, he eked out a living in the harsh post-war city. Some days he would walk the 12 miles to work and back to save his bus fare. It was certainly during this time that he became acutely aware of the day-to-day injustices that were an inevitable and indeed deliberate consequence of the system soon to be formally known as apartheid. As he described his awakening in his autobiography, *Long Walk to Freedom*:

'A thousand slights, a thousand indignities and a thousand unre-membered moments produced in me an anger, a rebelliousness, a desire to fight the system that imprisoned my people.'

It was during this time that he was introduced to a young cousin of Sisulu's by the name of Evelyn Mase. Evelyn was a nurse and Mandela was instantly attracted to her. They were married in 1944 and, after sharing a house for a short while with Evelyn's brother, moved into their own home in Orlando, near Johannesburg. The young couple had three children – a son, Thembi, a daughter who died in infancy, and another daughter, Makaziwe.

In spite of the tough conditions at home and war abroad, change was in the air during the 1940s. The Atlantic Charter signed by US President Teddy Roosevelt and British Prime Minister Winston Churchill 'reaffirmed faith in the dignity of each human' along with several other principles of democracy. This was soon adapted at home into the African Claims document, which was to become the found-ing basis of ANC policy and included a Bill of Rights together with a call for universal franchise. The 1940s also witnessed the African Mineworkers' Strike, the Alexandra Bus Boycott, the entrenchment of the 'Hertzog Bills' of the 1930s, the Durban race riots, the Passive Resistance Campaign and the coming to power, in 1948, of DF Malan's National Party.

All these developments were the backdrop to the creation of the ANC Youth League in 1944. During the 1940s, Mandela rubbed shoulders with some deeply influential political leaders and organis-ers such as Gaur Radebe, Anton Lembede, Sisulu, Oliver Tambo, and members of the Communist Party, Transvaal Indian Congress and Natal Indian Congress. The ANC, which had fallen back into a mod-erate slumber in the 1920s and 1930s, was catalysed into radical activism by the Programme of Action adopted by the Youth League in 1949. The Programme of Action spawned the Defiance Campaign and head-on confrontation with the apartheid state.

Mandela was elected to the executive committee of the Youth League, was appointed national volunteer-in-chief and chairman of the Action Committee and Volunteer Board of the Defiance Campaign. The campaign set out deliberately to break apartheid laws and court arrest. By the end of the campaign, 8 500 people of all races had been thrown in jail for defying apartheid laws.

Mandela suffered his first period in jail during the Defiance Campaign and was arrested again on 30 July 1952 under the

Suppression of Communism Act. In fact, Mandela never joined the Communist Party and, in his earlier days, enjoyed breaking up Communist Party meetings. He was, however, beginning to pay an increasing personal toll for his political involvement. He painfully remembers Evelyn being asked by five-year-old Thembi: 'Where does Daddy live?' Nor was the burden to lighten. Deeply saddened by his mother Nosekeni's continuing state of destitution, he 'wondered not for the first time . . . whether one was ever justified in neglecting the welfare of one's own family in order to fight for the welfare of others'. It was to be the one sacrifice that was to haunt him throughout his life.

As the passage of apartheid laws was intensified in the early 1950s and bills prohibiting mixed marriages, mixed residential areas and mixed voters' rolls were passed, so the intensity of resistance grew. By the time South Africa's famous Congress of the People met in Kliptown in 1955 to draft a charter for a nonracial, democratic future (the Freedom Charter), Mandela had been served banning orders and was not allowed to appear in public. He was to receive three such orders before he was arrested in front of his children at dawn on 5 December 1956 and charged with treason in a massively public trial involving 155 other defendants. On returning home on bail during the treason trial, he found his home empty and Evelyn and the children gone.

Mandela had opened a lawyer's practice in Johannesburg with his friend and ANC colleague Oliver Tambo. But the demands of political work on both Mandela and Tambo, including the incarceration and long trial period, undermined the financial viability of their business. They were the first two black lawyers to open their own practice in South Africa.

After separating from Evelyn, who became more interested in religion than politics and who struggled to accept the demands made on her husband's time and life by the ANC, Mandela drove past a young woman at a bus stop by the name of Nomzamo Winnifred Madikizela. 'At that moment I knew I wanted her as my wife,' Mandela wrote in his autobiography. On 14 June 1958, Mandela and Winnie, as she became known, were married. But marital bliss was never to be on the cards for this activist couple. Winnie herself was arrested in a protest against pass books and set off on her own course of anti-apartheid resistance. The couple had two daughters, Zindzi and Zeni.

Discussions about transforming from passive to violent resistance had taken place within the ANC throughout the 1950s. It was a deeply divisive notion. As the years passed, and the stayaways, strikes and marches were met by an 'iron hand', so Mandela began to rethink his own attitude to violence. 'Non-violence was not a moral principle but a strategy,' he wrote later.

In the wake of the Sharpeville killings in 1960 and following the banning of the ANC and other anti-apartheid organisations soon thereafter, Mandela and his colleagues agreed to forge ahead with a military structure, Umkhonto we Sizwe (Spear of the Nation) to up the ante in the struggle. After Mandela's final acquittal on treason charges in 1961, he went underground to work full time at the building of these military structures, of which he was commander in chief. 'I had no choice but to become an outlaw,' he wrote in *Long Walk to Freedom*. Nor was it something he especially relished: it was hazardous and he was kept apart from his family, 'But when a man is denied the right to live the life he believes in, he has no choice.'

For nearly two years, Mandela evaded the apartheid authorities. He went for military training in Ethiopia, visited Europe and several countries on the African continent and criss-crossed South Africa in disguise. He met with sugar workers in Natal, Muslims in the Cape and held secret meetings in townships and homes from one end of the country to the other. He would call newspapers from telephone booths after narrowly evading capture and soon became known as the Black Pimpernel. 'He was to become more famous in the shadows than he had ever been in broad daylight,' wrote Sampson.

But Mandela's dangerous, glamorous life underground soon came to an end after he was betrayed and captured by the authorities in 1962. Charged with travelling illegally out of the country and incitement to strike, he arrived at court in traditional dress, wearing a leopard-skin kaross, 'literally carrying on my back the history, culture and heritage of my people'. He was sentenced to three years for inciting and two years for leaving the country illegally, no parole.

In jail, Mandela protested the obligatory wearing of shorts by African prisoners. He was placed in solitary confinement for his troubles, in a cell perpetually lit by one bulb. For weeks he was utterly isolated. He had nothing to read, write on or with and no one to talk to. 'Every hour seemed like a year,' he wrote later. 'I found myself on the verge of initiating conversations with a cockroach.'

After six months in jail in Pretoria, Mandela was shipped off to the dreaded Robben Island. Mandela had heard tales of the Island since he was a child, listening to the elders around the fire at Mqhekezweni. He heard then how Makana, the six-foot, six-inch commander of the Xhosa army, had drowned while trying to escape the Island and how Autshumao, the Khoikhoi leader, had been banished there. Later, the Island had been used as a leper colony and as a lunatic asylum. In 1962, Robben Island was a tough, brutal place. But after only a few weeks, Mandela was back in Pretoria. The high command of MK had been arrested at Liliesleaf farm in Rivonia and Mandela and his fellow defendants were to be put on trial for their lives. At the outset of the trial, known as the Rivonia Trial, in October 1963, lawyers gave Mandela a 50:50 chance of escaping the hangman's noose. Mandela's famous statement from the dock, a four-hour speech delivered on Monday 20 April 1964, in which he told the court he was willing to die for his principles, echoed around the world.

On 12 June 1964, Mandela evaded the noose but received a life sentence. At midnight that evening, he was flown in an old military aircraft back to Robben Island. His monumental prison sentence, which would total some 27 years, had begun in earnest. The story of Mandela's prison sentence is one of great hardship mixed with great endeavour. It is a story of the indomitability of the human spirit, of the triumph of utter conviction and of the faith and collective strength of comrades. 'We were face to face with the realisation that our life would be unredeemably grim,' Mandela wrote of his early days on the Island. 'Prison life is about routine: each day like the one before; each week like the one before it, so that the months and the years blend into each other.'

The struggle against apartheid for Mandela and his colleagues shifted realms from the public to the private. Instead of speeches and rallies, the Islanders taught themselves and each other. Instead of defiance against the police and against apartheid laws, they waged a continual struggle with the prison authorities for better conditions, better food and more rights. Underpinning their actions was the unwavering belief that morality was on their side and that they would, one day, be free: 'I always knew that one day I would feel once again the grass under my feet and walk in the sunshine as a free man.'

From behind bars, Mandela heard of the travails that beset his family and especially Winnie. Her letters and visits were a lifeline to hope. Equally, they were a reminder of his incapacity and helplessness.

When Mandela heard his eldest son, Thembi, had been killed in a car accident, and was prevented from attending the funeral, 'it left a hole in my heart that can never be filled'. Prison, said Mandela, was a crucible that tests a person's character to its limit. The most terrible walls are the walls that grow up in the mind, he wrote of his trials on the Island.

In April 1982, after almost 20 years in prison, the commanding officer of Robben Island came to Mandela's cell and told him to pack his bags. He was being moved off the Island to Pollsmoor Prison on the mainland. In the real world, things were beginning to change. Unprecedented levels of civil insurrection and resistance were being met with similar levels of military force. South Africa during the 1980s became a battleground and Mandela increasingly was being considered the route out of the abyss.

The ANC had to contend with the collapse of the Soviet Union and the consequent loss of support. Its military operations against the apartheid state had been largely ineffective and the ANC was no nearer to provoking the spontaneous revolutionary insurrection it had initially believed was inevitable. The Nkomati Accord had damaged the ANC's capacity to operate from the frontline states. The organisation had reached its own kind of cul-de-sac and it too required Mandela to lead the way.

The discussions between Mandela and a range of officials of the apartheid state over how to move forward took place over many years. Progress occurred at glacial speed, but proceeded nonetheless. As time went by, Mandela's conditions improved until, in December 1988, he was moved into a prison warder's house at the Victor Verster Prison near Paarl. Then, after President PW Botha had suffered a stroke in January 1989 and FW de Klerk took the reins of apartheid power, the tide turned.

On 2 February 1990, De Klerk met the conditions necessary for negotiations about the future of South Africa to begin in earnest. He unbanned the ANC together with the other liberation movements, released political prisoners and suspended capital punishment. Mandela, at the age of 71 and after more than 10 000 days in jail, walked free.

For more than four years, the negotiations between the ANC, the apartheid government and the other party leaders and organisations in South Africa continued. At times, they were close to collapse. At others, it seemed the country was on the very brink of agreement.

Political violence and uncertainty plagued ordinary people and convinced the world that a racial civil war was imminent.

Then, on 27 April 1994, millions of South Africans voted in the first nonracial, democratic election in the country's history. Mandela was elected President with overwhelming support from the nation and from his party.

The five years in which Mandela held the supreme post were far from easy. Criminal violence, the developmental backlog of three centuries of racial oppression and the demands of governing a modern state at the turn of the twentieth century amounted to the severest of tests. Mandela divorced Winnie, from whom he had become irreconcilably estranged, and later fell in love and married once more. This time, he chose Graça Machel, the widow of Mozambique's late president, Samora Machel, and a Cabinet minister in her own right.

After a single term, Mandela stepped down as President of South Africa. It was an act many leaders of liberation movements in Africa have found almost impossible to carry through. But it was a passing gift that once again defined Mandela as a man of destiny and of conscience for whom principles will brook no opposition.

When Mandela was a small boy listening to stories by the fire, he dreamed one day of being an African hero like Makana or Autshumao whose feats of strength and endeavour would save his people. So things have turned out. He has done this not with the power to wield a spear or the strength to kill a foe, but with weapons far more powerful and far more enduring. He has put his enemies to flight and saved his nation with love, forgiveness and understanding.

REFERENCES

Hadland, A, 2003. *Nelson Mandela – The Prisoner Who Gave the World Hope.* London: Short Books.

Mandela, N, 1994. *Long Walk to Freedom – The Autobiography of Nelson Mandela.* London: Macdonald Purnell.

Sampson, A, 1999. *Mandela – The Authorised Biography.* London: HarperCollins.

Sisulu, E, 2002. *Walter and Albertina Sisulu – In Our Lifetime.* Cape Town: David Philip.

PROMETHEUS UNBOUND

FINTAN O'TOOLE

He walked, and was not driven, from jail. He was not set free, since for him there is no freedom for one man without the freedom of all, and that freedom remains to be won. He moved from a small prison to a larger one whose bars are truncheons, whose walls were poverty, contempt, indignity and the denial of common humanity. He chose the time when he would walk through the gates, defying the schedules, making the authorities and apparatchiks feel, for once, the powerlessness, the frustration, that they routinely inflicted on others. He neither exulted in his release nor complained of his years of deprivation.

Worst of all, he bore none of the marks of a man who had been isolated, cut off, shut away for a quarter of a century. For, of course, he had not been cut off from his country. He had merely lived a purer, clearer, more sharply defined version of the life outside the prison walls: a black man corralled by white men. In trying to remove him from his people, they had managed only to let him live their life in a more concentrated form, unadulterated by the necessary contingencies and compromises of ordinary life in a misshapen society.

This, perhaps, is why he emerged with such a clear mind and such sharp sight. In the stories, the operas, the histories, the parables, the prisoners emerging from the dark dungeon blink in the sunlight, unable to face with fully open eyes the torrent of sensations rushing towards them. In Plato's famous allegory, long imprisonment is a metaphor for the mind's inability to look at reality. The prisoners are chained up with their backs to the light and unable to turn their heads, so that all they see, projected on the wall they face, are shadows, distortions and illusions. Yet in apartheid South Africa, the metaphor could be reversed. The prison was the reality, and the world outside the flickering, distorted shadow of human truth.

So Mandela emerged unblinking, able to look full-on at all the colours under the sun. The long years in the cave have neither narrowed his vision nor dimmed the clarity with which he can see the reality that faces him. He remains that rarest of things: a clear-eyed visionary, neither lost in dreams of a better future for humanity nor in danger of losing those dreams in the hard manoeuvring for power by which change is won. And this is the worst defeat for his jailers.

Tyrants try to break people or, like petty gods, to re-make them in their own image. There was never much chance of Mandela being broken, but the danger, even in heroic defiance, is that it can make the world of the rebel as narrow as that of the oppressor, concentrate it so much on the struggle not to be broken that it becomes hard, unmoving, knotted. The tough shell of resistance grows thicker with every insult it must withstand and the person acquires the dignity but also the coldness of a monument. Thus the tyrant creates a mirror-image of himself, hate matching hate, contempt reflecting contempt. Mandela's greatness is that he remained bigger than his captors, that his mind stayed large enough to imagine for them what they had not dared to imagine for themselves: that they might become better than they had been, that they too might attain the only dignity worth having: the dignity of common humanity.

We are used to thinking that great men and women can attain the status of symbols, legends or myths. It is what we say when we want to indicate that a person has become truly extraordinary: a living legend. But Mandela has done something much more powerful, and much more significant. He has allowed a myth to attain the status of a man, has shown that a legend is elevated rather than diminished when it becomes human. Locked away so that we could not see or hear him, he was frozen into the face on the T-shirt, the ink on the poster, the syllables in the slogan, the nameplate on the streets in many parts of the world that were named after him, the chorus in the songs that were sung for his freedom. And then, quite suddenly, the symbol came alive. The face, older and thinner, was animated with passion. The ink of the slogans became the blood pulsing in his living heart. The words in the song turned into subtle speech, a voice speaking not just of past wrongs but of future possibilities.

This is something we have never experienced in this way. Normally, politicians, pop singers, film stars, celebrities, strive to become abstract images, mass-produced legends. When the images return to reality, it is because they are being diminished and reduced by scandal, becoming not just human but all too human. But Mandela has reversed this process and shown that a real, living man, alert and strategic, is infinitely more powerful than an abstract image. His great gift to his people, indeed, was to embody the revolution as a creature of humanity: frail, imperfect, real. When he walked out of prison, we saw at once what it sometimes takes bitter experience to learn: that justice would not appear in the sky waving a magic wand. It would have to walk slowly and steadily, with its head held high but its feet on the ground, one step at a time. In that moment, the fear of disillusionment was banished, for Mandela, emerging proudly from behind the frozen image, was replacing distant illusions with present realities.

In doing this, he has defied all the abstractions by which humanity is reduced: black and white, master and slave, our tribe and their tribe. He has shown that not one of them can hold a candle to the uniqueness of a man living in and through his times and his people. In an age that surfs on the day's sensations, Mandela has also reminded us that history has its own time frame, that one man's life can span immense changes on the surface while remaining true to an underlying anger and an underlying hope. Though he went into prison when most of the world's population today was very young or not yet born, he has never, since his re-emergence, seemed anachronistic. This is not just because he has remained steadfast in his adherence to timeless values, but also because he always carries within him the sense of being at the beginning of something rather than at the end. He is seeking to embody a new society rather than merely preside over the death of an old one.

He reminds us in this that the word 'confinement' has a double sense in the English language. It means both imprisonment and the period of waiting before the birth of a new child. Mandela's confinement, which his captors understood only in the first sense, was also the time in which a new country was preparing to be born. And like any birth, the joy transcended the pain.

'Unhappy the land', said the proverb, 'that has no heroes.' 'Unhappy the land', replied Bertolt Brecht, 'that needs heroes.' Mandela's heroism grew to match the scale of his land's unhappiness. It grew out of savagery and was shaped in reaction to inhumanity. It was moulded by the four walls of a prison cell. In that sense, it is a quality we would be happy not to need. Even as we salute this hero, we should also remember that his life's work was dedicated to making this kind of heroism redundant, to abolish the need from which it grows, to make his country a land fit, not for heroes, but for the courage and dignity of ordinary men and women living their daily lives in peace and freedom.

1

STRUGGLE

A SPIRIT OF LIBERATION

WILMOT JAMES

How extraordinary, even astonishing, it is to find passages written by Nelson Mandela in 1951 anticipating the nature of today's war on Iraq: 'Mankind as a whole is today standing on the threshold of great events – events that at times seem to threaten its very existence,' he told the annual conference of the African National Congress Youth League in December 1951, 'those groups, parties or persons that are prepared to go to war in defence of colonialism, imperialism and their profits', those 'who are determined to perpetuate a permanent atmosphere of crisis and fear in the world knowing that a frightened world cannot think clearly, these groups attempt to create conditions under which the common men might be inveigled into supporting the building of more and more atomic bombs, bacteriological weapons, and other instruments of mass destruction.'

It was 1951; three years after the National Party came to power, taking South Africa into a direction different to the tendency of the late colonial world, just a decade before the post-colonial independence movements reached their crescendo. The 1950s were a time in which the United States of America became strong, starting a post-war expansion extraordinary in its economic scale, and militarily awesome in its technological hardware. The US government was no friend to Mandela and the ANC during the difficult days of apartheid, but made up for it by Bill Clinton's support for democratic transformation after 1994.

The 1950s was for Mandela also a time of the ordinary person, 'the common man [who] is rising from being the object of history to becoming the subject of history', an expression strongly Hegelian in its philosophy of history. It was a time of growing defiance against injustice, of the 'oppressed all over the world' becoming 'creators of their own history', pledging 'to carve their destiny and not to leave it in the hands of tiny ruling circles – or classes'. The idiom used was clearly Marxist, though not because he was one, as Mandela later explained in his lonesome and compellingly powerful defence in the statement from the dock at the opening of the Rivonia Trial in April 1964: 'I have denied that I am a communist ... I have always regarded myself, in the first place, as an African patriot.' He was 'attracted to the idea of a classless society, an attraction which springs in part from Marxist reading' and is based on the egalitarianism with which pre-capitalist society treated land ownership, the promise of equality of which Marx spoke having a strong resonance with the – perhaps overstated in recollection – ethos of the 'tribe': 'There were no rich or poor and there was no exploitation.'

But where Marxists dismissed representative democracy as a mere shell for the expression of class interests, Mandela admired the Western parliamentary system; he had great respect for British political institutions, particularly the independence with which the judiciary was endowed, both in Britain and in the US, where the separation of powers, between the executive, Parliament or Congress and courts of law, provided for the just and fair representation of individual citizens on the basis of equality of citizenship. Individual representation was about human dignity, which next to poverty, were the two abiding issues that placed him and his people in bondage under apartheid. And therefore, Mandela gave himself the freedom to 'borrow the best from the West and the East' as he put it, to fight against poverty and the lack of human dignity, an intellectual liberation from dogma, powerfully stated.

The freedom to make up your own mind, to craft ideas for the problems of your own place and time and to find indigenous solutions by borrowing and not bowing to either the West or the East or both, was a quality Mandela and the ANC leadership brought to negotiations of the early 1990s, the settlement of 1994 and reconciliation politics of the post-apartheid democratic era. As Van Zyl Slabbert puts it elsewhere in this book: 'South Africa, as far as my knowledge goes, is the only country that negotiated itself out of domination into democracy without any outside assistance and/or interference.' From Marxism he took the class capacity this theoretical eschatology gave to the ordinary person, to use his or her 'labour power' as an instrument of resistance against unjust laws during the Defiance Campaign of 1952, empowering the masses by a recognition of its source: 'there is a mighty awakening among men and women of our country and the year 1952 stands out as the year of this upsurge of national consciousness', he told the Transvaal meeting of the African National Congress in 1953. The Defiance Campaign, like a lot of things in the political history of struggle, started in Port Elizabeth, and it awoke the 'political functioning of the masses'.

He was not a communist and counselled against open revolution and guerrilla warfare, widely regarded as their trademark. He was a democrat. The Defiance Campaign exemplified the 'passive resistance' against unjust laws inspired by Gandhi, the towering personality from the 'East', and respect for and admiration of the 'just laws' made democratically in the West. This was as much a question of analysis of class interests as it was a question of strategy moved by conscience, considerations of what is not only appropriate but what also is right: 'all South Africans are entitled to live a free life', Mandela told the Old Synagogue Court on the closure on the prosecution's case in 1962, 'on the basis of fullest equality of the rights and opportunities in every field, of full democratic rights, with a direct say in the affairs of the government', not simply because of an intellectual consideration of what is proper and just, but because Mandela felt 'driven to speak up for what we believe is right', because 'truth and justice' mattered to the dignity of the individual, to the emotional wellbeing of a person that neuro-psychologists today would associate with the power of the brain to have an inner-eye, a 'conscience'. It is here in Mandela's addresses that we first come across a phenomenon a colleague once described as an 'instinct for justice and democracy', and therefore a visceral reaction to injustice, the indignity of racial discrimination and to what Mandela characterised as the fascism of apartheid associated with an ideology of the *herrenvolk*, unsatisfactorily translated as a 'master race'.

Something else in his speeches and writings that we only see with hindsight, after having met him, we can now recognise as a quite extraordinary quality: an uncanny ability to lead by virtue of a self-reflective and deeply understood appreciation of the contradictoriness of human nature. Anthony Sampson in his biography, *Mandela,* describes the reflective self-understanding of dignity as a core of the humanity that framed his personality.[1] Anybody who has met him would know the feeling. Mandela receives any person with the greatest of respect. He makes you feel valued and important as a sincere expression of his person.

Mandela's approach to building the South African nation, to the reconciliation of diverse people with an awful history of oppression and repression, became a natural extension of a personality that lacked a sense of bitterness or vengeance. 'Mandela's capacity for forgiveness already amazed visitors', wrote Sampson, and '[M]any of his basic principles – his capacity for seeing the best in people, his belief in the dignity of man, his forgiveness – were essentially religious.'[2] The politics of these personality characteristics were, never to diminish your own dignity by diminishing that of others, and never to humiliate your adversary or do things to make them bitter beyond the reach of a future reciprocal embrace. This notion of an appreciation of our mutual humanity in the darkest hours of rage or despair is the quality that saved South Africa from self-destruction, articulated all too clearly in Mandela's statement from the dock at the opening of the defence case in the Rivonia Trial of 20 April 1964.

After countless efforts to petition and make representations to government, endless letters that went unanswered, of civil disobedience to convey unhappiness with unjust racial laws, Mandela explained that they either had to submit or fight. In a statement where he rejected PW Botha's offer of release with conditions, which was read out at a public meeting in Soweto by his daughter Zindzi Mandela in 1985, he recounted how 'My colleagues and I wrote in 1952 to Malan asking for a round table to find a solution to the problems of our country, but that was ignored. When Strijdom was in power we made the same offer. Again it was ignored. When Verwoerd was in power we asked for a national convention for all the people in South Africa to decide on their future. This, too, was in vain.'

Only then did the ANC form Umkhonto we Sizwe, and there was a choice to be made between four options: 'there is sabotage, there is guerrilla warfare, there is terrorism, and there is open revolution. We chose to adopt the first method and to exhaust it before taking any other decision.' Sabotage of installations and infrastructure was chosen because it did not involve the loss of life and because it would scare investors away, 'thus compelling [white] voters to reconsider their position'. And, in a series of phrases that anticipates his approach to post-apartheid nation building, sabotage 'offered the best hope for future race relations. Bitterness would be kept to a minimum and, if the policy bore fruit, democratic government could become a reality.'

Mandela sent a ringing letter of encouragement to the students who took to the streets of Soweto in 1976: The 'verdict of June 16 is loud and clear,' he said, 'apartheid is dead'. But in a long and considered treatment on the Black Consciousness Movement, he worried deeply about the wisdom of denigrating Afrikaners and the Afrikaans language. I remember the time. As an undergraduate student at the University of the Western Cape in the early 1970s the Black Consciousness Movement had great appeal because it celebrated the dignity of black humanity. But because there was no memory and political presence of the nonracialism of the ANC, given the incarceration and exile of its entire leadership, the assertion of black pride came at the cost of denigrating the culture of the oppressors, which included the language of Afrikaans, a tendency made worse when government imposed Afrikaans as a compulsory language in black schools which in turn sparked the Soweto revolt. In a powerful passage, Mandela had this to say about the implications of diminishing your adversary:

> Like many people inside and outside the liberation movement, BCM members have strong objections to the use of Afrikaans. The objection is quite understandable since Afrikaans is not only the language of the oppressor, but has also produced a literature that portrays the black man in a bad light. However, Afrikaans is the language of a substantial section of the country's blacks and any attempts to deprive them of their language would be dangerous. It is the home language of 95 per cent of the coloured population and is used by Indians as well, especially in the country dorps of the Transvaal. It is also widely spoken by the African youth in the urban areas. Even if only Afrikaners spoke the language it will still be unwise to abolish it. Language is the highest manifestation of social unity in the history of mankind and it is the inherent right of each group of people to use its language without restriction. Not only would its abolition be out of step with progressive developments in the enlightened world, but it would also be inviting endless strife. The question of minority rights has been of major concern to progressive forces throughout history and has often led to sudden and violent strife from the aggrieved community. Today South Africa has almost three million Afrikaners who will no longer be oppressors after liberation but a powerful minority of ordinary citizens whose co-operation and goodwill are needed in the reconstruction of the country.[3]

This approach, which Mandela strenuously insists is that of the ANC and not his, is what saved South Africa from civil war. It is an approach that would serve Israel and Palestine well in their search for peace and justice today. It is an ethos of avoiding the accumulated bitterness that has scarred the Balkans and delayed the resolution of the troubles of Northern Ireland. It is a powerful reminder of the folly of the US/UK-led war on Iraq, given the humiliation of the Iraqi people and the passionate identification of the entire Muslim and Arab world now with a severe feeling of insult: if in the conduct of war and struggle you humiliate your adversary, reconciliation and the achievement of democracy after the struggle is over become difficult, even impossible, certainly delayed. Mandela's profound wisdom of anticipating, premeditating perhaps, future outcomes as a guide for how you conduct your struggles and political conduct day-to-day, today, is the most telling legacy he leaves from his leadership.

And there is yet something more: the way in which South Africans negotiated their way out of the miserable corner of apartheid, the manner in which full equality of black and white was achieved by way of negotiating forums like the Conference for a Democratic South Africa (Codesa), can be found in writings penned during Rivonia. Mandela explained that the ANC turned to sabotage only after it had exhausted all legal and peaceful channels. In this the answer was always force and violence:

> It must not be forgotten that by this time violence had, in fact, become a feature of the South African political scene. There had been violence in 1957 when the women of Zeerust were ordered to carry passes; there was violence in 1958 with the enforcement of cattle culling in Sekhukhuniland; there was violence in 1959 when the people of Cato Manor protested against pass raids; there was violence in 1960 when the government attempted to impose Bantu Authorities in Pondoland. Thirty-nine Africans died in these disturbances. In 1961 there had been riots in Warmbaths, and all this time the Transkei had been a seething mass of unrest.

And, of course, there was Sharpeville, which resulted in the declaration of a state of emergency and banning of the ANC, the Pan Africanist Congress, the South African Communist Party and other organisations. When the Verwoerd government held a referendum to test (white) electoral support for a republic in their wish to break with the British monarchy, African, Indian and coloured South Africans were not consulted: 'All of us were apprehensive of our future under the proposed white Republic, and a resolution was taken to hold an All-In African Conference to call for a National Convention, and to organise mass demonstrations on the eve of the unwanted Republic, if government failed to call the Convention.'

It was an extraordinary moment in our history. The demand fell on deaf ears. But what if it had not? What if a Codesa had been held then? What if the ANC's tradition of 'non-violence and negotiation as a means of solving political disputes' had found its moral equal among a white leadership, what extraordinary possibilities would have been possible then? How many lives could have been saved? How much more quickly could we have improved our educational, health and housing problems? That it had to take 30 more years, the end of the Cold War and the fall of communism to have an FW de Klerk was a criminal waste of an opportunity, a testimony to the failure of white leadership, and, as Mandela had it, the weakness, even cowardice, of whites of liberal persuasion, who could not countenance majority rule. It is sad and perhaps pointless to speculate, but what a different place South Africa could have been today.

When Nelson Mandela became the first democratically elected President of South Africa he faced the daunting task of uniting a torn nation, of a continued right-wing Afrikaner threat embedded in the security forces, of Chief Mangosuthu Buthelezi's Inkatha Freedom Party at mortal loggerheads with the ANC in KwaZulu-Natal, and with minority groups fearful of the practical meaning of majority rule. I succeeded Alex Boraine as the executive director of the Institute for a Democratic Alternative for South Africa (Idasa) at the time, and we were asked by the Office of the President to assist in understanding the fears of coloured people in the new South Africa. The hidden conversation in coloured communities was that 'disadvantaged' meant African and that the working classes would, once again, be at the end of the job queue. There was talk of a *Kleurling Weerstandsbeweging* (a Coloured Resistance Movement) working in cahoots with Eugene Terre'Blanche's *Afrikaner Weerstandsbeweging* (AWB).

We met privately with the people involved and found them to be foolhardy loudmouths, full of bluster, not worth taking seriously. To deal with the real issues Idasa put together a conference to look at questions of employment and affirmative action, identity and nonracialism, citizenship and minority interests. President Mandela gave the opening address, and pledged his government's commitment to being open to hearing grievances and to a fair and just application of affirmative action as part of the Reconstruction and Development Programme (RDP).[4] He also asked us to help with the renaming of Westbrooke, the presidential residence in the Cape, since he wanted a name in deference to the coloured communities of South Africa. After some research we proposed *Genadendal* (Valley of Mercy). Izak Balie of the Genadendal Museum provided the background to a motivation that stressed the extraordinary importance of Genadendal, a Moravian mission located in the foothills of the Outeniqua mountains, a place that received individuals freed from slavery, and provided the education of generations of young people, who in turn became the teachers of many more. The late Vernon February and Franklin Sonn made their suggestions too.

Jakes Gerwel, then Director-General of the President's Office, liked the idea of Genadendal and presented the recommendation to President

Mandela, and so Westbrooke became Genadendal. I mention this in tribute to Nelson Mandela's unrelenting concern to recognise and honour
people, his wish born in struggle to live in *Ubuntu*, and to pay personal
attention to all communities, of the majority and the minorities. His
instinct for justice and democracy, his persistence, even stubbornness,
his sense of honour and dignity, trust and loyalty, were qualities of
resistance and defiance that brought continued life and inspiration to the
governance of the first democratic era that South Africa ever had since
the days of colonial settlement – and, certainly, the first modern representative democracy. They are qualities that made Nelson Mandela the
most popular and the most loved president of all South African times,
among black and white, someone who by example taught us to 'apply
our hearts unto wisdom',[5] a gift to us all.

NOTES
1 Anthony Sampson, 1999. *Mandela: The Authorised Biography*,
Johannesburg: Jonathan Ball Publishers, pp 226-45.
2 Sampson, *Mandela*, p 233.
3 Nelson Mandela, 2001. 'Whither the Black Consciousness Movement', in Mac Maharaj (ed.), *Reflections in Prison*. Cape Town: Zebra
Press and the Robben Island Museum, pp 47-8.
4 Wilmot James, Daria Caliguire & Kerry Cullinan (eds.), 1996. *Now
That We are Free: Coloured Communities in a Democratic South
Africa*. Boulder and Cape Town: Lynne Rienner Publishers and Idasa.
5 Psalm 90, v 12.

Full Democratic Rights

Selections from an address to the annual conference
of the African National Congress Youth League,
December 1951.

Mankind as a whole is today standing on the threshold of great events –
events that at times seem to threaten its very existence. On the one
hand, there are those groups, parties, or persons that are prepared to
go to war in defence of colonialism, imperialism, and their profits.
These groups, at the head of which stand the ruling circles in
America, are determined to perpetuate a permanent atmosphere of
crisis and fear in the world. Knowing that a frightened world cannot
think clearly, these groups attempt to create conditions under which
the common men might be inveigled into supporting the building
of more and more atomic bombs, bacteriological weapons and other
instruments of mass destruction.

These crazy men whose prototype is to be found at the head of
the trusts and cartels of America and Western Europe do not realise
that they will suffer the destruction that they are contemplating for
their innocent fellow beings. But they are desperate and become
more so as they realise the determination of the common men to
preserve peace.

Yes, the common man who for generations has been the tool of
insane politicians and governments, who has suffered privations and
sorrow in wars that were of profit to tiny privileged groups, is today
rising from being the object of history to becoming the subject of
history. For the ordinary men and women in the world, the oppressed all over the world are becoming the conscious creators of
their own history. They are pledged to carve their destiny and not
to leave it in the hands of tiny ruling circles – or classes.

Whilst the dark and sinister forces in the world are organising a
desperate and last-minute fight to defend a decadent and bankrupt
civilisation, the common people, full of confidence and buoyant hope,
struggle for the creation of a new, united, and prosperous human

11

family. That this is so can be gathered from the increasingly militant and heroic struggle that is being waged in all colonial countries against heavy odds. Our mother body has in clear and unmistakable terms indicated in which camp we are in the general world contest. We are with the oppressed all over the world and are irrevocably opposed to imperialism in any form.

In Africa the colonial powers – Great Britain, Portugal, France, Italy, Spain, and their servitors in South Africa – are attempting with the help of the notorious American ruling class to maintain colonial rule and oppression. Millions of pounds are pouring into the continent in the form of capital for the exploitation of our resources in the sole interests of the imperialist powers. So-called geological and archaeological expeditions are roaming the continent ostensibly engaged in gathering material for the advancement of science and the furtherance of humanity but being in reality the advance guard of American penetration. It is important for us and for the African people as a whole to realise that but for the support of American finance it would have been difficult if not impossible for the Western colonial powers to maintain rule in Africa, nor indeed anywhere in the world. In thinking of the direct enemies of the African people, namely, Great Britain, Spain, France, Portugal, Italy and South Africa, we must never forget the indirect enemy, the infinitely more dangerous enemy who sustains all those with loans, capital, and arms.

In common with people all over the world, humanity in Africa is fighting these forces. In the Gold Coast a situation exists which is capable of being translated into complete victory for the people. Events in Nigeria are leading to a similar situation. In French West Africa, the Democratic Rally of African People is leading the people into what is virtually open war against the French imperialists. In Egypt the heroic struggle is being waged which must receive the support of all genuine anti-imperialist forces, albeit with certain reservations. In Uganda the leaders of the Bataka Association who were condemned to 14 years of imprisonment have had to be released as a result of the attitude of the masses. In Central Africa the people saw through the tricks of the British imperialists who sought to foist a bogus federation scheme on them. What the rulers have reaped instead is a rejection of partnership, trusteeship and white leadership, and a clear demand for self-determination and independence. These are hopeful signs, but precisely because the African liberation movement is gaining strength the rulers will become more brutal and, in their desperation, will practise all manner of deception in order to stay on – at any rate to postpone the day of final victory. But history is on the side of the oppressed.

Here in South Africa the situation is an extremely grave and serious one. The plans of the Broederbond to set up an openly police state have so far almost run to schedule. About that there can be no question. This is in the interest of the ruling class in South Africa whether it is nominally in the United Party or the Nationalist Party.

The United Party represents the mining interests and also the rapidly rising industrialist power. The Nationalist Party represents farming interests and the growing Afrikaner commercial interest. The farming group as a distinct and separate interest is, of course, dying out – if it is not dead already! The financial lords are destroying the farmer group, and instead we have huge semi-industrial estates and plantations through which the big money power seeks to extend its monopoly of economic South Africa to the agricultural sphere. At one time it was thought that the development of a powerful industrialist class would produce a clash involving the primitive feudal-capitalist farming and mining interest on the one hand and the industrialist on the other. It was thought that this clash might result in a realignment of forces that might be advantageous to the oppressed people in the country. But it is becoming clear that there is no possibility of a clash between such groups. There is no chance that Sir Ernest Oppenheimer, the leading mining magnate, will clash with Harry Oppenheimer, the leading industrialist. There is also noticeable a growing affinity among the English, Jewish, and Afrikaner financial and industrial interests. It is quite conceivable that all their interests find the fascist policy of Malan suitable, as it will enable them to continue their bankrupt role by crushing the trade union movement and the national movements of the people. It is true that in the rank-and-file of the white parties are a number who whilst they support the maintenance of colour as an instrument of white political and economic supremacy are scared of a naked Hitlerite regime which might later turn out to be a danger to themselves; hence movements like the now thoroughly discredited Torch Commando. These are white South African people who have lost all their moral backbone. The possibility of a liberal capitalist democracy in South Africa is extremely nil. The propaganda among the whites and their desire to maintain what they imagine to be a profitable situation make it utterly unthinkable that there can be a political alignment that favours a liberal white group. In any case the political immorality, cowardice, and vacillations of the so-called progressives among whites render them utterly useless as a force against fascism.

The situation is developing in the direction of an openly fascist state. The Broederbond is the centre of the fascist ideology in this country, but like other things it is itself merely an instrument of the ruling circles which are to be found in all white parties. The commandos are the nucleus of a future Gestapo. The acts passed by the government, in particular the Suppression of Communism Amendment Act and the Group Areas Act, provide the readymade framework for the establishment of the fascist state. True to the pattern depicted for the rest of the imperialist world, South African capitalism has developed into monopolism and is now reaching the final stage of monopoly capitalism gone mad, namely, fascism.

But the development of fascism in the country is an indication of the fear they have of the people. They realise that their world is a dying world and that the appearance of impregnable strength is a mere facade. The new world is the one in which the oppressed Africans live. They see before their eyes the growth of a mighty people's movement. The struggles of 1950 were an indication that the leaders of the Africans and their allies were fully aware of the weakest link in the chain of white supremacy. The labour power of the African people is a force which when fully tapped is going to sweep the people to power in the land of their birth. True, the struggle will be a bitter one. Leaders will be deported, imprisoned, and even shot. The government will terrorise the people and their leaders in an effort to halt the forward march; ordinary forms of organisation will be rendered impossible. But the spirit of the people cannot be crushed, and no matter what happens to the present leadership, new leaders will arise like mushrooms till full victory is won.

. . .

Sons and daughters of Africa, our tasks are mighty indeed, but I have abundant faith in our ability to reply to the challenge posed by the situation. Under the slogan of FULL DEMOCRATIC RIGHTS IN SOUTH AFRICA NOW, we must march forward into victory.

No Easy Walk to Freedom

Selections from an address to the ANC Transvaal Congress,
21 September 1953.

Since 1912 and year after year thereafter, in their homes and local
areas, in provincial and national gatherings, on trains and buses, in the
factories and on the farms, in cities, villages, shanty towns, schools
and prisons, the African people have discussed the shameful misdeeds
of those who rule the country. Year after year, they have raised their
voices in condemnation of the grinding poverty of the people, the
low wages, the acute shortage of land, the inhuman exploitation and
the whole policy of white domination. But instead of more freedom,
repression began to grow in volume and intensity and it seemed that
all their sacrifices would end up in smoke and dust. Today the entire
country knows that their labours were not in vain for a new spirit
and new ideas have gripped our people. Today the people speak the
language of action: there is a mighty awakening among the men and
women of our country and the year 1952 stands out as the year of
this upsurge of national consciousness.

In June 1952, the African National Congress and the South
African Indian Congress, bearing in mind their responsibility as the
representatives of the downtrodden and oppressed people of South
Africa, took the plunge and launched the Campaign for the Defiance
of Unjust Laws. Starting off in Port Elizabeth in the early hours of
26 June with only 33 defiers in action, and then in Johannesburg in
the afternoon of the same day with 106 defiers, it spread throughout
the country like wild fire. Factory and office workers, doctors,
lawyers, teachers, students and the clergy; Africans, coloureds, Indians
and Europeans, old and young, all rallied to the national call and
defied the pass laws and the curfew and the railway apartheid regulations. At the end of the year, more than 8 000 people of all races had
defied. The Campaign called for immediate and heavy sacrifices.
Workers lost their jobs, chiefs and teachers were expelled from the

15

service, doctors, lawyers and businessmen gave up their practices and businesses and elected to go to jail.

Defiance was a step of great political significance. It released strong social forces which affected thousands of our countrymen. It was an effective way of getting the masses to function politically; a powerful method of voicing our indignation against the reactionary policies of the government. It was one of the best ways of exerting pressure on the government and extremely dangerous to the stability and security of the state. It inspired and aroused our people from a conquered and servile community of yes-men to a militant and uncompromising band of comrades-in-arms. The entire country was transformed into battle zones where the forces of liberation were locked up in immortal conflict against those of reaction and evil. Our flag flew in every battlefield and thousands of our countrymen rallied around it. We held the initiative and the forces of freedom were advancing on all fronts. It was against this background and at the height of this Campaign that we held our last annual provincial conference in Pretoria from the 10th to the 12th of October last year. In a way, that conference was a welcome reception for those who had returned from the battlefields and a farewell to those who were still going to action. The spirit of defiance and action dominated the entire conference.

Today we meet under totally different conditions. By the end of July last year, the Campaign had reached a stage where it had to be suppressed by the government or it would impose its own policies on the country.

The government launched its reactionary offensive and struck at us. Between July last year and August this year 47 leading members from both Congresses in Johannesburg, Port Elizabeth and Kimberley were arrested, tried and convicted for launching the Defiance Campaign and given suspended sentences ranging from three months to two years on condition that they did not again participate in the defiance of the unjust laws. In November last year, a proclamation was passed which prohibited meetings of more than ten Africans and made it an offence for any person to call upon an African to defy. Contravention of this proclamation carried a penalty of three years or of a fine of 300 pounds. In March this year the government passed the so-called Public Safety Act which empowered it to declare a state of emergency and to create conditions which would permit the most ruthless and pitiless methods of suppressing our movement. Almost simultaneously, the Criminal Law Amendment Act was passed which provided heavy penalties for those convicted of Defiance offences.

. . .

The cumulative effect of all these measures is to prop up and per-petuate the artificial and decaying policy of the supremacy of the white men. The attitude of the government to us is that: 'Let's beat them down with guns and batons and trample them under our feet. We must be ready to drown the whole country in blood if only there is the slightest chance of preserving white supremacy.'

But there is nothing inherently superior about the *herrenvolk* idea of the supremacy of the whites. In China, India, Indonesia and Korea, American, British, Dutch and French imperialism, based on the concept of the supremacy of Europeans over Asians, has been completely and perfectly exploded. In Malaya and Indo-China British and French imperialisms are being shaken to their foundations by powerful and revolutionary national liberation movements. In Africa, there are approximately 190 000 000 Africans as against 4 000 000 Europeans. The entire continent is seething with discontent and already there are powerful revolutionary eruptions in the Gold Coast, Nigeria, Tunisia, Kenya, the Rhodesias and South Africa. The oppressed people and the oppressors are at loggerheads. The *day of reckoning* between the forces of freedom and those of reaction is not very far off. I have not the slightest doubt that when that day comes truth and justice will prevail.

The intensification of repression and the extensive use of the bans are designed to immobilise every active worker and to check the national liberation movement. But gone forever are the days when harsh and wicked laws provided the oppressors with years of peace and quiet. The racial policies of the government have pricked the conscience of all men of goodwill and have aroused their deepest indignation. The feelings of the oppressed people have never been more bitter. If the ruling circles seek to maintain their position by such inhuman methods then a clash between the forces of freedom and those of reaction is certain. The grave plight of the people com-pels them to resist to the death the stinking policies of the gangsters that rule our country.

. . .

You can see that there is no easy walk to freedom anywhere, and many of us will have to pass through the valley of the shadow of death again and again before we reach the mountain tops of our desires.

Posterity Will Prove that I was Innocent

Selections from an address to the Court following the closure
of the prosecution's case, Old Synagogue Court, Pretoria,
15 October to 7 November 1962.

I am charged with inciting people to commit an offence by way of
protest against the law, a law which neither I nor any of my people
had any say in preparing. The law against which the protest was
directed is the law which established a republic in the Union of
South Africa. I am also charged with leaving the country without a
passport. This Court has found that I am guilty of incitement to
commit an offence in opposition to this law as well as of leaving the
country. But in weighing up the decision as to the sentence which is
to be imposed for such an offence, the Court must take into account
the question of responsibility, whether it is I who am responsible or
whether, in fact, a large measure of the responsibility does not lie on
the shoulders of the government which promulgated that law, knowing that my people, who constitute the majority of the population of
this country, were opposed to that law, and knowing further that
every legal means of demonstrating that opposition had been closed
to them by prior legislation, and by government administrative action.

The starting point in the case against me is the holding of the conference in Pietermaritzburg on 25 and 26 March last year [1961],
known as the All-In African Conference, which was called by a committee which had been established by leading people and spokesmen
of the whole African population, to consider the situation which was
being created by the promulgation of the republic in the country,
without consultation with us, and without our consent. That conference unanimously rejected the decision of the government, acting
only in the name of and with the agreement of the white minority
of this country, to establish a republic.

It is common knowledge that the conference decided that, in
place of the unilateral proclamation of a republic by the white
minority of South Africans only, it would demand in the name of the

18

African people the calling of a truly national convention representative of all South Africans, irrespective of their colour, black and white, to sit amicably round a table, to debate a new constitution for South Africa, which was in essence what the government was doing by the proclamation of a republic, and furthermore, to press on behalf of the African people, that such new constitution should differ from the constitution of the proposed South African Republic by guaranteeing democratic rights on a basis of full equality to all South Africans of adult age. The conference had assembled, knowing full well that for a long period the present National Party government of the Union of South Africa had refused to deal with, to discuss with, or to take into consideration the views of, the overwhelming majority of the South African population on this question. And, therefore, it was not enough for this conference just to proclaim its aim, but it was also necessary for the conference to find a means of stating that aim strongly and powerfully, despite the government's unwillingness to listen.

Accordingly, it was decided that should the government fail to summon such a National Convention before 31 May 1961, all sections of the population would be called on to stage a general strike for a period of three days, both to mark our protest against the establishment of a republic, based completely on white domination over a non-white majority, and also, in a last attempt to persuade the government to heed our legitimate claims, and thus to avoid a period of increasing bitterness and hostility and discord in South Africa.

At that conference, an Action Council was elected, and I became its secretary. It was my duty, as secretary of the committee, to establish the machinery necessary for publicising the decision of this conference and for directing the campaign of propaganda, publicity, and organisation which would flow from it.

The Court is aware of the fact that I am an attorney by profession and no doubt the question will be asked why I, as an attorney who is bound, as part of my code of behaviour, to observe the laws of the country and to respect its customs and traditions, should willingly lend myself to a campaign whose ultimate aim was to bring about a strike against the proclaimed policy of the government of this country.

In order that the Court shall understand the frame of mind which leads me to action such as this, it is necessary for me to explain the background to my own political development and to try to make

19

this Court aware of the factors which influenced me in deciding to act as I did.

Many years ago, when I was a boy brought up in my village in the Transkei, I listened to the elders of the tribe telling stories about the good old days, before the arrival of the white man. Then our people lived peacefully, under the democratic rule of their kings and their *amapakati*, and moved freely and confidently up and down the country without let or hindrance. Then the country was ours, in our own name and right. We occupied the land, the forests, the rivers; we extracted the mineral wealth beneath the soil and all the riches of this beautiful country. We set up and operated our own government, we controlled our own armies and we organised our own trade and commerce. The elders would tell tales of the wars fought by our ancestors in defence of the fatherland, as well as the acts of valour performed by generals and soldiers during those epic days. The names of Dingane and Bambatha, among the Zulus, of Hintsa, Makana, Ndlambe of the AmaXhosa, of Sekhukhuni and others in the north, were mentioned as the pride and glory of the entire African nation.

I hoped and vowed then that, among the treasures that life might offer me, would be the opportunity to serve my people and make my own humble contribution to their freedom struggles.

The structure and organisation of early African societies in this country fascinated me very much and greatly influenced the evolution of my political outlook. The land, then the main means of production, belonged to the whole tribe, and there was no individual ownership whatsoever. There were no classes, no rich or poor and no exploitation of man by man. All men were free and equal and this was the foundation of government. Recognition of this general principle found expression in the constitution of the council, variously called *Imbizo*, or *Pitso*, or *Kgotla*, which governs the affairs of the tribe. The council was so completely democratic that all members of the tribe could participate in its deliberations. Chief and subject, warrior and medicine man, all took part and endeavoured to influence its decisions. It was so weighty and influential a body that no step of any importance could ever be taken by the tribe without reference to it.

There was much in such a society that was primitive and insecure and it certainly could never measure up to the demands of the present epoch. But in such a society are contained the seeds of revolutionary democracy in which none will be held in slavery or servitude, and in

20

which poverty, want, and insecurity shall be no more. This is the inspiration which, even today, inspires me and my colleagues in our political struggle.

When I reached adult stature, I became a member of the African National Congress. That was in 1944 and I have followed its policy, supported it, and believed in its aims and outlook for 18 years. Its policy was one which appealed to my deepest inner convictions. It sought for the unity of all Africans, overriding tribal differences among them. It sought the acquisition of political power for Africans in the land of their birth. The African National Congress further believed that all people, irrespective of the national groups to which they may belong, and irrespective of the colour of their skins, all people whose home is South Africa and who believe in the principles of democracy and of equality of men, should be treated as Africans; that all South Africans are entitled to live a free life on the basis of fullest equality of the rights and opportunities in every field, of full democratic rights, with a direct say in the affairs of the government.

These principles have been embodied in the Freedom Charter, which none in this country will dare challenge for its place as the most democratic programme of political principles ever enunciated by any political party or organisation in this country.

. . .

I would say that the whole life of any thinking African in this country drives him continuously to a conflict between his conscience on the one hand and the law on the other. This is not a conflict peculiar to this country. The conflict arises for men of conscience, for men who think and who feel deeply in every country. Recently in Britain, a peer of the realm, Earl Russell, probably the most respected philosopher of the Western world, was sentenced, convicted for precisely the type of activities for which I stand before you today, for following his conscience in defiance of the law, as a protest against a nuclear weapons policy being followed by his own government. For him, his duty to the public, his belief in the morality of the essential rightness of the cause for which he stood, rose superior to his high respect for the law. He could not do other than to oppose the law and to suffer the consequences for it. Nor can I. Nor can many Africans in this country. The law as it is applied, the law as it has been developed over a long period of history, and especially the law as it is written and designed by the Nationalist government, is a law which, in our view, is immoral, unjust, and intolerable. Our consciences

21

dictate that we must protest against it, that we must oppose it, and that we must attempt to alter it.

Always we have been conscious of our obligations as citizens to avoid breaches of the law, where such breaches can be avoided, to prevent a clash between the authorities and our people, where such a clash can be prevented, but nevertheless, we have been driven to speak up for what we believe is right, and to work for it and to try and bring about changes which will satisfy our human conscience.

. . .

I wish again to return to the question of why people like me, knowing all this, knowing in advance that this government is incapable of progressive democratic moves so far as our people are concerned, knowing that this government is incapable of reacting towards us in any way other than by the use of overwhelming brute force, why I and people like me nevertheless decide to go ahead to do what we must do. We have been conditioned to our attitudes by the history which is not of our making. We have been conditioned by the history of white governments in this country to accept the fact that Africans, when they make their demands strongly and powerfully enough to have some chance of success, will be met by force and terror on the part of the government. This is not something we have taught the African people, this is something the African people have learned from their own bitter experience. We learned it from each successive government. We learned it from the government of General Smuts at the time of two massacres of our people: the 1921 massacre in Bulhoek when more than 100 men, women, and children were killed, and from the 1924 massacre – the Bondelswart massacre in South-West Africa, in which some 200 Africans were killed. We have continued to learn it from every successive government.

Government violence can do only one thing, and that is to breed counter-violence. We have warned repeatedly that the government, by resorting continually to violence, will breed in this country counter-violence amongst the people, till ultimately, if there is no dawning of sanity on the part of the government – ultimately, the dispute between the government and my people will finish up by being settled in violence and by force. Already there are indications in this country that people, my people, Africans, are turning to deliberate acts of violence and of force against the government, in order to persuade the government, in the only language which this government shows by its own behaviour that it understands.

Elsewhere in the world, a Court would say to me, 'You should have made representations to the government.' This Court, I am confident, will not say so. Representations have been made, by people who have gone before me, time and time again. Representations were made in this case by me; I do not want again to repeat the experience of those representations. The Court cannot expect a respect for the processes of representation and negotiation to grow amongst the African people, when the government shows every day, by its conduct, that it despises such processes and frowns upon them and will not indulge in them. Nor will the Court, I believe, say that, under the circumstances, my people are condemned forever to say nothing and to do nothing. If this Court says that, or believes it, I think it is mistaken and deceiving itself. Men are not capable of doing nothing, of saying nothing, of not reacting to injustice, of not protesting against oppression, of not striving for the good of society and the good life in the ways they see it. Nor will they do so in this country.

Perhaps the Court will say that despite our human rights to protest, to object, to make ourselves heard, we should stay within the letter of the law. I would say, Sir, that it is the government, its administration of the law, which brings the law into such contempt and disrepute that one is no longer concerned in this country to stay within the letter of the law. I will illustrate this from my own experience. The government has used the process of law to handicap me, in my personal life, in my career, and in my political work, in a way which is calculated, in my opinion, to bring about a contempt for the law. In December 1952 I was issued with an order by the government, not as a result of a trial before a Court and a conviction, but as a result of prejudice, or perhaps Star Chamber procedure behind closed doors in the halls of government. In terms of that order I was confined to the magisterial district of Johannesburg for six months and, at the same time, I was prohibited from attending gatherings for a similar period. That order expired in June 1953 and three months thereafter, again without any hearing, without any attempt to hear my side of the case, without facing me with charges, or explanations, both bans were renewed for a further period of two years. To these bans a third was added: I was ordered by the Minister of Justice to resign altogether from the African National Congress, and never again to become a member or to participate in its activities. Towards the end of 1955, I found myself free and able to move around once again, but not for long. In February 1956 the bans were again renewed, administrative-

23

ly, again without hearing, this time for five years. Again, by order of the government, in the name of the law, I found myself restricted and isolated from my fellow men, from people who think like me and believe like me. I found myself trailed by officers of the Security Branch of the Police Force wherever I went. In short, I found myself treated as a criminal – an unconvicted criminal. I was not allowed to pick my company, to frequent the company of men, to participate in their political activities, to join their organisations. I was not free from constant police surveillance.

I was made, by the law, a criminal, not because of what I had done, but because of what I stood for, because of what I thought, because of my conscience. Can it be any wonder to anybody that such conditions make a man an outlaw of society? Can it be wondered that such a man, having been outlawed by the government, should be prepared to lead the life of an outlaw, as I have led for some months, according to the evidence before this Court?

It has not been easy for me during the past period to separate myself from my wife and children, to say goodbye to the good old days when, at the end of a strenuous day at an office, I could look forward to joining my family at the dinner-table, and instead to take up the life of a man hunted continuously by the police, living separated from those who are closest to me, in my own country, facing continually the hazards of detection and of arrest. This has been a life infinitely more difficult than serving a prison sentence. No man in his right senses would voluntarily choose such a life in preference to the one of normal family and social life which exists in every civilised community.

But there comes a time, as it came in my life, when a man is denied the right to live a normal life, when he can only live the life of an outlaw because the government has so decreed to use the law to impose a state of outlawry upon him. I was driven to this situation, and I do not regret having taken the decisions that I did take. Other people will be driven in the same way in this country, by this very same force of police persecution and of administrative action by the government, to follow my course, of that I am certain.

. . .

I do not believe, Your Worship, that this Court, in inflicting penalties on me for the crimes for which I am convicted, should be moved by the belief that penalties deter men from the course that they believe is right. History shows that penalties do not deter men when their conscience is aroused, nor will they deter my people or the colleagues with whom I have worked before.

I am prepared to pay the penalty even though I know how bitter and desperate is the situation of an African in the prisons of this country. I have been in these prisons and I know how gross is the discrimination, even behind the prison walls, against Africans, how much worse is the treatment meted out to African prisoners than that accorded to whites. Nevertheless, these considerations do not sway me from the path that I have taken, nor will they sway others like me. For to men, freedom in their own land is the pinnacle of their ambitions, from which nothing can turn men of conviction aside. More powerful than my fear of the dreadful conditions to which I might be subjected is my hatred for the dreadful conditions to which my people are subjected outside prison throughout this country.

I hate the practice of race discrimination, and in my hatred I am sustained by the fact that the overwhelming majority of mankind hate it equally. I hate the systematic inculcation of children with colour prejudice and I am sustained in that hatred by the fact that the overwhelming majority of mankind, here and abroad, are with me in that. I hate the racial arrogance which decrees that the good things of life shall be retained as the exclusive right of a minority of the population, and which reduces the majority of the population to a position of subservience and inferiority, and maintains them as voteless chattels to work where they are told and behave as they are told by the ruling minority. I am sustained in that hatred by the fact that the overwhelming majority of mankind both in this country and abroad are with me.

Nothing that this Court can do to me will change in any way that hatred in me, which can only be removed by the removal of the injustice and the inhumanity which I have sought to remove from the political and social life of this country.

Whatever sentence Your Worship sees fit to impose upon me for the crime for which I have been convicted before this Court, may it rest assured that when my sentence has been completed I will still be moved, as men are always moved, by their consciences; I will still be moved by my dislike of the race discrimination against my people when I come out from serving my sentence, to take up again, as best I can, the struggle for the removal of those injustices until they are finally abolished once and for all.

. . .

I have done my duty to my people and to South Africa. I have no doubt that posterity will pronounce that I was innocent and that the criminals that should have been brought before this Court are the members of the Verwoerd government.

I am Prepared to Die

Statement from the dock at the opening of the defence case in the
Rivonia Trial, Pretoria Supreme Court,
20 April 1964.

I am the First Accused.

I hold a Bachelor's Degree in Arts and practised as an attorney in
Johannesburg for a number of years in partnership with Oliver
Tambo. I am a convicted prisoner serving five years for leaving the
country without a permit and for inciting people to go on strike at
the end of May 1961.

At the outset, I want to say that the suggestion made by the state
in its opening that the struggle in South Africa is under the influence
of foreigners or communists is wholly incorrect. I have done whatever I did, both as an individual and as a leader of my people, because
of my experience in South Africa and my own proudly felt African
background, and not because of what any outsider might have said.

In my youth in the Transkei I listened to the elders of my tribe
telling stories of the old days. Amongst the tales they related to me
were those of wars fought by our ancestors in defence of the fatherland. The names of Dingane and Bambatha, Hintsa and Makana,
Squngthi and Dalasile, Moshoeshoe and Sekhukhuni, were praised as
the glory of the entire African nation. I hoped then that life might
offer me the opportunity to serve my people and make my own
humble contribution to their freedom struggle. This is what has
motivated me in all that I have done in relation to the charges made
against me in this case.

Having said this, I must deal immediately and at some length with
the question of violence. Some of the things so far told to the Court
are true and some are untrue. I do not, however, deny that I planned
sabotage. I did not plan it in a spirit of recklessness, nor because I
have any love of violence. I planned it as a result of a calm and sober
assessment of the political situation that had arisen after many years
of tyranny, exploitation, and oppression of my people by the whites.

I admit immediately that I was one of the persons who helped to form Umkhonto we Sizwe, and that I played a prominent role in its affairs until I was arrested in August 1962.

In the statement which I am about to make I shall correct certain false impressions which have been created by state witnesses. Amongst other things, I will demonstrate that certain of the acts referred to in the evidence were not and could not have been committed by Umkhonto. I will also deal with the relationship between the African National Congress and Umkhonto, and with the part which I personally have played in the affairs of both organisations. I shall deal also with the part played by the Communist Party. In order to explain these matters properly, I will have to explain what Umkhonto set out to achieve, what methods it prescribed for the achievement of these objects, and why these methods were chosen. I will also have to explain how I became involved in the activities of these organisations.

I deny that Umkhonto was responsible for a number of acts which clearly fell outside the policy of the organisation, and which have been charged in the indictment against us. I do not know what justification there was for these acts, but to demonstrate that they could not have been authorised by Umkhonto, I want to refer briefly to the roots and policy of the organisation.

I have already mentioned that I was one of the persons who helped to form Umkhonto. I, and the others who started the organisation, did so for two reasons. Firstly, we believed that as a result of government policy, violence by the African people had become inevitable, and that unless responsible leadership was given to canalise and control the feelings of our people, there would be outbreaks of terrorism which would produce an intensity of bitterness and hostility between the various races of this country which is not produced even by war. Secondly, we felt that without violence there would be no way open to the African people to succeed in their struggle against the principle of white supremacy. All lawful modes of expressing opposition to this principle had been closed by legislation, and we were placed in a position in which we had either to accept a permanent state of inferiority, or to defy the government. We chose to defy the law. We first broke the law in a way which avoided any recourse to violence; when this form was legislated against, and then the government resorted to a show of force to crush opposition to its policies, only then did we decide to answer violence with violence.

But the violence which we chose to adopt was not terrorism. We who formed Umkhonto were all members of the African National Congress, and had behind us the ANC tradition of non-violence and negotiation as a means of solving political disputes. We believe that South Africa belongs to all the people who live in it, and not to one group, be it black or white. We did not want an interracial war, and tried to avoid it to the last minute. If the Court is in doubt about this, it will be seen that the whole history of our organisation bears out what I have said, and what I will subsequently say, when I describe the tactics which Umkhonto decided to adopt. I want, therefore, to say something about the African National Congress.

The African National Congress was formed in 1912 to defend the rights of the African people which had been seriously curtailed by the South Africa Act, and which were then being threatened by the Native Land Act. For 37 years – that is, until 1949 – it adhered strictly to a constitutional struggle. It put forward demands and resolutions; it sent delegations to the government in the belief that African grievances could be settled through peaceful discussion and that Africans could advance gradually to full political rights. But white governments remained unmoved, and the rights of Africans became less instead of becoming greater. In the words of my leader, Chief Luthuli, who became President of the ANC in 1952, and who was later awarded the Nobel Peace Prize:

> Who will deny that thirty years of my life have been spent knocking in vain, patiently, moderately, and modestly at a closed and barred door? What have been the fruits of moderation? The past thirty years have seen the greatest number of laws restricting our rights and progress, until today we have reached a stage where we have almost no rights at all.

Even after 1949, the ANC remained determined to avoid violence. At this time, however, there was a change from the strictly constitutional means of protest which had been employed in the past. The change was embodied in a decision which was taken to protest against apartheid legislation by peaceful, but unlawful, demonstrations against certain laws. Pursuant to this policy the ANC launched the Defiance Campaign, in which I was placed in charge of volunteers. This campaign was based on the principles of passive resistance. More than 8 500 people defied apartheid laws and went to jail. Yet there was not a single instance of violence in the course of this

campaign on the part of any defier. I and 19 colleagues were convicted for the role which we played in organising the campaign, but
our sentences were suspended mainly because the Judge found that
discipline and non-violence had been stressed throughout. This was
the time when the volunteer section of the ANC was established, and
when the word '*Amadelakufa*' [Death Defiance!] was first used: this was
the time when the volunteers were asked to take a pledge to uphold
certain principles. Evidence dealing with volunteers and their pledges
has been introduced into this case, but completely out of context. The
volunteers were not, and are not, the soldiers of a black army pledged
to fight a civil war against the whites. They were, and are, dedicated
workers who are prepared to lead campaigns initiated by the ANC to
distribute leaflets, to organise strikes, or do whatever the particular
campaign required. They are called volunteers because they volunteer
to face the penalties of imprisonment and whipping which are now
prescribed by the legislature for such acts.

During the Defiance Campaign, the Public Safety Act and the
Criminal Law Amendment Act were passed. These Statutes provided
harsher penalties for offences committed by way of protests against
laws. Despite this, the protests continued and the ANC adhered to its
policy of non-violence. In 1956, 156 leading members of the Congress
Alliance, including myself, were arrested on a charge of high treason
and charges under the Suppression of Communism Act. The non-violent policy of the ANC was put in issue by the state, but when the
Court gave judgement some five years later, it found that the ANC did
not have a policy of violence. We were acquitted on all counts, which
included a count that the ANC sought to set up a communist state in
place of the existing regime. The government has always sought to
label all its opponents as communists. This allegation has been repeated in the present case, but as I will show, the ANC is not, and never
has been, a communist organisation.

In 1960 there was the shooting at Sharpeville, which resulted in
the proclamation of a state of emergency and the declaration of the
ANC as an unlawful organisation. My colleagues and I, after careful
consideration, decided that we would not obey this decree. The
African people were not part of the government and did not make
the laws by which they were governed. We believed in the words of
the Universal Declaration of Human Rights, that 'the will of the
people shall be the basis of authority of the government', and for us
to accept the banning was equivalent to accepting the silencing of

the Africans for all time. The ANC refused to dissolve, but instead went underground. We believed it was our duty to preserve this organisation which had been built up with almost 50 years of un-remitting toil. I have no doubt that no self-respecting white political organisation would disband itself if declared illegal by a government in which it had no say.

In 1960 the government held a referendum which led to the estab-lishment of the Republic. Africans, who constituted approximately 70 per cent of the population of South Africa, were not entitled to vote, and were not even consulted about the proposed constitutional change. All of us were apprehensive of our future under the proposed white Republic, and a resolution was taken to hold an All-In African Conference to call for a National Convention, and to organise mass demonstrations on the eve of the unwanted Republic, if the govern-ment failed to call the Convention. The conference was attended by Africans of various political persuasions. I was the Secretary of the con-ference and undertook to be responsible for organising the national stay-at-home which was subsequently called to coincide with the declaration of the Republic. As all strikes by Africans are illegal, the person organising such a strike must avoid arrest. I was chosen to be this person, and consequently I had to leave my home and family and my practice and go into hiding to avoid arrest.

The stay-at-home, in accordance with ANC policy, was to be a peaceful demonstration. Careful instructions were given to organisers and members to avoid any recourse to violence. The government's answer was to introduce new and harsher laws, to mobilise its armed forces, and to send Saracens, armed vehicles, and soldiers into the townships in a massive show of force designed to intimidate the peo-ple. This was an indication that the government had decided to rule by force alone, and this decision was a milestone on the road to Umkhonto.

Some of this may appear irrelevant to this trial. In fact, I believe none of it is irrelevant because it will, I hope, enable the Court to appreciate the attitude eventually adopted by the various persons and bodies concerned in the National Liberation Movement. When I went to jail in 1962, the dominant idea was that loss of life should be avoided. I now know that this was still so in 1963.

I must return to June 1961. What were we, the leaders of our people, to do? Were we to give in to the show of force and the implied threat against future action, or were we to fight it and, if so, how?

31

We had no doubt that we had to continue the fight. Anything else would have been abject surrender. Our problem was not whether to fight, but was how to continue the fight. We of the ANC had always stood for a nonracial democracy, and we shrank from any action which might drive the races further apart than they already were. But the hard facts were that 50 years of non-violence had brought the African people nothing but more and more repressive legislation, and fewer and fewer rights. It may not be easy for this Court to understand, but it is a fact that for a long time the people had been talking of violence – of the day when they would fight the white man and win back their country – and we, the leaders of the ANC, had nevertheless always prevailed upon them to avoid violence and to pursue peaceful methods. When some of us discussed this in May and June of 1961, it could not be denied that our policy to achieve a nonracial state by non-violence had achieved nothing, and that our followers were beginning to lose confidence in this policy and were developing disturbing ideas of terrorism.

It must not be forgotten that by this time violence had, in fact, become a feature of the South African political scene. There had been violence in 1957 when the women of Zeerust were ordered to carry passes; there was violence in 1958 with the enforcement of cattle culling in Sekhukhuniland; there was violence in 1959 when the people of Cato Manor protested against pass raids; there was violence in 1960 when the government attempted to impose Bantu Authorities in Pondoland. Thirty-nine Africans died in these disturbances. In 1961 there had been riots in Warmbaths, and all this time the Transkei had been a seething mass of unrest. Each disturbance pointed clearly to the inevitable growth among Africans of the belief that violence was the only way out – it showed that a government which uses force to maintain its rule teaches the oppressed to use force to oppose it. Already small groups had arisen in the urban areas and were spontaneously making plans for violent forms of political struggle. There now arose a danger that these groups would adopt terrorism against Africans, as well as whites, if not properly directed. Particularly disturbing was the type of violence engendered in places such as Zeerust, Sekhukhuniland, and Pondoland amongst Africans. It was increasingly taking the form, not of struggle against the government – though this is what prompted it – but of civil strife amongst themselves, conducted in such a way that it could not hope to achieve anything other than a loss of life and bitterness.

At the beginning of June 1961, after a long and anxious assessment of the South African situation, I, and some colleagues, came to the conclusion that as violence in this country was inevitable, it would be unrealistic and wrong for African leaders to continue preaching peace and non-violence at a time when the government met our peaceful demands with force.

This conclusion was not easily arrived at. It was only when all else had failed, when all channels of peaceful protest had been barred to us, that the decision was made to embark on violent forms of political struggle, and to form Umkhonto we Sizwe. We did so not because we desired such a course, but solely because the government had left us with no other choice. In the manifesto of Umkhonto, published on 16 December 1961, we said:

> The time comes in the life of any nation when there remain only two choices – submit or fight. That time has now come to South Africa. We shall not submit and we have no choice but to hit back by all means in our power in defence of our people, our future, and our freedom.

This was our feeling in June of 1961 when we decided to press for a change in the policy of the National Liberation Movement. I can only say that I felt morally obliged to do what I did.

. . .

As a result of this decision, Umkhonto was formed in November 1961. When we took this decision, and subsequently formulated our plans, the ANC heritage of non-violence and racial harmony was very much with us. We felt that the country was drifting towards a civil war in which blacks and whites would fight each other. We viewed the situation with alarm. Civil war could mean the destruction of what the ANC stood for; with civil war, racial peace would be more difficult than ever to achieve. We already have examples in South African history of the results of war. It has taken more than 50 years for the scars of the South African War to disappear. How much longer would it take to eradicate the scars of inter-racial civil war, which could not be fought without a great loss of life on both sides?

The avoidance of civil war had dominated our thinking for many years, but when we decided to adopt violence as part of our policy, we realised that we might one day have to face the prospect of such a war. This had to be taken into account in formulating our plans. We required a plan which was flexible and which permitted us to act in accordance with the needs of the times; above all, the plan had to be one which recognised civil war as the last resort, and left the decision on this question to the future. We did not want to be committed to civil war, but we wanted to be ready if it became inevitable.

Four forms of violence were possible. There is sabotage, there is guerrilla warfare, there is terrorism, and there is open revolution. We chose to adopt the first method and to exhaust it before taking any other decision.

In the light of our political background the choice was a logical one. Sabotage did not involve loss of life, and it offered the best hope for future race relations. Bitterness would be kept to a minimum and, if the policy bore fruit, democratic government could become a reality. This is what we felt at the time, and this is what we said in our manifesto:

> We of Umkhonto we Sizwe have always sought to achieve liberation without bloodshed and civil clash. We hope, even at this late hour, that our first actions will awaken everyone to a realisation of the disastrous situation to which the Nationalist policy is leading. We hope that we will bring the government and its supporters to their senses before it is too late, so that both the government and its policies can be changed before matters reach the desperate state of civil war.

The initial plan was based on a careful analysis of the political and economic situation of our country. We believed that South Africa depended to a large extent on foreign capital and foreign trade. We felt that planned destruction of power plants, and interference with rail and telephone communications, would tend to scare away capital from the country, make it more difficult for goods from the industrial areas to reach the seaports on schedule, and would in the long run be a heavy drain on the economic life of the country, thus compelling the voters of the country to reconsider their position.

Attacks on the economic lifelines of the country were to be linked with sabotage on government buildings and other symbols of apartheid. These attacks would serve as a source of inspiration to our people. In addition, they would provide an outlet for those people who were urging the adoption of violent methods and would enable us to give concrete proof to our followers that we had adopted a stronger line and were fighting back against government violence.

In addition, if mass action were successfully organised, and mass reprisals taken, we felt that sympathy for our cause would be roused in other countries, and that greater pressure would be brought to bear on the South African government.

. . .

Umkhonto had its first operation on 16 December 1961, when government buildings in Johannesburg, Port Elizabeth and Durban were attacked. The selection of targets is proof of the policy to which I have referred. Had we intended to attack life we would have selected targets where people congregated and not empty buildings and power stations. The sabotage which was committed before 16 December 1961 was the work of isolated groups and had no connection whatever with Umkhonto. In fact, some of these and a number of later acts were claimed by other organisations.

The manifesto of Umkhonto was issued on the day that operations commenced. The response to our actions and manifesto among the white population was characteristically violent. The government threatened to take strong action, and called upon its supporters to stand firm and to ignore the demands of the Africans. The whites failed to respond by suggesting change; they responded to our call by suggesting the laager.

In contrast, the response of the Africans was one of encouragement. Suddenly there was hope again. Things were happening. People in the townships became eager for political news. A great deal of enthusiasm was generated by the initial successes, and people began to speculate on how soon freedom would be obtained.

But we in Umkhonto weighed up the white response with anxiety. The lines were being drawn. The whites and blacks were moving into separate camps, and the prospects of avoiding a civil war were made less. The white newspapers carried reports that sabotage would be punished by death. If this was so, how could we continue to keep Africans away from terrorism?

Already scores of Africans had died as a result of racial friction. In 1920 when the famous leader, Masabala, was held in Port Elizabeth jail, 24 of a group of Africans who had gathered to demand his release were killed by the police and white civilians. In 1921, more than 100 Africans died in the Bulhoek affair. In 1924 over 200 Africans were killed when the Administrator of South-West Africa led a force against a group which had rebelled against the imposition of dog tax. On 1 May 1950, 18 Africans died as a result of police shootings during the strike. On 21 March 1960, 69 unarmed Africans died at Sharpeville.

How many more Sharpevilles would there be in the history of our country? And how many more Sharpevilles could the country stand without violence and terror becoming the order of the day? And what would happen to our people when that stage was reached? In the long run we felt certain we must succeed, but at what cost to ourselves and the rest of the country? And if this happened, how could black and white ever live together again in peace and harmony? These were the problems that faced us, and these were our decisions.

Experience convinced us that rebellion would offer the government limitless opportunities for the indiscriminate slaughter of our people. But it was precisely because the soil of South Africa is already drenched with the blood of innocent Africans that we felt it our duty to make preparations as a long-term undertaking to use force in order to defend ourselves against force. If war were inevitable, we wanted the fight to be conducted on terms most favourable to our people. The fight which held out prospects best for us and the least risk of life to both sides was guerrilla warfare. We decided, therefore, in our preparations for the future, to make provision for the possibility of guerrilla warfare.

All whites undergo compulsory military training, but no such training was given to Africans. It was in our view essential to build up a nucleus of trained men who would be able to provide the leadership which would be required if guerrilla warfare started. We had to prepare for such a situation before it became too late to make proper preparations. It was also necessary to build up a nucleus of men trained in civil administration and other professions, so that Africans would be equipped to participate in the government of this country as soon as they were allowed to do so.

. . .

I turn now to my own position. I have denied that I am a communist, and I think that in the circumstances I am obliged to state exactly what my political beliefs are.

I have always regarded myself, in the first place, as an African patriot. After all, I was born in Umtata, 46 years ago. My guardian was my cousin, who was the acting paramount chief of Thembuland, and I am related both to the present paramount chief of Thembuland, Sabata Dalindyebo, and to Kaizer Matanzima, the Chief Minister of the Transkei.

Today I am attracted by the idea of a classless society, an attraction which springs in part from Marxist reading and, in part, from my admiration of the structure and organisation of early African societies in this country. The land, then the main means of production, belonged to the tribe. There were no rich or poor and there was no exploitation.

It is true, as I have already stated, that I have been influenced by Marxist thought. But this is also true of many of the leaders of the new independent states. Such widely different persons as Gandhi, Nehru, Nkrumah, and Nasser all acknowledge this fact. We all accept the need for some form of socialism to enable our people to catch up with the advanced countries of this world and to overcome their legacy of extreme poverty. But this does not mean we are Marxists.

Indeed, for my own part, I believe that it is open to debate whether the Communist Party has any specific role to play at this particular stage of our political struggle. The basic task at the present moment is the removal of race discrimination and the attainment of democratic rights on the basis of the Freedom Charter. In so far as that Party furthers this task, I welcome its assistance. I realise that it is one of the means by which people of all races can be drawn into our struggle.

From my reading of Marxist literature and from conversations with Marxists, I have gained the impression that communists regard the parliamentary system of the West as undemocratic and reactionary. But, on the contrary, I am an admirer of such a system.

The Magna Carta, the Petition of Rights, and the Bill of Rights are documents which are held in veneration by democrats throughout the world.

I have great respect for British political institutions, and for the country's system of justice. I regard the British Parliament as the most democratic institution in the world, and the independence and impartiality of its judiciary never fail to arouse my admiration.

The American Congress, that country's doctrine of separation of powers, as well as the independence of its judiciary, arouses in me similar sentiments.

I have been influenced in my thinking by both West and East. All this has led me to feel that in my search for a political formula, I should be absolutely impartial and objective. I should tie myself to no particular system of society other than of socialism. I must leave myself free to borrow the best from the West and from the East.

. . .

Our fight is against real, and not imaginary, hardships or, to use the language of the State Prosecutor, 'so-called hardships'. Basically, we fight against two features which are the hallmarks of African life in South Africa and which are entrenched by legislation which we seek to have repealed. These features are poverty and lack of human dignity, and we do not need communists or so-called 'agitators' to teach us about these things.

South Africa is the richest country in Africa, and could be one of the richest countries in the world. But it is a land of extremes and remarkable contrasts. The whites enjoy what may well be the highest standard of living in the world, whilst Africans live in poverty and misery. Forty per cent of the Africans live in hopelessly overcrowded and, in some cases, drought-stricken Reserves, where soil erosion and the overworking of the soil makes it impossible for them to live properly off the land. Thirty per cent are labourers, labour tenants, and squatters on white farms and work and live under conditions similar to those of the serfs of the Middle Ages. The other 30 per cent live in towns where they have developed economic and social habits which bring them closer in many respects to white standards. Yet most Africans, even in this group, are impoverished by low incomes and high cost of living.

The highest-paid and the most prosperous section of urban African life is in Johannesburg. Yet their actual position is desperate. The latest figures were given on 25 March 1964 by Mr Carr, Manager of the Johannesburg Non-European Affairs Department. The poverty datum line for the average African family in Johannesburg (according to Mr Carr's department) is R42.84 per month. He showed that the average monthly wage is R32.24 and that 46 per cent of all African families in Johannesburg do not earn enough to keep them going.

Poverty goes hand in hand with malnutrition and disease. The incidence of malnutrition and deficiency diseases is very high amongst Africans. Tuberculosis, pellagra, kwashiorkor, gastroenteritis and scurvy bring death and destruction of health. The incidence of infant mortality is one of the highest in the world. According to the Medical Officer of Health for Pretoria, tuberculosis kills 40 people a day (almost all Africans), and in 1961 there were 58 491 new cases reported. These diseases not only destroy the vital organs of the body, but they result in retarded mental conditions and lack of initiative, and reduce powers of concentration. The secondary results of such conditions affect the whole community and the standard of work performed by African labourers.

The complaint of Africans, however, is not only that they are poor and the whites are rich, but that the laws which are made by the whites are designed to preserve this situation. There are two ways to break out of poverty. The first is by formal education, and the second is by the worker acquiring a greater skill at his work and thus higher wages. As far as Africans are concerned, both these avenues of advancement are deliberately curtailed by legislation.

The present government has always sought to hamper Africans in their search for education. One of their early acts, after coming into power, was to stop subsidies for African school feeding. Many African children who attended schools depended on this supplement to their diet. This was a cruel act.

There is compulsory education for all white children at virtually no cost to their parents, be they rich or poor. Similar facilities are not provided for the African children, though there are some who receive such assistance. African children, however, generally have to pay more for their schooling than whites. According to figures quoted by the South African Institute of Race Relations in its 1963 journal approximately 40 per cent of African children in the age group between seven to 14 do not attend school. For those who do attend school, the standards are vastly different from those afforded to white children. In 1960–61 the per capita government spending on African students at state-aided schools was estimated at R12.46. In the same years, the per capita spending on white children in the Cape Province (which are the only figures available to me) was R144.57. Although there are no figures available to me, it can be stated, without doubt, that the white children on whom R144.57 per head was being spent all came from wealthier homes than African children on whom R12.46 per head was being spent.

The quality of education is also different. According to the *Bantu Educational Journal*, only 5 660 African children in the whole of South Africa passed their Junior Certificate in 1962, and in that year only 362 passed matric. This is presumably consistent with the policy of Bantu Education about which the present Prime Minister said, during the debate on the Bantu Education Bill in 1953:

> When I have control of Native education I will reform it so that Natives will be taught from childhood to realise that equality with Europeans is not for them. . . . People who believe in equality are not desirable teachers for Natives. When my Department controls Native education it will know for what class of higher education a Native is fitted, and whether he will have a chance in life to use his knowledge.

The other main obstacle to the economic advancement of the African is the industrial colour-bar under which all the better jobs of industry are reserved for whites only. Moreover, Africans who do obtain employment in the unskilled and semi-skilled occupations which are open to them are not allowed to form trade unions which have recognition under the Industrial Conciliation Act. This means that strikes of African workers are illegal, and that they are denied the right of collective bargaining which is permitted to the better-paid white workers. The discrimination in the policy of successive South African governments towards African workers is demonstrated by the so-called 'civilised labour policy' under which sheltered, unskilled government jobs are found for those white workers who cannot make the grade in industry, at wages which far exceed the earnings of the average African employee in industry.

The government often answers its critics by saying that Africans in South Africa are economically better off than the inhabitants of the other countries in Africa. I do not know whether this statement is true and doubt whether any comparison can be made without having regard to the cost-of-living index in such countries. But even if it is true, as far as the African people are concerned it is irrelevant. Our complaint is not that we are poor by comparison with people in other countries, but that we are poor by comparison with the white people in our own country, and that we are prevented by legislation from altering this imbalance.

The lack of human dignity experienced by Africans is the direct result of the policy of white supremacy. White supremacy implies black inferiority. Legislation designed to preserve white supremacy entrenches this notion. Menial tasks in South Africa are invariably performed by Africans. When anything has to be carried or cleaned the white man will look around for an African to do it for him, whether the African is employed by him or not. Because of this sort of attitude, whites tend to regard Africans as a separate breed. They do not look upon them as people with families of their own; they do not realise that they have emotions — that they fall in love like white people do; that they want to be with their wives and children like white people want to be with theirs; that they want to earn enough money to support their families properly, to feed and clothe them and send them to school. And what 'house-boy' or 'garden-boy' or labourer can ever hope to do this?

Pass laws, which to the Africans are among the most hated bits of

legislation in South Africa, render any African liable to police surveillance at any time. I doubt whether there is a single African male
in South Africa who has not at some stage had a brush with the
police over his pass. Hundreds and thousands of Africans are thrown
into jail each year under pass laws. Even worse than this is the fact
that pass laws keep husband and wife apart and lead to the breakdown of family life.

Poverty and the breakdown of family life have secondary effects.
Children wander about the streets of the townships because they
have no schools to go to, or no money to enable them to go to
school, or no parents at home to see that they go to school, because
both parents (if there be two) have to work to keep the family alive.
This leads to a breakdown in moral standards, to an alarming rise in
illegitimacy, and to growing violence which erupts not only politically, but everywhere. Life in the townships is dangerous. There is not
a day that goes by without somebody being stabbed or assaulted. And
violence is carried out of the townships into the white living areas.
People are afraid to walk alone in the streets after dark. House-
breakings and robberies are increasing, despite the fact that the death
sentence can now be imposed for such offences. Death sentences
cannot cure the festering sore.

Africans want to be paid a living wage. Africans want to perform
work which they are capable of doing, and not work which the
government declares them to be capable of. Africans want to be
allowed to live where they obtain work, and not be endorsed out of
an area because they were not born there. Africans want to be
allowed to own land in places where they work, and not to be
obliged to live in rented houses which they can never call their own.
Africans want to be part of the general population, and not confined
to living in their own ghettoes. African men want to have their wives
and children to live with them where they work, and not be forced
into an unnatural existence in men's hostels. African women want to
be with their menfolk and not be left permanently widowed in the
Reserves. Africans want to be allowed out after 11 o'clock at night
and not to be confined to their rooms like little children. Africans
want to be allowed to travel in their own country and to seek work
where they want to and not where the Labour Bureau tells them to.
Africans want a just share in the whole of South Africa; they want
security and a stake in society.

Above all, we want equal political rights, because without them our disabilities will be permanent. I know this sounds revolutionary to the whites in this country, because the majority of voters will be Africans. This makes the white man fear democracy.

But this fear cannot be allowed to stand in the way of the only solution which will guarantee racial harmony and freedom for all. It is not true that the enfranchisement of all will result in racial domination. Political division based on colour is entirely artificial and, when it disappears, so will the domination of one colour group by another. The ANC has spent half a century fighting against racialism. When it triumphs it will not change that policy.

This then is what the ANC is fighting. Their struggle is a truly national one. It is a struggle of the African people, inspired by their own suffering and their own experience. It is a struggle for the right to live.

During my lifetime I have dedicated myself to this struggle of the African people. I have fought against white domination, and I have fought against black domination. I have cherished the ideal of a democratic and free society in which all persons live together in harmony and with equal opportunities. It is an ideal which I hope to live for and to achieve. But if needs be, it is an ideal for which I am prepared to die.

We Shall Crush Apartheid

Response to the Soweto Uprising of 1976, smuggled out of
Robben Island Prison, published by the African National Congress,
10 June 1980.

The gun has played an important part in our history. The resistance of the black man to white colonial intrusion was crushed by the gun. Our struggle to liberate ourselves from white domination is held in check by force of arms. From conquest to the present the story is the same. Successive white regimes have repeatedly massacred unarmed defenceless blacks. And wherever and whenever they have pulled out their guns the ferocity of their fire has been trained on the African people.

Apartheid is the embodiment of the racialism, repression and inhumanity of all previous white supremacist regimes. To see the real face of apartheid we must look beneath the veil of constitutional formulas, deceptive phrases and playing with words.

The rattle of gunfire and the rumbling of Hippo armoured vehicles since June 1976 have once again torn aside that veil. Spread across the face of our country, in black townships, the racist army and police have been pouring a hail of bullets killing and maiming hundreds of black men, women and children. The toll of the dead and injured already surpasses that of all past massacres carried out by this regime.

Apartheid is the rule of the gun and the hangman. The Hippo, the FN rifle and the gallows are its true symbols. These remain the easiest resort, the ever-ready solution of the race-mad rulers of South Africa.

In the midst of the present crisis, while our people count the dead and nurse the injured, they ask themselves: what lies ahead?

From our rulers we can expect nothing. They are the ones who give orders to the soldier crouching over his rifle: theirs is the spirit that moves the finger that caresses the trigger.

Vague promises, tinkerings with the machinery of apartheid, constitution juggling, massive arrests and detentions side by side with renewed overtures aimed at weakening and forestalling the unity of us blacks and dividing the forces of change – these are the fixed paths along which they will move. For they are neither capable nor willing to heed the verdict of the masses of our people.

That verdict of 16 June is loud and clear: apartheid has failed. Our people remain unequivocal in its rejection. The young and the old, parent and child, all reject it. At the forefront of this 1976/77 wave of unrest were our students and youth. They come from the universities, high schools and even primary schools. They are a generation whose whole education has been under the diabolical design of the racists to poison the minds and brainwash our children into docile subjects of apartheid rule. But after more than 20 years of Bantu Education the circle is closed and nothing demonstrates the utter bankruptcy of apartheid as clearly as the revolt of our youth.

The evils, the cruelty and the inhumanity of apartheid have been there from its inception. And all blacks – Africans, coloureds and Indians – have opposed it all along the line. What is now unmistakable, what the current wave of unrest has sharply highlighted, is this: that despite all the window-dressing and smooth talk, apartheid has become intolerable.

This awareness reaches over and beyond the particulars of our enslavement. The measure of this truth is the recognition by our people that under apartheid our lives, individually and collectively, count for nothing.

We face an enemy that is deep-rooted, an enemy entrenched and determined not to yield. Our march to freedom is long and difficult. But both within and beyond our borders the prospects of victory grow bright.

The first condition for victory is black unity. Every effort to divide the blacks, to woo and pit one black group against another, must be vigorously repulsed. Our people – African, coloured, Indian and democratic whites – must be united into a single massive and solid wall of resistance, of united mass action.

Our struggle is growing sharper. This is not the time for the luxury of division and disunity. At all levels and in every walk of life we must close ranks. Within the ranks of the people differences must be submerged to the achievement of a single goal – the complete overthrow of apartheid and racist domination.

The revulsion of the world against apartheid is growing and the frontiers of white supremacy are shrinking. Mozambique and Angola are free and the war of liberation gathers force in Namibia and

Zimbabwe. The soil of our country is destined to be the scene of the fiercest fight and the sharpest battles to rid our continent of the last vestiges of white minority rule.

The world is on our side. The OAU, the UN and the anti-apartheid movement continue to put pressure on the racist rulers of our country. Every effort to isolate South Africa adds strength to our struggle.

At all levels of our struggle, within and outside the country, much has been achieved and much remains to be done. But victory is certain!

We who are confined within the grey walls of the Pretoria regime's prisons reach out to our people. With you we count those who have perished by means of the gun and the hangman's rope. We salute all of you – the living, the injured and the dead. For you have dared to rise up against the tyrant's might.

Even as we bow at their graves we remember this: the dead live on as martyrs in our hearts and minds, a reproach to our disunity and the host of shortcomings that accompany divisions among the oppressed, a spur to our efforts to close ranks, and a reminder that the freedom of our people is yet to be won.

We face the future with confidence. For the guns that serve apartheid cannot render it unconquerable. Those who live by the gun shall perish by the gun.

Between the anvil of united mass action and the hammer of the armed struggle we shall crush apartheid and white minority racist rule.

Amandla ngawethu! Matla ke a rona!

I Will Return

Response to a conditional offer of freedom, read on his behalf
by his daughter Zindzi, Jabulani Stadium, Soweto,
10 February 1985.

I am a member of the African National Congress. I have always been a member of the African National Congress and I will remain a member of the African National Congress until the day I die. Oliver Tambo is much more than a brother to me. He is my greatest friend and comrade for nearly 50 years. If there is any one amongst you who cherishes my freedom, Oliver Tambo cherishes it more, and I know that he would give his life to see me free. There is no difference between his views and mine.

I am surprised at the conditions that the government wants to impose on me. I am not a violent man. My colleagues and I wrote in 1952 to Malan asking for a round table conference to find a solution to the problems of our country, but that was ignored. When Strijdom was in power, we made the same offer. Again it was ignored. When Verwoerd was in power we asked for a National Convention for all the people in South Africa to decide on their future. This, too, was in vain.

It was only then, when all other forms of resistance were no longer open to us, that we turned to armed struggle. Let Botha show that he is different to Malan, Strijdom and Verwoerd. Let him renounce violence. Let him say that he will dismantle apartheid. Let him unban the people's organisation, the African National Congress. Let him free all who have been imprisoned, banished or exiled for their opposition to apartheid. Let him guarantee free political activity so that people may decide who will govern them.

I cherish my own freedom dearly, but I care even more for your freedom. Too many have died since I went to prison. Too many have suffered for the love of freedom. I owe it to their widows, to their orphans, to their mothers and to their fathers who have grieved and wept for them. Not only I have suffered during these long, lonely, wasted years. I am not less life-loving than you are. But I cannot sell my birthright, nor am I prepared to sell the birthright of the people to be free. I am in prison as the representative of the people and of your organisation, the African National Congress, which was banned.

What freedom am I being offered while the organisation of the people remains banned? What freedom am I being offered when I may be arrested on a pass offence? What freedom am I being offered to live my life as a family with my dear wife who remains in banishment in Brandfort? What freedom am I being offered when I must ask for permission to live in an urban area? What freedom am I being offered when I need a stamp in my pass to seek work? What freedom am I being offered when my very South African citizenship is not respected?

Only free men can negotiate. Prisoners cannot enter into contracts. Herman Toivo ja Toivo, when freed, never gave any undertaking, nor was he called upon to do so.

I cannot and will not give any undertaking at a time when I and you, the people, are not free.

Your freedom and mine cannot be separated. I will return.

2
FREEDOM

FREEDOM IN OUR LIFETIME

ALBIE SACHS

There is a pride that cometh not before fall, but before rising up. If ever we start to forget what seemed unforgettable, let us recapture the pride we felt as we heard the valiant words of Nelson Mandela to the huge crowd gathered on the Grand Parade in Cape Town hours after his release. No professional speech-writers here, no carefully launched flights of verbal imagination. Straightforward prose, direct and forceful in that voice that had been silenced since his famous speech from the dock nearly 30 years before (and that we have now come to know so well and feel so affectionately towards that even schoolboys whose voices have not broken imitate it). The emotion on that great occasion came not from the adjectives and the imagery of the address, but from the moment and the setting and the tears of happiness that each listener and viewer had. History itself provided the poetry. The hard, cruel period was over. Free, free at last. The prisoners were being released, the exiles could return. Conditions for free political activity were being created. The process of negotiating a new Constitution and of irreversibly dismantling the structures of apartheid was beginning.

In the 1950s as a young law student I had frequently appeared at meetings on the Grand Parade, and lustily joined in the shouting of the slogan: Freedom in Our Lifetime! Now, through the words of Nelson Mandela, our generation could shout: Freedom in our lifetime, at last. The dismemberment of our country into racially defined areas would be over. No more pass laws, no more prohibition of inter-racial sex or marriage, no more laws creating separate and inferior schools, hospitals, trains and buses for the majority, no more exclusion on grounds of race from sports teams, beaches and hotels. And soon we would achieve our central and all-defining goal of a nonracial franchise based on a common voters' roll, the key to all political transformation. This was the form that self-determination for the oppressed African majority would take in

51

South Africa, already an independent state: not secession and the creation of a new country, but the total de-racialisation of the state, the elimination of colonial-type forms of racial subordination and the creation of a common citizenship for all. Freedom in the lifetime of those who had survived. Freedom, joyous freedom, at last.

And those of us who had been entrusted with the task of laying the groundwork for a new Constitution felt our blood racing. We knew that everything would be contested: who should make the Constitution, how it should be made and what its content should be. It was not enough to talk about freedom and proclaim its arrival. It had to be guaranteed by creating rock-solid institutions for its protection and nurturing. We were particularly concerned that under the guise of ending apartheid new forms of safeguarding minority privilege would be established: race-group vetoes in government, and the privatisation of apartheid for perpetuity through giving constitutional protection to property rights and freedom of association. We were willing and eager to guarantee all universally accepted fundamental rights, but the Constitution had to be a nonracial one that opened the way for appropriate law-governed methods of dealing with the huge divisions and inequalities in our country. Our legal teams were scattered. We needed urgently to pool our ideas, to bring the ex-political prisoners together with those who would soon be the ex-exiles, together with the many democratic lawyers who had stayed on in the country and used what space had been available to them to further the struggle inside and outside the courts.

Free, free at last. The vast network of security laws giving the authorities powers to detain and repress opponents would be repealed, as would the laws restricting the press and empowering officials to state what we could read or see or how we could express ourselves artistically. If freedom was to be understood simply as the absence of oppression, the long walk to freedom would soon be over. Apartheid as a formal system of government would be a thing of the past and the massive structures of state oppression of the majority would be gone. People could express themselves freely, move freely, choose their governments freely, and get on with their lives freely both as individuals and as members of communities. Freedom of conscience and religion would be guaranteed while workers and employers would be free to advance their respective interests; women would be freed from discrimination, and barriers to their advancement removed.

And yet, as the run up to the great poetic speech four years later at the Inauguration of Nelson Mandela as first President of democratic South

Africa showed, as soon as one long walk to freedom ended, another long walk to freedom began. We were learning that triumph in relation to the past was one thing, but triumphalism in respect of the future was another. The apparent miracle of the negotiated revolution had not been the product of good chemistry between the leaders – in fact their great virtue was that they were able to remain steady even during periods of bad chemistry. On the contrary, it was the outcome of prolonged, painstaking and imaginative hard work in which consensus between different viewpoints was always sought and the innumerable details over which we fought were eventually always placed in the context of the large picture. Madiba was strong both on the importance of free speech in arriving at a consensus and in never losing sight of the overall view. As his predecessors as President of the ANC, Chief Albert Luthuli and Oliver Tambo, had done, he encouraged important policy positions to emerge from open and democratic debate rather than to be imposed from above. It was in this spirit that we embarked on the process of defining and securing the lineaments of our burgeoning freedom. We invited broadly based groups of legal people, political scientists and grassroots representatives to hold workshops on key areas, and then threw open all major proposals to intensive political debate. While Madiba often had his own point of view, he saw his role as leader as being that of holding the ring while hard issues were being freely debated. There was no question of declaring his own positions and then demanding adherence to them as a test of loyalty.

In fact there was one matter over which he had strong personal feelings, and where I was appointed to argue that he was plainly wrong, not once but three times. It related to the voting age. Madiba insisted that it be as low as fifteen or sixteen, pointing to the special role that the youth had played in resisting apartheid. The constitutional committee of which I was a member felt that we should go for eighteen, the age with the greatest international acceptance. At the meeting where the final decision had to be taken Madiba insisted on his position, while I contended for ours. One by one people spoke tactfully but firmly in favour of eighteen. A vote was not necessary. Stung and unhappy, Madiba conceded the point, declaring that the future would show that he had been right. Yet for all that he had been unpersuaded by the argument, and despite his pride having manifestly been wounded, not once thereafter during our many encounters did I ever feel that his defeat on the question of the voting age rankled with him or created a sense of distance between us. On the contrary, he made it clear with his warm body language and sly humour that our duty was always to speak the truth, to listen to others and to debate difficult issues honestly and openly. If a free person has the right and duty to speak truth to power, so does the free person in power have the right and duty to communicate candidly with those affected by his or her decisions. And on the subject of the voting age, history in fact has spoken, through the voice of Madiba himself: he said recently that he had been wrong in his position, and that Presidents should not balk at changing their minds!

It is both a virtue and a danger that our Constitution today is taken for granted, as if somehow it wrote itself. Yet every detail was laboured over and thought through. Madiba was such a popular figure that some harboured the idea of creating a powerful Presidency invested with vast authority to promote the transformation that the country needed. Yet with the full concurrence of Madiba himself this temptation was resisted. One of the recommendations of the constitutional committee that had been incorporated into the Constitution was that the President not be elected by direct suffrage, but instead be chosen by Parliament at its first sitting. Not only were we worried about possible institutional paralysis if one day the Presidency went one way and the legislature another, we were concerned that the traditions of highly personalised authoritarian rule of the past would re-assert themselves, that is, the practices of the colonial Governor General exercising power as the Supreme Chief of the African population, and those of the dictatorial traditional leaders who had sided with Pretoria against their communities. When the highly centralised and secretive forms of leadership that had been necessitated by underground resistance to apartheid were thrown into the mix, all the conditions conducive to an authoritarian Presidency would be there. So Parliament was given the central position in the governmental structures, with the President chosen by and answerable to Parliament. The swearing in of Nelson Rolihlahla Mandela as both head of government and head of state was a gloriously giddy moment for the nation and the world.

The beautifully spacious ambience of the Union Buildings up on the hill overlooking Pretoria provided a fitting scene for the sober but joyous ushering in of a new era of constitutional democracy in South Africa. How we had hated those buildings as the centre of oppression, and how often we had envisaged storming them and raising the flag of insurrection on the rooftop. Now, without warfare and through the negotiated processes of democracy, Nelson Mandela was taking the oath to uphold our new and admired Constitution. Calmer and far more lyrical than the speech after his release, and giving measured expression to measureless happiness, his carefully selected and cadenced words announced the arrival of two profound commitments that were to dominate his speeches thereafter.

The first was: never again. Never again should anyone, whoever they were, and whoever their ancestors had been, be treated with disrespect for their fundamental rights and disregard for their humanity. This was a philosophical commitment, emerging from years of struggle against racism, rooted in the African tradition of *Ubuntu* and drawing on universal notions of fundamental rights. It was central to the vision of those facilitating the emergence of a new society, and was constitutionally guaranteed by a strong Bill of Rights to be guarded by the Constitutional Court and the Commissions for Human Rights and Gender Equality respectively. It was also the basis on which the remarkable Truth and Reconciliation Commission was set up.

Some months later it was my turn, in the presence of Mandela, to swear the oath to uphold the Constitution. The occasion was the inauguration of the Constitutional Court. Madiba began his address with the striking words: 'The last time I stood up in court was to find out if I would be hanged. Today I rise to inaugurate South Africa's first Constitutional Court.' Institution-building, institution-building, institution-building. Freedom was not just a state of affairs. It had to be constantly nurtured in terms of general popular culture and permanently protected by strong and independent institutions. And institutions were not impersonal abstractions: the Court was us, eleven men and women, ourselves products of South African history, each with his or her own life experiences and personalities, but all together 'the Bench'. And later that year we were to find out directly how awesome in a constitutional sense our responsibilities were. We were asked by opponents of the government to declare invalid and strike down proclamations by President Mandela regulating the holding of the first democratic local government elections in the Western Cape, as well as to declare invalid the Parliamentary statute which authorised him to pass such proclamations. This was not a manifestly evil law left over from the apartheid past. It was a measure adopted by Mandela to enable people to exercise their full democratic rights as equal citizens for the first time at the local government level. Yet despite the manifestly beneficent objectives of the proclamations, the Constitutional Court struck them down, stating that Parliament had no authority to authorise the President to make such laws, but, following proper 'manner and form' in terms of Parliamentary procedure, had to do so itself. The immediate result was that elections in the Western Cape

had to be postponed and Parliament re-convened, but the enduring principle was that public power could only be exercised in the manner
envisaged by the Constitution. It has been said that that was the moment
when South Africa's new democracy was baptised in the font of consti-
tutionalism. Nelson Mandela immediately went on television. Despite
having suffered what the press referred to as a political setback, he stated that he fully accepted the decision of the Court, and emphasised that
he as President must be the first to show respect for the Constitution as
interpreted by the Constitutional Court. In this way, the supremacy of the
Constitution and the impossibility of separating freedom from the rule of
law and an independent judiciary were established. In the view of many
commentators, far from emerging with his reputation damaged, Madiba
came through with his standing enhanced, as if people were feeling:
what a marvellous country he is the President of.

The second Presidential commitment related to freedom from want.
We did not wish to have a society that merely guaranteed that a person
dying of hunger had the right to curse the government with his or her last
breath. Our goal was one where hunger, illiteracy and homelessness
would be banished, where everyone had access to food, clothing and
education, where freedom was seen as inseparable from human dignity
and equality. Though absence of undue restraint was central to any
notion of freedom, our aim to overcome the abuses of the apartheid past
and achieve negative liberty was to be seen merely as the starting point
and precondition, by no means expressive of the full content of a mature
democracy. Thus, the government was not only to be under a duty never
again to limit rights in a manner that could not be justified in an open
and democratic society. It was also to be obliged to create conditions to
enable people effectively to enjoy all their rights. The central idea of
rights is not simply that you have them and no one can take them away,
but that you are able to enjoy them. Thus, persons completely overwhelmed by necessitous circumstances could not be regarded as free,
however much they had the right to vote, to believe and to complain.
Our Constitution accordingly gave unique attention to ensuring that
social and economic rights could be enforced by the courts in a progressive and sustainable way.

The amplitude of the constitutional commitment to the enjoyment of
the fruits of freedom did not stop there. To ensure that no one should
arbitrarily have his or her moral citizenship diminished, the Bill of Rights
set out a long list of grounds of discrimination that would be presump-
tively unfair, including not only race, colour, creed and gender, but dis-

ability and sexual orientation. It also had strong and innovative provisions relating to environmental rights. Yet perhaps its most strikingly advanced feature as far as human dignity and freedom were concerned, was the way in which it placed nonsexism on a par with nonracialism as a foundational feature of the Constitution. We South Africans are so overwhelmed by the question of race that we can easily downplay the importance of sexism in our society. Yet sexism can be as pernicious in inhibiting freedom and self-determination as racism, sometimes even more so because it is presented as being a phenomenon of nature or an intrinsic part of the people's culture. And the overlap of gender and race can be particularly inhibiting.

How would Madiba conduct himself in this intensely complicated area of public and private life? Some declared that he was a natural patriarch, others a natural democrat, yet others that he was both. All agreed that what had traditionally been regarded as the manly virtues, such as courage and honour, played a strong role in his world view. Thus, in rejecting proposals during the early days of negotiations from the then government, he would say with distinctive patrician forcefulness: 'No man worth his salt would accept these terms.' Yet this phase did not last long. Perhaps because he staffed his office with women who were strong and not the silent type, and who, he said with characteristic playfulness, controlled him more rigidly and effectively than the guards had ever done, sexist expressions vanished from his speech. He used gender neutral terms, or, more affirmatively, language that indicated that both men and women were contemplated by what he was saying. And the manifest sense of equal companionship between himself and the eminently independent Graça Machel today shows that the values of nonsexism have been internalised, even if a patriarchal impulse pops out from time to time.

In the years that followed a sad new dimension entered into our understanding of freedom, freedom from fear. We had won our personal freedom, but not yet gained our personal security. The need to deal effectively with crime is repeated in speech after speech. In the past fear reigned amongst the people because the state was too powerful. Now there was fear because the criminals were seen to be too strong and the state was thought to be too weak. Measures were announced to deal with crime, not through executions, torture and whipping as in the past, but through a better equipped and trained police force and improved police–community relations. At times it seemed that we were extremely adept at doing the impossible but not always proficient in doing the ordinary. We had to learn to do ordinary things, and to do them well, without laying our bodies and our lives on the line each time. And we had to acknowledge that the paradox of our lives was that we had fought with all our passion to create a boring society, where humour and a bit of simple humanity could count for more than heroism and grandiose yet abstract plans.

One of Mandela's great accomplishments during the years of his Presidency was to link up the ordinary details of life with the great events of our history, and to do so with a light and intensely human touch. He has freed us from the rancour and the corrosive and belittling sarcasm of political life. The Madiba smile and the Madiba jive have brought a sense of achievement and satisfaction to all of us, enabling us to enjoy his sense of enjoyment, and to share in his pleasure of living as a free person in a free country.

Release from Prison

Speech on release from prison, Cape Town,
11 February 1990.

Friends, comrades and fellow South Africans. I greet you all in the name of peace, democracy and freedom for all. I stand here before you not as a prophet but as a humble servant of you, the people. Your tireless and heroic sacrifices have made it possible for me to be here today. I therefore place the remaining years of my life in your hands.

On this day of my release, I extend my sincere and warmest gratitude to the millions of my compatriots and those in every corner of the globe who have campaigned tirelessly for my release. I send special greetings to the people of Cape Town, this city which has been my home for three decades. Your mass marches and other forms of struggle have served as a constant source of strength to all political prisoners.

I salute the African National Congress. It has fulfilled our every expectation in its role as leader of the great march to freedom. I salute our President, Comrade Oliver Tambo, for leading the ANC even under the most difficult circumstances. I salute the rank and file members of the ANC. You have sacrificed life and limb in the pursuit of the noble cause of our struggle. I salute combatants of Umkhonto we Sizwe, like Solomon Mahlangu and Ashley Kriel, who have paid the ultimate price for the freedom of all South Africans.

I salute the South African Communist Party for its sterling contribution to the struggle for democracy. You have survived 40 years of unrelenting persecution. The memory of great communists like Moses Kotane, Yusuf Dadoo, Bram Fischer and Moses Mabhida will be cherished for generations to come. I salute General Secretary Joe Slovo, one of our finest patriots. We are heartened by the fact that the alliance between ourselves and the Party remains as strong as it always was.

I salute the United Democratic Front, the National Education Crisis Committee, the South African Youth Congress, the Transvaal and Natal Indian Congresses and Cosatu and the many other formations of the Mass Democratic Movement. I also salute the Black Sash and the National Union of South African Students. We note with pride that you have acted as the conscience of white South Africa. Even during the darkest days in the history of our struggle you held the flag of liberty high. The large-scale mass mobilisation of the past few years is one of the key factors which led to the opening of the final chapter of our struggle.

I extend my greetings to the working class of our country. Your organised strength is the pride of our movement. You remain the most dependable force in the struggle to end exploitation and oppression. I pay tribute to the many religious communities who carried the campaign for justice forward when the organisations for our people were silenced.

I greet the traditional leaders of our country – many of you continue to walk in the footsteps of great heroes like Hintsa and Sekhukhuni. I pay tribute to the endless heroism of youth, you, the young lions. You, the young lions, have energised our entire struggle. I pay tribute to the mothers and wives and sisters of our nation. You are the rock-hard foundation of our struggle. Apartheid has inflicted more pain on you than on anyone else.

On this occasion, we thank the world community for their great contribution to the anti-apartheid struggle. Without your support our struggle would not have reached this advanced stage. The sacrifice of the frontline states will be remembered by South Africans for ever.

My salutations would be incomplete without expressing my deep appreciation for the strength given to me during my long and lonely years in prison by my beloved wife and family. I am convinced that your pain and suffering was far greater than my own.

Before I go any further I wish to make the point that I intend making only a few preliminary comments at this stage. I will make a more complete statement only after I have had the opportunity to consult with my comrades.

Today, the majority of South Africans, black and white, recognise that apartheid has no future. It has to be ended by our own decisive mass action in order to build peace and security. The mass campaign of defiance and other actions of our organisation and people can only culminate in the establishment of democracy. The destruction caused by apartheid on our sub-continent is incalculable. The fabric of family life of millions of my people has been shattered. Millions are homeless and unemployed. Our economy lies in ruins and our people are embroiled in political strife. Our resort to the armed struggle in 1960 with the formation of the military wing of the ANC, Umkhonto we Sizwe, was a purely defensive action against the violence of apartheid. The factors which necessitated the armed struggle still exist today. We have no option but to continue. We express the hope that a climate conducive to a negotiated settlement will be created soon so that there may no longer be the need for the armed struggle.

I am a loyal and disciplined member of the African National Congress. I am therefore in full agreement with all of its objectives, strategies and tactics. The need to unite the people of our country is as important a task now as it always has been. No individual leader is able to take on this enormous task on his own. It is our task as leaders to place our views before our organisation and to allow the democratic structures to decide. On the question of democratic practice, I feel duty-bound to make the point that a leader of the movement is a person who has been democratically elected at a national conference. This is a principle which must be upheld without any exceptions.

Today, I wish to report to you that my talks with the government have been aimed at normalising the political situation in the country. We have not as yet begun discussing the basic demands of the struggle. I wish to stress that I myself have at no time entered into negotiations about the future of our country except to insist on a meeting between the ANC and the government.

Mr De Klerk has gone further than any other Nationalist president in taking real steps to normalise the situation. However, there are further steps as outlined in the Harare Declaration that have to be met before negotiations on the basic demands of our people can begin. I reiterate our call for, *inter alia*, the immediate ending of the State of Emergency and the freeing of all, and not only some, political prisoners. Only such a normalised situation, which allows for free political activity, can allow us to consult our people in order to obtain a mandate.

The people need to be consulted on who will negotiate and on the content of such negotiations. Negotiations cannot take place above the heads or behind the backs of our people. It is our belief that the future of our country can only be determined by a body which is democratically elected on a nonracial basis. Negotiations on the dismantling of apartheid will have to address the overwhelming demand of our people for a democratic, nonracial and unitary South Africa. There must be an end to white monopoly on political power and a fundamental restructuring of our political and economic systems to ensure that the inequalities of apartheid are addressed and our society thoroughly democratised.

It must be added that Mr De Klerk himself is a man of integrity who is acutely aware of the dangers of a public figure not honouring his undertakings. But as an organisation we base our policy and strategy on the harsh reality we are faced with. And this reality is that we are still suffering under the policy of the Nationalist government.

Our struggle has reached a decisive moment. We call on our people to seize this moment so that the process towards democracy is rapid and uninterrupted. We have waited too long for our freedom. We can no longer wait. Now is the time to intensify the struggle on all fronts. To relax our efforts now would be a mistake which generations to come will not be able to forgive. The sight of freedom looming on the horizon should encourage us to redouble our efforts.

It is only through disciplined mass action that our victory can be assured. We call on our white compatriots to join us in the shaping of a new South Africa. The freedom movement is a political home for you too. We call on the international community to continue the campaign to isolate the apartheid regime. To lift sanctions now would be to run the risk of aborting the process towards the complete eradication of apartheid.

Our march to freedom is irreversible. We must not allow fear to stand in our way. Universal suffrage on a common voters' role in a united, democratic and nonracial South Africa is the only way to peace and racial harmony.

In conclusion I wish to quote my own words during my trial in 1964. They are true today as they were then:

> I have fought against white domination and I have fought against black domination. I have cherished the ideal of a democratic and free society in which all persons live together in harmony and with equal opportunities. It is an ideal which I hope to live for and to achieve. But if needs be, it is an ideal for which I am prepared to die.

Election as President

Speech announcing the ANC election victory,
Carlton Hotel, Johannesburg,
2 May 1994.

My fellow South Africans – the people of South Africa:

This is indeed a joyous night. Although not yet final, we have received the provisional results of the election, and are delighted by the overwhelming support for the African National Congress.

To all those in the African National Congress and the democratic movement who worked so hard these last few days and through these many decades, I thank you and honour you. To the people of South Africa and the world who are watching: this is a joyous night for the human spirit. This is your victory too. You helped end apartheid, you stood with us through the transition.

I watched, along with all of you, as the tens of thousands of our people stood patiently in long queues for many hours, some sleeping on the open ground overnight waiting to cast this momentous vote. South Africa's heroes are legend across the generations. But it is you, the people, who are our true heroes.

This is one of the most important moments in the life of our country. I stand here before you filled with deep pride and joy – pride in the ordinary, humble people of this country. You have shown such a calm, patient determination to reclaim this country as your own. What joy that we can loudly proclaim from the roof-tops – free at last!

I stand before you humbled by your courage, with a heart full of love for all of you. I regard it as the highest honour to lead the ANC at this moment in our history, and that we have been chosen to lead our country into the new century. I pledge to use all my strength and ability to live up to your expectations of me as well as of the ANC.

I am personally indebted and pay tribute to some of South Africa's greatest leaders including John Dube, Josiah Gumede, GM Naicker, Dr Abdurahman, Chief Luthuli, Lilian Ngoyi, Helen Joseph, Yusuf

Dadoo, Moses Kotane, Chris Hani and Oliver Tambo. They should have been here to celebrate with us, for this is their achievement too.

Tomorrow, the entire ANC leadership and I will be back at our desks. We are rolling up our sleeves to begin tackling the problems our country faces. We ask you all to join us – go back to your jobs in the morning. Let's get South Africa working. For we must, together and without delay, begin to build a better life for all South Africans. This means creating jobs building houses, providing education and bringing peace and security for all.

The calm and tolerant atmosphere that prevailed during the elections depicts the type of South Africa we can build. It set the tone for the future. We might have our differences, but we are one people with a common destiny in our rich variety of culture, race and tradition. People have voted for the party of their choice and we respect that. This is democracy. I hold out a hand of friendship to the leaders of all parties and their members, and ask all of them to join us in working together to tackle the problems we face as a nation. An ANC government will serve all the people of South Africa, not just ANC members. We also commend the security forces for the sterling work done. This has laid a solid foundation for a truly professional security force, committed to the service of the people and loyalty to the new Constitution.

Now is the time for celebration, for South Africans to join together to celebrate the birth of democracy. I raise a glass to you all for working so hard to achieve what can only be called a small miracle. Let our celebrations be in keeping with the mood set in the elections, peaceful, respectful and disciplined, showing we are a people ready to assume the responsibilities of government. I promise that I will do my best to be worthy of the faith and confidence you have placed in me and my organisation, the African National Congress. Let us build the future together, and toast a better life for all South Africans.

Before Inauguration as President

Address to the people of Cape Town, Grand Parade,
on the day before his inauguration as President, Cape Town,
9 May 1994.

Today, we are entering a new era for our country and its people.
Today, we celebrate not the victory of a party, but a victory for all the
people of South Africa.

Our country has arrived at a decision. Among all the parties that
contested the elections, the overwhelming majority of South Africans
have mandated the African National Congress to lead our country
into the future. The South Africa we have struggled for, in which all
our people, be they African, coloured, Indian or white, regard themselves as citizens of one nation, is at hand.

Perhaps it was history that ordained that it be here, at the Cape of
Good Hope, that we should lay the foundation stone of our new
nation. For it was here at this Cape, over three centuries ago, that
there began the fateful convergence of the peoples of Africa, Europe
and Asia on these shores. It was to this peninsula that the patriots,
among them many princes and scholars of Indonesia, were dragged
in chains. It was on the sandy plains of this peninsula that the first
battles of the epic wars of resistance were fought.

When we look out across Table Bay, the horizon is dominated by
Robben Island, whose infamy as a dungeon built to stifle the spirit of
freedom is as old as colonialism in South Africa. For three centuries
that island was seen as a place to which outcasts can be banished. The
names of those who were incarcerated on Robben Island are a roll
call of resistance fighters and democrats spanning over three centuries. If indeed this is a Cape of Good Hope, that hope owes much
to the spirit of that legion of fighters and others of their calibre.

We have fought for a democratic Constitution since the 1880s.
Ours has been a quest for a Constitution freely adopted by the
people of South Africa, reflecting their wishes and their aspirations.
The struggle for democracy has never been a matter pursued by one

race, class, religious community or gender among South Africans. In honouring those who fought to see this day arrive, we honour the best sons and daughters of all our people. We can count amongst them Africans, coloureds, whites, Indians, Muslims, Christians, Hindus, Jews – all of them united by a common vision of a better life for the people of this country.

It was that vision that inspired us in 1923 when we adopted the first ever Bill of Rights in this country. That same vision spurred us to put forward the African Claims in 1946. It is also the founding principle of the Freedom Charter we adopted as policy in 1955, which in its very first lines places before South Africa an inclusive basis for citizenship.

In the 1980s the African National Congress was still setting the pace, being the first major political formation in South Africa to commit itself firmly to a Bill of Rights, which we published in November 1990. These milestones give concrete expression to what South Africa can become. They speak of a constitutional, democratic, political order in which, regardless of colour, gender, religion, political opinion or sexual orientation, the law will provide for the equal protection of all citizens. They project a democracy in which the government, whomever that government may be, will be bound by a higher set of rules, embodied in a Constitution, and will not be able to govern the country as it pleases.

Democracy is based on the majority principle. This is especially true in a country such as ours where the vast majority have been systematically denied their rights. At the same time, democracy also requires that the rights of political and other minorities be safeguarded. In the political order we have established there will be regular, open and free elections, at all levels of government – central, provincial and municipal. There shall also be a social order which respects completely the culture, language and religious rights of all sections of our society and the fundamental rights of the individual.

The task at hand will not be easy. But you have mandated us to change South Africa from a country in which the majority lived with little hope, to one in which they can live and work with dignity, with a sense of self-esteem and confidence in the future. The cornerstone of building a better life of opportunity, freedom and prosperity is the Reconstruction and Development Programme. This needs unity of purpose. It needs action. It requires us all to work together to bring an end to division, an end to suspicion and build a nation united in our diversity.

The people of South Africa have spoken in these elections. They want change! And change is what they will get. Our plan is to create jobs, promote peace and reconciliation, and to guarantee freedom for all South Africans. We will tackle the widespread poverty so pervasive among the majority of our people. By encouraging investors and the democratic state to support job creating projects in which manufacturing will play a central role we will try to change our country from a net exporter of raw materials to one that exports finished products through beneficiation.

The government will devise policies that encourage and reward productive enterprise among the disadvantaged communities – African, coloured and Indian. By easing credit conditions we can assist them to make inroads into the productive and manufacturing spheres and break out of the small-scale distribution to which they are presently confined.

To raise our country and its people from the morass of racism and apartheid will require determination and effort. As a government, the ANC will create a legal framework that will assist, rather than impede, the awesome task of reconstruction and development of our battered society.

While we are and shall remain fully committed to the spirit of a government of national unity, we are determined to initiate and bring about the change that our mandate from the people demands. We place our vision of a new constitutional order for South Africa on the table not as conquerors, prescribing to the conquered. We speak as fellow citizens to heal the wounds of the past with the intent of constructing a new order based on justice for all.

This is the challenge that faces all South Africans today, and it is one to which I am certain we will all rise.

Inauguration as President

Address to the nation at the inauguration of Nelson Mandela
as President of the Republic of South Africa,
Union Buildings, Pretoria,
10 May 1994.

Today, all of us do, by our presence here, and by our celebrations in other parts of our country and the world, confer glory and hope to newborn liberty. Out of the experience of an extraordinary human disaster that lasted too long must be born a society of which all humanity will be proud.

Our daily deeds as ordinary South Africans must produce an actual South African reality that will reinforce humanity's belief in justice, strengthen its confidence in the nobility of the human soul and sustain all our hopes for a glorious life for all. All this we owe both to ourselves and to the peoples of the world who are so well represented here today.

To my compatriots, I have no hesitation in saying that each one of us is as intimately attached to the soil of this beautiful country as are the famous jacaranda trees of Pretoria and the mimosa trees of the bushveld. Each time one of us touches the soil of this land, we feel a sense of personal renewal. The national mood changes as the seasons change. We are moved by a sense of joy and exhilaration when the grass turns green and the flowers bloom.

That spiritual and physical oneness we all share with this common homeland explains the depth of the pain we all carried in our hearts as we saw our country tear itself apart in a terrible conflict, and as we saw it spurned, outlawed and isolated by the peoples of the world, precisely because it has become the universal base of the pernicious ideology and practice of racism and racial oppression.

We, the people of South Africa, feel fulfilled that humanity has taken us back into its bosom, that we, who were outlaws not so long ago, have today been given the rare privilege to be host to the nations of the world on our own soil. We thank all our distinguished international guests for having come to take possession with the people of our country of what is, after all, a common victory for justice, for peace, for human dignity. We trust that you will continue to stand by us as we tackle the challenges of building peace, prosperity, nonsexism, nonracialism and democracy.

We deeply appreciate the role that the masses of our people and their political mass democratic, religious, women, youth, business, traditional and other leaders have played to bring about this conclusion. Not least among them is my Second Deputy President, the Honourable FW de Klerk.

We would also like to pay tribute to our security forces, in all their ranks, for the distinguished role they have played in securing our first democratic elections and the transition to democracy from bloodthirsty forces which still refuse to see the light.

The time for the healing of the wounds has come. The moment to bridge the chasms that divide us has come. The time to build is upon us. We have, at last, achieved our political emancipation. We pledge ourselves to liberate all our people from the continuing bondage of poverty, deprivation, suffering, gender and other discrimination.

We succeeded in taking our last steps to freedom in conditions of relative peace. We commit ourselves to the construction of a complete, just and lasting peace. We have triumphed in the effort to implant hope in the breasts of the millions of our people. We enter into a covenant that we shall build the society in which all South Africans, both black and white, will be able to walk tall, without any fear in their hearts, assured of their inalienable right to human dignity – a rainbow nation at peace with itself and the world.

As a token of its commitment to the renewal of our country, the new Interim Government of National Unity will, as a matter of urgency, address the issue of amnesty for various categories of our people who are currently serving terms of imprisonment.

We dedicate this day to all the heroes and heroines in this country and the rest of the world who sacrificed in many ways and surrendered their lives so that we could be free. Their dreams have become reality. Freedom is their reward.

We are both humbled and elevated by the honour and privilege that you, the people of South Africa, have bestowed on us, as the first President of a united, democratic, nonracial and nonsexist government. We understand it still that there is no easy road to freedom. We know it well that none of us acting alone can achieve success. We must therefore act together as a united people, for national reconciliation, for nation building, for the birth of a new world.

Let there be justice for all. Let there be peace for all. Let there be work, bread, water and salt for all. Let each know that for each the body, the mind and the soul have been freed to fulfil themselves. Never, never and never again shall it be that this beautiful land will again experience the oppression of one by another and suffer the indignity of being the skunk of the world. Let freedom reign. The sun shall never set on so glorious a human achievement!

God bless Africa!

Freedom Day 1995

Speech at the Freedom Day Celebrations,
Union Buildings, Pretoria,
27 April 1995.

As dawn ushered in this day, 27 April 1995, few of us could suppress the welling of emotion, as we were reminded of the terrible past from which we come as a nation; the great possibilities that we now have; and the bright future that beckons us. And so we assemble here today, and in other parts of the country, to mark a historic day in the life of our nation. Wherever South Africans are across the globe, our hearts beat as one as we renew our common loyalty to our country and our commitment to its future.

The birth of our South African nation has, like any other, passed through a long and often painful process. The ultimate goal of a better life has yet to be realised. But if any one day marked the crossing of the divide from a past of conflict and division to the possibility of unity and peace; from inequality to equality; from a history of oppression to a future of freedom, it is 27 April 1994.

On this day, you, the people, took your destiny into your own hands. You decided that nothing would prevent you from exercising your hard-won right to elect a government of your choice. Your patience, your discipline, your single-minded purposefulness have become a legend throughout the world. You won this respect because you made the simple but profound statement that the time had come for the people to govern. You turned our diversity from a weakness to be exploited for selfish ends into a richness to be celebrated for the good of all. Today, we meet to reaffirm that we are one people with one destiny, a destiny that we can now shape together from the sweat of our brows.

We have learnt over the First Freedom Year that there is no short-cut to making South Africa the country of our dreams. It requires hard work by those entrusted with positions of responsibility in government. It demands that workers and employers work together to produce efficiently and compete with the best in the world, to achieve equity and to help create more jobs.

It requires hard work on the part of farmers and farm-workers, to feed the nation and provide raw materials, even in the face of adversity. It requires hard work by students and teachers to build a literate, skilled and learned nation. It requires greater exertion by our sportspersons and artists to always offer the best for the country and its people. It demands of all of us, wherever we may be, to exercise our rights as citizens, and do so without infringing on the rights of others.

South Africa is firmly set on the road to peace and prosperity. In the spirit of *Masakhane*, we must, as a nation, strive to do better, and even better, all the time. This is the challenge that we face, as we enter the Second Freedom Year.

The rights that we now enjoy should be improved as we draft the new Constitution. And you, and only you, can ensure that the Constitutional Assembly produces what is best for the country. We must ensure that democracy reaches our localities, at work and everywhere we interact. To make the RDP work, we must all register for the November local government elections.

On its part, government is finalising guidelines for next year's budget: to ensure greater spending on education, health, housing and other needs. We are determined that public funds must be spent responsibly and in an open fashion. The projects we have started in Odi-Moretele, Weenen, Ibhayi, the East Rand, Kutama-Sinthumule, Mogopa and other areas have shown that the people, working together with government, can improve their lives. The phasing in of free education, free medical care to children under six and pregnant mothers, the school nutrition scheme, land restitution – all these and others are the beginnings of programmes to give freedom real meaning. In the Second Freedom Year, we must speed up these programmes; cut down on bureaucratic red tape; ensure that there are community structures to manage them; and direct more relief to the poor.

April 27 bequeathed us the supreme bodies to make laws and guard our democratic rights. As we move into the Second Freedom Year, our democracy will be strengthened by the welcome role of bodies such as the Constitutional Court, Human Rights Commission and the soon-to-be-established Truth and Reconciliation Commission, not only to correct past wrongs, but also to create a better future. In the same vein, we shall need more systematic work in Parliament to complete the legal framework needed for transformation.

But freedom would be meaningless without security in the home and in the streets. It is for this reason that government has set in motion a plan to deal firmly with crime and violence. Discussions have been completed to allocate more resources for the training of police officers, improving facilities in areas ignored under apartheid, and to facilitate the setting up of more police community forums. These funds will be acquired both from the shifting of priorities in the ministry concerned, and from the RDP Fund.

In the spirit of *Masakhane*, where communities succeed in co-operating with the police to bring down the levels of crime, and where they ensure that services are paid for, serious consideration will be given to increase the investment of public funds in these localities.

We thank the security forces, whose support for the process of change has been invaluable.

In the spirit of goodwill that accompanies this, our first Freedom Day, I have decided to grant amnesty to the following categories of prisoners: Firstly, a special remission of sentences of one quarter for all prisoners, with a maximum remission of six months. This amnesty will not apply to prisoners sentenced for child abuse. Secondly, a remission of sentences on all persons who were charged solely for the possession, before 6 December 1993, of arms, ammunition, explosives and explosive devices, associated with political conflicts of the past, irrespective of their political affiliation.

These measures will come into effect as soon as the departments concerned have completed the necessary administrative procedures. We hope that through this act of goodwill, we are sending a message to all prisoners that they should mend their ways and make a fresh start. We appeal to society to help them resettle in communities as responsible and law-abiding citizens.

Over the past year we have confounded the prophets of doom; and we shall do so for many, many more years to come.

On behalf of the Government of National Unity, I wish to thank all South Africans who have made this, our miracle possible. As a nation, we extend our gratitude to the international community whose force of example, encouragement and support has strengthened us in this difficult task. I also wish to congratulate Minister Ben

Ngubane and his team for the excellent work they have done to make this celebration the success that it promises to be. Theirs has been a lofty example of united action in the national interest.

As our nation did a year ago, let each community take its destiny into its own hands by ensuring that everyone registers as a voter by 1 June.

Enriched by the experience of the First Freedom Year, let us work together, with each other and for each other, in the spirit of *Masakhane!*

Freedom Day 1996

Speech at the Freedom Day Celebrations,
Union Buildings, Pretoria,
27 April 1996.

For generations to come, the abiding image of a patient citizenry in long voting queues on 27 April 1994 will remain deeply etched in the collective memory of the nation. As the world held its breath, South Africans together made their mark to bring into being one of the truly remarkable events of this turbulent century. Once more, we affirmed a truism of human history: that the people are their own liberators. And so today we meet here to pay tribute to you, the people – the midwives of the new South Africa; you, the true healers and builders of a nation once rent asunder by bigotry; you, the expert builders of a great future that beckons.

We are truly honoured today to play host in the ceremony to distinguished world leaders – UN General-Secretary Boutros Boutros-Ghali, His Majesty King Hussein bin Talal of Jordan, Presidents Jose Maria Figueres of Costa Rica, Benjamin Mkapa of Tanzania and Jean-Pascal Delamuraz of the Swiss Confederation, ministers from as far afield as Europe and Latin America, Africa and the Pacific, North America and Asia, and the heads of various multilateral agencies. Perhaps it was time that those who shared with us the trials and tribulations of struggle, those who helped break the back of apartheid, those whose presence during our historic negotiations and elections helped to stay the hand of backward elements – perhaps it was time that they joined us in this colourful Freedom Day tribute to our young nation, united in its diversity.

For the next two days, we shall all be witness to a celebration of unity in diversity: by our army and police; workers and industrialists; professionals and religious communities and others – all in honour of our common loyalty to our common motherland. The flowering of this new patriotism of the new South Africa will find even more vivid expression in the display of our distinguished artists, reflecting the rich tapestry of the sources that make up our national heritage.

Today, the friendship and harmony among South Africa's communities underlines that to us, diversity is becoming a source of strength and collective enrichment. Beyond matters cultural, this enrichment is becoming a living reality in the evolution of our democracy and human rights practices.

In some ten days from now, we shall adopt a new Constitution for our country. We say this with confidence because we know that, as we practised democracy in the past two years, as we strove to better our conditions, and as we pursued the collective interest in government, we all came to better appreciate what is truly common among us, and thus to clear the cobwebs of mutual suspicion.

We say this with a measure of certainty because as we recognised that the security of one community is the best guarantee of that of other communities, we became better placed to set the constitutional framework required to transform our society into one based on genuine equality.

We shall indeed be able to adopt the new Constitution in a matter of days, because the new patriotism infusing our society beckons us as leaders to fashion an appropriate basic law of the land. In a sense, there in the sportsfields and workplaces; in the farms and villages; in the institutions of learning and worship; there where young children play with gay abandon; where the women of our country endeavour to achieve genuine equality; there where the unemployed and the disabled sue for their rightful stake in society – that is where the new Constitution has been written.

Like any truly historic act of creation, this has not been and will not be easy. But we have the leaders and the collective wisdom to weather any storms. Yet, we dare remember every day and every minute of our lives, as we enter the Third Freedom Year, that the solemn undertaking we made two years ago was that we will work together to improve our lives. The feeling of freedom that infuses every South African heart, at last liberated from the yoke of oppression, underlines the fact that we have all, in one way or another, been victim to the system of apartheid.

In no other activity is this more lucidly captured than in the heart-rending evidence being led at the hearings of the Truth and Reconciliation Commission. It is only natural that all of us should feel a collective sense of shame for the evils that, as compatriots, we inflicted upon one another. But even in the few days of these hearings, even if its work is still tentative, we can all attest to the cleansing power of the truth. We wish on this occasion to congratulate the commission and the witnesses, and once more to urge all citizens to co-operate with it.

Within weeks, in metropolitan and rural Western Cape and, hopefully, in KwaZulu-Natal, voters who were excluded from last November's local government elections will join their compatriots as proud rulers of their own localities. It is our fervent wish that these elections should take place as soon as practicable in KwaZulu-Natal; and take place in an atmosphere free of violence, intimidation and fraud. Not one province, not a single one of our citizens, should be subjected to second-rate democracy. It is in this spirit that we shall be examining the report of the task group investigating conditions in that province.

The better life for which we all strive requires that all of us join hands to build a climate necessary for the growth and development of our economy. This imposes heavy obligations on the main role-players in the economy, government, labour and business. I wish therefore to report that the provinces and relevant departments are making substantial progress in working out concrete actions required to achieve the kind of growth that will create jobs and promote socio-economic improvements. The process is on track; and it has been profoundly enriched by the welcome contribution of the trade union movement and business organisations.

Needless to say, our society has long passed debating about the broad targets of economic policy. Rather, we need to ensure that the concrete measures we propose do indeed point in the direction of these targets. Already, in the first few months of the year great strides have been made in the field of education, health, the public service, water provisioning, municipal services and housing policy and delivery, to ensure that we carry out the programmes required to improve the people's quality of life. Only in this way can freedom have real meaning. Similarly, integrated mechanisms to fight crime are starting to bear fruit in many parts of the country. Improvements include the prodding of industry to ensure proper management and sharing of information, public education and participation, decisive deployment and action where required, and co-operation with foreign partners.

But as we make these short-term improvements, and finalise long-term strategies, we are again reminded that success depends above all on partnership among all sectors of society. The same applies to the measures required to deal with the pockets of political violence remaining in KwaZulu-Natal. Through joint efforts across the political spectrum, we should send a clear signal that, especially in a democracy, political violence does not pay.

To the extent that we were our own liberators in the process culminating on 27 April 1994, to that extent are we collective builders of a better life. Indeed, all the projects undertaken thus far have confirmed that success depends on community initiative and participation. The government has therefore decided to set up the President's Award for Community Initiative to acknowledge communities that have put their shoulders to the wheel; communities who, with scarce resources, took the initiative to uplift their conditions. This award will be presented annually to nine provincial communities. From them, a national winner will be selected, with prizes including further injection of resources. We hope that through this initiative we will be able further to draw out the best in all our communities, in the spirit of *Masakhane*, to build one another and together build a bright future.

Again on this our Freedom Day we should thank the international community for the solidarity they continue extending to us as we proceed with the difficult task of reconstruction and development. We are immensely gratified, in particular, that a glimpse at the programmes being undertaken by our departments reveals, without exception, references to practical projects involving Unctad, Unicef, the Food and Agricultural Organisation, the UNDP, the ILO, the Habitat housing initiative and many others. Such benefit as we derive from this association has further strengthened our resolve to help build the United Nations into a powerful force for good, as we enter the new millennium.

We once again wish to thank the United Nations for allowing us to host Unctad IX, an eloquent demonstration that, as a nation we have become an equal and proud participant in world affairs. We pledge to continue contributing, in our own humble way, to peace and development in Southern Africa, in Africa and further afield.

Freedom Day comes at a time when we are making progress on all fronts to build South Africa into a land of our dreams. Our confidence derives not from overlooking the real difficulties. But we know that now that we have redeemed our pledge to attain the freedom to be free, we have it in our power as a nation to march together to a better life.

As we enter our Third Freedom Year, infused with our new patriotism and with the spirit of *Masakhane*, we are confident that no obstacle will be large enough to block our path. A bright future beckons. The onus is on us, through hard work, honesty and integrity, to reach for the stars.

Freedom Day 1997

Speech at the Freedom Day Celebrations, Upington,
27 April 1997.

Three years have passed since the people of South Africa proclaimed their freedom; three years since we made a pledge to work together as a nation to bring a better life for all. On that day, too, by our votes, we gave birth to new provinces – including your Northern Cape Province – so that government should be closer to the people and reflect the diversity of our country. And in a process that we completed during our Third Freedom Year, we voted in our millions to create democratic and nonracial councils where they never existed before.

And so today we gather in Upington to celebrate our nation's three years of freedom with you: liberators who helped bring democracy to our land, to this province and to the communities where you live; patriots who turned their backs on division, oppression and conflict, in order to found a new South African nation whose watchwords are unity, peace and prosperity.

This year, we have added cause to celebrate. Our deepest aspirations are enshrined now in the basic law of our land. The new Constitution has strengthened our unity, both in the democratic manner it was written and in the hopes it embodies. It has become a cornerstone of the new patriotism. It is a framework for undoing the legacy of our divided past and improving the quality of life.

The strength of the new South African nation we are building lies in the room it gives for each and every language, culture and religion to flourish. These have the same power to unite us as the international achievements of our sportsmen and women. That is why we are celebrating our unity by giving free rein to the rich diversity of our cultures in every province. That is why we are here in Upington.

In holding the national Freedom Day celebrations in the Northern Cape we are paying tribute to a shining example of nation-building and reconciliation; to people from the legacy of neglect as great as anywhere else in our country; to a region with an inspiring history and richness of culture that has been too long hidden from view. In a part of our country almost as diverse as the whole nation, a new distinctive identity is being woven from the strands of Griqua and Tswana; Khoikhoi and Afrikaner; San and Xhosa; coloured, white, Indian and African.

Across our land communities and researchers are working to undo the distorted accounts of our history forced on us by colonialism and apartheid. Our legacy of hundreds, indeed thousands, of years of civilisation in South Africa is being recovered. The epic resistance of proud communities defending land, independence and dignity is being told for all to hear. Later today we will be commemorating the vision of Abraham September, a man born in slavery, who began the irrigation that makes this such a fertile area. In doing so, we will be helping give recognition to the skills and knowledge of ordinary people which over centuries have turned the rich natural resources of our country into the wealth of our nation.

As we seek to know the truth about our divided past nothing is more painful than confronting the terrible hurts that we inflicted on each other during the last decades of apartheid rule. But the work of the Truth and Reconciliation Commission has shown us, beyond what anyone could have foreseen, the power of the truth to heal. We should take this opportunity to congratulate the TRC for the work they are doing. We are encouraged by the growing numbers willing to help the commission uncover the truth about human rights abuses, and hope that their example will be followed by many more. The best recompense that can be made to the victims, and the most powerful substance for reconciliation, is our success in building a new society.

The new Constitution, and its place in the hearts of our people, is a powerful assurance that never again will South Africa allow such things to happen.

Today we will also be presenting a copy of this document to the Upington Fourteen. Their suffering, as part of a community afflicted by repression, represents that of many, many of our people, in the Northern Cape and in South Africa as a whole. When they were on Death Row the name of Upington became known across the world as the international community campaigned to save their lives. Today Upington is sending a different message to the world – that it is a town whose people have joined hands in striving to make a reality of the vision of a better life for all that is embodied in our Constitution. We are saying that the freedom they helped us achieve is being put to good use. This is a message that is heard across the country as communities get down to work with their new democratic councils to improve their lives.

It is right that we ask ourselves, now that we are halfway through our country's first democratically elected government: What progress have we made as a nation in fulfilling our pledge to work together to improve our lives?

We can say with confidence that the foundation for a better life has been laid. Government has the right policies for the challenges South Africa faces. Slowly but surely the policies are taking effect and making a difference to the way people live. As a government we have sharpened our programme of action and set ourselves concrete targets for this year and beyond to which you, the people, must hold us.

We take immense pride and joy in the fact that since 27 April 1994, millions have for the first time experienced access to clean water, electricity, housing subsidies, free health care, nutrition programmes and land. In the budget that the government has just adopted we shifted still more resources to social spending so that these programmes can be extended during the coming year.

In this regard we should congratulate the Northern Cape provincial government – and other provinces – for their plans to use funds provided by the national government, to speed up delivery of basic needs. We also congratulate the Northern Cape police for their work in uncovering the province's largest organised crime syndicate.

Such breakthroughs, here and elsewhere, are helping us turn the tide against crime. They will be boosted by the increased resources which government is providing to the criminal justice system. They will be strengthened by the high-density crime prevention operation by police and 10 000 members of the SANDF throughout the country which is taking place right now.

The successes that are being made are the result of dedicated work by our police service. The great majority are men and women committed to the safety and security of our people. We acknowledge the work they are doing, often under difficult and dangerous conditions. And we urge every community and each sector of our society to join hands with them to defeat the criminals. Lasting and long-term solutions to the problem of crime will come from the improvements in living conditions and the eradication of poverty. In turn, that will be made possible by the success of our economic policies.

All the signs point to our being on track. The stagnant economy we inherited is now on a path of sustained growth as investment, productivity and exports increase. Our provinces are facing up to the challenge of devising their own growth and development strategies within the national framework, so that they can deal with the special needs and contribute to the country's economic success.

We admire the determination of your province to find ways of breaking from dependence on agriculture and a shrinking mining sector by diversifying into manufacturing and tourism. With the help of the private sector your plans to establish more factories to add value to the products of mining could not only create jobs in the province – they can help us in one of the primary economic goals of boosting exports.

However good the policies of the government are, national or provincial, nothing will come of them without the active participation of each and every one of us. Our democracy will become a living reality and a force for transformation only when communities become involved, calling their elected representatives to account, voicing their needs and their ideas for improving things, and paying for services.

Our shared vision of a nonracial society will be realised through bold and conscious action by communities and councils to deracialise our towns and cities so that they reflect the character of the Rainbow Nation we are building. The response to the renewed Masakhane Campaign encourages us to believe that communities and councils are indeed joining hands in order to repair the tattered fabric of our society.

As our new nation matures the challenges we face are shifting to the provinces and the localities in which we live. The call now on each and every one of us as we enter our Fourth Freedom Year is to roll up our sleeves. Let us build on what has been achieved, for the sake of Unity, Peace and Prosperity.

Umanyano, Uxolo neNkqubela;
Tshwaragano, Kagiso le Katlego.

The foundation for a better life has been laid – Forward Ever!

Freedom Day 1998

Speech at the Freedom Day Celebrations, Cape Town,
27 April 1998.

When we gathered here on the Grand Parade in February 1990 we knew that our march to freedom was irreversible, that nothing could stop our dream of a free South Africa coming true. The people had opened the prison doors and we knew that it would not be long before we found the way to peace and democracy.

We knew that apartheid had devastated our society and that it would be no easy and short-term task to eradicate the poverty and inequality it had created. But on that day we understood that we could overcome whatever obstacles lay ahead, because the great majority of South Africans had recognised that they had a common future.

Four years later, on 27 April 1994, the people of South Africa in all their millions declared before the world that they would govern themselves. On that day we founded our nation upon the pledge that we would undo the legacy of our divided past in order to build a better life for all our people.

Today we meet here again, with four years of freedom to celebrate. We meet to reaffirm that we are one people with one destiny; and to recommit ourselves to the achievement of the goals that define us as a people. The history of what is now the Western Cape – like that of all our country – taught us that freedom is indivisible. The freedom of one is the freedom of the other, and where one is unfree, no one is free.

The rule of a minority could last only as long as it could force people into the acceptance of which Adam Small speaks in his poem:

Die Here het geskommel en die dice het verkeerd geval vi' ons daai's maar al
So dis allright, pellie, dis allright

But now that all the oppressed have united and taken their destiny into their own hands; and oppressed and former oppressors have together accepted responsibility for a common future, Adam Small can say with more hope:

> dis allright, pellie, dis allright.

On this Freedom Day, the Parade and the streets of Cape Town are alive with the unity in diversity of a society at peace with itself because the rights of all are respected. The diversity of colours and languages once used to divide us are now a source of strength. The basic law of our land, our Constitution, declares that we are all one. We have been liberated from a system that held us all in its chains, free at last to be who and what we really are, secure in the respect others have for our cultures and religions.

The languages of this province, like all our country's languages, are no longer distinguished as official or unofficial. They are no longer associated with injustice and oppression on the one hand or with disadvantage and deprivation on the other. All are free to flourish as languages of all our people in all their diversity.

We cherish our Constitution and want to ensure that its rights become a living reality for all our people. That is why government has declared this week Constitution Week. All of us should play our part in popularising this manifesto of our democracy, in our workplaces; in our schools and universities; in our communities and in our homes. Political parties should also take care, in the cut and thrust of the coming election campaign, that they do not stir up baser emotions which were created by our divisive past and which are yet to fully disappear from our society.

Our freedom and our rights will only gain their full meaning as we succeed together in overcoming the divisions and inequalities of our past and in improving the lives of especially the poor. Planning and policy development have long since given way to implementation, and we are moving at an increasing pace. We take great pride in the fact that basic amenities which were once only a dream to most communities are beginning to change the lives of millions. But this task is far from completed. Though the old lines no longer have the force of law, they are still visible in social and economic life – in our residential areas, in our workplaces, between rich and poor.

When we celebrate the start that we have made in undoing that legacy, it is in the knowledge there is still much to be done. That requires hard work by all of us – employers and workers; teachers and students; government and communities. On the part of government it requires special attention to the efficient and disciplined use of the public resources. On the part of all of us, wherever we stand in society, it requires us to work together to reverse the disparities of the past. Amongst other things it means giving greater effect to our policies for opening opportunities at work to those previously excluded or disadvantaged. As we finalise details of the Employment Equity Bill, as an instrument to correct historical wrongs caused by discrimination and prejudice against Africans, coloureds, Indians, women and the disabled, we must make it absolutely clear that anyone who tries to apply such action to favour only one group is acting contrary to the principles underlying this bill.

Our freedom is also incomplete as long as we are denied our security by the criminals who prey upon our communities; who rob our businesses and undermine our economy; who ply their destructive trade in drugs in our schools; who do violence against our women and children. Even though government's strategy is beginning to take effect and, with your support, has begun to turn the tide, crime is at an unacceptable level and we must do more. In particular we must break once and for all the long hold which organised gangs have had on so many communities. The way in which the Western Cape is uniting to fight this scourge is encouraging.

Today's launch of a campaign that brings community structures and government agencies together in narrowing the space for the gangs will boost the fight. To the extent that this mass campaign succeeds in mobilising communities to work with the police and the courts, the Western Cape Commission on Gang Violence will expand the freedom which we celebrate today. I will also be discussing with my ministers proposals made to me two days ago by a delegation from the Inter-Religious Committee on Crime and Violence in the Western Cape. The gains we make will have lasting effect as we eradicate the socio-economic conditions that allow the criminal masterminds to implement their sinister plans.

To achieve all these goals requires sustained economic growth. The groundwork has been laid in our economic policies and in our new place in the world. Together we must seize the opportunities to produce the resources and create the jobs that will transform our people's lives.

As we enter our Fifth Freedom Year, we have taken great strides along the path that stretched out before us when we gathered here eight years ago at the start of our transition from a painful past to a bright future. We face challenges which in many ways are even greater. As we overcame the obstacles that lay before us then, we will meet those of today. The foundation for a better life has been laid, and the building has begun. Today let us renew our pledge to work together, to make South Africa into a land of our dreams!

Freedom Day 1999

Speech at the Freedom Day Celebrations, Umtata,
27 April 1999

On this Freedom Day, one short month before our second democratic elections, the sense of history is overwhelming. We have gathered in Umtata to celebrate our nation's five years of freedom with you: the people of a region that has helped shape our nation with all the pain and suffering, with all the courage and heroism that have marked our country's path to democracy.

On the horizon lie the rural hills amongst which generations of South Africans began on that long walk to freedom that has taken our nation ever closer to the fulfilment of our dreams. It was there in the hills and valleys of Qunu; in the rolling hills of KwaDlangezwa; in the Genadendal settlement; and along the Gariep, the Lekoa and the Luvuvhu Rivers that we first understood that we are not free. It is there that we were inspired with pride in our history. There, among the humble but proud rural folk, we learnt of the courage of our forebears in the face of superior force.

We meet today in the town that not long ago hosted the first of the bantustans that were created to suppress the proud resistance of South Africa's rural masses. It is from this soil across the rural areas of our land, washed bare by the erosion of over-population and over-grazing, that we converged in our millions to the mines and factories that consumed our labour and spawned the towns and cities of South Africa.

It is from surroundings such as these, that we understood that we were in the grip of a system that divided us one from the other; a system that set a few above the majority by virtue of skin colour alone. Millions were deliberately reduced to poverty. And to perpetuate itself, a system that claimed to be ordained from on high, could be sustained only by brute force, robbing us all of our humanity – oppressed and oppressor alike.

The Eastern Cape knows this fearful history as well as any other part of our country. Amongst the sons and daughters of this province are many who helped open the way for our freedom. It is therefore a weakness on our part, that we have yet to create a monument to remember them, and all South Africans who sacrificed so that we should be free. With the recent Cabinet decision on this matter, the day should not be far off when we shall have a people's shrine, a Freedom Park, where we shall honour with all the dignity they deserve, those who endured pain so we should experience the joy of freedom.

On 27 April five years ago, we knew that nothing could stop the people's declaration that the time had come to govern ourselves. We had then fully understood that none of us could be free unless we were all free; and that none of us could enjoy lasting peace and security while countless South Africans were cursed by hunger, homelessness and ill-health.

When for the first time we voted in our millions, as equals – men and women of every colour, language and religion; rich and poor – our nation was reborn. As we pledged to undo the legacy of our divided past, we rekindled the hope of a South Africa that would rise from the ashes of apartheid. We gave new life to the world's hopes that peace and unity will everywhere prevail over division and conflict, and that justice, freedom and dignity will everywhere prevail over oppression, poverty and discrimination.

Today in Umtata, as everywhere in our land, we celebrate five years in which we have tasted peace, freedom and dignity. We recommit ourselves to make a reality of the vision that lit the dawn of freedom. In these five years we have as a nation laid the foundation for a better life. Increasingly South Africans are reaching out to one another to make ours a winning nation. Across the land our communities are seizing responsibility for their own upliftment, in partnership with government.

It is right on this day that we honour communities that distinguish themselves as nation-builders in the spirit of *Masakhane*. That is why, three years ago on Freedom Day, we launched the Presidential Award for Community Initiative. It is with admiration and pride that I announce today eight of the nine provincial winners of the award for this year. They have been selected from over 500 nominated community projects. Their presence here today tells us of a nation that has its shoulder to the wheel to change life for the better.

I therefore have the privilege to acknowledge: the Lerato Feeding Scheme from Campbell in the Northern Cape; Itsuseng Self-Help Organisation in the Free State and the Khanyisa Day Care Centre in the Eastern Cape, all of which look after and train disabled children; Multi Purpose Centres of the Makgaung community in the Northern Province, the Koinonia Centre in Paarl in the Western Cape and Bhongweni in KwaZulu-Natal; as well as the Doornkop Environmental Community Organisation in Gauteng, all of which created jobs and services to their communities; and the Sizi Misele Project for the Disabled in Mpumalanga which provides jobs for the disabled and services local schools with uniforms and other needs. The North West Province's submission will be made in the next few days. And the national winner from amongst these nine communities will be announced by our new President at the opening of the first session of the Parliament which you will elect on 2 June.

Even as we take pride in our progress, we know it is only a start. Though many are feeling the fruits of government programmes, there are many needs still to be met. We must improve service delivery to the people. We must improve our attitudes towards citizens, as public servants. Together, we must work harder to root out crime and corruption, and to create jobs. We must fight the scourge of Aids by breaking the silence that encourages its quiet devastation. We must fight the fear and prejudice that can only worsen the suffering of those who live with Aids.

Great as these problems are, we draw hope from the way that all sectors of our society are now joining hands to tackle them; in the Jobs Summit; in Business Against Crime and Community Policing Forums; in the Partnership Against Aids; in the Morals Summit of religious leaders; and the Anti-corruption Summit. Out of these partnerships is born the hope that we can and shall succeed. It is this hope and warmth that I have felt wherever I go, as I visit communities across the land. And, though the end of our first democratic government is near, the task of building a better life for all cannot stop, even for a single day.

In the five weeks before the elections, we must build more houses to provide shelter to the homeless beyond the three million houses since 1994. We must make clean water accessible to more people beyond the three million who have gained access since 1994. More houses must be connected with electricity and telephones beyond the millions connected since 1994. We must continue the work of building relations with the world. From this gathering I will be going on a visit to countries that are home to more than a billion of the world's population: to Russia, China, Pakistan and Hungary. Through these visits we strengthen friendship with nations that are our partners in building a better world. We expand economic ties to our benefit and theirs, and strengthen our partnership for a better quality of life for all.

The achievements we have made would not have been possible without the staunch loyalty of our armed forces; without their unwavering dedication to the country and its people. Like our new democracy, the South African National Defence Force is today five years young. This morning it was my privilege as Commander-in-Chief of the SANDF, for the last time, to take the national salute of our armed forces. And today we pay tribute to all the members of our Defence Force. They have distinguished themselves not by conquest or suppression. We are proud of them for their success in uniting former foes in an integrated force, and by their contribution to crime-fighting and regional peace. Residents of this region, among others, will attest to the role of the armed forces in disaster management when natural tragedies struck towns and villages. We thank them, along with tens of thousands of civil servants and many members of the public for their assistance to the IEC in the registration of voters.

We know that we can count on our Defence Force and all our security services to safeguard our second democratic elections. They will do so because they know that, as we come out in our millions to vote on 2 June, we will be confirming our commitment to democracy. We will emerge strong and more united, true to our pledge that, whatever our political affiliation, we are one people with one destiny – ready to speed up the changes that we started in 1994.

Together let us make a reality of the hopes to which we gave birth five years ago.

3

RECONCILIATION

NEGOTIATING RECONCILIATION

F VAN ZYL SLABBERT

Reconciliation is one of those cosy, warm words; it exudes obvious virtue. Like truth, it is a 'good value'. At the same time, moral dilemmas seldom arise when good and bad are juxtaposed; one does not struggle to choose between reconciliation and hatred, truth and deceit. But try and choose between truth and reconciliation and think of situations where this could pose an acute moral dilemma. Does truth lead to reconciliation? The divorce courts seem to prove otherwise. Can reconciliation occur without truth? White lies seem to help sometimes!

These are not trivial points to make. Reconciliation on an individual/relationship level keeps a wide diversity of professionals occupied on a daily basis in most industrialised societies of the world. What I wish to evaluate here is the contribution of one man to bringing about reconciliation in the country of his birth – South Africa. In doing so one has to consider the person, the context in which he worked, and the process that evolved.

It is commonplace to single out Nelson Mandela as the individual who had the most profound personal impact on reconciliation in South Africa. One tends to forget that until 1990 the vast majority of South Africans – and, for that matter, countries in the world – had never laid eyes on him, or knew what he was like. From 1979 to 1986 I was Leader of the Opposition in the racist House of Assembly, and tried every year to get permission to visit him on Robben Island. This was regularly refused and only Helen Suzman was allowed to visit him. However, this was to be strictly a 'Red Cross' visit and no politics discussed. In the meantime, the government of the day spent an enormous amount of time and energy demonising Mandela and the ANC.

For many, he became a disembodied myth – a repository of dreams and fears. For millions he was the symbol of liberation from oppression, for a few he epitomised terror and destruction. Irrespective of who he really was, he became appropriated into a process of brutalised polarisation in South Africa over which he had no control. I had left Parliament quite abruptly in February 1986 and became involved in promoting dialogue inside and outside South Africa about a future democracy for the country. This was done through an NGO called Idasa (Institute for a Democratic Alternative for South Africa), which still exists today. Idasa organised the 'Dakar Meeting'. One of the offshoots of this meeting in July 1987 was a visit to Burkina-Faso, where we met President Thomas Sankara. He gave us a reception in his palace gardens one evening. There was a band playing and the song they were singing was 'Libere Mandela'. I remember standing in the humid hot night thinking: 'Who is this man? What is he like? How can I meet him?'

There is only one word to describe him when he was released in February 1990 for those who heard, saw and met him for the first time – 'disarming'. I was 50 years old when I met him face to face for the first time in Abuja, Nigeria (not even in South Africa). I was completely disarmed by him and felt immediately that I would like to do anything to help him achieve his vision for South Africa. This must have been the most common response to the person of Mandela immediately after his release, and even today. His personality, as it became more and more revealed in his actions after his release, was an indispensable element in the unfolding process of reconciliation in South Africa. To the extent that reconciliation happened and deepened in South Africa, it is unimaginable that it could have happened without the person of Nelson Mandela.

And it is not just about pulling a No 6 Springbok jersey over one's head at the final of the World Rugby Cup in South Africa, or visiting Betsie Verwoerd for a cup of tea in Orania. Most of my intelligent life I have spent trying to make sense of the political, social and economic context of South Africa. It was not a pretty or happy country that Mandela stepped into on his release. Politically it was extremely repressive, socially it was extraordinarily racially polarised and economically, fundamentally unequal. Reconciliation seemed an impossible dream. That is why commentators still scramble for words in trying to describe what happened. The most overused one is 'miracle'.

It serves no purpose to go back too far in trying to describe and analyse the South African context. There are countless scholars and analysts who have done so, far more comprehensively and competently than I can hope to do in the space allotted to me in this book. Suffice to say that for me, the worst decade before liberation was the last one – the eighties. From 1980 to 1986 I sat in Parliament and saw and experienced the brutalisation of South Africa. Parliament itself became a passive, impotent and increasingly abused spectator to a process that it was part of, but could not influence in any way. The securocratic regime of PW Botha combined military/police repression with co-optive domination to unfold a 'total strategy' in order to meet a 'total onslaught' from the 'communist-supported ANC'.

The apex of co-optive domination was the Tri-Cameral Parliament for whites, coloureds and Indians and the Homeland Policy for blacks. The 'urban blacks' could have limited municipal autonomy as envisaged in the so-called Koornhof Bills. It was farce descending into tragedy. In the 1983 'white' referendum a substantial majority of whites voted for this nonsense as a 'step in the right direction'. I left Parliament soon after it was implemented and remember on the day of my resignation saying to Hendrik Schoeman, a Nat Cabinet Minister of Transport: '*Hendrik, dis mos nonsens hierdie* (This is pure nonsense).' '*Nee van Zyl!*' he said, '*Dis nie nonsens nie. Dis 'n pot kak* (This is not nonsense, this is a bucket of shit).'

During 1985 I had taken some executive members of the PFP, the party of which I was leader, to Lusaka to meet some members of the leadership of the ANC in exile. The first one to meet me was Mac Maharaj; later on Alfred Nzo, Thabo Mbeki, Penuell Maduna, and others. This was my first exposure to 'real live' members of the ANC. I came away from this meeting deeply aware that I did not have the faintest clue about what was going on amongst the vast majority of people in my country. If it was true of me, it was so also for the vast majority of whites, and maybe coloureds and Asians.

After my resignation (Alex Boraine followed me a week later), and after Idasa had been formed, I contacted Thabo Mbeki in Lusaka and said we would like to promote interaction between predominantly Afrikaans-speaking youth and people in the townships, and could he help us get in touch with the 'underground'. He said they would get in touch with us – and so they did. That is how we got to meet Pro-Jack (assassinated), Eric Mtonga (assassinated), Ernie Malgas, Stone Sisane and many others who worked with us. Important as it was to contribute in some way to an internal dialogue, I felt it imperative to engage the ANC in exile. The lies and propaganda spread about them could be exposed and secularised if interaction with 'the exiles' could be seen as normal. Towards the end of the 1980s a number of such initiatives were on the go, much to the chagrin of the PW Botha government. I subsequently learnt that he had himself initiated confidential and private talks, and Niel Barnard, then head of the National Intelligence Service, told me himself how irritated the regime was with private initiatives such as ours. From July 1987 to October 1989 Idasa arranged at least six major conferences between prominent, predominantly Afrikaans-speaking professionals inside South Africa with the ANC in exile. The first was the Dakar Meeting in July 1987, but this was followed with meetings in Leverkusen in Germany, Paris, Lusaka, Harare, Victoria Falls, Frankfurt and London.

I mention this not to claim any credit for bringing about reconciliation in South Africa. On the contrary, if anything persuaded me that reconciliation in South Africa was going to be very, very difficult, it was my interaction with the Nationalist government in Parliament, and the ANC in exile. Each defined the solution to South Africa's conflict as the total destruction of the other. The 'total strategy' of the NP government vs. the national democratic revolution of the ANC. Another thing they had in common was the view that a liberal democratic constitution would be the most inappropriate form of government for a future South Africa. One of our current learned judges on the Constitutional Court wrote an impassioned paper arguing that a Bill of Rights would be an 'obscenity' in the new South Africa, as it would simply entrench existing inequalities.

What also came out very clearly was the enormous divide on future economic policy. The NP government favoured authoritarian capitalism, whereas a strong prevailing view within the ANC was democratic centralism, where the state would be the primary instrument of economic development, with a strong emphasis on redistribution. One of our current Cabinet ministers, at the Paris meeting, argued passionately for the abolition of private property. Wagging his finger at those who came from inside South Africa, he said: 'You fat cats have had your chance.'

The very notion of a negotiated transition in South Africa was a highly controversial and contested issue. For the NP under Botha it was inconceivable that negotiations would even take place other than on their terms and with whom they chose. I had personal discussions with Ramaphosa, Hani, Slovo, Tambo and Mbeki on the likelihood of negotiations. Almost without exception there was deep scepticism about this coming about, and transition through attrition was seen, if not as the preferred route, then the most likely one.

PW Botha was no more the President. De Klerk replaced him. Then, in November 1989, the Berlin Wall came down and the context in international relations, as well as within South Africa, began to change fundamentally. Three months later, on 2 February 1990, De Klerk made 'that speech'. I was at All Souls, Oxford, that day and could not believe what I was hearing. The next day I met Aziz Pahad and Thabo Mbeki in London and they were as close to a state of shock as one could get. I think it is fair to say that the ANC in exile was totally unprepared for negotiations. Domestically, Cyril Ramaphosa, as the leader of NUM (the National Union of Mineworkers), had been eyeballing it out with Anglo American and was regarded as an expert negotiator.

But if anybody, or any organisation, was even less prepared for negotiations, it was De Klerk and the National Party itself. I saw De Klerk two weeks after the speech (one on one in his office in Cape Town) and asked him one simple question: 'Why?' He replied that he had undergone a 'spiritual leap' and after a pause he said: 'I would have been a fool not to take the gap that the fall of the Berlin Wall gave me.' It is my honest conviction that De Klerk was convinced he could take charge of and control the process he had unleashed because of the loss of Soviet and East German patronage for the ANC. (If one reads Shubin, *Moscow and the ANC*, this is not an entirely unreasonable assumption.)

However, De Klerk had miscalculated on two vital issues. One was the popular support for the ANC domestically. The other was the person of Nelson Mandela. It was in this context that he released Mandela, and within a month Mandela had obliterated De Klerk as an international figure and a national leader. De Klerk had let the genie out of the bottle and from then on, until 27 April 1994, he was playing a futile game of catch-up.

The process of negotiation and the process of reconciliation became flipsides of the same coin. It is important to stress here that the reconciliation I am talking about is not quite the same as that of the TRC. There was a powerful redemptive personal element to the TRC process. I am talking here about a political, social and economic reconciliation. Given the past that I have alluded to, how did South Africans, across the spectrum, reconcile themselves politically, with a liberal democratic state; socially, with the ideals of an open society; and economically, with a market-driven economy? Some clues to the process that made this possible can be found in extracts from speeches by Mandela following immediately after this introduction. An example: 'Negotiations must be viewed as the culmination of all our efforts on different levels, through the use of a variety of methods, under different conditions to achieve our strategic objective – the transfer of power from the minority to the majority' (3 September 1993). In the old South Africa, this position would have been a provocation for violence and repression. In the new South Africa, majority rule was a non-negotiable for reconciliation.

The central point I am making is that throughout the process of negotiation Mandela was not going to reconcile 'at any cost'. There were clear non-negotiables for him. He would rather go back to prison than concede on majority rule. Roelf Meyer, a key negotiator for the De Klerk side, told me in conversation that right up to the Boipatong massacre in June 1992 De Klerk fought against majority rule. After Boipatong, he reluctantly accepted it, and this was seen as the ultimate betrayal by many of his followers. At the same time, Mandela took the sting out of majority rule by his emphasis on constitutional government and the rule of law.

The ultimate triumph of reconciliation is the way the negotiation process resulted in finally creating a situation in South Africa where certain key values were (and still are) held in creative tension in relation to one another. Liberal democracy and economic growth, law and order and respect for human rights, fiscal discipline and delivery of services, modernity and traditionalism. The very fact that they are held in tension is testimony to the absence of dogma and a willingness to compromise. And without compromise there can be no reconciliation. Mandela epitomises the willingness to compromise without sacrificing principle. Because of that, South Africans can explore a new future in an entirely different and unanticipated context.

South Africa, as far as my knowledge goes, is the only country that negotiated itself out of domination into democracy without any outside assistance and/or interference. Certainly, it is the only country on the African continent that has done so. And it was not simply a walk in the park that brought it about. There were moments when we were perilously close to failure: Boipatong, Bisho, KwaZulu-Natal, the Siege of Mmabatho, right-wing bombings in Braamfontein, train murders, the De Klerk referendum after his loss to Treurnicht – these are shorthand references to events and incidents that very nearly derailed the process of transition. It is a tribute to the resilience and maturity of our political leadership, across the spectrum, that we survived and succeeded. However, I have no doubt that history will record that the final accolades for the success of our transition will go to Nelson Mandela as the individual who held us all together when the dark days threatened us. Through his example, he made a critical mass of South Africans want to make the new South Africa work. It is still so today!

A New Era of Hope

New Year message from the President of the ANC
to the people of South Africa,
30 December 1991.

A New Year is upon us. A New Year that, in the last decade of this century, could usher in a new era of hope for all South Africans. While we have achieved a great deal, we should not, however, mark this New Year in a spirit of self-congratulation, but rather as an occasion for calm and sober reflection. We need to take stock of the tasks and challenges that still lie ahead. Yet it is an index of the advances we have made that the opportunity to set South Africa firmly on the road to democracy is with us.

1991 saw many new developments, including the formation of the Patriotic Front. We can all justly take pride in the success of the first meeting of the Conference for a Democratic South Africa, Codesa, which brought together the overwhelming majority of political parties, organisations and formations in our country. The commonly agreed objective of Codesa, subscribed to by all but two of the participants, is the attainment of a nonracial democracy.

The tragedy of South Africa is that Codesa comes after eighty years of costly struggles by the majority of South Africans who had been excluded from the so-called National Convention that took place in 1909. After the innumerable missed opportunities of the past eight decades, Codesa represents a promising window of opportunity for all South Africans to map out the future of our country together.

As 1991 draws to a close, there remains the painful, fruitless and tragic bloodshed that has been the source of so much grief in Natal and other parts of the country. There is little merit today in attempting to determine who fired the first shot. But it is abundantly clear that no one – other than those who wish to preserve the apartheid order – benefits from the continuation of this bloodletting.

During Christmas and New Year, dedicated to peace and goodwill to all, I appeal to all the leaders of our people, be they in the civics,

101

the mass movement, the trade unions, women's or youth organisations, cultural or educational bodies, the churches or business, to spare no effort to make the Peace Accord work and bring peace into our lives. For the sake of our children, for the future of our country, and to ensure that the democratic order so many have sacrificed so much to achieve is not still-born, the killing must stop now. Not another life should be lost in this futile violence.

As we enter the New Year, we cannot forget those of our fellow citizens whose lot is the despair of homelessness, hunger and poverty. Millions of our people are still denied fundamental human rights – shelter, food and the right to a full and productive life. The future we seek to build will be seriously flawed if it cannot address this national problem. The ANC has its own proposals to resolve the socio-economic problems afflicting the people of our country. I would appeal to others to give the matter the priority it deserves.

We realise that many South Africans are deeply concerned about the future, particularly the question of creating a vibrant and growing economy. The speed with which we can achieve this is dependent on progress made towards fundamental change. We have proposed, and the world has endorsed, the phased lifting of sanctions. The achievements to date have enabled us to lift people-to-people sanctions, and the benefits are there for all to see and enjoy – in cricket and other sports, in the cultural sphere and in tourism. The establishment of a democratic constitution would allow for all remaining sanctions, including financial sanctions, to be lifted and enable us to take our place with pride in the international community. Investors are keenly interested in the progress we make. If we accomplish these goals, the world is open to us.

This New Year will be the first that many who have engaged in struggle will observe outside prison. I take this opportunity to renew my heartfelt, warm welcome to these former political prisoners. I embrace these comrades, fully confident that they will find their rightful place in the ranks of the struggle they have served with such distinction, even while they were behind bars. The release of the majority of political prisoners, fought for and won by the people of South Africa, supported by millions throughout the world, is a great victory. But it is not complete, for outstanding patriots like Robert McBride, Mthetheleli Mncube and Mzondeleli Nondula are among the over 400 political prisoners who still remain in jail and on death row.

The harsh reality is that irrespective of the numbers that we, through our collective strength and efforts, can release from apartheid's jails, no one in South Africa can be truly free as long as the racist consti-tutional order remains in place. In our view, the foundations laid at Codesa make it possible for an Interim Government of National Unity to be established to oversee the transition process and super-vise free and fair elections for a Constituent Assembly, on the basis of one person, one vote. A democratic constitution is, therefore, one of our priority goals to be achieved for this coming year.

1992 can be the year in which our country takes this giant step, which is necessary to realise our goal of democracy and win inter-national acceptance. But all this can be achieved through our actions alone. For the sake of our country and our future, we dare not fail!

Let us begin this New Year by resolving not to perpetuate distinct racial, ethnic and language groups, which are the legacy of apartheid, but to act as fellow South Africans, ready and willing to work togeth-er. Let us seize this opportunity to make a new beginning by cre-atively harnessing what is best in our past to build for the future. There is a role and place for everyone in our country. Let us set aside narrow sectoral and party political interests to serve the greater national interest that will guarantee a future of peace, stability and prosperity for all.

To the extent that we all do this, 1992 can indeed become a Happy and Prosperous New Year.

Negotiations

Selection from the opening address to the 48th national
conference of the African National Congress, Durban,
2 July 1991.

As a result of the struggle that we waged for decades, the balance of
forces has changed to such an extent that the ruling National Party,
which thought it could maintain the system of white minority domination for ever, has been obliged to accept the fact that it has no
strength to sustain the apartheid system and that it must enter into
negotiations with the genuine representatives of the people. Negotiations constitute a victory of our struggle and a defeat for the ruling
group which thought it could exercise a monopoly of political power
forever.

When we decided to take up arms, it was because the only other
choice was to surrender and submit to slavery. This was not a decision we took lightly. We were always ready, as we are now, to seize
any genuine opportunity that might arise to secure the liberation of
our people by peaceful means.

We are very conscious that the process could not be smooth since
we are dealing with a regime that is steeped in a culture of racism,
violence and domination. We are dealing with a group of politicians
who do not want to negotiate themselves out of power and representatives of the state who fear the impact of democratic change.

The point which must be clearly understood is that the struggle is
not over, and negotiations themselves are a theatre of struggle, subject to advances and reverses as any other form of struggle.

Despite our own heroic efforts, we have not defeated the regime.
Consequently, we see negotiations as a continuation of the struggle
leading to our central objective: the transfer of power to the people.
There are therefore some issues that are non-negotiable: among others our demands for one person one vote, a united South Africa, the
liberation of women and the protection of fundamental human rights.

As a movement we recognise the fact that apart from ourselves there are other political formations in the country. These are as entitled to exist as we are. They have a right to formulate their own policies and to contest for support for their policies and organisations. We have agreed to enter into talks with all these, and have been talking to most of them, because we have no desire whatsoever to impose our views on everybody else.

We have never claimed that we have a monopoly of wisdom and that only our views and policies are legitimate. As a democratic movement we shall continue to defend the right of all our people to freedom of thought, association and organisation. It is precisely because of this that we have firmly committed ourselves to the per- spective of a multi-party democracy.

We say all this to contribute to our preparations for the period ahead of us when we shall enter into negotiations which will deter- mine the destiny of our country for the foreseeable future. We must participate in these processes with a clear vision of what we want to achieve, with a clear view of the procedures we must follow to ensure that our representatives are properly mandated and that they report back to us, and with a clear view of the process of negotiations.

Negotiations and Armed Struggle

Selection from the keynote address to the Umkhonto we Sizwe
National Conference, Eastern Transvaal,
3 September 1993.

It is with great honour that I stand here before you at this critical
juncture in the history of our country. You, the combatants of our
people's army, Umkhonto we Sizwe, have left an indelible mark on the
history of our struggle for freedom and democracy. We are gathered
here today to look back on that history, to acknowledge both our
strengths and weaknesses and more importantly to consolidate our
gains in order to face the challenges ahead.

MK from its inception has played a significant role both politically
and militarily in the process of liberating our people from apartheid
oppression and economic exploitation. MK was and is the embodiment of the fighting spirit of our people and came to represent the
highest aspirations and ideals of our struggle. It was by way of example that MK inspired generations of our fighting youth to swell the
ranks of our army and the African National Congress.

It must be acknowledged that the post-February 1990 period did
affect the ANC organisationally at different levels in an adverse way. MK
was no exception to this process of reorganisation and restructuring.
The reality is that any period of transition is characterised by change,
and it is inevitable that this process will be accompanied by some
degree of uncertainty and require adaptation to the new situation.

The most important point to note in relation to negotiations and
their relationship to other forms of struggle is that they are not mutually exclusive. Negotiations must be viewed as the culmination of all
our collective efforts on different levels, through the use of a variety
of methods, under different conditions, to achieve our strategic
objective – the transfer of power from the minority to the majority.

The decision to suspend armed activity did not mean an acceptance on our part of the irreversibility of the process of negotiations,
but rather a genuine commitment to the process of peace and

106

democracy. The African National Congress has more than any other organisation or political party blazed the trail of democracy in this country. The suspension of armed activity should also not be viewed as a sign of weakness on our part; it should be viewed as a process of strengthening our position at the negotiating table and our commitment to creating the most favourable conditions for the democratisation process to succeed.

The most significant point in relation to the suspension of armed activity is that it in no way negates either the existence of MK or the need to strengthen and build our army for the future. In fact, it places greater responsibility upon and poses new challenges for our army.

It is also important to recognise that negotiations are an advance for our struggle. It is the combined efforts of all our people and that of MK in reinforcing the mass struggles of our people which forced the regime to engage in the negotiation process.

We must end the violence, the death and destruction, the oppression and exploitation, and build a secure future for us all in peace and democracy.

Codesa

Address to the Convention for a Democratic South Africa,
20 December 1991.

Today will be indelibly imprinted in the history of our country. If we who are gathered here respond to the challenge before us, today will mark the commencement of the transition from apartheid to democracy. Our people, from every corner of our country, have expressed their yearning for democracy and peace. Codesa represents the historical opportunity to translate that yearning into reality.

For 80 years, the ANC has led the struggle for democracy in South Africa. Along the route traversed during this period, many sacrifices were made by thousands upon thousands of our people. In the arduous battle between the people and oppression, positions hardened and polarisation developed between the people and the state. Even when, in the absence of any other recourse, the ANC took up arms, our objective was to secure a political settlement in South Africa. In the past few years an environment more conducive to establishing mutual trust has been established.

South Africans of many persuasions recognise that this environment, and its constitutional product, Codesa, is the fruit of their sacrifices and struggle. They have a justifiable expectation that Codesa will set our country on the road to democracy.

Inasmuch as apartheid has been declared a crime against humanity and the problems of our country have engaged so much of the attention of the international community over decades, the presence of esteemed observers from the key international organisations as guests of Codesa is most appropriate.

We welcome the guests from the United Nations organisations, the Organisation of African Unity, the Commonwealth, the European Economic Community, and the Non-Aligned Movement. We trust that they will avail to the process now unfolding, their wisdom, insights and experience gained in many similar initiatives across the world.

All South Africans share the hope and vision of a land free of apartheid, where internal strife will have no place.

The ANC initiated the search for peace in our country. Since 1987 the ANC has intensively campaigned for a negotiated transfer of power. This campaign reached new heights in 1989 when the OAU, the Non-Aligned Movement and the UN General Assembly all adopted declarations supporting the position. All three declarations stated:

> ... that where colonial, racial and apartheid domination exists, there can be neither peace nor justice.

In keeping with this spirit, Codesa must therefore lay the basis for the elimination of racial and apartheid domination.

It is only by decisive action in this regard that South Africa will be granted entry to the community of nations as a full member.

The strength of the Codesa initiative lies in the range of political parties and persuasions represented here. The presence of so many parties augurs well for the future. The diverse interests represented speak of the capacity to develop consensus across the spectrum and of the desire to maximise common purpose amongst South Africans. Many parties here have already invested so much by way of preparing their constituencies for transformation. Above all else, the investment already made must spur us on to total commitment for the successful outcome of this convention.

We regret the fact that there are still parties who exclude themselves from this important process. After Codesa the situation in our country is irreversible. Threats about civil war are irresponsible and totally unacceptable. The time for such talk is long past. If they execute these the world will see that they are prolonging the suffering of all South Africans, and poisoning the search for peace in our country.

But one thing stands fast: the process of moving towards democracy is unstoppable. History grants all of us a unique opportunity. To exchange this opportunity for a bowl of lentil soup of the past, and negative bravado, is to deny the future. We continue to call on such parties to join Codesa now, even at this late stage.

The message of the ANC through Codesa is straightforward, clear, and for all South Africans: the time for one South Africa, one nation, one vote, one future is here.

The National Convention in 1909 was a gathering of whites

representing the four British colonies. It was also a betrayal of black people and a denial of democracy. The Act of Union entrenched colonial practices and institutions constitutionally. In its wake, our country has lived through eight decades of wasted opportunity. Codesa provides the first opportunity since to attempt to establish democracy in our country.

It is imperative that we also reach consensus on the definition of democracy. From the ANC's perspective, democracy entails:

- That all governments must derive their authority from the consent of the governed.
- No person or groups of persons shall be subjected to oppression, domination or discrimination by virtue of their race, gender, ethnic origin, colour or creed.
- All persons should enjoy the right to life.
- All persons should enjoy security in their persons and should be entitled to the peaceful enjoyment of their possessions, including the right to acquire, own or dispose of property, without distinction based on race, colour, language, gender or creed.
- All persons should have the right to express whatever opinions they wish to subscribe to, provided that in the exercise of that right they do not infringe on the right of others.

This quality of democracy will indeed only be possible when those who have borne the brunt of apartheid oppression exercise their right to vote in a free and fair election on the basis of universal suffrage. We can see no reason why an election for a Constituent Assembly should not be possible during 1992.

When oppression necessitated a struggle in South Africa the ANC never retreated but was in the vanguard. Now that the situation is conducive it is the ANC again that leads the way in the effort to bring peace to the land of our ancestors.

Of all the people who need freedom in South Africa it is the black people. They need it now because their economic and welfare situation deteriorates daily.

The right to vote is the essence of the struggle for freedom. 1992 is the year that must bring the first democratic elections in South Africa.

Codesa, on its own, will not deliver democracy. In recording this fact, there is no attempt to demean Codesa. Even absolute consensus during the life of Codesa will still leave an apartheid Constitution in place. We need to be reminded that this very Constitution was declared null and void by the UN Security Council in 1983.

The invalidation of the prevailing Constitution is the most persuasive argument in support of the view that the incumbent government is unsuited to the task of overseeing the transition to democracy and we must now compel it to make way for an Interim Government of National Unity to supervise the transition.

This is the only cogent outflow from our deliberations at Codesa. The consensus which we arrive at will certainly have far-reaching implications for the birth of a new nationhood. None of us could be satisfied with circumstances where the consensus struck at this is not translated into full legal force.

An interim government, important as it may be, is but the product of agreement between ourselves as political parties and organisations. It will not be the outcome of full participation by the people of our country. Negotiations, to be successful, must be owned and supported by the majority of South Africans.

In the absence of full participation, we must commit ourselves to open negotiations to ensure that notions of secret deals do not arise. This process will also hinge on the confidence by each participating party that the communication of developments be absolutely non-partisan. Consideration therefore needs to be given to the immediate establishment of the necessary mechanisms to ensure that the state-controlled media accurately and fairly represent the views of all participants.

The means of establishing an interim government will not be participatory. Therefore the consensus at Codesa should curtail both its mandate and its lifespan.

The ANC remains fully committed to the installation of a government which can justly claim authority because it is based on the will of the people. This reality will have to be underpinned by a Constitution which both engenders respect and enjoys legitimacy. There is a compelling urgency about this task. It is inconceivable that such a democratic Constitution could be reached in any way but through the portals of an elected constitution-making body, namely a Constituent Assembly

It is tragic that our country, so well endowed with natural resources, has been reduced to an economic wasteland by the system of apartheid, based on greed and mismanagement. It is also distress-

111

ing to note that the deplorable violence has reached such alarming proportions, and others threaten still more. These features are a direct consequence of the determination of a minority to maintain the power and privilege accrued by apartheid. There are large parts of our country where free political activity is still not possible, where law and order are still ruled by the jackboot and a large number of political prisoners remain incarcerated. In the spirit of our Convention we call upon the government to proclaim an immediate Codesa amnesty before Christmas for all remaining political prisoners throughout the country.

Nothing could be more irresponsible than for those of us gathered here to deny our people the right to peace and freedom of association and deny our country its due economic growth.

As everybody here is aware, the ANC and the government have been involved in bilateral discussions since May last year. There are still some matters dealt with in these bilateral talks which have not been finalised. We will continue these discussions, among other things, seeking to resolve the question of the control of armed formations in the country, including Umkhonto we Sizwe.

We can only reverse the situation if we set our sights on establishing true democracy. The national interest is far, far more important than the sectional interests represented by any party here. Everybody wants a place in the sun of a post-apartheid South Africa. No delegation here could possibly have been mandated by its constituency, however small, to attend Codesa in order to annihilate itself.

Recognising this, however, we want to make a strong appeal to everybody present to place the compelling national concerns above narrow sectional interests.

History will judge us extremely harshly if we fail to turn the opportunity which it now presents us with to the common good. The risks of further pain and affliction arising from violence, homelessness, unemployment and gutter education are immense. The approach which we adopt at Codesa must be fundamentally inclusive. The price of Codesa's failure will be far too great.

We must not trample on the confidence which our people have in the successful conclusion to these negotiations. It would be foolhardy to spurn the world for its efforts in assisting to secure peace and prosperity for South Africa. Our people and the world expect a nonracial, nonsexist democracy to emerge from the negotiations on which we are about to embark.

Failure of Codesa is inconceivable, so too is consensus without legal force. There is absolutely no room for error or obstinacy. The challenge which Codesa places before each one of us is to unshackle ourselves from the past and build anew.

Codesa can be the beginning of reconstruction. Let our common commitment to the future of our country inspire us to build a South Africa of which we can all be truly proud.

ANC and the National Party

Statement at the opening of the ANC/NP Summit,
26 September 1992.

Allow me to express my appreciation that we have finally been able
to meet. At the very least, the simple act of our coming together at
this level is bound to send a signal of hope among all South Africans.
We are duty bound not to disappoint them.

I would like to congratulate Secretary-General Cyril Ramaphosa,
Minister Roelf Meyer and their assistants for their outstanding work
in preparation for the summit. The ultimate accolade, however, goes
to the people of South Africa who, in their various ways, have
ensured that the issues of peace and democracy remain high on the
political agenda.

There were moments when the temptation to despair seemed
most attractive. Indeed, the issues would not have been critical, and
the urgency to address them not acute, if difficulties did not arise on
the way.

Now we have assembled – representatives of the ANC and the
government – to seek practical solutions to the most urgent questions facing our country. I take this opportunity to welcome back to
our midst the political prisoners who have just been released, and hope
that the others will join us soon. This important step, and practical
measures to address violence, will help create the climate so necessary
for substantive negotiations to resume.

We have come here in the hope that by the time this summit ends,
a firm basis will have been laid for the resumption of negotiations.
This is what all our people want. This is what our economy needs.
This is what our country yearns for.

The African National Congress has not come here to claim victories. We have come to earnestly tackle the problems facing our country. We must emerge with a firm resolve to clear the path to a new
and democratic order. South Africa must be the winner.

We believe that if negotiations are to succeed, all parties and organisations should be able to strengthen themselves. As difficult as it is, it would be a grave mistake for any organisation to behave in negotiations blinded by sectarian interests.

Certainly, the National Party and the African National Congress are products of specific backgrounds. We must try to regulate the emotions arising from these backgrounds in the interest of our common future. We have to be proactive in the face of the current situation and dispassionately address the objective realities of the day.

Recently we have had a spate of massacres like Boipatong and Bisho. We have been blaming each other for these events. It is our duty to ensure that an Interim Government of National Unity is brought about speedily. This will go a long way in addressing many of these problems. I hope that when next we meet, we will be able to agree on dates for elections for a Constituent Assembly and the installation of an Interim Government.

Our economy has been badly damaged. Starvation, lack of jobs, the education crisis, poor services and crime infect our society like the plague. The longer these problems remain unsolved, the more they feed upon themselves to drag the country further down the precipice. And the longer the transition to democracy takes, the more are solutions to these problems postponed.

But to reach that stage, we have to attend to violence and political intolerance with a new determination. All members of our society – including those in the so-called homelands – must enjoy freedom of speech and association. They deserve, without exception, the right to life.

By tackling with serious intent the matters on the summit's agenda we shall strengthen the National Peace Accord and contribute immensely to national reconciliation.

This summit has the potential to lay a firm basis for speedy movement towards democracy. The adoption of a Constitution to which all South Africans pay allegiance and a government truly representative of all the people are the most important milestones in this process.

My delegation and I will do all in our power to ensure that the summit succeeds. There is no alternative for South Africa.

ANC and the Inkatha Freedom Party

Opening address at the African National Congress/
Inkatha Freedom Party Summit,
29 January 1990.

Allow me, on behalf of the National Executive Committee of the African National Congress, and indeed our entire membership, to express my profound gratitude to all gathered here for this historic encounter between our two organisations.

Our ultimate praise should indeed be reserved for the masses in the province of Natal and other parts of the country whose yearning for peace is the driving force of our deliberations today. It is on their behalf that we crown the local and regional initiatives such as the Lower Umfolozi Accord with a meeting of this nature. It is to satisfy their yearning and facilitate their efforts that we have gathered here.

The fact that we have traversed a long and tortuous road before this opportunity availed itself gives this august meeting its special significance. For us this meeting represents the culmination of our persistent efforts to bring an end to the confrontation which has plagued our two organisations and our people.

Right at the outset we want to make one thing crystal clear. We have not come here to apportion blame for the fact that it has taken so long before we managed to sit around a table of peace and reconciliation. Nor do we think that it would benefit the cause of peace if we spent our time in this meeting pointing fingers to identify those responsible for the terrible carnage which has left so many thousands or our people dead and wounded.

If we are to fulfil the true purpose of our get-together, there must be no victors or losers between the ANC and Inkatha. Only our people must be the victors. And the only losers should be those whose racist policies are served by carnage among blacks.

The eyes of the world are on us. The majority of the people in this ravaged province and other parts of the country certainly wish us success. The angels of death and destruction – the defenders of white minority rule – will the opposite. We must satisfy and disappoint in equal measure. We must deliver.

It is ironic that a meeting between organisations of the oppressed should require such a special effort to accomplish. Be that as it may, it is certainly a tragedy that the land of Kings Shaka, Dingane and Cetshwayo should drown in the self-inflicted bloodletting of its own sons and daughters.

We meet in the province which has mothered some of the greatest liberation figures of our whole country. Among the unforgettables are the great warrior Bambatha of the last armed revolt before modern South African history. King Dinizulu, John Dube and Josiah Gumede were founder members of the ANC. We owe these and other heroes, including Chief Albert Luthuli and Bishop Zulu, peace in their graves.

Their sacrifices were for the unity of the people against the common enemy of all the oppressed – the apartheid system. They shed their blood so that peace can finally prevail with the destruction of the apartheid system.

This is what the African National Congress was formed to achieve. And this is what it strives to attain today. The yoke of white colonial domination still rests on the shoulders of our people. To throw it off is the profound wish of every African, no matter what station he or she might occupy in life.

The foundation stone laid by our forebears is the rock upon which our encounter today must be based. The attempts to divide our people along ethnic lines, to turn their rich variety into a dagger with which to pierce their hearts, must be made to fail.

There can be no salvation for our beleaguered country but the realisation by all and sundry that we are one people – black and white. Cast in a mould that can be different, but one interdependent people all the same – irrespective of the political and ideological creed that each one of us might hold dear.

Thanks to the untiring efforts of the people, the grim and infamous era of apartheid is coming to an end.

Our people had to sacrifice generously to bring the administrators of apartheid to the realisation that they have no future as South Africans if they do not accept the reality that the fate of our country needs to be determined by all its people, as equals.

Many thousands have died in inter-communal violence in Natal and other parts of the country. In the final analysis, we are justified to lay the blame at the door of the apartheid regime which has created conditions of such squalor and degradation among our people. We are certainly right to assert that the removal of this system is a basic precondition for an end to violence in our country. But generalities of this nature will not take us very far.

Among ourselves, we could point fingers and apportion blame in all directions. Perhaps that would satisfy an ego. But deflecting criticism, however justified we may be in doing so, would not help resolve the problem. Therefore, whatever the concrete outcome of our meeting today, contact among us must continue, precisely to nurture areas of agreement and seek lasting solutions to areas of conflict.

The African National Congress believes that the efforts of our people have brought about a situation in which apartheid can be eradicated by peaceful means.

This requires an atmosphere of free political activity in which all people can freely canvass their positions within the rest of society. The use of force against others and the denial of access to public facilities, be it in inter-communal strife or by means of instruments of the state, simply because they hold differing views, can only make the views of the perpetrator the more despicable. Such free political activity and the peace that we seek require that the security forces of this land act impartially and in a way that promotes peace.

We also firmly hold the view that movement to that new South Africa is the business of all South Africans. It should be undertaken on the basis of mass involvement and broad consultation among all interested organisations. Our proposal for an all-party congress derives from this belief. So do our calls for an impartial supervisory mechanism as well as an elected body to draft a new Constitution. Otherwise the final product and the process itself will lack popular support.

The ANC does not demand of the Inkatha Freedom Party complete agreement with these our views. If we are to reach the prosperous South Africa to which we all aspire, we must let the culture of debate flower in full bloom. We must ensure that every South African, including those in the security forces, helps to build a nation of which all of us can be proud. More immediately, we must rebuild and develop communities in a manner that removes the potential for violence and heals the wounds of conflict.

This challenge faces us as we start our historic deliberations. In struggle, we have achieved the possibility of movement forward to a democratic future with a minimum of bloodshed.

Today we are called upon to cement this. If we do play our role as a catalyst to this process we shall have accomplished our mission. To all intents and purposes we cannot afford to fail. Violence must end. Let peace prevail.

Patriotic Front

Statement at the opening of the Patriotic Front
Summit Meeting, Port Elizabeth,
29 October 1992.

It is an excellent thing that we meet here today as part of our process of regular consultation about matters which are of critical importance to the future of our country and people. I thank you for the opportunity you have given me to speak at this opening session.

I want to take this opportunity to present some ideas directed at the central objective we all share of taking our country forward towards its speedy transformation into a nonracial democracy.

The reality we all have to face is that our people are bleeding as they have never done before. They bleed from the criminal political violence which has already claimed too many lives and whose most recent manifestations are the heinous massacre at Folweni in Natal, the persisting destruction of the Sabelo family and the murder of Reggie Hadebe, Deputy Chairperson of the ANC in the Natal Midlands.

They bleed from the criminal violence perpetrated by robbers, thugs, rapists, racists, the abusers of women and children, ritual murderers, people unbalanced by intense social pressures, and are victims of the demented frenzy of other ogres in our communities.

They bleed from the pestilence of poverty which has thrown people out of jobs, denied them access to food, accommodation, clothing and health.

They bleed from the drought which ravages humans, beasts and the environment, compounded by the crimes of those who intercept drought relief and thus derive personal gain from the desperate suffering of those who were already abjectly poor but are now thrown into the pit of hopelessness because the rains refused to come.

A fetid cloud of despair envelops our country. Its stench has begun to be felt by many nations beyond our borders and beyond our continent.

People begin to ask – what happened to the hopes that the events of recent years inspired? What has dimmed, or perhaps eclipsed, the rainbow that lit and decorated our skies with such promises of joy? Whence the soulless and soul–destroying and fetid cloud of despair?

Many questions are asked and to each an answer must be given.

When we promised the people freedom were we offering them a mirage? When we held out a future that will be crowned with happiness and prosperity were we seeking to blind them to the continuing reality of growing misery and poverty? When we proclaimed that we represent their true interests, were we hiding from the people our inability to deliver what life itself demands?

Many more questions are asked and to each an honest answer must be given.

To be honest in our answers we will each as leaders have to disrobe ourselves of the mantle of self-righteousness. We will each have to open our minds to critical self-examination and examination. We will each have to admit past wrongs and admit to public correction. We will each have to question the truths that we considered given and learn to live with a reality which demands that we change the assumptions which inform our action.

We will have to, each one of us and those we lead, accept that we must break out of a mould which constrained and stultified when we should have evolved a frame which injected freedom and dynamism to what we had to do to promote the public good.

We shall have done all our people and all humanity an historic service, carrying with it a priceless reward, if at the end of our meeting we shall have identified the problems our nation faces and said what it is that we should do to turn those problems into a record of the past.

We must, then, admit that the process of transformation has been slow, lethargic and insufficiently responsive to the sense of urgency which we all know should be the hallmark of our approach to the process of change.

If we accept this, as I am convinced we must, then we will also have to accept that we shall have to elaborate the ways and means by which we can expedite the process leading to the formation and adoption of a new Constitution by an elected Constituent Assembly.

Among other things, this must mean that we should resist with all the energy we can muster the notion that we should enter into protracted negotiations on a new negotiating forum in order to accommodate certain groupings which, for reasons of myopia, decided not to board the train when it left the station many months ago. It also means that we should contest vigorously the idea that agreements already reached in the Codesa process should be discarded and the process of negotiations started from the beginning.

An agreement exists between the ANC and the National Party according to which these two organisations will engage in an intensive and extensive bilateral discussion to find common ground on all the outstanding issues on the Codesa agenda. We meet here today because it is the firm belief of the ANC that prior to this meeting, we should consult as broadly as possible so that the views we present at the forthcoming meeting should be as representative as possible.

In keeping with this view we are therefore presenting to this important meeting two major documents for your approval. One details our proposals for the agenda of the bilateral meeting. The other contains a strategic perspective which we would like this meeting to adopt as its common position.

Further, we are convinced that if we proceed in the manner we have described, as part of a thorough process of preparation for the resumption of the formal multilateral negotiations, we will, together, create the conditions for the success of these negotiations, for speedy movement forward, as well as avoidance of the deadlock that confronted all of us at the second plenary session of Codesa.

Consequently, what we request of you today is both endorsement of this approach and all the necessary input on a continuing basis to ensure that we carry your broad mandate as we go into the process of detailed bilateral negotiations.

The meeting might also find it fit to consider the organisational steps it should agree upon to ensure a continual process of consultation among ourselves so that, after this meeting, we do indeed use both legs, the one being of multilateral consultations and the other being the preparatory bilateral negotiations.

At the meeting between ourselves and the government on 26 September we entered into agreements which relate to the issue of violence, and which must be implemented. Nevertheless, important as these agreements were, we cannot pretend that they address this matter comprehensively. We need to reflect on this matter of violence continuously to determine what needs to be done to reduce it and hopefully bring it to an end.

We, for ourselves, have accepted the urgent need for a meeting of the signatories of the National Peace Accord to find practical ways to end the shame of the debilitating bloodletting that has been imposed on the people.

As we examine this matter we must surely look at our own conduct, going beyond narrow partisan considerations, and play our rightful roles as the leaders of the process of democratic transformation, the principal guardians of peace and militant combatants for the protection of life itself.

We must re-examine many questions – not necessarily at this meeting – including how to stop the process of retribution for past wrongs, the burning of coffins in public and whether the burning of effigies is not too evocative of earlier scenes of people killed by burning.

I give these only as examples to make the point that we must really be engaged in ways that we may not have been able to before to contribute the maximum we can to end the terrible violence which afflicts our society.

We must aim to arrive at the situation whereby by the end of the year we have reached all the necessary agreements that will enable us to move forward speedily to the election of a Constituent Assembly and the Interim Government of National Unity.

We must confront any tendency which seeks further delays in the process of transformation. Our people want freedom. The country desperately requires to be put on a new footing so that we can address the enormous problems we will inherit from the apartheid system.

The world waits for the change that is overdue, ready to engage with us in the process of reconstruction and hopeful that what we will do with our own country will vindicate the hopes of the nations who joined us in the struggle against apartheid and make an important contribution to the rebuilding of our world as a place of peace, democracy, equality, and prosperity.

As we conduct our work here today, I trust we shall all be inspired by the conviction that we must move our country forward speedily in conditions of peace, so that it too can, at last, begin to experience the joys of peace, democracy, equality and prosperity.

Transition

Address to the summit of the Patriotic Front, Mahlangu,
KwaNdebele, 24 November 1993.

The Patriotic Front as a whole can truly be proud of the results produced in the negotiations process. Our country at last has put together through negotiations a package of instruments which enable all South Africans, black and white, to put aside the past and travel the high road to democracy.

Through the four bills including the one setting up the TEC [Transitional Executive Council], which were enacted by Parliament earlier, we have the necessary instruments to ensure that free and fair elections take place. We have made certain that the De Klerk government is not both player and referee. This was one of the first objectives contained in the declaration of the Patriotic Front adopted in Durban in 1991.

It is now up to us to use these instruments to level the playing fields, guarantee free political activity and enable the country to hold free and fair elections.

In the recent decision of the plenary meeting the Constitution for the transition has taken shape. This Constitution provides for a Government of National Unity which would govern the country for a maximum of five years. This government will be the outcome of elections to be held on 27 April 1994. Through this means we can now say firmly that the votes of the people will enable us to remove the architects of apartheid from the seat of political power. This was another objective the Patriotic Front set for itself.

The Constitution for the transition also provides that while the country is governed by a Government of National Unity, the Constitutional Assembly will sit in order to draft the final Constitution of a nonracial, nonsexist democratic South Africa. This was a third and central objective of the declaration of the Patriotic Front.

In this way, the mandate we gave ourselves is being fulfilled. The negotiations process has produced an interim Constitution which opens the road for South Africa to move without interruption to a true democracy in which majority rule prevails.

We have reached this point through immense effort and steadfastness of purpose. We have produced a package which all South Africans can be proud of. In the course of negotiations there has been much give and take. Whatever we have given has been done in the interests of the country and without sacrificing our principles.

I would like to pay tribute to all members of the Patriotic Front for the way in which we have worked together to register these achievements. The lesson of this co-operation should not be minimised. In the negotiations process we took on the might of the apartheid state. We produced an outcome which lays the basis for uniting our country and our people into one nation.

Whatever our problems, we must take encouragement and redouble our efforts to work together so that on 27 April we finally and completely put paid to white minority rule and launch our country on a path of peace, reconstruction and democracy.

The road ahead is not going to be easy. The forces which tried and failed to stop the negotiations process have not given up. In fact, many of them are becoming even more desperate. To handle these problems we must have confidence in ourselves. We must have confidence in the capacity of the Patriotic Front to work together as a united force. Above all, we must have confidence in the people whose servants we are.

There are formations in the extreme right – and here I include both white and black – who cannot face the test of the electorate. They, especially the white right, pose a serious threat. They know they cannot stop the change. They however do have the capacity to create all sorts of destabilisation.

We are able to deal with this threat. In the first place, we must find the correct political answers which will leave them as an isolated tiny minority. We must never allow them the capacity to grow and develop into a social force. We must be flexible and firm at the same time. We must be willing to accommodate without abandoning our principles. We must be ready to adjust our tactics and never lose sight of our main goal.

One of the main reasons why this extreme right poses a real threat is because the De Klerk government has always recoiled from acting with firmness against them. The same is true about the way in which the De Klerk government has failed and refuses to act decisively against those who are fomenting violence.

In addition to our own strength as a people we have managed to keep the support of the international community on the side of our struggle for democracy. Despite the changes that have taken place on the international scene, we have maintained their support not only for the purposes of eliminating apartheid but also to help us in the reconstruction of our economy and society.

We now have to fix our eyes firmly on the immediate period ahead. This is from now until the elections on 27 April 1994. The central focus of this period is the forthcoming elections. All the other parties in the elections have one thing in common. They share a common platform of being anti-ANC. They want to stop a runaway victory for the ANC.

The ANC has been the architect of multi-party democracy in South Africa. And yet these parties have come to put a unique meaning to multi-party democracy. They are trying to sell the idea that it is good for the country if there is not an overwhelming majority party. They know that they are going to lose the race so they want to plead with the electorate not to give a verdict which will overwhelmingly underscore the unity of our nation. And yet, what this country needs for its transition is the unequivocal evidence that the people as a whole are united behind the one organisation which has been the champion of unity, peace and democracy.

We are facing a no-holds-barred battle. The parties ranged against the ANC are going to stop at nothing to reduce our strength. They will do everything in their power; they will use fair means and foul means to confuse the electorate, to scare them away from the ANC and its allies. They will do all they can to drive wedges between us.

As certain as we are of victory we cannot take our people for granted. We must carry our message to every corner of our land. The elections of 27 April are going to be the most highly developed form of mass action in which our people participate.

The Constitution for the transition provides for strong central government and strong provincial government. One of the greatest dangers we face is that we may focus our minds on capturing central power and by default leave provincial power in other hands. This would be a terrible mistake. It would weaken the centre and leave it cut off from the masses. In terms of the Constitution, good governance, the delivery of socio-economic upliftment, will depend and be perceived by people to depend on their interaction with provincial government.

Our aim must therefore be to win power at the centre, to win power in all nine provinces and to provide the forces who will establish effective local government. In deploying ourselves we must never lose sight of all three tiers of government. None of these can be left to accident or chance.

I am confident that we will be able to reach the people and convince them to support us. I am convinced that whatever tricks the National Party has in store we can outmanoeuvre them. From our foundation in 1912 we have learnt one cardinal lesson in mobilising support: never mislead the people. Speak to them with honesty and with clarity. Understand their concerns and find ways to address these. That is the road to victory.

Multi-Party Negotiations

Address to the plenary session of the Multi-Party Negotiations Process,
World Trade Centre, Kempton Park,
17 November 1993.

We have reached the end of an era. We are at the beginning of a new era. Whereas apartheid deprived millions of our people of their citizenship, we are restoring that citizenship. Whereas apartheid sought to fragment our country, we are re-uniting our country.

The central theme of the Constitution for the Transition is the unity of our country and people.

This Constitution recognises the diversity of our people. Gone will be the days when one language dominated. Gone will be the days when one religion was elevated to a position of privilege over other religions. Gone will be the days when one culture was elevated to a position of superiority and others denigrated and denied.

We emerge from a conflict-ridden society; a society in which colour, class and ethnicity were manipulated to sow hatred and division. We emerge from a society which was structured on violence and which raised the spectre of a nation in danger of never being able to live at peace with itself.

Our agreements have put that era behind us. This shameful past dictates the crucial need for a Government of National Unity. We are firmly on the road to a nonracial and nonsexist democracy.

For the first time in the history of our country, on 27 April 1994, all South Africans, whatever their language, religion and culture, whatever their colour or class, will vote as equal citizens. Millions who were not allowed to vote will do so. I, too, for the first time in my short life, will vote.

There are some people who still express fears and concerns. To them we say: You have a place in our country. You have a right to raise your fears and your concerns. We, for our part, are committed to giving you the opportunity to bring forth those views so that they may be addressed within the framework of democracy.

The democratic order gives to each and all of us the instruments to address problems constructively and through dialogue.

Let this, however, be clear: there is no place in a democracy for any community or section of a community to impose its will at the expense of the fundamental rights of any other citizen.

Let us all grasp the opportunities that democracy offers. Democracy has no place for talk of civil war. Those who persist with such threats do not care for human life.

Democracy is about empowerment. Now together we can begin to make the equality of education the right of all our children; to begin to remove homelessness, hunger and joblessness; to begin to restore land to those who were deprived by force and injustice; to break the cycle of stagnation in our economy.

Together, we can build a society free of violence. We can build a society grounded on friendship and our common humanity – a society founded on tolerance. That is the only road open to us. It is a road to a glorious future in this beautiful country of ours. Let us join hands and march into the future.

Commissioning the TRC

Address to the Interfaith Commissioning Service
for the Truth and Reconciliation Commission, Cape Town,
13 February 1996.

Allow me to congratulate the chairperson and other members of the Truth and Reconciliation Commission on your appointment, and to wish you well. Yours is a task of extreme difficulty and of great consequence to the future of our nation.

All South Africans face the challenge of coming to terms with the past in ways which will enable us to face the future as a united nation at peace with itself. To you has been entrusted the particular task of dealing with gross violations of human rights in a manner that ensures that the painful truth is laid bare and that justice is done to the victims within the capacity of our society and within the framework of the Constitution and the law. By doing so, and by means of amnesty, your goal is to ensure lasting reconciliation.

South Africa's transition from apartheid has seen the accomplishment of one step after another that sceptics judged impossible. The once-mighty apartheid state machine is no more. Forces locked in apparently irreconcilable conflict found a negotiated path to a democratic Constitution. The first democratic elections took place on the appointed day, 27 April, despite formidable challenges. Just 18 months later the local government elections put in place yet another critical element of our democratic system of government. The spectre of civil war has receded from South Africa's vision of its future. After years of stagnation and economic decline, we are experiencing growth beyond expectation.

Time and again the prophets of doom have been confounded by the capacity and determination of South Africans to solve their problems and to realise their shared vision of a united, peaceful and prosperous country. And I am confident that the members of the Truth and Reconciliation Commission, together with whole nation, will in the same way succeed in building national unity and reconciliation through confronting one of the most complex and sensitive aspects of our past.

There is a view that the past is best forgotten. Some criticise us when we say that whilst we can forgive, we can never forget. They do not agree that perpetrators of human rights violations should make full disclosure and acknowledge what they have done before they can be granted amnesty. There are also those who urge interference in prosecutions in progress.

Even if politicians could agree to suppress the past in these ways, they would be mistaken in doing so. Ordinary South Africans are determined that once the past be known the better it will be to ensure that it is not repeated. They seek this, not out of vengeance, but so that we can move into the future together. The choice of our nation is not whether the past should be revealed, but rather to ensure that it comes to be known in a way which promotes reconciliation and peace. This will also impact on our ability to end violent crime and establish the rule of law today.

Essential to the work of the Commission is its independence. It must, and it will, operate free from interference by political authority. And I call on all South Africans to respect its independence and impartiality. The importance of the Commission's work demands that it should have the co-operation of all of us.

The Truth and Reconciliation Commission affords all South Africans an opportunity to participate in reconciliation and nation building. There is a role for community-based organisations and non-governmental organisations to play their part. There is a role, too, for individuals to make a contribution.

Perhaps the most important role player is not the politician or the Commission, but the victim. Too often, victims have been neglected in our society. It is necessary that we identify the individuals who have suffered and their families, as well as communities.

But the whole South African nation has been a victim, and it is in that context that we should address the restoration of dignity and the issue of reparation. The healing process is meant for the individual, the family and the community. However, above all the healing process involves the nation, because it is the nation itself that needs to redeem and reconstruct itself.

In conclusion, may I say that I have come here today not to prescribe to the Commission, but to reiterate our commitment to respect your independence; and to wish you well.

We hope that our words of encouragement, but particularly the blessings of the religious leaders who have graced this occasion, will ensure that your work is crowned with success.

Receiving the Report of the TRC

Statement on receiving the report of the
Truth and Reconciliation Commission, Pretoria,
29 October 1998.

South Africa is no longer the country it was when we adopted the Interim Constitution in 1993, when together we resolved to overcome the legacy of our violent and inhuman past.

Out of that negotiation process emerged a pact to uncover the truth, the better to build a bright future for our children and grandchildren, without regard to race, culture, religion or language.

Today we reap some of the harvest of what we sowed at the end of a South African famine. And in the celebration and disappointment that attend such a harvest, we know that we shall have to sow again, and harvest again, over and over, to sustain our livelihood; to flourish as a community; and for our generation to know that when we finally go to rest forever, our progeny will be secure in the knowledge that two simple words will reign: Never Again!

Today we receive a report whose creation has itself been a part of what has brought us to where we are. It represents the toil of nurturing the tender fields of peace and reconciliation and the plodding labour of opening the bowels of the earth to reveal its raw elements that can build and destroy.

The report we receive today – and which is to be completed when the amnesty process has run on its course – cannot but help signal the end of one season and the beginning of another.

And so as we observe this stage of the TRC process, we should pay tribute to the 20 000 men and women who relived their pain and loss in order to share it with us; the hundreds who dared to open the wounds of guilt so as to exorcise it from the nation's body politic; indeed the millions who make up the South African people and who made it happen so that we could indeed become a South African nation.

That so many have taken part in the Commission's work so far – individuals, organisations and institutions – and that our media provided us with such extensive coverage and commentary which the public followed with interest, tells us that we were and are engaged in a truly national process.

At the helm of it all has been the Most Reverend Desmond Tutu, who has, during the hearings, conveyed our common pain and sorrow, our hope and confidence in the future.

To you and all the commissioners and staff of the TRC we say on behalf of the nation: Thank you for the work you have done so far!

If the pain has often been unbearable and the revelations shocking to all of us it is because they indeed bring us the beginnings of a common understanding of what happened and a steady restoration of the nation's humanity.

The TRC that is guiding us on this journey is the TRC of all of us. It flows from our Interim Constitution. It was established by an act of Parliament with overwhelming support. It is composed of individuals from all backgrounds and persuasions. It has put the spotlight on all of us.

Though the interim report is formally given to me as President, it is in reality a report to all of us. For that reason it is being released to the public and given to our elected representatives without a moment's delay. Its release is bound to reawaken many of the difficult and troubling emotions that the hearings themselves brought.

Many of us will have reservations about aspects of what is contained in these five volumes. All are free to make comment on it and indeed we invite you to do so. And for those who feel unjustly damaged, there are remedies.

It will seem artificial to some to place those fighting a just war alongside those whom they opposed. It will be difficult for the victims of gross violations of human rights to accept the philosophical account of the trade-off between punitive justice and a peaceful transition. It may be difficult for many to accept the finding that the apartheid state was the primary perpetrator of gross human rights violations.

Yet, if we are true to our founding pact, we cannot equivocate about a system which exacted such inhumanity. There can be no dissonance with regard to the clarion call: Never Again!

Such is the injunction of our democratic Constitution and Bill of Rights. Such is the logic of our survival and prosperity as a nation.

I therefore take this opportunity to say that I accept the report as it is, with all its imperfections, as an aid that the TRC has given to us to help reconcile and build our nation.

The Commission was not required to muster a definitive and comprehensive history of the past three decades. Nor was it expected to conjure up instant reconciliation. And it does not claim to have delivered these either. Its success in any case depended on how far all of us co-operated with it. Yet, we are confident that it has contributed to the work in progress of laying the foundation of the edifice of reconciliation. The further construction of that house of peace needs my hand. It needs your hand.

Reconciliation requires that we work together to defend our democracy and the humanity proclaimed by our Constitution. It demands that we join hands, as at the Jobs Summit tomorrow, to eradicate the poverty spawned by a system that thrived on the deprivation of the majority.

Reconciliation requires that we end malnutrition, homelessness and ignorance, as the Reconstruction and Development Programme has started to do. It demands that we put shoulders to the wheel to end crime and corruption, as religious and political leaders committed themselves to doing at the Morals Summit last week.

More particularly, we will start consultations with all sectors of society on how to contribute to the variety of programmes required to restore the dignity of those who suffered and to give due recognition to those who paid the supreme sacrifice so that our nation could be free.

This report contains material that could sustain endless finger-pointing and gloating at the discomfort of opponents whom the TRC has pronounced to be responsible for gross violations of human rights. And in the brevity and the pattern of media reports, the fundamental principles it raises may be missed, creating an impression that the honourable thing to do would have been to acquiesce in an inhuman system. But we should constantly keep our minds on the broad picture that has emerged.

We are extricating ourselves from a system that insulted our common humanity by dividing us from one another on the basis of race and setting us against each other as oppressed and oppressor. In doing so that system committed a crime against humanity, which shared humanity we celebrate today in a Constitution that entrenches humane rights and values.

In denying us these things the apartheid state generated the violent political conflict in the course of which human rights were violated.

The wounds of the period of repression and resistance are too deep to have been healed by the TRC alone, however well it has encouraged us along that path. Consequently, the report that today becomes the property of our nation should be a call to all of us to celebrate and to strengthen what we have done as a nation as we leave our terrible past behind us forever.

Let us celebrate our rich diversity as a people in the knowledge that when the TRC in its wisdom apportions blame, it points at previous state structures, political organisations, at institutions and individuals, but never at any community. Nor can any individual so identified claim that their brutal deeds were the result of some character inherent in any community or language group.

All of us are therefore now more free to be who we really are; no longer forced to experience some of those things which are most precious to us – language, culture or religion – as walls within which we are imprisoned. Above all, we should remember that it was when South Africans of all backgrounds came together for the good of all that we confounded the prophets of doom by bringing an end to this terrible period of our history.

Though the liberation movement was the primary agent of this change, it could not have done so on its own. To the extent that popular resistance stirred all of South Africa into action, to that extent are we all responsible for an outcome that did not take us deeper into the horrors of a wasteland.

Now the challenge is for all of us to protect our democratic gains like the apple of our eye. It is for those who have the means to contribute to the efforts to repair the damage wrought by the past. It is for those who have suffered losses of different kinds and magnitudes to be afforded reparation, proceeding from the premise that freedom and dignity are the real prize that our sacrifices were meant to attain.

Free at last, we are all masters of our destiny.

A better future depends on all of us lending a hand – your hand, my hand.

Reconciliation Day

Message on Day of Reconciliation,
16 December 1995.

There are few countries which dedicate a national public holiday to reconciliation. But then there are few nations with our history of enforced division, oppression and sustained conflict. And fewer still, which have undergone such a remarkable transition to reclaim their humanity.

We, the people of South Africa, have made a decisive and irreversible break with the past. We have, in real life, declared our shared allegiance to justice, nonracialism and democracy; our yearning for a peaceful and harmonious nation of equals.

The rainbow has come to be the symbol of our nation. We are turning the variety of our languages and cultures, once used to divide us, into a source of strength and richness. But we do know that healing the wounds of the past and freeing ourselves of its burden will be a long and demanding task. This Day of Reconciliation celebrates the progress we have made; it reaffirms our commitment; and it measures the challenges.

The Government of National Unity chose this day precisely because the past had made 16 December a living symbol of bitter division. Valour was measured by the number of enemies killed and the quantity of blood that swelled the rivers and flowed in the streets.

Today we no longer vow our mutual destruction but solemnly acknowledge our interdependence as free and equal citizens of our common motherland. Today we reaffirm our solemn constitutional compact to live together on the basis of equality and mutual respect.

Reconciliation, however, does not mean forgetting or trying to bury the pain of conflict.

Two terrible defects weakened the foundations of the modern South African state that were laid in the great upheaval at the beginning of the century. Firstly, it rested on the treacherous swamps of

137

racism and inequality. The second defect was the suppression of truth.

Now, at the end of the century, South Africans have the real chance to strike out along a glorious path. The democratic foundations of our society have been laid. We must use our collective strengths to carry on building the nation and improving its quality of life.

The Truth and Reconciliation Commission, which will soon begin its work, is one important institution created by our democratic Constitution and Parliament in order to help us manage the more difficult aspects of healing the nation's wounds. Thus we shall free ourselves from the burden of yesteryear; not to return there; but to move forward with the confidence of free men and women, committed to attain the best for ourselves and future generations.

Reconciliation means working together to correct the legacy of past injustice. It means making a success of our plans for reconstruction and development. Therefore, on this 16 December, National Day of Reconciliation, my appeal to you, fellow citizens, is: Let us join hands and build a truly South African nation.

INTEGRITY AND INTEGRATION

GJ GERWEL

Thematic compartmentalisation of the life, work and thought of Nelson Mandela is more a measure of convenience to make a mass of information organised and readable than something approximating the nature of that life, work and body of thought. If pushed to offer a single word that would capture most fully the character of Nelson Mandela, it would be integrity. His is a life in which things cohere, are dynamically integrated to wholeness and wholesomeness.

This is not to suggest an absence of contradiction, an unchanging uniformity or unilinear progression. The achievement of integrity resides exactly in the manner in which a diversity of experiences, modes and means are rendered morally coherent in a life that inspires through the sense of purposeful wholeness it exudes. For me, the Mandela life always reminds of the great modernist novel in which aesthetic and ethical quality lies in the wealth and diversity of material integrated.

Some of us who worked in Nelson Mandela's personal office during his presidency with responsibility for his public appearances at first felt the rhetorician's reservations about his habit of repeating the same stories, anecdotes and themes almost verbatim from one occasion to another. We soon came to realise that this habit in fact represented a narrative manifestation of that integrity of a life of consistent moral purpose. For him not the studied rhetorical trick of a different story for each occasion; rather, the truthful reliability of the same story. Such was his life, such would be the narrative he conducted and such the organisation of his thoughts and teachings.

This chapter on nation building, for example, cannot be read and understood independent from those on reconciliation, development, peace, freedom or culture, amongst others. These aspects – in the attention he paid them in political practice or as themes of his speeches and thinking – were all interwoven and inextricably linked parts of one integrated project and mission: the building of a united South Africa, nonracial, nonsexist, based on the values of dignity, equality and freedom, and with a better life for all its people, especially the poor and marginalised.

There is sometimes a temptation to portray Mandela as the one-dimensional 'reconciliator' who glossed over the other challenges and dimensions of nation building. A facile dichotomy between reconciliation and transformation is posited with Mandela pictured as primarily embodying and advocating the former while according fundamental social changes a lower priority. The extracts from speeches collected in this chapter and in the entire book will clearly show up the fallacy of such an interpretation and portrayal.

Nelson Mandela will of course in very large measure be remembered, and certainly not only in South Africa, for his monumental role in holding a racially divided society together through his personal efforts at political reconciliation across racial and ethnic divides, his constant advocacy of inclusive unity, his living of a life of forgiveness and a total absence of bitterness. As he so frequently reminds us in his speeches, the world was expecting the South African conflict to escalate into a bloody racial war; that it was averted came to be widely described as a miracle. South Africa symbolises to many people across the world the almost miraculous achievement of racial reconciliation, and Nelson Mandela is the icon representing that national achievement.

Mandela frequently points out also that the achievements for which he receives credit would not have been possible without a broader framework of people, organisations and groups with whom he worked and by whom he was shaped and assisted. This is characteristic humility, but also the wisdom that recognises collective leadership and action as well as the compassion that places human solidarity at the centre of his guiding set of values.

In a moving speech at the last opening of Parliament during his presidency (included in this chapter), he locates himself within these broader social networks: as belonging to that generation of leaders for whom the achievement of democracy was the defining challenge; a product of the people of South Africa, the rural masses, the workers, South Africa's intelligentsia of every colour, South Africa's business entrepreneurs; a product of the people of the world, of Africa; and in a final invocation, a product of the African National Congress, 'the movement for justice, dignity and freedom that produced countless giants in whose shadow we find our glory'.

These expanding circles of identification are characteristic of Mandela's world view and provide the basis for his understanding of and belief in national unity.

He opens and closes this 'ode of tributes' by acknowledging his primary bases of social and political thought, the generation of ANC leaders from which he springs and the ANC as the organisation that formed him. It is from that generation of political leadership that South Africa inherited its strong sense of a single nationhood in spite of all the perverted efforts to divide its people into separate quasi-nations. It was that organisation that over decades kept alive and defended the ideal of a nonracial South Africa that belongs to all who live in it. It was that generation and that organisation that gave birth to the Freedom Charter, the early precursor of a Constitution for a united South Africa.

Nelson Mandela's inclusive sense of South African nationhood is firmly and unshakeably rooted in his identification of himself as a member of the African National Congress – 'a loyal and disciplined member of the ANC', as he so often introduces himself. For him there is no contradiction between this (potentially sectarian) party political emphasis and the broad inclusiveness he pursues. On the contrary, the sincerity of his inclusiveness derives from being self-confidently rooted in an organisation that prides itself on having been for so long a 'broad church' of political opinion and 'the parliament of the people'; an organisation that mobilises people where it finds them instead of demanding prior acts of fundamental conversion.

The rest of that 'ode of tributes', captured between the opening and closing tributes to the ANC and its veteran generation of nation builders, gives a glimpse of the breadth of Mandela's national vision. He proclaims himself the product of the people of South Africa in all their various class formations and racial and ethnic origins. He finds his vision informed by the ideas and ideals of freedom-loving people in the world and on the African continent.

While Mandela has that unwavering and unapologetic allegiance to the ANC, he was also always very attentive to not confusing national or non-party political occasions with party events. He more than once took severe public issue with members of the ANC for ostentatiously displaying symbols of the organisation at public events he organised for a wider community audience, believing that national unity did not demand uniformity of political allegiance. My own experience with him was similar; as his Director-General and Secretary of the Cabinet of the Government of National Unity, he required of me to abstain from overt party political

143

(ANC) activities and to remain equally accessible for the leaders of the other two parties in the government.

In many of his speeches Mandela pays tribute to other political parties for their contribution to the national progress made. He saw the strength of multi-party democracy as crucial for national unity. As he continued to emphasise the importance of a vigilant and critical press, he always extolled the democratic virtues of good, strong political opposition.

At times one had cause to smile at the delightful clash between the deep commitment of a multi-party democrat and the instincts of the eternal party organiser – one who proclaims publicly that his first act after arrival in the next world would be to look for the nearest ANC branch office. The Democratic Party was once offered seats in the Cabinet, only to discover the offer was dependent on their party merging with the ANC; and attempts to unite the PAC and the ANC were well reported. It was Tony Leon, in his tribute to President Mandela at the final session of Parliament, who captured this best; he sang the praises of the President as great statesman and nation builder and at the same time expressed appreciation and respect for him being such a superb party political animal.

Mandela's approach to matters like multi-party democracy is informed by his deep-seated appreciation of difference and diversity as the constituent parts of national unity. At one point after the attainment of democracy a discourse surfaced arguing that the concept of nation building contained a denial of diversity and was therefore democratically flawed. No more unequivocal refutation of those arguments can be found than in the published thoughts and lived deeds of Nelson Mandela.

There are in fact those on the other side of that diversity debate who argued that Mandela over-emphasises and over-accommodates diversity. From these quarters, his approach to the national question is criticised as an outdated restatement of the traditional 'four nations' approach of the Congress Movement that recognised Africans, coloureds, Indians and whites as discernible national groups with possible distinctive concerns that should be accommodated.

Once more on the anecdotal level, I had personal and amusing experience of the Mandela notion of diversity accommodation. In his very polite manner, typically starting with a reaffirmation of his belief in what a good person I generally am, he more than once expressed to me his difference of opinion about the pace at which the University of the Western Cape under my leadership changed from an institution predominantly attended by coloured students to one with at least an equal number of African students. For the inauguration ceremony of my successor, at which the President was scheduled to speak, I helped write what I thought was a delicately crafted piece that would accommodate the sensitivities of my boss and remain suitably nuanced and politically correct. He obediently read the text up until just before the concluding 'thank you', put it down, famously removed his reading spectacles and declared: 'Now I wish to add personally,' and proceeded to expound on the insensitivity displayed towards minorities, the University of the Western Cape being a case in point!

This concern for what he calls 'the minorities' is genuine and consistently present. Like most of his approaches and actions it is based on an observation, often taken from his reading of history, that runs as a consistent theme through his pronouncements and reflections: in this case, that in all periods of profound social and political change, minority groups (of whatever nature that is relevant in a particular society and age) experience grave uncertainty and anxiety. If these are not sensitively and constructively dealt with, he states, they could fester and lead to destabilisation of the entire social or political order.

The integrity of this life of action and thought can, once more, be read from the restatement of this theme throughout important moments of his life. For example: in his speech from the dock, as an accused facing the possibility and imminence of a death sentence, he expresses himself as opposed to white domination as well as black domination; in a letter referred to in one of the speeches contained in this chapter he (still in prison at the time) writes to the then president of the apartheid state to point out the two central issues to be addressed – 'firstly, the demand for majority rule in a unitary state; secondly, the concern of white South Africans over this demand'.

The speeches collected in this book will demonstrate equal concern for the interests, anxieties and wellbeing of all minority groups, including non-ethnic ones such as women and children, the elderly and handicapped, the rural poor.

This sensitivity also expresses itself in the concern he has about perceptions of Xhosa dominance in party political and governmental affairs. Mischievous deductions are sometimes made from his disclosure that he proposed Cyril Ramaphosa rather than Thabo Mbeki as Deputy President to the ANC's senior officials in 1994. This proposal in fact had little to do with the respective merits of the two men – both of whom he holds in high regard as hugely capable leaders – but with his concern about

145

allegations of a Xhosa dominance while a non-Xhosa of Ramaphosa's capabilities was available.

In his school and clinic building programme, persuading business people to erect or renovate educational and health facilities in under-privileged areas across the country, a similar concern for ethnic and geographical diversity surfaces. He insists on being seen to spread, as he does, his efforts way beyond his native Transkei and Xhosa-speaking Eastern Cape.

Even-handed as he might be (and in fact is) in his concerns for and attention to the various 'minorities', the poignancy of his reconciliatory attitude towards Afrikaners could not fail to draw special attention. In a very concrete, specific and unmediated sense, the Afrikaner people were his jailers and the architects and operators of the racial state against which he struggled and at whose hands he suffered. To be so totally for-giving to members of this group and the group as a whole came to sig-nify the quintessential morality of the man.

When elements within his party, in government or in society general-ly tended towards provocative impetuosity, President Nelson Mandela would warn against the dangers of an arrogance that wishes to mistak-enly regard Afrikaners as a foe defeated in battle. His special approach to Afrikaners was, however, based on factors and considerations much more complex and profound than a concern for relative military or para-military capacities.

He has special warmth for Afrikaners growing from, I believe, his basic anthropology. He genuinely believes, and acts on the belief, that human beings are essentially good-doing beings. When they err, it is a deviation, not the norm. His experience of and with members of the Afrikaner group – ironically, it might be said – contributed to the valida-tion of this attitude in his view of humankind. He recounts examples from his time as a practising attorney when Afrikaner officials demon-strated humaneness and reason in situations where the contrary was expected. His experiences with Afrikaner prison warders and prison offi-cials in this regard are well documented.

His particular sense of history also plays a role. That Afrikaners fought an anti-imperial war counts hugely in his esteem of them as a people. Paradoxically, their period as 'oppressors' adds to his sense of their pecu-liar role in South African history. They are, he often said, the only group in South Africa that combines in its history the experiences of being oppressed, of fighting a war for liberation and of then brutally oppress-ing its fellow countrymen and women. This, in his view, equips them to

146

understand the yearning for freedom, the suffering of an oppressed people and the depravity of being oppressors.

One suspects that his attitude might also be a product of his missionary education with its strong Enlightenment elements and the belief in human progress from backwardness to enlightenment. Never have I heard him suggest that the Afrikaner people were evil, as some are wont to do. I recall moments of talking about some of the preposterous claims and statements apartheid leaders made in the past, he turning his gaze inwards to those hidden depths of solitude, and then remarking with pained compassion that the Afrikaners allowed themselves to be misled to incomprehensible communal craziness. Never the condemnation of people; always the Enlightenment man who takes pity on those in conditions of backwardness, striving to facilitate progress.

The highest respect he could pay Afrikaners was learning to speak Afrikaans, which he does with an impeccable grammatical correctness. He, who seldom shows pride, is quite proud of his speaking and reading command of the language. At one meeting with a range of Afrikaner leaders conducted in English, he commented on what a central role a certain figure was playing. He then turned to Ferdi Hartzenberg next to him, proudly plucking from his vocabulary one of those schoolbook Afrikaans idioms: '*Hy is die spil waarom alles draai!* [He is the pivot around which everything turns!]'

A favourite saying of Nelson Mandela's will be found in the speeches collected here, namely that there are good men and women to be found in all communities, groups and political parties. That simple precept he repeated over and over, from one platform to the other. The simplicity of that self-evident yet often ignored truth drove and directed the complex task of nation building for Nelson Mandela.

South Africans, Africans, and Citizens of the World

Selections from the State of the Nation address,
Houses of Parliament, Cape Town,
24 May 1994.

The time will come when our nation will honour the memory of all the sons, the daughters, the mothers, the fathers, the youth and the children who, by their thoughts and deeds, gave us the right to assert with pride that we are South Africans, that we are Africans and that we are citizens of the world.

The certainties that come with age tell me that among these we shall find an Afrikaner woman who transcended a particular experience and became a South African, an African and a citizen of the world.

Her name is Ingrid Jonker.

She was both a poet and a South African. She was both an Afrikaner and an African. She was both an artist and a human being.

In the midst of despair, she celebrated hope. Confronted with death, she asserted the beauty of life.

In the dark days when all seemed hopeless in our country, when many refused to hear her resonant voice, she took her own life.

To her and others like her, we owe a debt to life itself. To her and others like her, we owe a commitment to the poor, the oppressed, the wretched and the despised.

In the aftermath of the massacre at the anti-pass demonstration in Sharpeville she wrote that:

> The child is not dead
> the child lifts his fists against his mother
> who shouts Africa! ...
>
> The child is not dead
> Not at Langa nor at Nyanga
> nor at Orlando nor at Sharpeville

nor at the police post at Philippi
where he lies with a bullet through his brain ...

The child is present at all assemblies and law-giving
the child peers through the windows of houses
and into the hearts of mothers
this child who only wanted to play in the sun at Nyanga
is everywhere.

The child grown to a man treks on through all Africa
the child grown to a giant journeys
over the whole world
without a pass!

And in this glorious vision, she instructs that our endeavours must be about the liberation of the woman, the emancipation of the man and the liberty of the child.

It is these things that we must achieve to give meaning to our presence in this chamber and to give purpose to our occupancy of the seat of government. And so we must, constrained by and yet regardless of the accumulated effect of our historical burdens, seize the time to define for ourselves what we want to make of our shared destiny.

The government I have the honour to lead, and I dare say the masses who elected us to serve in this role, are inspired by the single vision of creating a people-centred society.

Accordingly, the purpose that will drive this government shall be the expansion of the frontiers of human fulfilment, the continuous extension of the frontiers of freedom. The acid test of the legitimacy of the programmes we elaborate, the government institutions we create, the legislation we adopt must be whether they serve these objectives.

Our single most important challenge is therefore to help establish a social order in which the freedom of the individual will truly mean the freedom of the individual. We must construct that people-centred society of freedom in such a manner that it guarantees the political and the human rights of all our citizens.

As an affirmation of the government's commitment to an entrenched human rights culture, we shall immediately take steps to inform the Secretary-General of the United Nations that we will subscribe to the Universal Declaration of Human Rights. We shall take steps to ensure that we accede to the International Covenant on Civil and Political Rights, the International Covenant on Social and Economic Rights and other human rights instruments of the United Nations.

Our definition of the freedom of the individual must be instructed by the fundamental objective to restore the human dignity of each and every South African. This requires that we speak not only of political freedoms. My government's commitment to create a people-centred society of liberty binds us to the pursuit of the goals of freedom from want, freedom from hunger, freedom from deprivation, freedom from ignorance, freedom from suppression and freedom from fear.

These freedoms are fundamental to the guarantee of human dignity. They will therefore constitute part of the centrepiece of what this government will seek to achieve, the focal point on which our attention will be continuously focused. The things we have said constitute the true meaning, the justification and the purpose of the Reconstruction and Development Programme, without which it would lose all legitimacy.

When we elaborated this programme we were inspired by the hope that all South Africans of goodwill could join together to provide a better life for all. We were pleased that other political organisations announced similar aims.

. . .

Tomorrow, on Africa Day, the dream of Ingrid Jonker will come to fruition. The child grown to a man will trek through all Africa. The child grown to a man will journey over the whole world – without a pass!

Tomorrow, on Africa Day, our new flag will be hoisted in an historic ceremony at the OAU Headquarters in Addis Ababa, with the OAU having already agreed to accept us as its latest member.

Tomorrow, on Africa Day, the UN Security Council will meet to lift the last remaining sanctions against South Africa and to position the world organisation to relate to our country as an honoured, responsible and peace-loving citizen.

As such, the government is involved in discussions to determine what our contribution could be to the search for peace in Angola and Rwanda, to the reinforcement of the peace process in Mozambique, to the establishment of a new world order of mutually beneficial co-operation, justice, prosperity and peace for ourselves and for the nations of the world.

Yesterday the Cabinet also decided to apply for our country to join the Commonwealth. This important community of nations is waiting to receive us with open arms.

We have learnt the lesson that our blemishes speak of what all humanity should not do. We understand this fully that our glories point to the heights of what human genius can achieve.

In our dreams we have a vision of all our country at play in our sportsfields and enjoying deserved and enriching recreation in our theatres, galleries, beaches, mountains, plains and game parks, in conditions of peace, security and comfort.

Our road to that glorious future lies through collective hard work to accomplish the objective of creating a people-centred society through the implementation of the vision contained in our reconstruction and development plan.

Let us all get down to work!

Serious Work

Selection from the State of the Nation address,
Houses of Parliament, Cape Town,
17 February 1995.

We have gathered in this hallowed chamber to begin the work of the second session of our democratic Parliament, nine months after its first members were sworn in.

Let me say this from the beginning, that the challenges ahead of us require that we move away from spectacle and rhetoric, and bend our backs to the serious work ahead of us.

I would like to take this opportunity to extend my sincere appreciation to the leaders of all the parties represented in Parliament, the members of Parliament, the presiding officers, the whips, the chairpersons of committees, the Secretary of Parliament and his staff for the sterling work that was done from the day that this first democratic and nonracial Parliament convened.

Of necessity, much of this work had to do with the establishment of our organisational structures and evolving a rhythm of work which would enable us to discharge our responsibilities in an effective and efficient manner.

All of us, precisely because we had never sat in any democratic Parliament before, had to begin the continuing process of learning how to carry out our functions as people's deputies. We had to educate ourselves in an atmosphere characterised by a critical public focus which did not necessarily allow for the reality of that inexperience.

Undoubtedly, many of us, both in the legislature and in the executive, have made mistakes. But mistakes are an inevitable element of any process of learning. It is always the case that the spectators are better than the players on the field. None of us should therefore feel ashamed for having committed errors. We must, however, learn from these mistakes so that we do indeed improve our performance.

Whatever it is that our critics might have to say, we can take pride in the fact that not only did we succeed in establishing our two houses of Parliament, as required by the Constitution, but we also ensured that they play their role in the governance of our country.

We are pleased that the honourable members of both the National Assembly and the Senate have not been satisfied merely to endorse the bills that have been presented to them. They have participated actively in improving such draft legislation with the aim of ensuring that our laws are consistent with the glorious vision we share of creating a truly humane and people-centred society.

Of particular importance is the fact that you, the legislators, have worked in a manner consistent with the objective of ensuring that ours should be a Parliament of the people. This we have done by opening our proceedings to the public to ensure that the people know what we are doing. We have also opened the doors to the people to address the legislative committees of Parliament directly.

This has also been replicated in our provincial legislatures, consistent with our objective of bringing government as close to the people as possible. We can therefore claim with justification that such legislation as has been approved is representative of the will of the people. It therefore enjoys a degree of legitimacy and enforceability which all previous laws could never have.

Undoubtedly, we must continue to look for ways and means of ensuring that the people as a whole are better informed of what we are doing and are given ever-improved capacity to intervene in our proceedings in an informed and purposive manner.

In the recent past, much has been said about corruption among some Members of this Parliament and other leading political figures in the country. Many within and without this chamber and among the mass media have been very keen to condemn and to propel us into precipitate action on the basis of mere allegations.

We have resisted this and will continue to do so. We have a responsibility to act on the basis of fact and not allegations, however strident the voice that makes those allegations. Furthermore, we firmly believe that it is important that we build a society based on justice and fairness. At all times we must guarantee the right of the accused to be heard, without making any concession to a primeval instinct to pillory and burn people at the stake.

As South Africans, with our particular history, we must be extremely careful not to reintroduce the McCarthyist atmosphere which resulted in people being herded into unthinking hordes that sought the blood of anybody who was labelled a communist.

We must also make this clear that we need no educators with regard to the matter of rooting out corruption, which we will deal with firmly and unequivocally, whoever may be involved. We are conscious of the reality that corruption in many forms has deeply infected the fibre of our society. It is not possible to have a society based on a lie and patent injustice, as apartheid society was, without this spawning corrupt practices.

Precisely because we face the challenge of dealing with systemic corruption we need a dispassionate and systematic approach to this question and not allow ourselves to be stampeded by responses which are not very different from a witch-hunt.

Healing and Building

Selections from the State of the Nation address,
Houses of Parliament, Cape Town,
9 February 1996.

Today in the streets of Johannesburg, the new patriotism of our new democracy once again asserts itself as citizens of that city express their appreciation for the feat of our soccer team in the African Nations Cup. This is bound to replay itself in other cities, adding to the crowning glory of our rugby world champions.

Our sportspersons are performing beyond the nation's wildest expectations. On and off the field, they are uniting our nation like never before, by their determination to do the best for their country.

Such is the true character of South Africans. We do possess the inner strength to achieve excellence. We have the will to persevere against all odds.

We enter 1996, as Cabinet and the rest of the Executive, as parliamentarians, as workers and managers, as professionals, traditional leaders, security forces, students and communities in general, faced with the challenge of bringing these positive qualities to bear on everything we do: to make South Africa a winning nation.

We must bring out the best in all of us; and, like our sportspersons, perform better everywhere, to expand the economy and create jobs; to improve the quality of life for all; to expand the frontiers of freedom; and to ensure comprehensive security for all citizens. These are the critical challenges that we face within and outside these hallowed chambers.

In October this year we shall pass the half-way mark of the present legislature and its Executive. The nation and the world will judge us not on whether we mean to do good; but, above all, on whether we have mobilised South Africans to work together to improve their quality of life.

Indeed, we can say with confidence that steadily but surely the great majority of South Africans do feel that things are improving for the better. We are on our way – South Africa is on its way – to a better future.

Life has started to have real meaning for the hundreds of thousands who now have access to clean and safe drinking water. The benefits of democracy have a tangible impact for the 400 000 homes which have been supplied with electricity during the course of last year. To the millions of children who benefit from the school nutrition scheme, free medical care and free and compulsory education, not only has the present become better, but there is also great confidence in the future.

This is the case with communities where the clinic-building programme and the district health system are taking root; the workers in public works programmes; the communities who can, at least, feel secure on a piece of land they can call their own and the families who, for the first time, are benefiting from the farm support programme and extension of agricultural credit.

At last, millions who had no hope in the future can look ahead with confidence in the full knowledge that they have a government prepared to work together with them to build a better life for all.

. . .

Yes, South Africa is not only on the right road. We are well on our way to making this the country of our dreams. I take the opportunity to congratulate all South Africans, in the public and private sectors – the most prominent in the land as well as the humble members of the community – all of whom are striving to add another brick to the edifice of our democracy. We have set out on this road together, and we should together aim for the stars.

If these achievements are something to be proud of, this is because they have laid the foundation to make a real impact on the inequities of the past. For we are only at the beginning of a long journey, a journey we should undertake with expedition, if our consciences are not impervious to the cries of desperation of millions. But this is a journey, too, that requires thorough planning and tenacious industry if we are to remain on course and capable of sustaining our march.

Let me preface the identification of the challenges of the coming year by saying that all of us, all South Africans, are called upon to become builders and healers. But, for all the joy and excitement of creation, to build and to heal are difficult undertakings.

We can neither heal nor build, if such healing and building are perceived as one-way processes, with the victims of past injustices forgiving and the beneficiaries merely content in gratitude. Together we must set out to correct the defects of the past.

We can neither heal nor build if, on the one hand, the rich in our society see the poor as hordes of irritants; or if, on the other hand, the poor sit back expecting charity. All of us must take responsibility for the upliftment of our conditions, prepared to give our best to the benefit of all.

We can neither heal nor build, if we continue to have people in positions of influence and power who, at best, pay lip service to affirmative action, black empowerment and the emancipation of women, or who are, in reality, opposed to these goals; if we have people who continue with blind arrogance to practise racism in the workplaces and schools, despite the appeal we made in our very first address to this Parliament. We must work together to ensure the equitable distribution of wealth, opportunity and power in our society.

We cannot build or heal our nation, if – in both the private and public sectors, in the schools and universities, in the hospitals and on the land, in dealing with crime and social dislocation – if we continue with business as usual, wallowing in notions of the past. Everywhere and in everything we do, what is now required is boldness in thinking, firmness in resolve and consistency in action.

The message I am trying to convey is that all of us must take the national project of accelerated and fundamental transformation of our country very seriously indeed. The achievement of the objectives of equity, nonracialism and nonsexism constitute the very essence of the new society we seek to build.

In the history of nations, generations have made their mark through their acumen to appreciate critical turning points, and with determination and creativity, to seize the moment. South Africa is well on its way to a new and better life. This we will achieve only if we shed the temptation to proceed casually along the road; only if we fully take the opportunities that beckon.

We must unite in a new patriotism to achieve the goal of creating a new society.

. . .

There is a new patriotism abroad in our land. Whatever the social stations they occupy, no matter how humble, South Africans are showing a determination to work together and make our country a winning nation. Our task is to harness these energies into a mate-

157

rial force for growth and development, safety and security, nation building and reconciliation.

Such are the demands of this historical moment. Such are the demands of the new South Africa.

New Patriotism

Selections from the State of the Nation address,
Houses of Parliament, Cape Town,
7 February 1997.

A new year is upon us, once more affording us the opportunity to account in a comprehensive manner to the citizens on the awesome responsibilities they have mandated us to fulfil.

All of us, in the Executive and legislatures, the majority party and Members in the opposition benches, are called upon to outline practical programmes to improve the nation's quality of life.

Again and again over the past year the people showed remarkable commitment to the country's wellbeing. They took advantage of resources offered through RDP projects. They turned adversity into opportunity in the export market. They excelled in international sporting events, including the Olympics and Paralympics. And they joined hands to raise awareness around crime, and actually to work together to combat it.

In practical action, a new nation is being forged; a nation whose new patriotism and sense of pride derive not only from ideas in our hearts, but also from concrete progress made in improving the wellbeing of all.

Our task is to mobilise all our people, to create more and more opportunities to ensure that the citizen's potential is given the fullest expression. We have to do this and more, sensitive to the feelings of the majority and the minority, the haves and the have-nots, those who have the media to communicate their ideas and those deprived of such resources.

We can all derive pride from the fact that we took a historic step in this direction last year through the adoption of the new Constitution: the basic law of our land reflecting the nation's yearning for a rising quality of life, in circumstances of democracy, peace and respect for human rights.

In a sense this is the first session of the new Parliament.

And allow me to take this opportunity to welcome members of the National Council of Provinces, the living embodiment of co-operative governance. Their presence here already starts to redefine relations between government and the people: not abstract national or regional or local people, but South Africans requiring and deserving of the highest professional service from their elected representatives.

Last Friday, I had the honour to thank our erstwhile Senators for their service to the nation. I wish to reiterate that today. At the same time as they infused the debate in these chambers with their unique knowledge and expertise, they were also pioneers at an important moment of creation, the culmination of which is the national Parliament as we have it today.

The major restructuring of Parliament represented by these changes epitomises the maturing of our democracy. Of no less significance is the process that led to the adoption of the Constitution: including mass involvement on the one hand, and the meticulous approach of the Constitutional Court on the other. With each major judgement, this court grows in stature and places our democracy on a higher pedestal.

Co-operative governance and the new patriotism also mean a loyal opposition: an opposition that opposes, but remains loyal to the Constitution; an opposition that takes part in the major national programmes to reconstruct, to develop, to reconcile, to improve South Africa's standing in the world, to enhance business confidence, to put shoulders to the wheel in the fight against crime: in brief an opposition that takes full part in the efforts to build a better life for all. We are encouraged that all parties in this chamber have committed themselves to this national consensus.

Through the new Constitution we have laid the foundation for a peaceful and prosperous nation. But it is just that: a foundation. And it will not amount to much if its provisions are not felt in the daily life of our people. We must and will popularise the Constitution. But, above all, we need to act together to implement its provisions.

. . .

Our young democracy is still grappling with the challenge of its positioning in the international milieu.

It is understandable that at times this debate will be heated and acrimonious; because it is a debate more than just about how we relate to the world. It is part of the process of defining who we are. It is part of the resolution of past divisions within South African society – divisions which informed our divergent views of the world.

Within the Southern African Development Community, the first steps have been taken towards a free trade area within eight years. Historic initiatives exemplified by the Maputo Development Corridor are gradually going to become the norm as we bring our collective strength to bear to meet common challenges. It is a measure of our collective destiny that even bilateral negotiations between ourselves and the European Community had to be underpinned by regional realities.

Welcome progress was made in bilateral trade arrangements with Zimbabwe, and we aim to move faster this year to complete negotiations on the Customs Union.

We were honoured last year to be elected as chairperson of the SADC for three years; and we will continue to work to strengthen the Community and enhance its standing in Africa and abroad. In this context, we shall continue to make our humble contribution to the resolution of the crisis in the Great Lakes Region and to assist in facilitating the peace process in Angola.

Over the past year, we strengthened our relations with countries such as India and others in Asia, Brazil and others in Latin America, Saudi Arabia and others in the Middle East.

We are all only starting to appreciate the full meaning of these relations in terms of exports, opportunities for investments and sources of capital. And evolving quietly from this is a special relationship that is more or less natural among countries with broadly the same level of development, socio-economic challenges and interests.

How this will impact on South–South co-operation, assist in redefining the world balance of forces and enhance the unique potential of each of the countries are matters that still require further examination.

Our commitment to the strengthening of the Organisation of African Unity is a matter of course. We also wish to congratulate UN Secretary-General, Kofi Annan, and offer our co-operation as this august body restructures itself. As President of the United Nations Conference on Trade and Development we will continue to contribute to building the bridges of co-operation between the North and the South. We shall also start in earnest this year to prepare for the next Summit of the Non-Aligned Movement which we shall be honoured to host in 1998.

In the next few days, we shall play host to the King of Sweden as well as the Vice-President of the United States of America. These visits epitomise the intimate relations we have forged across the spectrum before and since our democratic elections. Bi-national commissions with the US, Russia and the Federal Republic of Germany, and our special relations with countries of Northern and Western Europe, Japan and others speak of the positive climate that we have to pursue South Africa's interests, which are in many respects the interests of the majority of the world's peoples.

We shall not falter in our contribution to the resolution of conflict and promotion of peace throughout the world. In this context, and in the context of our own principles, we shall continue to approach the issue of the manufacture and sale of weapons with circumspection. And as in everything else we do, we shall always defend our right as a nation independently to take decisions.

In all areas of endeavour, we have laid the foundation for success. At work, in sport and leisure, in business and the professions, in the schools and places of worship, we are forging a resilient nation; a nation conscious of its responsibilities to itself, to future generations and to the world in which we live.

The government has got the practical programmes in place to contribute decisively to the attainment of the nation's objectives. At the same time as we intensify the implementation of reconstruction and development, we shall improve co-operative governance as well as capacity and management at all levels.

The foundation for a better life has been laid. In the spirit of the new patriotism we can only rise to new heights.

Building Together

Selections from the State of the Nation address,
Houses of Parliament, Cape Town,
6 February 1998.

I should start by expressing my appreciation for this opportunity to exchange views with you at the beginning of this penultimate sitting of our first democratic Parliament. I wish all of you a productive New Year in the service of the people.

As government, we are confident of the progress being made to meet our mandate. We are resolved to build on the solid foundation that has been laid over the past three-and-half years. As always, the most critical challenge is whether we are succeeding as leaders to mobilise the people in actual practice to be their own liberators.

We know too well that on our own we cannot succeed. We know that the programmes of government are not the panacea for all the ills of our terrible past. They are but a platform for South Africans to let their strengths shine through.

By our own pronouncements and actions, we could relate to these citizens as passive recipients of 'government delivery', as if government were a force on high. Worse still, we could turn some constituents into passive critics, their own rationality drowned in the chorus of regret that the past has passed. On both counts, this would be a recipe for sure failure.

That is why, during the course of last year, we once again put the Masakhane Campaign at the centre of our activities. And our performance should be judged above all on the basis of whether our programmes are positively affecting the lives of especially the most vulnerable sections of society: the poor, women, the disabled, children and the rural masses – the primary victims of the iniquitous system from which we have just emerged. We are proud to answer this question in the affirmative.

. . .

There is no magic in numbers as such. But we are proud that,

through these and many other projects, our programmes are impact-
ing on the lives of particularly the poor. This applies to varying degrees
with regard to other challenges to which we shall later return.

And it is all a result of a clear strategy, properly managed plans,
good governance and, more than anything else, the determination of
the overwhelming majority of our countrymen and -women to change
their lives for the better. It is therefore understandable that, unlike
some of us, those who bore the brunt of apartheid oppression say
that things are a lot better.

But they also say, and are justified to say so, that what has been
done is not enough. Not because they expect the legacy of centuries
of colonialism to be eradicated in a few years, as we ourselves have
said on countless occasions before. Not because they are frustrated
with government. But because they appreciate that together we need
to do much more, over many years, to realise a truly just and prosperous society. They do recognise that in this government, they have
a serious, committed and caring institution – a government that they
can call their own.

We are at the beginning of an arduous and protracted struggle for
a better quality of life. In the course of this struggle, we shall have
immediate successes; we shall have setbacks; but we shall certainly
progress, inch by inch, towards our goal.

From time to time, incidents do happen which bring out in bold
relief the enormity of the challenges we face. As the saying goes, one
falling tree makes more noise than millions that are growing. As
such, for both good reasons and bad, occasional problems are seized
upon by our detractors as the stock-in-trade of this government,
indeed as the essence of democracy.

. . .

We must be ready to give back to society part of what we gain
from it. In this respect, the words of one eminent citizen who has
actively joined the campaign against crime are worth repeating in
this august Assembly:

> This country, warts and all, has been good to me – it is unbelievable. It
> has fed me; it has clothed me; it has educated me; it has given me
> opportunities in the business world that were unthinkable when I was
> a kid in Brits. I think the very least I could do is put something back.
> And this is my kind of national service and I am enjoying it.

This is a challenge to all of us, especially those whose past privileges have afforded them skills that are in high demand in public service, to volunteer skills to help improve the lot of the nation.

Indeed, on the vexed question of crime, we could do more if each South African of integrity consciously ask themselves every day whether they may have assisted in the commission of crime:

- as a parent who conceals the activities of a child who is taking drugs, without assisting the police to track down the suppliers;
- as a customer who co-operates in a transaction which allows you a large discount because the seller will not pay VAT;
- as a trade unionist or ordinary worker who turns a blind eye to pilfering on the shop-floor, or worse still, to corruption in government service;
- as a politician who stands behind individuals who break the law, in the name of challenging bodies such as the Truth and Reconciliation Commission;
- as a parent or spouse who avoids asking questions when a relative is suddenly awash with money, and behaves like a fugitive from justice.

Don't many of us do this and more, and yet express bewilderment at the high rate of crime?

What this emphasises is that we need a campaign of moral regeneration. As we reconstruct the material conditions of our existence, we must also change our way of thinking, to respect the value and result of honest work, and to treat each law of the country as our own.

This is our call to all South Africans to firm up the moral fibre of our nation. It is a call to artists and musicians and sportspersons, to religious leaders and traditional institutions, to intellectuals, to the media and to all those who should give leadership as we establish new symbols and role models: all of us to join hands in a new patriotism, not because the government says so, but because it is in our common interest to do it.

In this regard, it is encouraging that the youth of our country through the National Youth Commission have taken important steps to define a youth policy that will give all – irrespective of the skin colour that is the accident of birth – a stake in our new society. Particularly heartening is the proposal for youth community service, which can be broadened to encompass most of society, be it in helping to clean streets, volunteering services in schools and so on.

Civic duty is the central purpose behind the Masakhane Campaign, whose awareness week last year was fairly successful. We shall continue this year and beyond to intensify this drive, including the mobilisation of, and assistance to, non-governmental and community-based organisations who truly have the interests of the community at heart.

. . .

Wherever we go internationally, we are always moved by the appreciation of the world for our efforts in resolving problems that seemed intractable.

These international forces are always willing to assist in our exciting transition. But they recognise that, in the final analysis, our success will depend on our own efforts. They appreciate and have confidence in our economic environment, and equally they expect the same among South Africans themselves.

They respect our nation because they know we are contributing to the collective efforts of humankind redefining itself and reclaiming its humanity as we move into the new millennium.

This, our programme for 1998, is a humble contribution to the quest for a better world. As always, we are encouraged, first and foremost, by the fact that South Africans are ready, and they have rolled up their sleeves to build a society that cares.

These millions of South Africans are joining hands to sustain their democratic achievement; and they will protect it like the apple of their eye. They are filled with hope about the bright future that beckons. They shall not be distracted by the noise of a falling tree amidst the dignified silence of a new future starting to blossom, because they know that:

The foundation has been laid; and the building has begun!

Building the Country of Our Dreams

Selections from the State of the Nation address,
Houses of Parliament, Cape Town,
5 February 1999.

Today we start the ultimate session of our first democratic Parliament.

The profound changes of the past four-and-a-half years make the distance traversed seem so short; the end so sudden. Yet with the epoch-making progress that has been made, this period could have been decades.

South Africa is in a momentous process of change, blazing a trail towards a secure future. The time is yet to come for farewells, as many of us − by choice or circumstance − will not return. However, there is no time to pause. The long walk is not yet over. The prize of a better life has yet to be won.

Allow me to cast my eyes further back than the period under review. Ten years ago, in a letter to the head of the apartheid state, in an attempt to launch negotiations, one humble prisoner said that, at a first meeting between government and the ANC, two central issues needed to be addressed:

> . . . firstly, the demand for majority rule in a unitary state; secondly, the concern of white South Africans over this demand, as well as the insistence of whites on structural guarantees that majority rule will not mean domination of the white minority by blacks.

In yet another letter, it was emphasised:

> The very first step on the way to reconciliation is obviously the dismantling of apartheid, and all measures used to reinforce it. To talk of reconciliation before this major step is taken is totally unrealistic.

These are some of the matters that I will address today.

Our transition has been managed with such success that some generously invoke the imagery of 'miracle'. Things such as equality,

167

the right to vote in free and fair elections and freedom of speech, many of us now take for granted. Many past difficulties are now mere footnotes of history.

There can be no equivocation that the majority of South Africans, coalesced around our founding pact, are outgrowing the apprehensions which required the convoluted 'structural guarantees' of the first few years. Though we might differ on method, it has become a national passion to pronounce commitment to a better life for all.

. . .

I referred at the beginning to the letters written by a notorious prisoner. In one of them, he said:

> I am disturbed, as many other South Africans no doubt are, by the spectre of a South Africa split into two hostile camps: blacks on one side ... and whites on the other, slaughtering one another; by acute tensions which are building up dangerously in practically every sphere of our lives.

As I said earlier, we have collectively managed the transition in a commendable manner. But it is matter of public record that elements of these divisions remain. We slaughter one another in our words and attitudes. We slaughter one another in the stereotypes and mistrust that linger in our heads, and the words of hate we spew from our lips. We slaughter one another in the responses that some of us give to efforts aimed at bettering the lives of the poor. We slaughter one another and our country by the manner in which we exaggerate its weaknesses to the wider world, heroes of the gab who astound their foreign associates by their self-flagellation. This must come to an end. For, indeed, those who thrive on hatred destroy their own capacity to make a positive contribution.

To the extent that the apprehensions about the meaning of democracy relate to real fears about matters such as language and culture we are proud that progress is being made towards the establishment of the commission on these and other issues so that all can feel secure as part of a united nation. To the extent that some of the apprehensions are imagined or based on opposition to change, to that extent we are convinced that history will be the best teacher.

We hope, though, especially as we go into the election campaign, that real leaders will emerge who base their messages on hope rather than fear, on the optimism of hard work rather than the pessimism of armchair whining.

Dealing with these challenges also means accepting the facts of our history. As I said when I received the TRC Interim Report last October, the government accepts it with its imperfections. We recognise that it is not a definitive or comprehensive history of the period it was reviewing; neither was it a court of law. It was an important contribution on the way to truth and reconciliation.

The critical act of reconciliation, to come back to the letters I referred to earlier, is the dismantling of what remains of apartheid practices and attitudes. Reconciliation without this major step will be transient, the ode of false hope on the lips of fools.

It will therefore be critical that when we go into the detail of the TRC report's recommendations in the coming period we must elaborate concrete plans about how together we can make practical contributions. This applies particularly to reparations, not so much to individuals, but to communities and the nation as a whole.

Let me reiterate that we shall all assist that process of nation building and reconciliation, reconstruction and development, by protecting the institutions which guarantee the checks and balances that make social and political aberrations impossible. Our word of acknowledgement to the Human Rights Commission, the Gender Commission and others for the sterling work they are doing to strengthen democracy.

. . .

As we reflect on the years of transition and beginnings of transformation, we have cause to draw inspiration from what South Africans can do. We dare to hope for a brighter future because we are prepared to work for it. The steady progress of the past few years has laid the foundation for greater achievements. But the reality is that we can do much, much better.

In the discussions that I have had with Deputy President Mbeki, we have posed to ourselves the question whether we should be satisfied with steady progress. Is South Africa not capable of breaking out of the current pace and moving much faster to a better life?

As the Deputy President has often said, the policies we have accord with the needs of the moment. There is no need to change them. Yet the speed and style of implementing them can be improved. There are a few ingredients to this that need further attention. To elaborate on some of them:

The first ingredient is partnership. If we examine the major successes that have been made this year in addressing the most serious problems we face, one factor stands out above all others, and that is partnership among various sectors of society. The Jobs Summit, the new Aids Awareness Campaign, the summits on morality and corruption, and the issue of security in the farming communities are concrete examples from recent months. So too was last year's successful Masakhane Focus Week. And it is in this spirit that we shall on Freedom Day announce this year's winners of the President's Award for Community Initiative.

These initiatives have resulted in major advances as society mobilises hand-in-hand with government to tackle the issues head on. As such, one of the launching pads to faster progress has to be the mobilisation of South African society to act in unison on critical issues facing the nation.

The second element is discipline – the balance between freedom and responsibility. Quite clearly, there is something wrong with a society where freedom is interpreted to mean that teachers or students get to school drunk; warders chase away management and appoint their own friends to lead institutions; striking workers resort to violence and destruction of property; businesspeople lavish money on court cases simply to delay implementation of legislation they do not like; and tax evasion turns individuals into heroes of dinner-table talk.

Something drastic needs to be done about this. South African society – in its schools and universities, in the workplace, in sports, in professional work and all areas of social interaction – needs to infuse itself with a measure of discipline, a work ethic and responsibility for the actions we undertake.

Thirdly, and related to the above, is the question of reconstruction of the soul of the nation, 'the RDP of the Soul': by this we mean first and foremost respect for life; pride and self-respect as South Africans rather than the notion that we can thrive in senseless self-flagellation.

It means asserting our collective and individual identity as Africans, committed to the rebirth of the continent; being respectful of other citizens and honouring women and children of our country who are exposed to all kinds of domestic violence and abuse. It means building our schools into communities of learning and improvement of character. It means mobilising one another, and not merely waiting for government to clean our streets or for funding allocations to plant trees and tend school-yards.

These are things that we need to embrace as a nation that is nurturing its new patriotism. They constitute an important environment for bringing up future generations. They are about the involvement of South Africans in building a better life.

Thus we shall take not just small steps, but giant leaps to a bright future in a new millennium. As we confounded the prophets of doom, we shall defy today's merchants of cynicism and despair. We shall, as we said in those letters of ten years ago, fully dismantle apartheid and achieve true reconciliation. Our hopes will become reality.

The foundation has been laid – the building is in progress. With a new generation of leaders and a people that rolls up its sleeves in partnerships for change we can and shall build the country of our dreams!

The Long Walk Continues

Speech at the final sitting of the first democratically
elected Parliament, Cape Town,
26 March 1999.

Today does not mark the end of our country's first democratic
government. Nor does it bring to an end the term that I have the
profound privilege to be serving as President. The business of government continues for some months to come and the high responsibilities which our Constitution confers on the President must still be
exercised in the interests of our nation.

But this day is a moment of deep significance for all of us whom
the people of South Africa have entrusted with representing their
needs and interests, their aspirations and hopes. And so it comes to
pass that we who have collectively accepted the role of political leadership of our nation today take leave of one another as members of
this, our country's first democratically elected Parliament.

Because the people of South Africa finally chose a profoundly
legal path to their revolution, those who frame and enact the Constitution and law are in the vanguard of the fight for change. It is in
the legislatures that the instruments have been fashioned to create a
better life for all. It is here that oversight of government has been
exercised. It is here that our society in all its formations has had an
opportunity to influence policy and its implementation.

In brief, we have laid the foundation for a better life. Things that
were unimaginable a few years ago have become everyday reality.
And of this we must be proud.

Questions have been raised, we know, as to whether this House is
not a carriage on the gravy train, whose passengers idle away their
time at the nation's expense. To those who raise such questions we
say: Look at the record of our Parliament during these first years of
freedom. Look at the work of the nation's representatives when they
formed themselves into a Constitutional Assembly.

With a breadth of consultation and public participation that few

172

would have imagined possible, and in a spirit of unprecedented consensus-seeking, it was here that a Constitution was formulated and adopted to enshrine our people's deepest aspirations.

Look at the 100 laws on average that have been passed by this legislature each year. These have been no trivial laws nor mere adjustments to an existing body of statutes. They have created a framework for the revolutionary transformation of society and of government itself, so that the legacy of our past can be undone and put right. It was here that the possibility was created of improving the lives and working conditions of millions.

Look at the work of the committees that have scrutinised legislation and improved it, posed difficult questions of the Executive and given the public insight and oversight of government as never before.

This is a record in which we can take pride. But even as we do so, we do need to ask whether we need to re-examine our electoral system, so as to improve the nature of our relationship, as public representatives, with the voters!

I raise this question with great pride in what has been done to lay the foundation of democracy in our country. Personally, I dare to say that moments in my life have been few and far between when I have sensed the excitement of change as in this august chamber.

Each historical period defines specific challenges of national progress and leadership; and no man is an island. As for me personally, I belong to the generation of leaders for whom the achievement of democracy was the defining challenge.

I count myself fortunate in not having had to experience the rigours of exile and decades of underground and mass struggles that consumed the lives of such giants as Oliver Tambo, Anton Lembede, Duma Nokwe, Moses Kotane, Robert Sobukwe, Oscar Mpetha, Lilian Ngoyi, Bishop Alpheus Zulu, Bram Fischer, Helen Joseph, Alex La Guma and Yusuf Dadoo. I count myself fortunate that, amongst that generation, history permitted me to take part in South Africa's transition from that period into the new era whose foundation we have been laying together.

I hope that decades from now, when history is written, the role of that generation will be appreciated, and that I will not be found wanting against the measure of their fortitude and vision. Indeed, I have noted with deep gratitude, the generous praise that has often been given to me as an individual. But let me state this:

To the extent that I have been able to achieve anything, I know that this is because I am the product of the people of South Africa.

I am the product of the rural masses who inspired in me the pride in our past and the spirit of resistance.

I am the product of the workers of South Africa who, in the mines, factories, fields and offices of our country, have pursued the principle that the interests of each are founded in the common interest of all.

I am the product of South Africa's intelligentsia, of every colour, who have laboured to give our society knowledge of itself and to fashion our people's aspirations into a realisable dream.

I am the product of South Africa's business people – in industry and agriculture, commerce and finance – whose spirit of enterprise has helped turn our country's immense natural resources into the wealth of our nation.

To the extent that I have been able to take our country forward to this new era it is because I am the product of the people of the world who have cherished the vision of a better life for all people everywhere. They insisted, in a spirit of self-sacrifice, that that vision should be realised in South Africa too. They gave us hope because we knew by their solidarity that our ideas could not be silenced since they were the ideas of all humanity.

I am the product of Africa and her long-cherished dream of a rebirth that can now be realised so that all of her children may play in the sun.

If I have been able to help take our country a few steps towards democracy, nonracialism and nonsexism it is because I am a product of the African National Congress, of the movement for justice, dignity and freedom that produced countless giants in whose shadow we find our glory.

When, as will be the case in a few months, I once again become an ordinary citizen of our land, it shall be as one whose concerns and capacities are shaped by the people of our land.

I will count myself as amongst the aged of our society; as one of the rural population; as one concerned for the children and youth of our country; and as a citizen of the world committed, as long as I have strength, to work for a better life for all people everywhere. And as I have always done, I will do what I can within the discipline of the broad movement for peace and democracy to which I belong.

I will then count myself amongst the ordinary men and women

whose wellbeing must, in any country, be the standard by which democratic government must be judged.

Primary amongst these criteria is the Reconstruction and Development Programme aimed at building a better life for all.

Primary amongst these criteria are national unity and reconciliation amongst communities and citizens whose destiny is inseparable.

It is a measure of our success as a nation that an international community that inspired hope in us, in turn itself finds hope in how we overcame the divisions of centuries by reaching out to one another. To the extent that we have been able to reciprocate in renewing hope amongst the people of the world, we are grateful indeed and feel doubly blessed. And it goes without saying that we should all live up to those expectations which the world has of us.

As I was reminded yet again on the visit which I have just made to The Netherlands and the four Nordic countries, the world admires us for our success as a nation in rising to the challenges of our era. Those challenges were to avoid the nightmare of debilitating racial war and bloodshed and to reconcile our people on the basis that our overriding objective must be together to overcome the legacy of poverty, division and inequity.

To the extent that we still have to reconcile and heal our nation; to the extent that the consequences of apartheid still permeate our society and define the lives of millions of South Africans as lives of deprivation, those challenges are unchanged.

I would like to take this opportunity to pay tribute to all the parties represented in this Parliament for their contribution to the progress we have made. Though we have our differences, often important and sometimes profound, we have as a collective demonstrated our overriding commitment to the new order that we have together established. You have ensured that this Parliament is no rubber stamp in the hands of government and given birth to a new democratic political culture.

And so, in the spirit of that democracy we are today taking leave of one another so that our parties can once again submit themselves to the judgement of the people.

Many of us will return to the second democratic Parliament. Others will not return to this hallowed institution, whether because of the electorate's judgement on our parties, or because of our own choice, or because of the imperatives of advanced age.

For my part, I wish to say that it has been a profound privilege to be accountable to this Parliament. Though there is sadness in leave-taking, I am filled with contentment by the sounds of voices that I have heard in the many debates that I have attended in this National Assembly, in the Senate, and in its successor, the National Council of Provinces.

Yesterday's debate on issues affecting Afrikaners and other communities was no exception. Amongst the principles which the liberation movement pursued from the beginning of negotiations is that out of any debate we must emerge stronger and more united, and that there should be no winners or losers.

Deputy President Thabo Mbeki, whom we all expect to be the President of South Africa, exemplifies this approach which is critical to the unity of our country. I call on all to give their support to his leadership, across all political parties.

His and other voices are those of a new generation of leaders that are emerging in answer to new historical challenges. They are the voices of the good men and women who exist in all communities and all parties, and who define themselves as leaders by their capacity to identify the issues that unite us as a nation. Together, we must continue our efforts to turn our hopes into reality.

The long walk continues.

Ndlelanhle! Mooi loop! Tsela tshweu!

5
DEVELOPMENT

RISING TOGETHER

CYRIL RAMAPHOSA

Long before I met Nelson Mandela, I felt I knew him. From his speeches, from his writings and, yes, from his legend, I had long known and identified Mandela as one of the towering leaders of our struggle against apartheid and the foremost exponent of the aspirations of the oppressed majority people of South Africa.

This, I have found, is not uncommon. Millions of people in South Africa – and indeed across the world – have long identified closely and personally with the vision of humanity for which Madiba has fought, which he has articulated and which he has represented.

For a person who spent almost three decades in prison, it is not surprising that Madiba is a person preceded by his reputation. It is a reputation built on his famous statement from the dock in the Rivonia Trial; from his courage and unrelenting commitment to the struggle; and from articles he wrote and speeches he made in the 1950s and early 1960s. It was built on the stories told about him in the townships and villages of this country. Most of them were true. Others, I am sure, had been embellished. It was a reputation fuelled by the underground pamphlets, the 'bush telegraph' and the publications which circulated among activists, workers and intellectuals. And, as we have learned since his release from prison, it was a reputation well earned.

The Mandela that we came to know, admire and love – even before we had seen him – was a person whose entire being was dedicated to the plight of humanity. This dedication was most directly evident in his struggle for the liberation of South Africa's black population: the African people, coloureds and Indians.

He spoke about the oppressed; he spoke for the oppressed, the poor, and the downtrodden of South Africa. But he was never parochial. As discrimination, oppression and exploitation defy national boundaries, so too did Mandela's message echo across the globe. Couched in the language of national liberation, Mandela's voice made a compelling case for the liberation of all humanity. It is not therefore surprising that in the last decade, as the myth Mandela has become the man Mandela, his message and his work have defied national boundaries.

In the years that we have come to know Mandela, as we have heard him speak the words that appear in this volume, and as we have all worked with him and under his leadership in building a new South Africa, his unbending dedication to the plight of the poorest and most vulnerable has both impressed and inspired.

He is fond of saying that poverty is the greatest assault on human dignity. It is a revolutionary position. For it recognises that human dignity cannot be achieved simply by its inclusion in a Bill of Rights. It cannot be achieved merely through the promulgation of laws or by changing the relationship of the state to its people, important though these are. It has to be achieved through the eradication of all that undermines human dignity. It requires a thoroughgoing transformation of society; a fundamental change in economic and social power relations; and earnest attention to the basic material needs of all people. In short, it requires development.

The speeches contained in this chapter offer an insight into Mandela's thinking not only on the significance of development to the struggle for human dignity, but also on the shape and content of that programme of development. Together, they provide an overview of the component parts of the struggle against poverty and underdevelopment – a 'theory', if you will, of sustainable human development.

But this is not the stuff of textbooks. The speeches each reflect a part of an actual programme of development undertaken by South Africa's first democratic government, which he led after 1994. Each contribution refers to the work done by South Africans to build a better life for all.

These speeches form part of the record of social progress made during Mandela's presidency and later during the presidency of Thabo Mbeki. They are testimony to the achievements and challenges of the greater part of the first decade of liberation.

What resonates throughout these speeches is the conviction that the theory and practice of development cannot be separated from democracy.

Democracy requires development. For unless people are given control over the basic activities of human existence, the effect of their hard-won right to choose people to represent them in structures of governance will remain limited. The value of electing public representatives and even participating in government decision making is severely undermined if people have few resources and even less opportunity to make of their lives what they want.

For Mandela, the democratic election of 1994 was the first, crucial step in the process of building democracy in South Africa. Each subsequent election further entrenches the culture of democracy. But it is the development of communities and the empowerment of the people which deepens and enriches democracy.

If democracy requires development, then it is equally true, Mandela suggests, that development requires democracy. Any despot can build a million houses. But to truly meet the needs of the people demands the involvement of the people in the development process. The intended beneficiaries are best placed to identify the areas of greatest need, to understand local conditions and challenges, and to reflect on the suitability of any proposed development.

The people need therefore to be integral to the processes of planning, design and delivery. This places an onus on structures of governance to involve communities in the allocation of resources for development, to consult thoroughly and continually, and to provide opportunities for reporting and feedback.

This gives expression to a view that has long been the mainstay of Nelson Mandela's political philosophy, and that of the liberation movement: that the people are their own liberators. It is a position which was at the heart of the anti-apartheid liberation struggle, which saw millions of South Africans being mobilised to confront the apartheid state, and which ultimately led to its collapse. It is the position which Mandela and others are now working to inject into the struggle for development. In the Reconstruction and Development Programme, adopted in 1994, it was described as people-centred and people-driven development. This concept has been augmented by the notion of *Vuk'uzenzele*, which is a call to all South Africans to 'arise and act' in together building a better life.

This spirit has informed a new volunteer movement for social development. Arising from the ANC's *Letsema* volunteer campaign, this broad national effort carries echoes of the volunteers of the 1950s, who risked imprisonment to defy unjust apartheid laws. It is fitting that Nelson Mandela was the volunteer-in-chief during that campaign.

Just as Nelson Mandela's life and work find resonance across the world, so too has his contribution to development not been limited to the immediate challenges of his home country.

As South Africa works to address the legacy of its apartheid and colonial past, much of the world is also working to tackle poverty and underdevelopment. It is a testament to Mandela's global view that South Africa has played such an important and prominent role in international efforts to promote development, whether at the Copenhagen Summit on Social Development or as host to last year's World Summit on Sustainable Development.

This view is reflected in something Mandela said at the Copenhagen Summit: 'We either rise together as humanity, or together fall.' This perspective recognises that many of the challenges being faced by South Africans are indeed being faced by peoples across the world. All humans have the same basic needs – water, shelter, food, skills – and billions find themselves unwittingly linked by their common lack of these essentials.

It is not only what they lack that links these people. The dire situations in which they find themselves also share the same cause: global inequality. While exacerbated by war and conflict, economic mismanagement and corruption, climatic failure and famine, at the root of global poverty and underdevelopment is the unequal distribution of resources and capacity between the developed North and the underdeveloped South.

As Nelson Mandela is seen as the person who led the struggle to overthrow apartheid in South Africa, so, in many ways, does the world look to Mandela to provide leadership in the effort to confront 'global apartheid'.

South Africa continues to make every effort possible to contribute what it can to global efforts to reshape international relations in the cultural, social and economic spheres. It does so, as Mandela suggested in Copenhagen, because the needs of South Africa's poor cannot be met in isolation from progress in meeting the needs of the people of Southern Africa, of the continent more broadly, and of the developing world.

It is for this reason that South Africa has been so active in efforts to stimulate an economic, political and social renaissance across Africa. The formation of the African Union and the development of the New Partnership for Africa's Development (Nepad) are both tangible responses to the question Mandela posed in 1995: 'How does humanity cooperate to build a better life for all.'

A thread which runs through all Nelson Mandela's speeches and statements on development is the particular role that women have to play in development, and the specific benefits which development efforts need to bring to the lives of women.

As in many other developing countries, women in South Africa tend to be disproportionately affected by poverty. Women generally have lower levels of education than men; they have lower levels of income; they have less access to resources; and they generally bear a greater burden of responsibility for care of children and the elderly.

Any efforts to tackle poverty therefore need to take into account the conditions in which women find themselves, as well as the broader benefits of directing efforts at empowering women. The provision of cheap and sustainable energy sources to households often has a profound effect on the quality of life of women, who in many instances are responsible for the collection of wood for cooking and heating purposes. The provision of clean water has a similar effect in households where the collection of water previously required travelling some distance each day.

Women are not merely beneficiaries of development, however. They are themselves active and energetic agents of development. This has been borne out in numerous projects in South Africa over the last few years. Women have formed collectives to build their own houses, investing their own savings to buy materials, contributing their time, their labour and, with time, their growing skills. They have removed alien vegetation to preserve South Africa's water resources. They have built roads and bridges, clinics, schools and community centres.

Mandela must be credited with recognising and embracing the importance of the positive impact women can make on governance and in decision-making structures at all levels. Together with Thabo Mbeki, Mandela provided crucial leadership when the ANC grasped the nettle on the issue of empowering women by deciding that at least a third of its candidates for the 1994 elections would be women.

This decision had a profound effect on the form and content of South Africa's post-apartheid political landscape. Mandela appointed a number of women to Cabinet positions, making a powerful statement about the role, capacity and centrality of women to transformation. As a result, South Africa is one of the leading countries in the world when it comes to the representation of women in Parliament, legislatures and executive structures.

Through his words and his work, Mandela has sought to draw attention to this dual role of South African women – both as among the most important beneficiaries of development, and as significant agents for development and progress.

Whether because he still sees himself as a 'country boy' at heart, or because he recognises that rural South Africa remains largely poverty-stricken and underdeveloped – or both – Nelson Mandela has always placed great store in efforts to tackle rural poverty.

Soon after his release from prison, he spoke of what he observed as he travelled around the country. He found that the conditions in which our people lived in 1990 had become a lot worse than the conditions they lived in during the 1960s. This to him meant that apartheid had had a much more devastating impact on our people than what appeared on the surface. Incomes had declined, the gap between rich and poor had increased, and Bantu Education had eroded the skills of the population.

He spoke with knowledge and passion about how decades of apartheid policies have stripped so much of the South African country-side of its potential, and how it has condemned rural people to eke out an existence on land that is over-populated, environmentally degraded and devoid of the most basic infrastructure.

During his years as President he championed programmes to restore land to those from whom it had been forcefully taken and to redistribute land among those who needed it. These programmes, which have continued and indeed accelerated, have been accompanied by efforts to ensure that people have the resources, skills and support necessary to make effective use of the land they have recovered.

Since his presidency, he has spent much of his time and his amazing and impressive powers of persuasion to mobilise business to invest in the building or renovation of schools and clinics in rural areas. As many a chief executive will testify, Mandela firmly believes that the challenge of development, whether rural or urban, is not the sole responsibility of government. He has always maintained that the private sector has both a moral responsibility and a commercial interest in using its resources for the development of the country's people.

The upliftment of South Africa's poor, the education of its children, and the health of its workforce are all goals which the private sector should, working with government, seek to achieve. Not only because it's the right thing to do, but also because it is what's needed to build a successful country and a strong and growing economy.

Nelson Mandela has an uncanny ability to demonstrate to even the most sceptical that their interests are inextricably entwined with the interests of all. We either rise together, or together fall.

On this, the occasion of his 85th birthday, it is not unreasonable to ask why it is that so many people identify so closely and passionately with Nelson Mandela. What accounts for the millions of messages of support and admiration which pour in from around the globe each day?

It is in great part due to the story of his life, a remarkable journey of hardship, struggle and liberation which mirrors the journey of an entire people. It is a real-life parable of the triumph of good over evil, of humility over arrogance, of nonracialism over exclusion. It is at once a celebration of human goodness and a powerful reason for hope.

But there is more. Perhaps what appeals so much about Nelson Mandela is that he is able to express in words and actions so precisely what much of humanity feels and thinks. In the speeches contained in this volume, he is able to give voice to the sentiments that we all feel, but have neither the means nor the language to say ourselves.

Nelson Mandela gives voice to the thoughts and aspirations of the voiceless. And in doing so, his life work continues to challenge the material conditions which keep so many people in silence. His words express what so many people feel, while his actions create the possibility for those millions of people to start speaking for themselves.

If ever there was a suitable tribute for Nelson Mandela, it is to hear, loudly and unhindered, the myriad voices of the people that his work has helped empower. It is to see how development has given rise to democracy, vibrant in its activity and brilliant in its diversity.

Happy birthday, Tata.

Masakhane

Speech at the launch of the Masakhane Campaign,
Marconi Beam, Koeberg,
25 February 1995.

Here at Marconi Beam we see the Reconstruction and Development Programme at work. What is happening here is the product of the kind of partnership which is needed to transform our country.

It is a partnership of a community determined to take responsibility for its own upliftment; and a government which has assumed the responsibility of planning for the most efficient use of the country's resources in order to address the legacy of the past. The Masakhane Campaign will build partnership, so that we can build one another.

This does not mean that such projects are without problems. But provided there is proper consultation, we can be confident that problems will be solved, and that all the plans will be turned into the basic things that people need. What is happening here is happening in more and more places each day. Soon it will be happening everywhere in our country.

From Soweto to Mitchell's Plain, from Chatsworth to Khayelitsha, democracy brings to neighbourhoods and communities the power to make sure that the changes working through our country will reach them. The Masakhane Campaign will help communities turn government programmes into the projects they need.

With freedom comes responsibility, the responsibility of participation. Each brick that is used to build a wall, every drop of water from a tap, is the result of many people's work and uses our country's resources. Government is putting massive investment into programmes for housing and services. We all have the responsibility to pay for what we use, or else the investment will dry up and the projects come to an end. We must ensure that we can, as a nation, provide for the millions still without the basic needs.

The laying of this brick symbolises the building of our nation, by

186

all of us, working togther in partnership to bring a better life for all South Africans.

Let us all build together and let us build each other.

Masakhane!

Joining Hands

Speech during Masakhane Focus Week, Bothaville,
14 October 1998.

South Africans have shown a tremendous capacity to join hands
when facing difficulty. The apartheid system eventually fell because
of the unity of those who were denied their rights; and because all
sectors of society recognised that they had more to gain from working together than from fighting each other. It is that same quality that
has helped us so quickly to lay the foundations for a better life.

When apartheid ended we faced the difficult task of reconstructing our shattered society and providing the most basic of services for
our people. We had to build schools and hospitals; to provide housing and jobs; to boost our economy; to protect our peoples' rights
through our Constitution and our courts; to help South Africa deal
with the division of its past and start the healing process; to deal with
abuse and damage which engulfed most of our communities.

Essentially our task was to create the conditions in which every
South African has the opportunity to create a better life for themselves. But government cannot meet these challenges by itself. It requires of us all to pull together into a partnership in order to bring
about the necessary changes.

In order to achieve these goals, we also needed to transform government from a system serving minority interests to one that meets
the needs of all South Africans. And all these things had to be done
in a country where most people were denied experience of government or proper education and training. This is why we have placed
a heavy emphasis on building capacity in government.

In spite of all the difficulties, we have succeeded as a nation in
beginning to change life for millions of people in ways they could only
dream about a few years ago. Over the past four years government has
been acting together with the private sector, non-governmental
organisations, workers and communities to rebuild and develop our
country. It is this spirit of partnership and consultation that has allowed

us to bring clean water to over 2.5 million people, build over 600 clinics and electrify 2 million homes. This is only a start, we know, and there are many needs still to be met. But it gives us confidence that we will meet the challenge we now face of speeding up delivery.

Today we have come together to celebrate some of the fruits of democracy and partnership in Bothaville/Kgotsong. Here the democratically elected local authority and an increasingly united community have been working together with national and provincial government to normalise life in a community that previously had little infrastructure, poor housing, crime, unemployment and boycotts of payment and services.

The two projects I have visited here in Bothaville/Kgotsong demonstrate what can be achieved when we work together.

The off-site housing project has brought together many different role-players: farmers, farmworkers, the departments of land, agriculture and housing for the eventual benefit of 1 000 people. Though the project was conceived many years ago, it could only come to fruition with democracy. Farmers involved in this project must be commended for their hands-on approach to the development of their employees' land and housing needs. It is by joining hands, across the old divides, in practical action to overcome the legacy of our past, that we will find true reconciliation and nation building.

We have all been disturbed of late to hear about the increasing violent attacks on farmers. In the Bothaville area, no less than five separate attacks have taken place in the last year. The Rural Safety and Security Summit we have just held has, we are convinced, laid a sound basis for stabilising the situation on farms.

But the complex problems of crime on our farms, as elsewhere, demand long-term solutions. In the meantime, we all need to commit ourselves to doing everything in our power to stop that kind of violence. Efforts to secure more stable farming environments by normalising labour relations and providing security for workers will make an important contribution.

As the test case for the policy of providing off-site housing for farm dwellers under the Extension of Security of Tenure Act, the Bothaville housing project has been designed to allow easy access to facilities such as clinics, libraries and sports complexes, while securing land and housing. This kind of effort can only enhance stability.

The infrastructure project is no less important. Apart from bringing water to over 14 000 people, it has boosted the local economy by employing local people in the construction phase.

We should not forget that this infrastructure project in Bothaville is just one among thousands of other such projects, across the country's 850 municipalities, under the Municipal Infrastructure Programme. This programme, now in its third phase, has brought improvements to about 11 million people and there are another 600 projects in the pipeline.

Your housing project is contributing to a national effort which is now seeing about 1 000 houses brought into construction or completed every day.

Both these and other local projects have been initiated, built and are being maintained by you, the people of Bothaville/Kgotsong. You have done it together as a community. You have consulted and gone about responsibly creating a partnership to give real meaning to *Masakhane*, that tradition of building one another. I would like to say: Congratulations to you all!

During this Masakhane Focus Week, people all over the country are celebrating similar achievements in building our nation. *Masakhane* is about people taking responsibility for their own upliftment and participating in the governing of their own lives. It is about empowering ourselves by creating good working relations between government and communities, for the benefit of everybody, just as you have done here and just as other communities have done.

It is about helping to build the capacity of our councillors and our provincial governments so that they, in turn, can best service our needs. We are celebrating progress in the implementation of our programmes for improved services and living conditions. We are also gathering together to commit ourselves further to tackling these and other challenges before us, like crime, unemployment and Aids.

When we say that the best solutions to these challenges can only be found when we work with each other, it requires a commitment of each and every one of us. Today we should all ask ourselves; what have I done to improve the surroundings in which I live? Do I litter or do I protect my surroundings? Do I spread racial hatred or do I promote peace and reconciliation? Do I buy stolen goods or do I help reduce crime? Do I pay my dues or do I cheat on my taxes, service fees and licences? Do I expect everything to be delivered to me or do I work with my local councillors to create a better life for myself and my community?

Co-operation between government, business, workers and other sectors brings a lasting relationship that benefits all. It is the road to creating jobs and business opportunities, reducing crime and improving the lives of people where they live.

These partnerships helped us lay the foundations for reconstruction. The building has begun. Together we can turn our villages and towns, our cities and rural areas, into parts of a new South Africa that we can all be truly proud of.

Masakhane!

Turning the Tide of Poverty

Speech at the SA Institute of International Affairs/
University of the Western Cape Conference, 'Southern Africa
into the Next Millennium,' Johannesburg,
19 March 1998.

In a few short years Southern Africa has taken great strides towards the vision of co-operation for development conceived in the struggle for liberation. Yet we are still in our infancy as a region of free and equal nations striving for better life for all our citizens. Indeed, the twenty-first century brings challenges even greater than those we have overcome.

It is therefore a great pleasure to join you as you gather to deliberate on the future of Southern Africa. May I congratulate the two organisations involved for their foresight in staging an event on this important topic.

As President of the United World Colleges, I am delighted to see so many students here from the Waterford Kamhlaba College. You belong to a unique global educational institution that brings together students from all corners of the world to live and work together. For South Africans, Waterford shone in the night of apartheid as a beacon of hope. For me personally Waterford has special meaning because two of my daughters attended the college while I was on Robben Island, as did the children of many of my colleagues.

The realisation of our dreams for our country and our continent depends on the values that the United World Colleges strive for – international understanding; development and leadership through education; peace and justice for all.

In an era increasingly defined by the interdependence of nations, a grasp of international trends is indispensable. As an independent organisation promoting appreciation of international issues through education and research, the South African Institute of International Affairs is ideally placed to make a major contribution.

By bringing together the worlds of government, research and education, this conference highlights the positive role non-governmental organisations can play alongside government.

192

The success of our programme for the reconstruction and development of South Africa depends also on the people of Southern Africa and of Africa as a whole achieving our common goals of democracy, peace and social progress.

Such is the interdependence of the countries of our region and our continent that the globalisation that is integrating the nations of the world is at the same time impinging on their sovereignty and helping to widen disparities between rich and poor.

In stating these facts we are touching on the most profound influences on South Africa's foreign and trade policy into the next century: the imperatives of development; the phenomenon of globalisation; and our relationship with the rest of the African continent, in particular the SADC states.

Conferences like this allow us to reflect on how well we have used the opportunities that freedom has brought to eradicate the poverty that afflicts the mass of our people; to take stock of how far we have to go; and to appreciate if changing conditions require new responses. You have spent the day traversing these issues in depth and with analytic skill far beyond what I could muster.

Suffice it to say that Southern Africa's interest in peace and stability is reflected in a collaborative approach to security and the resolution of such tensions as might occur; that a preference for democracy and the peaceful resolution of disputes has become the norm; that co-operation in combating crime is narrowing the space for criminals; that the pace of economic policy is being set by a commitment to disciplined use of public resources in pursuit of far-reaching programmes of reconstruction, and by measures to encourage the flourishing of enterprise.

These practices are nurturing a climate for sustained growth and development. They are reflected in a rising trend of growth in the region and falling inflation.

We are proud of these achievements, but we do not underestimate the difficulties. Aligning countries afflicted by historic imbalances is no easy task nor one that can be accomplished in a short time. Creating the single market to which SADC is committed will require a phased approach accompanied by measures to address the imbalances between and within countries.

In like manner SADC has initiated the challenging process of its own rationalisation as we pursue the evolution from Co-ordination Conference to Development Community. We need to find the right institutional forms to take full advantage of the new possibilities for integrated development through co-operation, including the potential for private sector contribution to development.

We must succeed in these matters if we are to meet our most urgent challenges, such as ensuring that economic growth translates into increased employment; that investment into the region matches the favourable conditions that exist; and that our trade relations with the world are put on an equitable basis.

As we succeed, we will be turning our region into the powerful engine for development it has the potential to be – a building block of an African economic community and a vital force in helping to make the twenty-first century the African century.

The imperatives of development define our destiny not only as an African nation, but also as a nation of the South. South Africa therefore seeks every opportunity to keep development issues high on the agenda, whether it be in our co-operation with nations at a similar stage of development or in the partnerships we are building with developed countries.

In this regard we see the selection of South Africa to chair Unctad [United Nations Conference on Trade and Development], and soon the Non-Aligned Movement, as an affirmation of our commitment to addressing the problems facing developing nations. The summit of the Non-Aligned Movement which South Africa will be hosting later this year will be an opportunity to promote our common concerns.

As we pursue these goals we will count on the Institute to help keep our nation alert to global developments. And we expect graduates and students of the University of the Western Cape, wherever they are, to play an active role in creating a better world.

At the end of a century which has seen unparalleled advances in political freedom, poverty still burdens the lives of millions who live in our region; in our continent; and indeed the world. That is an indictment of the past from which we are emerging. The widening disparities are a challenge defined by the process of globalisation in its current form.

As we enter the next millennium, we must know that history will judge us by our success or failure in turning the tide of poverty.

Social Development

Speech at the UN World Summit for Social Development,
12 March 1995.

We are gathered here to answer one question: how does humanity co-operate to build a better life for all? If this question sounds trite in its simplicity and too familiar in its rhyme, it is because this challenge has been with us for millennia.

More often, however, the need to pursue the good of all has been subsumed under the narrow interest of the self or the corporate unit. The endless cycle then becomes: better circumstances for a few, precarious ones for many, and indeed, worse for the majority.

That age-old question confronts us today under conditions which require of us an abiding consensus. Technological advance has narrowed the plains and oceans dividing nations. The era, in inter-state relations, in which military considerations were placed above pertinent socio-economic imperatives has come to an end. Our common habitat is in danger. We either rise together as humanity, or together fall.

It is appropriate that a major effort to re-order world affairs should take golden place as we celebrate the United Nations golden jubilee. We therefore join others in congratulating the Secretary-General and the UN's specialised agencies for this epoch-making initiative.

Above all, ours is a challenge issuing from the voices of the peoples, who are uniting across artificial boundaries for real and lasting security. They are asserting themselves more and more, particularly in structures of civil society. The choice before us, who call ourselves their leaders, is either to bend to that will or continue to flounder in the morass of circumlocution.

We in South Africa have learnt through bitter experience that security for a few is in fact insecurity for all. To the extent that the world taught us to understand and to challenge discrimination; to that extent we are apt to observe that to be born in the South, to be born a woman, disabled or amongst the poor – all these circumstances often define one's life possibilities as part of the wretched majority. The simple facts reflect the present untenable division of power and wealth, within and among nations.

The core challenges facing this summit undoubtedly require international solidarity. But they also demand from each one of us, national responsibility.

The South is justified in citing history and current international practices as the cause of our woes. However, our efforts to build open democracies and respect human rights, to improve efficiency and implement sustainable policies, will be a resounding voice which compels the North to listen.

On the other hand, it is to perpetuate difficulties of the South for the North to relate to us as consumers of arms and finished goods, as passive recipients of project assistance without transfer of skills and technology, as hapless victims to dictate to regarding loans and employment of aid.

Certainly, protectionism cannot survive. Certainly, basic rights, including a social clause in international arrangements, are desirable. We therefore need to co-operate in making the transformation easier for countries lagging behind.

South Africa is fortunate to emerge into the world in such interesting times. If our recent successes in building an inclusive democracy and knitting together a deeply divided nation are broadly appreciated, this is because we did what humanity taught us to do. But from the exalted heights of that success we now enjoy a better view of the mass we have inherited. This has spurred us even more to pursue integrated and sustainable objectives of economic growth and equity, fiscal discipline, human resource development, open and transparent government and popular involvement in our Reconstruction and Development Programme. The central strategy of our whole nation is a developmental one, aimed at creating full employment and ending poverty. National consensus around major policies, among both political parties and sectoral formations, is central to our approach.

We are thankful that the donor community is receptive to our view that aid should be in line with our priorities and budgetary plans. In particular, we believe that we must commit ourselves to finding a way of ending the marginalisation of Africa. The measures that are required to do this must be addressed urgently by all of us in very concrete terms.

The irony of democratic South Africa's late entry into international affairs is that we can reap the fruits of a world redefining itself. And in our naivety we are perhaps better placed, and even duty-bound, to ask the question: how do we emerge from here inspired not merely to attend future summits, but, under the aegis of the UN, to implement programmes that the world and its inhabitants demand and deserve?

Homes for the Homeless

Selection from the closing ceremony of the United Nations Habitat II
African Housing Ministers' Conference, World Trade Centre,
Johannesburg, 18 October 1995.

Let me begin by thanking the United Nations for giving South
Africa the opportunity to host this historic gathering. It has been an
honour for our new democracy to be able to play this role.

I am informed that you have reached an African consensus on this
critical matter that will be presented at Habitat II in Istanbul next
June. I want to compliment you on this important achievement.

The world can be divided into those countries where the nation is
comfortably housed, and those where housing is part of a daily struggle for survival. Most countries in Africa, including South Africa, fall
into the latter category. And this is a reflection of the challenges we
face to ensure that our peoples do indeed enjoy a better life.

Our approach to housing in South Africa, as in other parts of
Africa, embodies the principle that the government has an important
role to play. But it recognises too that government cannot solve the
problem on its own. We fully endorse the need for a full and meaningful partnership of government, the private sector and homeless
communities.

The very specific challenge that Africa faces is that of poverty; quite
simply, most of our people are too poor for a pure market solution
to the housing problem. Yet poverty does not mean hopelessness. The
greatest single resource we have in solving this challenge is the energy
and creativity of the homeless themselves. It is an energy that can be
mobilised in an effective partnership that helps communities to help
themselves.

In tackling the task of housing the nation, we are presented with
an historic opportunity to fundamentally challenge economic and
social relations. For, housing is not neutral. Our own country has in
the past known only too well how the provision and non-provision
of housing can be used as a form of social and political control. Here

and elsewhere it has often been the means of dealing with the urban and rural poor – to hide them, evict them, harass them and trample on their self-esteem.

As such, a successful housing programme can at one and the same time become a force for economic and social liberation. Built into this there are in our situation some fundamental requirements.

The first deals with security of tenure. The absence of such security is one of the most consistent reasons for the non-improvement of housing conditions. Granting such security leads to a completely different response from communities.

Another critical issue is that of the provision of credit to people who do not attract the interest of the formal banking sector. One of the most important ways of changing this negative relationship lies in the mobilisation of people's own savings. There are significant initiatives under way in South Africa that are proving the viability of this approach.

A third key issue is one that is often overlooked or even scoffed at. Very simply put: the success of our housing programme – of any housing programme – is directly related to the extent to which women are directly involved. When we talk about people-centred development, we should understand that the involvement of women is often the difference between success and failure.

The last issue I would highlight as critical to any effective housing programme, or indeed any programme, is good and clean governance.

It is very difficult to build a democracy when daily living is such a struggle. The reality we face in South Africa is that the housing programme has essentially to be implemented by the poor themselves. The state has a vital role in facilitating and complementing this process. It has a central role in infrastructural development. But by involving the people, we shall not only ensure that they get jobs, but also that they will claim ownership of the process and the final product.

In just a moment a South African school pupil will read to you an essay which he wrote. David Dladla lives in KwaZulu-Natal, and in his entry for the competition organised by our Department of Housing for World Habitat Day he speaks of the hopes and dreams of many of our continent's children.

It is our task as leaders to ensure that the dreams of Africa's children become a reality.

Housing as a global issue is also about resources – about the judicious use of the world's natural resources, as well as about their just allocation. Our decisions on these matters determine our living environment and, ultimately, whether we are creating cities or slums.

Africa, as a continent, must play its part in creating a new world vision of shelter at Habitat II. We must recognise that the provision of shelter is a process that can both create and maintain the democratic process.

The Africa delegation that goes to Istanbul must know that they have the most important mandate on this issue. That mandate comes from the homeless.

You have our full backing; and we wish you every success.

The World in Soweto

Speech at the launch of 'The World in Soweto,' Soweto,
1 December 1995.

Today the world has descended on Soweto. Not to monitor the police violence or other infamous abuses of the apartheid regime which made this township an international household name. On the contrary, we are all here to give her residents a hand in transforming Soweto into a decent suburb.

Throughout the apartheid years the world community was appalled by the South African townships. These areas were built for third-class citizens, people whom the powers-that-be regarded as sub-humans. The architects of these townships didn't care what became of their residents, their health, the potential for crime, or the general welfare. With the dawn of a new era these residential areas must be upgraded.

Soweto became a symbol of these townships. Over the years foreign dignitaries who visited our country always came here to pledge their solidarity not only with Soweto residents, but with all the oppressed.

Upgrading of residential areas is the responsibility of municipalities. But for Soweto, with its millions of inhabitants and its vast area, it would take decades because of the limited available financial resources. Joining forces with international partners was the only option.

'The World in Soweto' is, therefore, an opportunity for governments and civic bodies around the world to make a real difference to the lives of Sowetans who live amid garbage heaps and dust storms.

Gathered with us today are representatives of governments, international organisations, and foreign cities. They are here to hold our hands in the drive to better the lives of our people.

In doing so they will not assume the responsibility of the municipalities we elected a month ago. Those will remain responsible for normal municipal services like provision of water and electricity and garbage removal. Rather 'The World in Soweto' will assist with things which otherwise would have been pushed to the bottom of the priority ladder, like the paving of sidewalks, provision of rubbish bins, planting of trees, parks development, and the general beautification of the area.

'The World in Soweto' will provide us with an opportunity to link up with still more foreign governments, cities and civic bodies. Most were involved in our fight for freedom. They campaigned against the apartheid regime and raised funds for our struggle. Some came here to pledge their solidarity. They sustained our morale by assuring us that we were not alone.

Now they are returning to help us to help ourselves. They are launching this project because they have confidence in our determination to succeed. It is not their objective to do our work for us. They know that they are helping a hard-working nation, ready to assume responsibility for our own upliftment. They are joining with us in the spirit of *Masakhane*.

'The World in Soweto' will also be a window through which the international community views our reconstruction process. Our response to their assistance will either spur them to more joint projects or may discourage them from further involvement. The responsibility is on all Sowetans to exploit this opportunity to the fullest. Success will open similar ventures for other townships across the country. If we fail, we shall be letting our entire nation down. As pioneers we must excel.

It is encouraging to see our local business fraternity joining up, strengthening the bonds with the communities they serve. It is a sign that they are not simply in business to line their pockets. I would therefore urge the rest of the business community to associate themselves with such efforts. During the apartheid era most of them voiced their opposition to the system. Now is the time to correct the wrongs of that system. Our people will be waiting for concrete actions. As the local business community they are expected to do more than our foreign friends because they will be helping themselves as well.

'The World in Soweto' is another sign that we are indeed now part of the world community of nations. May I thank all our foreign guests for having made this function such a resounding success and for putting their faith in us.

As a Sowetan myself, I pledge to spare neither strength nor effort to ensure the smooth running of this venture.

Rural Anti-Poverty Programme

Speech on the Rural Anti-Poverty Programme,
13 October 1998.

I am deeply moved and honoured to be here today. We first planned to come here in April to launch the Rural Anti-Poverty Programme. But in truth it is even more satisfying to be able to see for myself the progress you have made in implementing the programme on the South Coast of KwaZulu-Natal where the needs are so great.

Being here awakens feelings of both sadness and joy. The name of Shobashobane recalls one of the most gruesome experiences of a province that has suffered untold and unnecessary pain as a result of political conflict and intolerance. It brings to mind the men, women and children who died in that incident, the families displaced, and the children left homeless. It reminds us of how conflict and tension only worsened the poverty that gripped the area.

But today we have cause for celebration, because communities are now working together to uplift themselves and rebuild confidence in the area. By doing so you are bringing back the businesses and the people who fled because of the violence. You are showing that you too have understood the lesson of our times, that peace is the most powerful weapon that any community or people has to bring about stability and development.

I would make a plea today that your practical message of peace should be heard by all. I would in particular urge all political leaders and *Amakhosi* to work together for peace. The leadership in KwaZulu-Natal can take pride in the progress they have together brought for peace, and I would like to encourage them all to continue in their efforts and to speed up the process.

Events in recent months in this province tell us that those who seek to take us back to war talk and conflict are still at work. Let us not allow the province to slip back into political violence. We should not give even the slightest opportunity to the forces of violence to derail the peace progress.

We are therefore proud to be here today. We are not here to try and calm a volatile situation of the kind that feeds perceptions that Africa and Africans are somehow prone to violence, but rather to reinforce the message that Africa and Africans are united for social upliftment.

This official launch of the Rural Anti-Poverty Programme, and the opportunity to review its progress, is indeed a joyous occasion.

At the heart of our democratic government's mandate is the reconstruction and development of our country, with the central objective of transforming our society in order to improve the lives of our people whose basic needs were so cruelly neglected by apartheid.

For that reason we are steadily shifting resources towards social services over a number of years and ensuring that our economy grows in order to sustain these improvements. At the same time we are also taking special measures to address urgent needs of the poorest of the poor. That includes allocating R300 million towards poverty relief in last year's Budget, including R85 million for the Rural Anti-Poverty Programme of the Department of Public Works.

It is for that reason too that this programme focuses in particular on KwaZulu-Natal, Eastern Cape and Northern Province, where so much of the poverty in our country is concentrated.

Equally important is the emphasis in the Rural Anti-Poverty Programme on opportunities for women; on participation by communities in their own upliftment; and on building the capacity of our local authorities to work with national and provincial government to meet the needs of communities.

These are the goals and the values that make up the spirit of *Masakhane*, and so it is highly appropriate that we are highlighting this programme during Masakhane Focus Week when partnership and joint responsibility for upliftment are celebrated in communities across the country.

From the reports I have been given on progress in the implementation of the Rural Anti-Poverty Programme it is clear that it is making a lasting difference where it really matters to our rural areas – by concentrating on such basic things as access roads, multi-purpose community centres, school buildings and infrastructure for agriculture, as well as training and capacity building.

These are fruits of our young democracy, along with the electricity and clean water supplies; the health care and telephones which are already changing the lives of millions, especially amongst those who live in the rural area. Achievements of this nature are only possible through the joint partnership of government and communities.

It touches my heart to see how ordinary men and women have seized the chance that democracy brings to participate actively in shaping and building these projects. In doing so you are not only building assets for your communities and for your children. You are also building our nation and making a living reality of democracy by bringing government closer to the people it serves. This programme has already clearly strengthened this spirit of partnership on which the future of our country must be built.

I would therefore like to take this opportunity to thank Premier Ngubane whose province is hosting us today, as well as the premiers of the Eastern Cape and Northern Cape for their contribution to the success of the programme.

I wish to pay a special tribute to all those in national, provincial and local governments, and to the communities and traditional leaders, who have worked together in designing, planning and implementing the programme as well as in securing the delivery of the projects.

Congratulations to you all!

If today we lay particular emphasis on the gains that have been made in partnership and co-operative governance, in training and capacity building, and in the creation of infrastructure and productive assets, it is because we will need all these things as we continue to tackle the immense task of many years, to address the legacy of poverty that blights the lives of millions of our people.

Much as we take pride in our achievements, we are not resting on our laurels and are gearing ourselves for still greater efforts. That is why in this year's Budget we increased the poverty relief funds from R300 million to R500 million, and altogether put R274 million in the hands of Public Works to spend especially on access roads in rural areas.

That is also why I personally continue to encourage the private sector to join with rural communities in meeting their needs. The response to my requests to business has always been positive, and as a result communities across the country today have schools, clinics or other facilities they would not otherwise have.

On all the major challenges facing our country, government is busy strengthening the partnerships of all social sectors that will allow our nation to meet its goals. This month alone has seen the Rural Safety Summit, which will help eliminate the attacks in our farming areas; the launch of a Partnership against Aids; and intensive preparations for the Jobs Summit which will strengthen our efforts to defeat the scourge of unemployment. We will also be having a national summit on fighting corruption.

Like rural development, these issues transcend whatever political differences there may be among us. I would therefore in conclusion return to my appeal that the transformation of Shobashobane from a symbol of the horrors of political violence to a lesson in development through peace should be taken to heart by all.

Especially as we approach a new election, we should remember the fundamental importance of political tolerance, and the spirit of nation building, to our future. Whatever political party we belong to, IFP or ANC or any other, we should conduct ourselves so that we emerge from the election even more united as a nation in our determination to improve the lives of our people.

We have laid the foundation for a better life for all, and through programmes like the Rural Anti-Poverty Programme the building has begun. Together, let us turn South Africa into the land of our dreams.

A Road for Development

Speech at the opening of the Noluntu Project, Bumbane,
14 August 1998.

When I was a young boy, I learned the value of education in this very area. I am pleased to return to the place I spent many of my formative years in. And I am honoured to be part of a project which will enable teachers to reach the children of this area once again and teach them too the value of a good education.

The opening of a new road in our country is always a cause for celebration. The new access road to the Sitebe–Komkulu area opens up a world to communities who have been cut off through years of neglect.

The opening of new roads is part of the earnest progress we are making in righting the wrongs of apartheid: we are confronting our evil past; we are building and growing for the future. Here, as elsewhere, it is part of a much broader programme to improve the lives of our people. This programme has already seen the delivery of clean water to nearly 2.5 million people; over 600 clinics built and the connection of electricity to some two million homes. All over the country people are gaining access to health services, good education opportunities and much more. There are still years of hard work ahead of us all before we complete the task, but we can be proud of the fact that democracy is already changing the lives of millions.

For the villages in this area, this road means health services, schools, shops and other facilities are within reach. It means mobility and choices for people who have been forced to spend many hours walking or forced to pay high transport costs because their homes are far from any roads.

And in this case, the new road is special because it means access to Bumbane, the Great Place: home of the late King Sabata Dalindyebo, who fought for the liberation of our country and who was forced into exile as a result.

As a result of his courage, the apartheid government and its servants punished all those who were loyal to King Sabata and to democracy by neglecting their needs. The infrastructure deteriorated so badly that many people could only reach health services, food supplies and schools through walking. Even taxis and buses could not service the area.

By the construction of this road we are finally able to empower Dalindyebo's people once again. One of the standards by which our democratic government must be judged is how much it does to empower those who have been most weakened by apartheid. This empowerment comes in many forms. By ensuring that this was a labour-intensive project, job opportunities were created for people of this region which brought training and skills development as well as work.

Another way in which this project has empowered people is that it was built primarily by women. The contract for this road reflected the fact that this is an area populated chiefly by women. It is thus fitting that there were 70 women for every 30 men engaged in building this project.

Given this opportunity, the women of this area have risen to the challenge. That is clear from the fact that out of the 22 employees who qualified for Civil Engineering Training Board certification, 16 were women. To them and to the five women who gained additional accredited training in project management, as well as to everyone else, I wish to say: congratulations on your sterling efforts.

This project has been a model of reconstruction and development: redressing the legacy of the past, opening new opportunities, and developing vital skills for building our nation.

Today as we celebrate the completion of the Noluntu project and officially mark the opening of the road, we can say with confidence: together, through hard work, we will continue to build a better life for all.

Business

Speech at the Black Management Forum,
24 November 1995.

When the oppressed and disadvantaged take their destiny into their own hands, and when those divided in bitter conflict turn towards peace and reconciliation, that is indeed a collective act of extraordinary leadership. It is this achievement of our whole nation which you are honouring tonight. It is in that spirit that I humbly accept the award, on their behalf.

The theme of your conference – Black Economic Self-empowerment – reaffirms that faith in the capacity of those who have been excluded to take the lead in shaping a new and equitable order. It resounds as a pledge to join hands with government in its endeavours to address the legacy of apartheid, whether in business or more broadly.

The achievement of our shared objectives will depend on the fulfillment of that pledge, since they cannot be achieved by government alone.

For its part, government has a range of initiatives in place to ensure that the vast business and managerial potential which apartheid left untapped is now released for the benefit of our society.

The major programme for the expansion of small, micro- and medium enterprises is making good progress as it builds on the foundation laid in the policy conference held in March this year.

Government policy on the restructuring of state assets will follow guidelines approved by Cabinet in August. They take into account the need to encourage the growth of small and medium enterprises, and to do so in ways which help create an opening into the business world for those hitherto marginalised.

Foreign investors are being strongly encouraged to engage in joint ventures with emerging business. So, too, are the established sectors of South African business, whose power and resources owe much to their privileged position under apartheid. Such partnerships will not only open doors – they are also a highly effective way of transferring skills and knowledge.

Government is committed to a review of its procurement and tendering policy. One of the objectives is to provide opportunities for those disadvantaged by previous policies to catch up and help provide efficient services to people.

Black business is in a position to make a special contribution to reconstruction and development, and built into the RDP are measures to ensure such participation.

The transformation of the public service places representativeness and affirmative action amongst the highest priorities for achieving a public sector that truly serves the people of this country.

In short, government is ensuring that the opportunities are there for black business and management. But it will need boldness in seizing opportunities. It will demand a readiness to face the challenges of the competitive world market to which we now belong. It will mean accepting the rigours of pursuing far-reaching goals with limited resources in a society that is eager for new standards of morality, accountability and professionalism in both the public and private sectors. One instance of which we should all be mindful in this regard is that of the African Bank. In putting over R200 million into the bank, government is counting on those qualities in management to ensure that a similar crisis does not recur.

The profits and the access to resources and decision-making power which flow from the opportunities that are opening should be used not only to reward enterprise and achievement. They should also be used to enhance the productive capacity and efficiency of companies and institutions, and their employees. Affirmative action, likewise, is a responsibility that must be embraced by its beneficiaries themselves, and extended to others.

For the most effective implementation of these policies and their further development there is a further requirement. While the number of black business organisations is a sign of vitality, it is also a weakness. A single and co-ordinated voice will increase the effectiveness with which needs are addressed. We hope that this conference will find a way to make decisive progress in achieving this objective, which has so far proved vexingly elusive.

This goes more broadly for business as a whole. One of our objectives in overcoming the legacy of apartheid must be the unification of each sector of our society, including business. No doubt, there will be difficulties on the path. But our society is moving towards solutions in the broader interest.

I raise these issues because I am confident that the Black Management Forum, which represents a sector of society that formed itself under the most difficult of circumstances and when opportunities were few, has a critical leadership role to play under the favourable conditions of today.

Though still few in number, as professionals and managers you are well placed to contribute to policy formation for the development of our enterprises, private and public.

One of our most urgent priorities is the rapid and extensive development of management expertise amongst the majority of our population who were excluded from such responsibility in the past.

The challenge for the BMF, and for black professionals generally, is to use the voice which their achievements have given them to help enlarge their own ranks. In so doing they will contribute to the realisation of the vision of a better life for all South Africans.

Labour

Address at the Fifth National Congress of Cosatu,
7 September 1994.

First, let me express my profound gratitude for the invitation to take part at this, the Fifth National Congress of Cosatu. Much has already been said about the significance of this Congress for Cosatu in particular, and indeed for the entire trade union movement of our country. I however wish to say that for me personally this is one of the high watermarks of my engagements since the elections and the inauguration of the Government of National Unity. To take part in a gathering of this nature, bringing together part of the core of cadres of the democratic movement, is for us a homecoming.

So, we speak to you not simply as representatives of a different organisation; nor merely as allies; less still as government to the governed. We stand before you fully conscious of the fact that, together, we spared neither life nor limb to ensure that South Africa is where it is today. We shared the trials and tribulations of struggle so that South Africa should be free.

The temptation is to say thank you for ensuring that the ANC secured a decisive electoral victory. But this would be wide off the mark. For you did what you had to do for none other than yourselves and your families, for your country and for your nation, so that we could break the chains of oppression.

The ideal of a nonracial, nonsexist and democratic South Africa in which there is social equity is the mission the ANC set itself over the decades. This is the mission of our alliance. It is a mission that should continue to guide us, no matter how steep the road and how rugged the terrain in which we have to operate.

That the broad perspectives of the Reconstruction and Development Programme have become the property of the whole nation is thanks to the correctness of its content and the creative leadership of the alliance. We are proud that organised workers have been and remain at the centre of efforts to define and realise national tasks. It is crucial that this should continue to be the case. Otherwise, what is essentially a programme to uplift the conditions of the poor, could easily be misappropriated to serve the interests of those who have all along benefited from the system of apartheid.

This, however, cannot subtract from the strategic task of winning over various sectors of society to become part of this effort. This means, among other things, that we should broaden our horizons.

It will always be crucial for the trade union movement to play the role of a critical extra-parliamentary force. But today you also have to take active part in determining and implementing government policy. It is fundamental that the trade union movement should jealously guard its independence. But today you also have to use, to maximum effect, the elements of political power that we have together achieved in struggle.

What does this mean in actual practice?

I understand that many government ministers will take part in your discussions on matters affecting their line functions. I encourage you not to pull your punches. Fortunately my task is much easier, and I will confine myself to a few general remarks.

What sets this Congress apart from all others before it is the fact of the elements of political power that the democratic movement as a whole is wielding. The challenge therefore is to use this power to consolidate democracy at the same time as the union movement promotes its own interests.

The presence at this Congress of government ministers demonstrates the influence that you have. But it would be unproductive if this interface were to end in special gatherings. Lines of communication should always be open between various government departments and the labour movement. Like other sectors of society, you should endeavour as far as possible to influence what they do. The same applies to the parliamentarians. On my part, I should reiterate that my door will always be open for such consultations.

The platform of the liberation movement, which entails more than just the frills of political office, is yet to be fully realised. If only for this reason, it is even more important today that we should strengthen the Tripartite Alliance, while redefining its form under the new conditions. In as much as the ANC needs a strong Cosatu, Cosatu needs a strong and vibrant ANC.

The kind of democracy that we all seek to build demands that we deepen and broaden the rights of all citizens. This includes a culture of workers' rights. Already, progress has been made, through joint consultation between government and the trade union movement, to start implementing a plan of action to achieve this.

Among the central questions that require urgent attention are the basic conditions of employment, regulations on collective bargaining and the right to strike. Combined with issues such as the democratisation of the workplace, an end to discrimination and central industrial bargaining, all these initiatives will help to improve labour relations and therefore economic growth and development.

To achieve this requires a partnership that will now find expression in statutory arrangements involving all the major role-players in the economy. The decision to set up the National Economic, Labour and Development Council is an important part of this process.

Among the many urgent tasks that face this council is the question of industrial restructuring so necessary for us to become a full and competitive partner in international economic relations.

We say this task is urgent because we shall never fully enjoy the benefits of our international standing as a democracy, if we do not bring our industries to international standards. Rather, we will become a victim of our own achievements. Yet it is crucial, as the various tripartite forums have indicated, that this should be implemented with due regard to human resource development and all-round strategies to improve productivity. It should be carried out with maximum consultation, and at a pace that will not adversely harm our economy in general and workers in particular.

The council will also have to examine as a matter of urgency the issue of a social consensus among the various economic role players.

The government is fully committed to the protection of the integrity of the collective bargaining system. Yet, among the lessons that we have all learnt from recent industrial actions is that this system should be improved, particularly with respect to mechanisms of mediation that should help resolve disputes before they come to a head.

It is quite instructive that major sectors such as mining, clothing and textile, and the iron, steel and metallurgical industries concluded their negotiations without recourse to strike action. Besides the fact that the number of strikes in this period this year was much lower than in previous years, this goes to demonstrate that we have healthy industrial relations in South Africa. The psychology of crisis, fanned by some enthusiasts in the media, has little to do with reality.

At the same time, we need to challenge the notion that strikes are, as a rule, inimical to the task of reconstruction and development.

Reconstruction and development entails more than just creating jobs or building houses. It means the fundamental restructuring of society as a whole, including relations at the workplace. The more labour, business and government interact in working out individual and collective contributions to reconstruction and development, the more will some of the industrial actions become unnecessary.

Much progress has already been made in kick-starting the implementation of the RDP. While the Presidential Projects are an important measure of this, our basic standard to gauge progress is the rate at which various departments are changing their priorities in line with the programme as a whole. Along with this, is the challenge of ensuring fiscal discipline and efficiency, so that the RDP can be implemented in a sustainable manner. The RDP White Paper, to which the trade union and other formations have made an important contribution, seeks to address these issues.

To achieve these objectives requires, among other things, rapid and systematic restructuring of the apartheid state structures, to ensure that the public service is representative of society as a whole and to eliminate wastage, mismanagement, duplication and corruption. We are pleased that Cosatu-affiliated unions are taking an active part in the forums set up to address these matters.

The success of the RDP will depend, above everything else, on the extent to which we involve all sectors of society in carrying it out. We need to involve more than just business and labour in the work of planning and co-ordinating socio-economic strategies. All sectors of civil society should take part through sectoral and multi-sectoral forums. The wisdom, initiative and creativity of the people is required to ensure that the RDP becomes a people-centred and people-driven programme in fact.

Circumstances might have changed. But the task of mobilising the people to become masters of their own destiny remains. This is a task that falls squarely on the shoulders of the political as well as mass democratic organisations. We therefore welcome the many proposals from workers on how they can drive the RDP in the workplace and within communities. Without such work, the RDP will remain a good programme on paper, but a damp squib in actual practice.

What this requires is that we should strengthen organisational structures of the democratic movement as a whole, ensure that members are properly serviced and extend our organisational reach. At the same time, leadership structures have to conduct themselves in such a way that they maintain and deepen the confidence of the masses they represent. We should also urgently tighten co-ordination in the Tripartite Alliance and among all sectors of the democratic movement. This is made the more urgent by the coming elections for local government, an institution which is critical for the implementation of the RDP.

In so far as the labour movement is concerned, the question of unity among various federations has come to the fore. In the final analysis, the strength of organised labour depends on its ability to articulate and promote the interests of workers as a whole. This will also contribute immensely to the strategic task of de-racialising South African society.

The challenges that we face are many and they are daunting. But this is the price we have to pay for our victories. As in the past, we do have the will and the creativity to carry out our mission.

I am confident that this Congress will meet the expectations of your members and broader society. You were among the front troops in the battle against apartheid. You were in the front ranks in charting the path out of the mess this system created. We are confident that Cosatu will be at the forefront of the successful implementation of the Reconstruction and Development Programme. Only then shall we be able to say that power is truly in the hands of the people.

I wish you all the best in your deliberations.

Long live Cosatu!

Long live the Alliance!

Business and Labour

Speech at a farewell luncheon for business and labour,
Pretoria, 26 March 1999.

Only days before the election that will usher in a new democratic government it is most gratifying to be able to play host to such a galaxy of leaders of business and labour. Your kindness in giving up some of your precious time to one so soon to become a former president is heartening, and I hope that members of the government here present will take note.

There is a special significance in this event which allows me to take leave as President of a critical part of the leadership of our economy after five momentous and historical years.

A large part of that significance is defined in those we wished to share this occasion with us.

Amongst you are leaders of our corporate world who have responded to my personal call, since I left prison, to contribute directly towards meeting urgent and immediate basic needs of some of our most disadvantaged communities. Your response has meant new or upgraded clinics, schools and hospitals for hundreds of thousands who would otherwise have to wait for the effects of longer-term programmes to reach them.

Amongst you are members of the Job Creation Trust set up by organised labour to mobilise resources amongst employed workers and business to help fund the creation of jobs for our fellow citizens who are unemployed. Those to whom democracy has brought workers' rights have responded by affirming in the most practical way their responsibility for the wellbeing of the nation as a whole.

Amongst you are members of the Business Trust, responsible for the initiative by business to mobilise resources and guide their use for job creation and skills development, in partnership with government. Here we see a direct and organised engagement of the private sector in social transformation.

217

In short, this gathering reflects the organised involvement in reconstruction and job creation of the two principal forces in our society. Locked until only a few years ago in an unremitting conflict, they have been liberated to work together to create a society which reflects the fact that we are one people with one destiny.

It has been an immense privilege for me to have been a participant over these five years in the process that has brought us to this point. Many in the international community, seeing from afar how our society defied the prophets of doom and their predictions of endless conflict, have spoken of a miracle.

You who have been closely involved in the transition as it affected the economy will know that it has been the product of human decisions.

There has had to be a series of often difficult compromises that allow each constituency to pursue its specific interests within a framework that is shaped by the interests of the nation as a whole. The establishment of Nedlac [National Economic Development and Labour Council], the Jobs Summit and the initiatives which this gathering represents are some of the landmarks of the process.

Amongst other things this has brought stability to our country and created conditions for progress that are quite remarkable, considering the odds against which we had to work. Without the preparation required for governing a modern economy, our first democratic government has brought about a quiet revolution in our institutions and laws. We have begun the delivery of services to millions of people and turned our economy from stagnation towards a path of sustained growth based on sound foundations.

It is not necessary in such a gathering to lay out the details of these changes. Nor is it necessary to state that proud as we may be of the progress that has been made, we face far greater challenges. The projects for job-creation and reconstruction have made a good start.

But compared with the need and the potential, there is no reason that what has so far been done should not be dwarfed by what lies ahead in the next five years of government under a new generation of leaders.

You will not need me to tell you that the person whom we all expect to be the next President of South Africa is Thabo Mbeki. He is someone who is steeped in the ANC's approach to matters which seeks to ensure that out of every debate and every challenge we should emerge more united. Much of what has been achieved in these first years of freedom, in particular in the economic field, is owed to the fact that the day-to-day business of government has been largely in his hands.

I will therefore take leave of government fully confident that there is hope for our economy; that there is hope for South Africa. The future cannot be brighter.

Conservation

Address at the launch of the Kruger National Park
Centenary Celebrations, Skukuza,
26 March 1998.

Conservation in its nature is directed both to the past and the future, to preserving our heritage and ensuring that it benefits generations to come. So it is a great pleasure to celebrate the centenary of this premier conservation area with men and women whose decisions and actions will be critical to its future.

We are also proud to welcome our visitors from abroad and representatives of governments from so many countries. For we are aware that we are entrusted with a priceless asset that is valued not only by our own people, but by our region and people across the world.

In commemorating this historic day, we do not forget those who had to surrender their land to make it possible, often through forcible removal, nor those who for generations were denied access to their heritage except as poorly rewarded labour.

We recall these threads in our history not to decry the foresight of those who established the park, nor to diminish our enjoyment of it. We do so rather to reaffirm our commitment that the rural communities in and around our parks should also benefit from our natural heritage, and find in it an opportunity for their development.

Tourism occupies a strategic place in our overall strategy for reconstruction and development. The rapid growth of this sector since our country was freed from apartheid confirms our confidence that tourism is destined to play a critical role in earning much-needed foreign exchange and creating jobs. It can help produce wealth which will strengthen our efforts to provide clean water, electricity, health-care and adequate housing to those who have been so long denied these basic amenities.

Such assets as the Kruger National Park and our many other parks and tourist attractions, if developed within a framework of regional co-operation, can make a major contribution not only to our own country but to the whole of Southern Africa. Visitors who come to experience the wonders of this park are in easy reach of many spectacular offerings elsewhere in our region.

In this regard it is satisfying to learn of the progress in discussions with Mozambican authorities to establish a single park that links our countries and our peoples. That would be a victory not only for more cohesive management of our region's ecology, but a concrete symbol of regional unity and a spur to development.

If we are to succeed in fully realising the potential of eco-tourism to contribute to development, it will be by embracing the spirit of partnership that underlies all our achievements as a newly liberated nation.

A new generation of leaders has the responsibility for enhancing conservation and public service standards. Theirs is the task of bringing together all stakeholders in a broad partnership.

Rural communities not only have the opportunity now to become involved as entrepreneurs. They can also be active agents in meaningful programmes of conservation and environmental community education. In so doing they will contribute to the sustainable use of our environment, and at the same time dispel the myth that this is a preserve of a rich elite. These efforts will be strengthened by co-operation between communities, conservation authorities and private operators.

The private sector, whose generosity has made this event possible, has a major role to play, whether it be through the promotion of conservation; direct assistance in the upliftment of communities neighbouring on parks; or as business with an interest in the sustainable growth of the industry.

Our guests from beyond our borders represent an international community that played a crucial role in making it possible for South Africans to join hands with each other in re-building our country. Our own efforts to preserve our natural heritage and develop it for the benefit of all our citizens will depend also on your support and co-operation.

Whether it is through contributions to international conservation efforts, as investors, or as tourists enjoying our sunny beaches and our rich cultural and natural heritage, you are part of our endeavours to create a better life for all our people.

Long may you continue as partners for conservation and development.

Oceans

Speech at the opening of the Fifth Session of the
Independent World Commission on the Oceans, Cape Town,
11 November 1997.

It is a great honour to have the Independent World Commission on the Oceans hold its Fifth Session here in South Africa.

We are proud to welcome so many distinguished visitors to our shores, in particular your chairman, Dr Mario Soares. His leadership contributed to the efforts of the people of this region to end colonial rule and apartheid in Southern Africa. Today we welcome him as the architect of a body dedicated to ensuring that the world's oceans, once under the sway of seafarers imposing Europe's colonial rule upon the world, should be used for the benefit of all peoples: the South as well as the North; future generations as well those living today.

Your Commission touches on matters of great urgency for us all. It becomes clearer with each passing year that our destiny in the next century is linked with the availability and purity of water.

The Law of the Sea Treaty recognises that the wealth of the oceans is part of the common heritage of humanity. Yet without a regulatory authority or enforceable law, alarming threats to the oceans face us because of such practices as the dumping of toxic wastes, over-fishing or transnational crime like drug trafficking. The efforts to establish a workable legal order for the oceans must not fail.

Democratic South Africa is eager to make its humble contribution to this endeavour. Hence our recent ratification of the United Nations Law of the Sea Treaty. And hence our support for the pledge, at the recent session of the Zone of Peace & Co-operation of the South Atlantic, to co-operate in dealing with drug trafficking in the region.

We share the commitment, from that same session, to address the urgent threats of environmental deterioration and illegal fishing activities that, if left unregulated, could deprive us of a critically important source of protein-rich foods for all peoples.

We need, too, to address the continuing militarisation and nuclea-risation of the seas by a few naval powers. The international effort to demilitarise the oceans and make them nuclear-free, of which the Treaty of Pelindaba is part, must succeed. Action by the commission to highlight this problem, and to offer directions for making the oceans peaceful as well as sustainable, will be of lasting benefit.

The protection of the oceans requires both knowledge and polit-ical effort; it demands an informed public and the involvement of all spheres of civil society in working with and putting pressure on the institutions of government and the private sector.

We look towards the Commission to give leadership in efforts to raise public awareness about the oceans, as well as giving advice and assistance to governments.

We do all know that there are no easy solutions. We have to strike some difficult balances in the use of the oceans.

It is, of course, helpful for developing countries to have preferred access to the resources of the coastal waters in their Exclusive Economic Zones in order to develop their economies and guarantee food security. The activities of distant fishing fleets must not impede the access to fisheries upon which local populations depend for their livelihoods. But individual nations must also respect the rights of others within the framework of international treaties.

We have to balance the exploitation of sources of much-needed energy on the continental shelf with the recreational pleasures of our beaches and seaside resorts.

Such competing interests, and many more, highlight the fact that nowhere is the concept of sustainable development more important than in relation to activities affecting the oceans.

Our policy on the oceans must rest on the solid moral foundation of dedication to the primacy of people and their long-term well-being. We have to be on guard against temptations of short-term benefits and pressures from powerful forces at the expense of the long-term interests of all. We cannot afford to bargain away the birthright of future generations.

South Africa's achievement of democracy has allowed it to work with others for these shared goals. By virtue of geographic gift we find ourselves strategically located between two great bodies of ocean waters, the Indian and the Atlantic, with immense potential for co-operation. This potential is given concrete expression in regio-nal organisations such as the Indian Ocean Rim Association, the

Southern African Development Community and the Valdivia Group of Temperate Southern Hemisphere Countries on the Environment. These bodies all help us to use the oceans of the region in ways that promote sustainable development and great equity.

The oceans of the southern hemisphere provide exciting opportunities for linking Africa, the Indian Subcontinent, Latin America and Australasia in ever closer ties that promise many rewards. Ultimately, this will enhance the contribution of the South, in partnership with the rest of the world, towards a more peaceful and prosperous future for humanity.

Our future as human beings depends upon our intelligent and prudent use of the oceans. And that in turn will depend on the determined efforts of dedicated women and men from all parts of our planet.

Your commission carries a great responsibility on behalf of the international community to summon our energies to this great undertaking. I am confident that with members of such calibre, it is equal to the task. I hope that this meeting in Cape Town provides you with the opportunity to take important steps along this path as you prepare to write your Lisbon Declaration on the Oceans.

May I in conclusion take this opportunity to thank the government of India and the donors from the private sector whose generous financial support has made this session possible.

Planet and Humanity

Address to the International Geographical Union
upon receiving the Planet and Humanity Award, Durban,
4 August 2002.

It is with a special sense of humility that we stand here to receive the Planet and Humanity Award. We are aware of how much correspondence and intervention it took to finally secure our presence here this afternoon. We need to indicate that the effort it entailed to finally conclude the discussions about our participation had nothing to do with an unwillingness to accept this prestigious award, or an attitude of playing 'hard to get', as the colloquial saying goes. We ourselves, as well as our office, long ago indicated to our Minister of Arts, Culture, Science and Technology that we would be extremely honoured to receive the award. The vagaries of leaving official office and having to establish a home as an unemployed pensioner contributed to the uncertainty of not knowing where and in what condition one would be when the event comes around at last. Employed people and those in office can never imagine how chaotically unscheduled the lives are of those who find themselves in the idleness of retirement and pension. We are very happy that out of that chaos, our office could contrive to have us here at this most prestigious event and occasion.

I am a simple country boy, and I remain astounded and overawed by the awards and honours that people, for some incomprehensible reason, decide to bestow upon us. A colleague of mine often asks me how it is that I remember so distinctly people I have met, days on which events have occurred, and the details of occurrences. My consistent and truthful reply to him is the following: I am a simple country boy, unacquainted with all of these marvellous and strange things of the world. Every time I encounter people, things and events, they remain indelibly stuck in my overawed mind.

I left the country in April 1941, and many people may wonder why I call myself still a country boy. But although I left the country in

1941, the country has not left me. This visit will be such an occasion that I will never be able to forget, and it is furthermore an occasion that takes me back to concrete memories of and present-day knowledge about my origins as a country boy.

When I go to the place and area of my birth, so often as I do, the changed geography of the place strikes me with a force that I cannot escape. And that geography is not one of mere landscapes and topography, it is the geography of the people. Where once there were trees and even forests, we now see barrenness. I can no longer walk those distances, but until a few years ago I would traverse the miles of land I knew as a child and young man, and one was saddened at the poverty of the people – poverty lived out in the geography of the place. It is the geography of women and young people, walking miles and miles to find the paltriest pieces of wood for fire to cook mealie meal, and to keep a shelter warm.

The trees and forests were destroyed exactly because our people were so dependent upon them as sources of energy. And in turn, people are today cold and in want of energy for cooking, cleaning and basic comforts because the trees and forests are destroyed. I walked and I saw in the land of my youth, women walking, but walking in poverty and destitution. The streams of my youth that were places of beauty and inspiration were now clogged up and dirty. I saw the descendants of the mothers of our people bowing down to secure with their bare hands the cleanest of the dirty and dangerous water in those streams and pools.

How would they get that water clean enough to use it for household purposes? I often ask them. They would boil it, they reply, if only they had wood or other sources of energy to do so.

I was taking a walk a few days ago in my country village, and I came across a stream which was polluted and where the water was moving very slowly. And then I found three women fetching water. And I asked them: 'What are you going to do with that water?'

They said: 'We are going to use it for domestic purposes. We are going to cook with it, drink it, clean ourselves.'

I said: 'But the water has tadpoles moving around, it has algae, this green stuff that covers stagnant water.' And I said: 'Up there, you see people washing their bodies and their clothes. That water comes here.'

They say: 'That is our life.'

And then I asked this question: 'What do you do with this water before you use it?'

226

They say: 'We do nothing. We use it as it is.'

And then I asked a foolish question. I was born in that area and I am supposed to know the conditions, but for me 27 years of prison life was sufficient to make me forget about the living conditions of my people. I then asked the question: 'Don't you boil it before you use it?'

They all exclaimed simultaneously: 'Boil it with what? Look up, right up to the horizon, there is not a single tree. We have no electricity. With what must we boil it? We use cow dung, and that gives more smoke than heat.'

I felt humiliated because I should never have asked that question, but I did. The alternatives seem clear: use what they have and suffer the consequences. And the consequences were and remain cholera and other environmentally induced diseases.

On 9 May, I was in New York and I met one of the most powerful businessmen in the world, who has supported us in the past, and who built a school and a clinic. And when I formed the Nelson Mandela Foundation, he invited me and my wife to his place in the United States of America. He then gave my wife five million dollars, and gave me ten million. And his partner gave my wife seven-and-a-half million, gave me seven-and-a-half million too [for charity work in South Africa].

Now I said to him: 'I want you to build forty-five schools in the countryside in South Africa, because there are vast areas in the countryside where there is no school, where there is no clinic.'

He said: 'No, I concentrate on health. I propose building so many clinics in your country.'

And we had an argument. I said: 'No, clinics are all right. But in the countryside the situation, the thinking of the people, is that the sangomas are more reliable than the clinics, modern clinics. We therefore want an educated core of people who are going to campaign in the countryside to say, these clinics are much better than sangomas. So that's why I want you to build your forty-five schools.'

We couldn't resolve the argument. He said: 'No, I am prepared to respond, but only in the field of health.'

'Well,' I said, 'let me go back and go to consult.'

I came back home and I consulted the Minister of Education, Professor Kader Asmal. He overruled both of us, and he said: 'No, there are many schools throughout the country without water, without sewerage, where the school children have to go to the veld to relieve themselves. They have nothing to clean themselves so they use grass and then their fingers are soiled. With soiled hands, without washing because there is no water, they go and handle food. Bread, sandwiches, hard mealie pap, meat, fruit, and in that way cholera spreads.' And then Professor Asmal said: 'What we want is the installation of water in all the schools. And it's going to cost a lot of money.'

Well, I have written to the businessman to say this is what the man who knows this field thinks we should do. No schools, no new schools, no new clinics, but water for the schools that are there. Because that will go a long way in preventing cholera.

These conditions I have seen repeated all over our country, our continent, and the developing world.

We accept the honour you bestow upon us today, not as an honour in the usual sense of that word. We accept it as an acknowledgement of our common lack of honour, as humanity, for the manner in which we are destroying our mother planet and the chances for our children to have a sustainable future on earth. Your award is, however, also a source of encouragement to take up and continue the struggle for a world in which we can live in dignity, not only among ourselves as human beings, but also as human beings in relationship with our natural environment.

South Africa will soon be hosting the all-important World Summit for Sustainable Development. As your Union gathers here and now, it is part of the challenge to our country, its leaders and its people to be seen to be in the vanguard of the modern-day struggle to render our environment a liveable and sustainable one for our children. I try to live by the simple precept of making the world one in which there is a better life for all, particularly the poor, marginalised and vulnerable. A devastated geography makes for a devastated people. It renders people vulnerable, and the traditionally vulnerable — women, children, the aged and disabled — will always be bearing the brunt of that suffering.

Let us stand together to make of our world a sustainable source for our future as humanity on this planet.

6
EDUCATION

OPENING THE DOORS OF LEARNING

MAMPHELA RAMPHELE

The most devastating aspect of the legacy of apartheid was the state of education for the majority population. Verwoerd was indeed a genius in designing a system of education that ensured that 'Education must train and teach people in accordance with their opportunities in life ... the Bantu must be guided to serve his own community in all respects. There is no place for him in the European community above the level of certain forms of labour.' He knew that even when those children get to take their place in the world alongside the rest of the human race as equals, they would be hobbled by the legacy of four decades of inferior education. Madiba's tough assignment as the first democratically elected President was to open the doors of learning so that all children can aspire to graze not only on the greener pastures within their sights, but beyond.

But how has the new democracy done in tackling this task? What have been the successes? What have been the failures and lessons learnt? How can South Africans work together to put Verwoerd's ghost finally to rest by freeing the potential of all children to develop to its fullest? Successful collaboration in this regard would be the greatest tribute we could pay to Madiba, the man who continues to work tirelessly to enhance opportunities for all South Africans to become the best they can ever be.

We need to stop and celebrate how well we have done as a society in tackling the legacy of apartheid. We often forget that our democracy is very young by any standard – less than a decade old. It has taken mature democracies in Europe and America centuries to get to where they are today. We need to be gentle on ourselves. There is much that we have accomplished that should serve as a platform for greater strides in the future.

First, bringing order to an education system with 17 departments serving the segregated elements of our divided society was no mean feat. It took courage and lots of tears and sweat to loosen the bureaucratic grip of traditionalists over the Byzantine system that was designed for divide

231

and rule rather than to promote high quality education. Minister Sibusiso Bhengu fought a heroic struggle against that bureaucracy. His gentle manner was sorely tested on many occasions. We now have a single department of education that can set standards and monitor progress in the learning of all of South Africa's children.

Second, curriculum reform. We have scored many successes in this regard. Young people can now learn about the history of their country without the blinkers of ideology. Gender sensitive texts are the order of the day. Outcomes-based education, appropriately modified, has helped focus the learning and teaching process on the purposes of their efforts. We have also introduced some ethics and discussion of values in our education process. This is essential to civic education. Over time this should pay off handsomely in a more informed and engaged citizenry.

Third, we have transformed separate higher education institutions into South African institutions. It was very tempting for many to hang on to the historical divides between institutions set up for black and white members of the population – indeed, between Afrikaans- and English-speaking institutions. Here Madiba led by example. The most important intervention he made was in 1996 when he discouraged attempts by some in government to slash the subsidies of historically white institutions in order to redress the imbalances between them and historically black institutions. No one could argue against the need to provide adequate financing for institutions that were struggling. But the assumption that it could simply be done by robbing Peter to pay Paul could not stand scrutiny. This would have had particularly serious implications given that many of the historically white institutions were admitting black students in larger and larger numbers. How could one punish black students who voted to get educated at the University of the Witwatersrand and reward those who chose to go the University of Venda? How could one justify perpetuating the historical divides founded on such a false premise? What would be the logic? Redressing the legacy of funding inequities needed to be done in a much more sophisticated way to ensure meeting the larger purposes of enhancing quality and access. That process is ongoing.

Madiba also made sure that no institution was ignored by his office. He visited institutions across the spectrum. He did not discriminate between English versus Afrikaans institutions. On the contrary, he bent over backwards to attend occasions in many Afrikaans institutions and spoke Afrikaans with a heavy isiXhosa accent! He did not shy away from reaching out. He visited technikons as much as universities. He was even-handed in signalling support for the teaching, research and learning enterprise.

Unlike many other African heads of state, Madiba truly believes in the power of ideas and the role of intellectuals in national and international development. He did not just engage with the higher education system because he was courting potential voters. He was in the business of signalling the priority he attached to knowledge as an engine of development.

I recall a discussion we had as staff and students from the University of Cape Town in Genadendal during my tenure as Vice Chancellor. He had invited us for dinner and discussion on the challenges facing the young democracy. He was keen to hear from all of us how we saw the role of institutions like UCT in civic life. He was particularly keen to hear from students and younger staff members. He wanted to see greater collaboration between government and higher education institutions. What were the impediments to greater collaboration? Issues raised pointed to the need by both sides to learn to work together within the boundaries of their distinct mandates. But it takes self-confidence and maturity on both sides to venture into such an engagement. One can only hope that his successors will take advantage of the goodwill in the higher education sector and tap its expertise to address the daunting challenges we face.

It is this love for learning that shines through when he talks to students about the need to persevere even if the going gets tough. Using self-deprecating humour about his own failures as a law student at Wits University, he enabled many to see failure as an opportunity to learn rather than as a personal condemnation. He also sent a strong message that it is not where you start but how high you aim that matters for success.

The timing of our transition to democracy could not have been worse. The longer the segregated system of education lasted, the deeper became the problems it left in its wake. Four decades of Bantu Education and poor quality education for other segments of the population has left a fatally flawed human capital base. It is not just the poor physical infrastructure that is not up to the job of educating young people for the twenty-first century, it is particularly the psychological scars of an inferior degrading system that continue to plague our society. The inferiority complex that has been bred in black people runs deep. So too the superiority complex amongst white people. Both are impediments to working together to create opportunities for tapping into the widest pool of talent possible and promoting its development for the common good.

The global environment of the twenty-first century is unforgiving in punishing those not appropriately positioned to take advantage of the competitive knowledge-driven economy. The gap between those economies that are reaping the benefits of investing in high-level skills and the promotion of science and technology and the rest is growing. Take South Korea. It was at the same level of development as Ghana in the 1960s, yet today it has streaked ahead of Ghana due to its deliberate high-level investment in science and technology over four decades. The same applies to the other Asian Tigers. The so-called Asian Miracle can be gleaned from an analysis of the deliberate investments in human capital these countries made over decades from which they are now reaping high rewards. Finland is another example of an economy that transformed itself from a paper and pulp focus of the 1960s to the high technology giant it is as the home of Nokia. South Africa should take lessons from these examples to leapfrog into the twenty-first century.

We must face our failures squarely. First, we have shied away from acknowledging the wounds that inferior education has left in many of our people. We have bought into the lie that equates lack of knowledge with intellectual inferiority. This equation plays into racist stereotypes of black inferiority. Four decades of Bantu Education that fostered an education devoid of mathematics and science focus has simply left many people without the basic scientific knowledge of how the world works. This includes how the human body works. This is not a reflection on the intellect of these people. It is a sign of how far-reaching Verwoerd's social engineering has been. By denying the wound he inflicted on generations of our people we are denying ourselves the opportunity to start the healing process. The longer we nurture this denial, the more we play into racial stereotypes. After more than a decade after apartheid what excuse would we be able to offer for the persistent gaps in knowledge in our society? It would become harder and harder to simply blame apartheid. We have to wrestle Verwoerd's ghost and put it finally to rest.

Second, many of the teachers in the classrooms catering for the poorest children are poorly qualified and unmotivated. It has been estimated that, in 2001, 27 per cent of African school pupils were taught mathematics by teachers with no qualifications in mathematics, 38 per cent were taught science by teachers with no science qualifications. Drastic steps need to be taken to upgrade teacher qualifications. Computer-aided learning makes this task less daunting. But it has to be driven by performance targets that are closely monitored. Unmotivated teachers who came into the profession by default should be encouraged to explore other career opportunities. Our society cannot afford free riders.

The risks are too high. Teacher unions should focus on the future of their society and discourage unprofessional behaviour. Trade unionism cannot just be about protecting short-term member interests. It is in the interest of every teacher to develop professional pride in their work.

Third, we have been too slow to take advantage of information technology to enhance access and quality of education. There are good developments with the recently launched Digital Partnership Programme that aims at putting refurbished computers in every school. It is a partnership between government, the private sector and the education institutions. We dare not fail. Bringing fun into learning has the benefit of motivating both teachers and learners.

Fourth, the high level of illiteracy is an impediment to progress. Illiteracy rates remain unacceptably high in a society that is committed to eliminating this scourge that does not belong in the twenty-first century. Given the high levels of unemployment amongst graduates and other young people, what stops us from creating opportunities for young people to partner with illiterate adults to enhance the quality of our human capital base? There are many young adults who sacrificed their education during the anti-apartheid struggle. Why must they continue to suffer the humiliation of not being able to function in a knowledge-based economy?

Parents who are illiterate are also in a weak position to participate in civic life. They are not empowered to make informed decisions about public policy and to hold public officials accountable for the rights that they are entitled to under the Constitution. Improving the quality of school governance and community life also requires an informed citizenry. The link between education and good health is clear. With the HIV/Aids epidemic that is affecting 4.7 million South Africans we need to ensure that citizens are properly informed about its nature, prevention and treatment opportunities. There is no excuse to continue to deny poor South Africans the right to know.

Finally, South Africa must hold a record with respect to foot dragging around higher education reform. Enough consultation has gone into exploring options for reform. We started with the National Commission on Higher Education in 1995. We then asked the Council on Higher Education to develop proposals for the way forward on some of the proposals made. We have had Minister Kader Asmal's Committee to take this matter further. At the end of the day tough decisions have to be made. Change is not possible without learning to live with compromises one might not like. But again the focus has to be on what is best for the future and less on short-term interests of individual institutions.

Institutions are there to serve the system and the society. Reshaping their purposes accordingly is what matters.

Joining the competitive global knowledge economy requires innovative approaches. We have to set benchmarks for ourselves against appropriate comparators in the rest of the world. There is much we can learn from other developing countries. India, China, Brazil, Mexico, Chile are but a few examples. These countries are developing closer linkages between their higher education systems and their national development strategies. Higher education systems are seen as assets to help strengthen the entire education enterprise to provide a stronger base for human development. Academies of Sciences are becoming active in advising and assisting governments to promote quality science and mathematics curriculum reforms and to institutionalise fun teaching of these key subjects. What stops us from learning from these examples?

The best tribute we can pay Madiba is to learn from his example. He has shown us that with determination nothing is impossible. He has taught us the value of focusing on the ties that bind us together as South Africans rather than the lines that divide us.

His campaign to promote collaboration between the private sector, local communities and the government in tackling social facilities gaps is a celebration of an enduring commitment. He uses his formidable stature for the common good. He has made South Africans of all walks of life join him in affirming the right of the least amongst us to access to facilities that promote and uphold their dignity.

Madiba does what he does out of a deep love for his people. An enduring image shown on television about a year ago was that of Madiba standing in a crowd of school pupils at a ceremony to open a new school facility in some rural area. It was raining and he was wearing his Burberry raincoat. He leaned over to speak to one of the children who must have been ten years old or so. He reached into one of his pockets and gave this child a note – it could have been R10 or R20 – what matters is the gesture. So grandfatherly! Politicians kiss babies to garner votes. Madiba kisses babies and children because he truly cares.

Education Crisis

Selection from an address to a rally in Soweto,
13 February 1990.

Comrades, friends and the people of Soweto at large, I greet you in the name of the heroic struggle of our people to establish justice and freedom for all in our country.

I salute the courage and the heroism of the youth of South Africa, organised under the South African Youth Congress. At this point I wish to pay tribute to comrade Hector Petersen who together with hundreds of young activists was mowed down by apartheid bullets in 1976. We gained inspiration by your courage and conviction during our lonely years on the Island.

Today, my return to Soweto fills my heart with joy. At the same time I also return with a deep sense of sadness. Sadness to learn that you are still suffering under an inhuman system. The housing shortage, the schools crisis, unemployment and the crime rate still remain.

The crisis in education that exists in South Africa demands special attention. The education crisis in black schools is a political crisis. It arises out of the fact that our people have no vote and therefore cannot make the government of the day responsive to their needs. Apartheid education is inferior and a crime against humanity. Education is an area that needs the attention of all our people, students, parents, teachers, workers and all other organised sectors of our community. Let us build disciplined structures, student representative councils, a united national teachers' organisation, parent structures and parent–teacher–student associations and the National Education Crisis Committee.

It has been the policy of the ANC that though the school and the entire education system is a site of struggle, the actual process of learning must take place in the schools. I want to add my voice, therefore, to the call made at the beginning of the year that all students must return to school and learn. We must continue our struggle for People's

Education within the school system and utilise its resources to achieve our goals. I call on the government to build more schools, to train and employ more teachers and to abandon its policy of forcing our children out of the school system by use of various measures such as the age restrictions and their refusal to admit those who fail their classes. We have consistently called for a unitary nonracial education system that develops the potential of all our youth.

Spirit of 16 June

Selection from a speech on the 17th anniversary of
the 1976 Students' Uprising, Orlando Stadium, Soweto,
16 June 1993.

Once again, freedom-loving South Africans and democratic mankind the world over commemorate 16 June, the day on which unarmed student protesters were massacred in Soweto, 17 years ago.

The rally this morning is one amongst many gatherings organised through the length and breadth of this country to mark this occasion.

Looking back at the events of the last 17 years, we can say without fear of being contradicted by history, that 16 June 1976 heralded the beginning of the end of the centuries-old white rule in this country. The response of our people to the massacre of unarmed students was to rally behind their organisations for liberation.

Through its brutal response, the apartheid regime hoped to suppress all resistance to its diabolic schemes. However, the events of 16 June and after injected a new life into the struggle against apartheid rule. Hundreds of thousands of our people committed themselves to the struggle. Thousands took the decision to join the ranks of the liberation movement. The ranks of Umkhonto we Sizwe and the underground presence of the ANC were swelled by the best sons and daughters of our motherland.

Through our sacrifices and struggle we have advanced to a point where a nonracial democracy is no longer simply a craving of those who have been victims of apartheid but a demand of all South Africans. In the struggle for the last 17 years, our youth have made a magnificent contribution, be it in our people's army, Umkhonto we Sizwe, in our underground work or in the mass struggles waged under the banner of the UDF, Cosatu and many other democratic formations.

Many of our youth and students laid down their lives on 16 June 1976. Many thousands more of our people have, in the last 17 years, paid that supreme sacrifice in pursuance of democracy and the liberation of our motherland. How many more should still lose their lives before it can dawn on the powers that be that enough is enough? How many more should still lose their lives or face a bleak future without education and work before it is realised that we need democratic rule now in this country?

As we meet here today to mark this occasion, the causes of the Soweto uprisings continue to be with us. The education crisis has in the last 17 years continued to deepen. A few irresistible questions must be put to the government.

Firstly, what accounts for the fact that 17 years after a crisis of the magnitude of the 1976 protests, the quality and conditions of black education have further deteriorated? Why 17 years later the attitude of government authorities to education grievances and demands is still typical of the behaviour which plunged this whole country into a crisis? Why has the government adopted an uncaring attitude as education increasingly became a preserve of those families who could afford to pay? And why is the government refusing to move away from separate development in education while at the same time continuing to claim that apartheid is dead and buried? There is indeed little doubt that if left unattended the recent demands by teachers and students would have effectively led to a total collapse in what remains of apartheid education. It is not an overstatement to say this problem was fast approaching proportions similar to the 1976 crisis if not worse.

While the government has met some of the demands raised by students and teachers there are still several other important problem areas in education that must be addressed. In this regard, the speedy convening of the proposed National Education Forum is of critical importance. Once more let us hasten to warn the government that this forum can only succeed in its function if it enjoys sovereignty from the incumbent authorities and is unhindered in its duties. If this forum has to make a meaningful contribution to the resolution of the immense problems plaguing the education system in this country, it must necessarily be vested with powers congruent with this job.

Comrades, we wish to see the convening of a representative and empowered forum on education which will bring all stakeholders together so that the task of dismantling the present fragmented education authorities can commence in earnest; a forum that will begin to work towards a centralised education body designed to meet the needs of all. This need can no longer await the resolution of all other problems. The truth is that the longer we take to address this problem, the more we drift towards an abyss of despair and the more is the future of our children undermined. In this regard, the challenge we face as a people is more than the simple restoration of a culture of learning in our nation and to a tradition of valuing academic achievement among our youth.

As we move closer to a democratic order in this country, education becomes one of the most important occupations for the millions in whose name we have prosecuted this struggle. It is therefore no longer enough to criticise. The value of our youth should be measured by their level of discipline and commitment to their studies.

It is with this in mind that we take this opportunity to call upon the students to approach their studies with all seriousness. Education is very crucial for your future as it will enable you to better serve your communities and our country during the difficult period of reconstruction.

Youth Day

Selection from a speech on South Africa Youth Day,
Ladysmith, 16 June 1995.

Today, in various parts of the country, local communities – students, parents and teachers – have come together to clean schools. They are committing themselves to make teaching and learning a fulfilling and rewarding experience.

This is one of the central messages as we mark the second South Africa Youth Day under conditions of democracy. Through these activities, we are driving home a central message: that education is the most important asset that our youth should acquire; and that for the government to succeed in improving education, it must have the support of students, teachers and parents alike. That is what the spirit of *Masakhane* is all about. We can only succeed as a nation if we build one another and build our country together.

For its part, the government is taking the education system out of the crisis it has been in for years. We have abolished apartheid education departments. We have started phasing in free education. We have taken the first steps to improve conditions in technikons, training colleges and universities. Through the Public Works Programme, we aim to impart skills to our youth.

We are doing all this because we know that, without education, our efforts to provide jobs, better health facilities, water, electricity and other needs will not be sustained. The RDP requires youth with skills. But remember: at the end of the day, your progress will depend on how you apply yourselves to your work. The road to a better life demands hard work. It demands discipline, patience and responsibility.

This generation of youth stands at the borderline between the past of oppression and repression, and the future of prosperity, peace and harmony.

On behalf of the government, I wish to say once more, that no one receives the attention of our government more than the youth.

You are our future. In your hands is the key to make South Africa a great country; to make our society a prosperous and caring nation.

. . .

I am confident that South Africa's youth is more than ready to meet the challenge of freedom. Wherever you are – in the schools, in religious institutions, at work, in the army and police services, in sporting bodies, as cultural workers – be assured that we love you all and you shall always remain in our hearts. We are firm in our conviction that you deserve a better future.

Together let us build that bright future. *Masakhane*!

Joint Education Trust

Speech at the Joint Education Trust Annual Review,
Johannesburg, 29 March 1996.

On its establishment, South Africa's first democratic government faced daunting challenges in the education sector. The lack of proper educational facilities and resources along with apartheid's devastating effect on our social fabric had created a crisis in education and training of immense proportions. The problem required a new multi-faceted approach to co-ordinate the efforts of different sectors of society, within an overall framework for fundamental change.

Thus we welcomed the formation of the Joint Education Trust in 1992 as a move inspired by patriotism and vision. Eighteen leading South African companies joined hands with our political parties, labour unions and educational organisations. This dynamic partnership of government, business, NGOs and community organisations has facilitated a practical programme within a common vision for peace, prosperity and opportunity for all South Africans.

The focus of the Joint Education Trust's activities locates it in areas that were most severely neglected historically – such as early childhood development, youth development, vocational training, and adult basic education and training. These are sectors which by working with government and communities can make a marked impact, especially as catalysts for innovation.

By directing these activities towards those who have been pushed to the margins of our society, and by doing so in such a way that they are empowered to change their own conditions, we are making a very special contribution to the building of our nation.

One project that is close to my heart encapsulates the strengths of this partnership. It is the Ekuseni Youth Development Centre, an initiative aimed at piloting a new approach to the rehabilitation of young convicted persons.

Government will provide the running costs once the facility is established. However, without the capital injection of R33.6 million by the Private Sector Initiative, government's capacity to create an environment conducive to learning and rehabilitation would be severely limited.

Construction and upgrading is underway and I have full confidence that the project will replicate itself throughout the country and in so doing revolutionise youth rehabilitation policy.

Multiplied across almost 400 projects, the principles represented by the trust are forging a partnership for development that bodes well for the new patriotism that is shaping our nation. It is a practical and significant investment in our youth and therefore in our future.

Presidential School Project

Speech at the launch of the Warrenton Presidential School Project,
Warrenton, 30 August 1996.

One of the most heartening things about our new South Africa is our people's commitment towards education. This is partly because education is associated with our children who are very close to our hearts. Equally it is because we all understand that education is the key towards realising our vision of a better life for all.

Today's function is all the more important because of the urgent educational needs of this province. With severe shortages of school buildings, close to 60 per cent of the province's young people are not attending school. For many of those at school the learning conditions are so bad that the annual matriculation exemption rate hovers around 10 per cent.

The province is also short of teachers. As we consider recruiting teachers from other overstaffed provinces we have to address the question of their living conditions. In the past many teachers quit local farm schools here because of transportation and accommodation problems. Consequently, most pupils had to make do with unqualified teachers.

Apart from there being too few schools, many African and coloured schools were also built along a clay belt that runs across this province. The movement of this belt has caused most of the buildings to crack and deteriorate. Schools that were built less than 15 years ago are already falling apart. To rub salt into the wound, though communities were promised proper schools in the past, few were built. Hence Ms Tina Joemat [MEC for Education in the Northern Cape] is left with a huge backlog of school buildings.

These things, we do know, are legacies of apartheid. But it is now our responsibility to correct those wrongs. Blaming things on the past does not make them better. Our immediate task is to provide our young ones with proper education.

Nelson Mandela, a 42-year-old political activist, in 1961. *(AP Photo)*

Below: Mandela *(back row, second left)* was the only black student at the Law School at the University of the Witwatersrand in 1946. He and Oliver Tambo opened the first black law practice in Johannesburg in 1952. *(PictureNET Africa)*

The front page of the *Cape Argus* displaying the outcome of the Rivonia Trial and the subsequent sentencing of ANC leaders, including Nelson Mandela, to life imprisonment.
(PictureNET Africa)

Below: Nelson and Winnie Mandela sing *Nkosi Sikelel' iAfrika* at the ANC Welcome Home rally at the FNB stadium near Soweto, shortly after his release from jail.
(Paul Velasco / PictureNET Africa)

Deputy President FW de Klerk
and President Nelson Mandela are
awarded a joint Nobel Peace Prize
in Oslo on 10 December 1993.
(AP Photo)

Right: President Nelson Mandela
signs into law the new South
African Constitution in a special
ceremony held in Sharpeville on
10 December 1996, while the
Chairman of the Constitutional
Assembly, Cyril Ramaphosa,
looks on. *(Adil Bradlow/AP Photo)*

Nelson Mandela takes the oath of office in Pretoria on 10 May 1994 and becomes the first black President of South Africa. *(David Brauchli/AP Photo)*

Nelson Mandela, his new wife Graça Machel and Michael Jackson applaud well-wishers during Mandela's 80th birthday celebrations at Gallagher Estate, Midrand, 19 July 1998. *(Tsheko Kabasia/PictureNET Africa)*

Nelson Mandela joins George Washington and Winston Churchill as recipient of an honorary Doctor of Laws degree at Harvard University on 18 September 1998. *(Elise Amendola/AP Photo)*

President Nelson Mandela casts his ballot in the second all-race elections in Johannesburg, Wednesday 2 June 1999. *(Peter Dejong/AP Photo)*

Nelson Mandela, Harry Oppenheimer and James McNamara sit together as Graça Machel is installed as Chancellor of the University of Cape Town on 6 December 1999. *(Private collection)*

Nelson Mandela strolls through the stone quarry in which he once laboured as an inmate of Robben Island prison, where he spent 27 years incarcerated under the apartheid regime.
(Benny Gool/PictureNET Africa)

Below: As part of the millennium celebrations in Cape Town on 31 December 1999, Mandela lit a candle to symbolise freedom, in the cell in which he was imprisoned for so long on Robben Island.
(Obed Zilwa/AP Photo)

Former presidents Boris Yeltsin of Russia and Nelson Mandela of South Africa kiss during a signing ceremony in Moscow's Kremlin in 1999. Yeltsin and Mandela signed a declaration pledging to boost economic ties in areas such as gold and diamond production and to improve political contacts between Russia and South Africa. *(AP Photo)*

Below: President Mandela delivers his last opening speech to Parliament on 5 February 1999. *(Shaun Harris/PictureNET Africa)*

Mandela's love for children is legendary. Together with Graça Machel, he enjoys a children's party after the launch of the African Cultural Centre. *(Giacomo Piozzi/PictureNET Africa)*

Right: In London to meet the Queen. A radiant Nelson and Graça Machel arrive at Heathrow airport in 1997, en route to Buckingham Palace. *(Tim Ockenden/AP Photo)*

Former president Nelson Mandela raises the hand of the newly sworn-in president Thabo Mbeki at the inauguration ceremony in Pretoria on 16 June 1999. *(Jean-Marc Bouju/AP Photo)*

A bereaved Nelson Mandela arrives for the funeral of his mentor, ANC stalwart Walter Sisulu, in Soweto on 17 May 2003. *(Obed Zilwa/AP Photo)*

Nelson Mandela shakes hands with United Nations Secretary-General Kofi Annan, 15 November 2001, before heading to a Security Council meeting at United Nations headquarters. *(Stephen Chernin/AP Photo)*

Archbishop Desmond Tutu and Nelson Mandela pray together on World Aids Day, 2001.
(Ruvan Boshoff/Sunday Times)

American entertainer Bill Cosby *(right)* and Mandela meet the press in Cape Town, on 20 March 1997. Cosby was to give a charity performance on Robben Island later that day. *(PictureNET Africa)*

Below: Mandela and American talk show host Oprah Winfrey during a sod-turning ceremony at the Oprah Winfrey Academy for Girls at Meyerton, South Africa, on 6 December 2002. The academy is an initiative of the Oprah Winfrey Foundation which plans to provide exemplary education and leadership training for the disadvantaged. *(Themba Hadebe/AP Photo)*

Nelson Mandela and Queen Elizabeth II at a banquet in Cape Town. *(Adil Bradlow/PictureNET Africa)*

With Britain's Prince Charles at an official banquet in November 1997, at Mandela's Cape Town residence during a week-long southern African tour. *(Adil Bradlow/AP Photo)*

President Nelson shows the way to Diana, Princess of Wales during her visit to Cape Town, 17 March 1997. *(PictureNET Africa)*

Posing for photographers with talk show host Larry King *(left)* on 16 May 2000 in New York, after a recording of CNN's 'Larry King Live' show. *(PictureNET Africa)*

Bill Clinton and Nelson Mandela emerge after bilateral discussions to address a news conference at Tuynhuis in 1998. *(Sasa Kralj/AP Photo)*

Tony Blair and Mandela at the Commonwealth Heads of Government summit in Edinburgh. *(Max Nash/AP Photo)*

New York City Mayor Rudolf Giuliani illustrates the collapse of the World Trade Centre towers in the 11 September terrorist attacks, during a tour of Ground Zero on 15 November 2001. *(Ezio Petersen/AP Photo)*

Shaking hands with Microsoft Chairman Bill Gates at a global health discussion, December 1999. Mandela was invited to Seattle by the Bill and Melinda Gates Foundation and spent three days meeting with community leaders. *(Jeff Christensen/AP Photo)*

Nelson Mandela and Pope John Paul II sit side by side at the President's Pretoria residence shortly after the Pontiff's arrival for his first visit to South Africa, 16 September 1995. *(Joao Silva/PictureNET Africa)*

President Mandela meets United States first lady Hillary Rodham Clinton in Cape Town, March 1997.
(PictureNET Africa)

Mandela hugs his old friend and comrade Walter Sisulu on his 90th birthday while Thabo Mbeki looks on.
(Sunday Times)

This is a challenge for all of us – teachers, parents, pupils, the business community and government. The problems must be addressed urgently, and they must be addressed in a joint effort. Government cannot solve the problems on its own.

It is with this in mind that I would like to extend our heartfelt gratitude to Shell South Africa for its magnificent contribution to this project. When last year I approached the chairman of this company, Mr John Drake, for assistance with one of the Presidential Lead Projects of the RDP, he readily agreed. He did so because Shell shared the government's ideals of the Reconstruction and Development Programme.

In true RDP spirit, Shell didn't regard the project as its own, but placed it in the hands of a school building association comprising different stakeholders. Development is a joint responsibility. What we are witnessing today is the success of the entire community. The Warrenton community, Shell and the Northern Cape Province have provided a model of the kind of partnership that is rebuilding South Africa.

That spirit will stand us in good stead as we enter a truly exciting period for education in our country. The South African Schools Bill which is now before Parliament has widespread support. It will establish for the first time in our history the framework for a single, national public school system. When it is passed, this bill will usher in changes for the benefit of all school communities. We shall all be able to work together to realise our ideal of a nonracial, nonsexist and fair system of schooling.

The school we are launching today will become a part of that new system of schooling. Let us congratulate the children who will be occupying the school and those who will be following them as the second and third phases of the project are completed.

And let me say to the children: the best and only way to show your gratitude to your parents and teachers, to Shell South Africa and to the government, is for you to study hard and excel. Your performance in the new school must be clearly better than your previous records at the hostel. Make the best of this opportunity.

Our nation needs you. Our future depends on the education you will receive here and what you make of it. Good luck.

It is now my privilege to unveil the plaque which will commemorate the official opening of the launch of the Rolihlahla Primary School.

National Campaign for Learning and Teaching

Address at the launch of the National Campaign
for Learning and Teaching, Soweto,
20 February 1997.

Our country is well endowed with natural resources. But our most valued treasure is our people, especially the youth. It is our human resources that enable us to reap the benefits of all our other assets.

Our fight against poverty, crime, and all the maladies of our society requires us to invest in the development of our human resources. The immense potential of our people must be turned into the specific skills and capacities needed for the reconstruction and development.

At the forefront of this effort is education and training. As government we are obliged to make it possible for everyone to develop their potential to the full; to provide opportunities for everyone to learn and nurture their talents. We have a duty to create a conducive environment, and to provide the necessary tools and the mechanisms to support people in their endeavours to better themselves.

In our first two-and-a-half years of democracy we have laid a solid foundation on which to build. Out of the previously separate education departments has been created a single national department. Our once-segregated schools are now open to all. The Schools Act creates the framework for a single national schooling system providing quality education to all our children. The National Qualifications Framework will allow everyone to progress through the education and training system without obstacles. There are programmes to ensure that millions of our young children are not hungry in school, and to renovate old schools and to build new ones.

Today's campaign launch is a challenge to the nation to combine all its forces in building on that foundation. The spirit of the new patriotism that is shaping the new South Africa must make itself felt in the proud resurgence of a culture of learning and teaching.

The potential to be reclaimed is immense. The millions of our adults who never had the chance to learn to read and write; the hundreds of thousands of our youth displaced from education without any meaningful skills; the nation's workers who must ensure that our country embraces the world's new technologies – we can tap this power to build a better life by using every opportunity to ensure that our nation learns.

Our message to teachers on this occasion is this: Let your watchword be unqualified commitment to the interests of those whose education has been entrusted to you. Amongst other things, this means meticulous punctuality; thorough preparation for every lesson; dedication to ensuring that every student learns something from each lesson. It involves keeping abreast of developments in your subject areas and working co-operatively with both colleagues and management to ensure that our schools truly educate the nation. In short it means upholding the highest standards so that dignity is fully restored to the teaching profession.

On your shoulders lies an enormous national responsibility, especially for teachers in historically black schools. All our students should be able to compete with their counterparts, not only in South Africa, but in the rest of the world. While affirmative action helps us redress the neglect of the past, it will not be a permanent feature of our society. If you fail our children you fail our country.

To students this campaign is a call to make learning your main, if not your only, priority. For you too, punctuality, attendance and diligence in study must be the order of the day. Active participation in lessons and inquisitive probing to aid your own learning; respect for fellow students and for teachers; and a resolve never to use drugs or take dangerous weapons to school – all these, and many more, make up the fabric of the culture of learning.

South Africans have made tremendous sacrifices, and many have given their lives, to ensure that you have access to the best education your country can afford. Redeem their sacrifice by acting to ensure that effective learning occurs in our schools. Youth and students were in the forefront of the struggle for freedom. By educating yourselves today you act as leaders of reconstruction and development.

To parents we say today that taking an interest in your children's education is as important as their own efforts and those of teachers. You can help educate the nation by participating in the activities of schools and protecting them from vandals; by supporting them, by working with teachers and students; and by constant guidance which ensures that your children always attend school and do their school work.

I am mindful of the untenable conditions in some of our schools, and the shortage of classrooms and other facilities. The government has committed itself to improve these conditions within a short space of time.

There is therefore also a message today to government in all its spheres, to elected representatives and public servants. Though we can take pride in what has so far been achieved, it is only a start. We must make sure that we effectively and efficiently implement the policies that have been adopted; that the different spheres of government co-operate in the interests of citizens; and that where problems do occur we acknowledge them and deal with them.

In the same way that we waged war against apartheid education, government and communities should together combat those factors which militate against effective learning and teaching. Amongst other things, this means firm action against those students and teachers whose conduct undermines the efforts of the dedicated and committed majority.

We can no longer afford to sit by while some schools are turned into havens of drug abuse, violence or vandalising of valuable property. We can no longer sit and watch while any of our country's children are held back in the mire of ignorance and lack of skills which apartheid decreed should be their lot.

We need a South Africa that prides itself on being a learning nation. I am therefore honoured to now formally launch this National Campaign for Learning and Teaching.

May the campaign inspire all South Africans, in the spirit of the new patriotism and in the spirit of *Masakhane*, to make our institutions of learning hives of activity that enrich and build our nation and its people.

Let us join hands, and work to make our schools work for us.

Education Awards

Speech at the Education Africa, Presidential,
and Premier Education Awards, Pretoria,
22 November 1997.

It is a great honour to join you in celebrating the contribution which our award winners have made to our people's quality of life. This ceremony highlights the role of education in realising our goals as a nation.

At the outset I should confess my delight at the impact these awards are beginning to make in the educational fraternity. For the first time in three years, there is a marked increase in the number of entries.

These entries and the unprecedented number of guests gracing this ceremony, from South Africa and further afield, tell us that more people are joining hands in efforts to improve the quality of education, and to make it accessible to the majority of South Africans. They show that we are all beginning to recognise in the most practical way that education is central to the success of a whole range of other human endeavours.

Our own reconstruction and development effort, the renaissance of the entire continent and our successful interaction in the global village depend largely on the progress we make in educating our populations.

In South Africa the challenges are as stark as they are real. The recently compiled School Register of Needs provides us with hard and cold facts. The majority of our children, especially in rural provinces, still either do not have access to basic education or depend on institutions that lack the teaching media and equipment needed for effective learning and teaching.

Such conditions continue to hinder the progress of the Campaign for Effective Learning and Teaching that we launched earlier this year. This campaign and the school building programme are vital elements in government's progress in dealing with the legacy of unequal distribution of resources.

251

Of course, try as it might, government on its own cannot achieve our nation's educational goals. We need to harness the energies and resources of the whole nation. It is precisely for this reason that we cannot repeat too often our appreciation of the role of business, non-governmental organisations and community organisations in the transformation of education. Very encouraging too is the increasing participation of parents and students in the management of our schools and tertiary institutions.

Government will continue to create the statutory framework to allow all stakeholders to participate meaningfully in policy formulation and in the education of our nation.

The power of education extends beyond the development of skills we need for economic success. It can contribute to nation building and reconciliation. Our previous system emphasised the physical and other differences of South Africans with devastating effects. We are steadily but surely introducing education that enables our children to exploit their similarities and common goals, while appreciating the strength in their diversity. We need to educate our young people to become adults who cherish the values of respect for women and children proclaimed in the National Men's March today. In short, we need a system, as envisaged by Curriculum 2005, that is geared to the realities of our country and the ideals of our people.

All efforts to improve our people's access to education are noble. Today we honour a few of the most outstanding examples. We give deserved recognition to men and women who have made not only their communities, but the whole nation proud; patriots whose selfless sacrifices have impacted positively on the lives of many; unsung heroes and heroines who sought neither glory nor recognition.

We present these awards as a pledge of permanent partnership. In honouring you tonight, we join thousands of workers who can now read and write thanks to your efforts; children who now have access to early childhood education facilities; and those whose special educational needs have been satisfied.

It is our fervent hope that these awards, and your educational projects, will inspire many more South Africans to contribute to this critical aspect of nation building.

Let us join hands, as government, business, NGOs and communities. Let us work together to educate our nation!

The Rock of Our Future

Speech at the dedication of Qunu and Nkalane Schools,
Qunu, 3 June 1995.

To be at one's first school of 70 years ago is a humbling experience. To share in the renewal of its fabric is an inspiring one.

Our children are the rock on which our future will be built, our greatest asset as a nation. They will be the leaders of our country, the creators of our national wealth, those who care for and protect our people. But if they are to take on this great responsibility, the rich potential in every child must be developed into the skills and the knowledge that our society needs. Education is the key to that process. It is also a door which opens from every village and city onto our larger society and indeed onto the whole world.

That lesson is spelt out with shocking clarity in the legacy of apartheid. This system also gained its notoriety for marginalising the majority of children as far as educational resources are concerned. Poverty, unemployment and illiteracy combine with lack of education to draw the same broad lines through our society as the divisions created by apartheid.

And this Eastern Cape Province is amongst the worst affected. The provincial government is busy renovating schools and even renting accommodation, in order to provide basic facilities for tens of thousands more children. But this is only the start of a long journey.

The cost to our whole society of these discriminatory policies is now clear for all to see. The lack of skills in our economy is holding the nation back from sustained economic growth. Education, therefore, stands amongst the highest priorities for our country. It needs to be at the forefront as the emphasis in government shifts from planning to visible change.

For all these reasons the upgrading and extension of the Nkalane and Qunu schools is something which we welcome as a contribution to the lives of the two communities. But more than that, it has national importance. The project whose completion we are marking today provides an example of the spirit of partnership which must be our guiding principle. The government has taken important steps to define and start phasing in an education policy which meets the needs of our people and our times. This can only succeed in co-operation with communities, the private sector and the donor community. *Masakhane!* Let us build each other and build together.

Success requires that communities should play their part in fostering an appreciation of the importance of education amongst their young people and in caring for the education facilities which they have. It demands that teachers dedicate themselves to the solemn responsibility that society has placed upon them of nurturing the potential in our young people. It requires that young people themselves make the most of the opportunity which education provides to become builders of our new society. To achieve this, they must apply themselves purposefully to their studies.

On the part of the private sector it means engaging its substantial capacity to contribute to the reconstruction of the education system. This includes steps to facilitate the enhancement of the skills of employees through training programmes, as well as making an input into the development of technical training generally. But the private sector can also add directly to the resources available for meeting the most fundamental need of providing classrooms for our children.

I would like to express my heartfelt appreciation to Dr Venter, Chairman of Altron, for the opportunity to share in the regeneration of these schools. You have set others who have the capacity to do so, a model of practical contribution to our national goal of building a better life for all.

I am deeply honoured to join with you in dedicating the renewed and enhanced facilities of this Junior Secondary School to the community of Qunu and its children.

Leaders of Tomorrow

Speech at the opening of Dalindyebo Senior Secondary School,
Qunu, 14 August 1998.

I feel honoured and deeply touched to be part of this remarkable event. The opening of this school is a matter that is close to my heart because children and youth education are at the top of the government's list of priorities. We can only make a better life for all South Africans if our young people get the skills and the training that we need to make our economy grow and make our democracy work. That is why our new education policy makes general education compulsory for all children.

We must therefore ensure that all our children have access to decent and formal education. If our education system is to produce the capable, skilled and empowered people who can turn South Africa into the just and prosperous nation of our dreams, we must overcome the years of neglect which left most of our children without proper facilities for their education.

I am therefore proud to officiate at the opening of the Dalindyebo Senior Secondary School. It is well named after a great leader of the Thembus, King Dalindyebo, whose grandson, King Sabata Dalindyebo, showed himself a true leader of his people by his concern for their education.

Partnership between government, the private sector and communities is critical in the development of our country. No one sector on its own, least of all government, can succeed in ensuring that we do improve the quality of life of our people. BP South Africa – and the local BP dealers in Umtata who have also contributed – have set a shining example of such partnership. I thank them for having responded to my request to help renovate the school. The funds spent to renovate and build boarding facilities for the Dalindyebo school are an investment in the community of Qunu and in the South African nation as whole. You should know that this school forms part of BP's larger Social Investment Projects which include a number of other refurbishments of schools.

You should also know that BP is not alone in our private sector, in joining hands with government and communities. Across our land there are clinics and schools which communities now have thanks to such projects. This is part of the investment back into our communities, especially those which are poor, which is needed to eradicate the legacy of apartheid and build the future of our country. It is also an inspiring demonstration of what reconciliation must mean in practice, and it gives one great hope for the future.

Amongst the steps government has taken to upgrade our education system, the Culture of Learning, Teaching and Services campaign is one of the most important. I urge teachers and learners to commit themselves to education and to ensure discipline in schools.

You must make your schools work for you. Parents and communities must participate in the education of their children through school governing bodies. Our traditional leaders also have a role to play. Such a partnership will help eradicate the problem of crime and violence in schools. It will help turn our children into the engineers and scientists, the teachers and lawyers, and the skilled workers and business leaders our country needs.

Once again, I thank BP for having done such a good job in helping to give Qunu a school it can be proud of. I also congratulate the school governing body, the principal and the entire school, as well as the Qunu community, on their upgraded school. Please cherish and treasure it, because it belongs to you. Make good use of it. We expect to have leaders of tomorrow out of this school.

Universities

Speech on receiving honorary degreees from the Universities of Bristol,
Cambridge, De Montfort, Glasgow Caledonian, London, Nottingham,
Oxford, and Warwick, Buckingham Palace, London,
10 July 1996.

Universities, it is well known, do not lightly confer honorary degrees
and thereby commit their own status and esteem. It is therefore a
singular privilege and pleasure for me to be in this illustrious company
on this memorable occasion, and to have such accolades bestowed
on me.

I do understand, however, that it is not individual achievements
which are being honoured. Rather it is the remarkable way in which
South Africans have turned from division and conflict to reconciliation and the peaceful pursuit of a better life. In this spirit, and on
their behalf, I express my gratitude for these magnanimous awards
and accept them with deepest humility.

The honour you do us as a nation is magnified by the fact that
these high honours express a warmth and commitment which is also
practical. The support which we received from the universities of
Britain during our struggle was an inspiration to us. I am aware too
that each and every university represented here is involved with
South Africa in a positive and constructive fashion.

Had time allowed, it would have been my wish to visit personally
each of the universities which has chosen to honour me in this manner today. It would have been a special privilege to cross the length
and breadth of your country and discuss with each institution what
you are doing – to go from Glasgow Caledonian in the north to
London; from Bristol in the west across to Cambridge. At the universities of Warwick, Oxford, Nottingham and De Montfort we could
have shared ideas on how the South African government could best
facilitate co-operation with respect to tertiary education. Unfortunately the vagaries of fate have dictated otherwise, and I am therefore not at liberty to fulfil my wish.

Empathy, support and assistance from the tertiary sector in Britain have been forthcoming over the past two years to a staggering degree. For this I wish from the bottom of my heart to voice my gratitude and that of all those for whom I speak today. South Africans have been overwhelmed by your goodwill, and we intend to respond to the many kind offers in a fitting fashion.

We appreciate in particular the assistance rendered by way of generous scholarship and funding programmes. I am made to understand that within our legislatures and in our organs of state, including the delegation present here today, there are many who are benefiting from these programmes, upgrading their skills as they contribute practically to transformation.

Apartheid imposed disastrous restrictions on the pool of skills available to our nation. This has not only been politically unjust, but it has had a massive impact on the possibilities for expanding and modernising our economy. Massive investment in people, in particular through education and training, is therefore one of the priorities we have set ourselves. Your programmes not only enlarge the body of trained people, but they also provide a channel for the infusion of new knowledge into South African society.

We are busy transforming our higher education system from one that was oriented towards serving the interests of a small and privileged minority to one that is geared to helping meet the needs of all South Africans. As we do so we are faced with many choices and decisions.

One of these challenges is to find the right balance between research and teaching activities aimed at producing useful results in the short-term and those which may not produce applications for decades. We have to develop South Africa's capacity to innovate and draw effectively from the whole world's scientific and intellectual activities. But our universities must also make a decisive impact in addressing the nation's basic needs. We must ensure that the paradigm of teaching and learning accords with the country's social conditions and position in the world arena.

In this regard we have a great deal to learn from your own experience. And the honour you have bestowed on me, and through me, to the people of South Africa, is an injunction for us to drink from the well of your experience and that of others, at the same time as we make our own humble contribution to the repository of world academic excellence. I am confident that we have a solid foundation on which to build, in the universities of our two countries and in our shared aspirations and values.

The honour, from so many distinguished centres of thought and wisdom, is an act that has overwhelmed me. A single honorary degree from any one of the institutions here would be a humbling experience. My gratitude and appreciation defy words.

In conclusion, may I join you in thanking our hosts, Their Royal Highnesses, for so graciously accommodating our capricious needs.

Fort Hare

Selection from an address on receiving an Honorary LLD degree
at the University of Fort Hare, Alice,
9 May 1992.

It is a great honour that this university bestows on me and through
me on the African National Congress and all democratic organisations dedicated to the creation of peace.

This happens at a time of transformation, a time of change or
prospective change in South Africa as a whole as well as in this university. We all have a responsibility, wherever we are, to contribute to
the successful outcome of this process in the institutions where we
are as well as in the country as a whole.

. . .

It is in this context that the transformation of Fort Hare attains its
full significance. The transformation of your university into a truly
people's university is itself a contribution to building the new South
African nation. It is also a return to the motivating factors for the
establishment of Fort Hare.

The movement for the founding of an African institution of high-
er learning began in 1902 with famous leaders of the South African
Native Congress as prime initiators – leaders of the calibre of Dr
Walter Benson Rubusana and Alan Kirkland Soga, editor of *Izwi
Labantu* newspaper. The initiative also involved prominent mission-
aries such as Dr Henderson of Lovedale.

Virtually every famous leader of the period became involved –
Tengo Jabavu, Joel Goronyana, Thomas Mapikela, Rueben Twala, Sol
Plaatje, Pixley Seme, Enoch Mamba, John Alfred Sishuba, Martin
Luthuli, Abner Mtimkulu – leaders of the newly formed ANC.

Through their combined efforts the University College of Fort
Hare was established in 1916. This response to the absence of a higher educational institution for Africans was a parallel development to
the exclusion of Africans from the Union of South Africa and the
political unification of Africans through the formation of the ANC.

This parallel development is being continued today, as Fort Hare marches forward as one of the institutions that will play a significant role in building a democratic education system that serves all the people of South Africa.

Let me say a little more about Fort Hare and the community. The people who are graduating today and the people who are still studying represent a very privileged sector of our community. You have acquired skills that can either be used purely to enrich yourselves, benefit yourselves, or they can be put at the service of our community.

I want to appeal to you to acknowledge that the community has a claim on your skills. I want to appeal to you to use those skills to help empower our people. Democracy is not fully established with a democratic government. That is just one step, albeit a crucial one.

One of the lessons of our times is that a transfer of power to a democratic organisation does not mean that ordinary people necessarily have the opportunity to exercise their democratic rights. One of the things that we have learnt is the necessity to encourage popular organs of civil society, that is institutions outside of the state that contribute to the overall democratic process, and the social and economic development of all our peoples.

Fort Hare is itself such a popular institution of civil society. The products of this university can play a crucial role in the professions and in society in general in developing popular organs in every sphere of existence. We cannot build a strong, vibrant, democratic culture merely from a government department. We need strong cultural organisations of the communities.

We cannot build a strong and democratic economy from a ministry in government buildings. It needs the participation of the trade unions and all other organs representing people in their various spheres of interests.

The list is endless but the realisation of this type of democracy is not easy. Our people have not only been denied the vote but have been disempowered in numerous other ways. By virtue of your education you have some of the skills that can empower these people, you have in your hands what a future government cannot do. I urge you not to fail our people. I urge you to act as true patriots and build our new nation, reach our people wherever they are and help them play a part in their own future.

In a more specifically educational manner, Fort Hare can make a very significant contribution to future developments in this country. Much of the research conducted in South African universities is not directed to solving the problems that are most pressing. The most serious problems are those relating to the social and economic disabilities of our people. We do not always have the data on which to develop adequate policies. Researchers can obtain this. We do not always know of all the alternative ways of tackling problems and those least interested in the betterment of our people have long researched these questions. Fort Hare can help us develop answers that truly address the questions most pressing to our people.

. . .

We want to move swiftly to an environment where Fort Hare can truly thrive. But that is a process. Democracy is a process and democracy in a university is a process that we will have to work at every day. This is not the time for complacency. This is the time for hard thinking about difficult problems and clear and decisive action. I am confident that this university and the men and women who graduate today can be relied on to do what the community expects of them.

University Transformation

Speech at the installation of Dr Mamphela Ramphele as
Vice-Chancellor of the University of Cape Town, Cape Town,
11 October 1996.

It is a privilege to share in this historic event in the life of a great institution. The installation of a university vice-chancellor is always an occasion of great moment. At an institution like the University of Cape
Town – our oldest university and a world-renowned centre of learning
and science – it evokes both the enduring character of the university
and the constant renewal of scholarship and scientific inquiry.

This evening's ceremony has additional significance. Dr Mamphela
Ramphele is a South African of exceptional talent, ability and stature.
With such a person at its helm, the University of Cape Town can face
the future with confidence. The nation can rest assured that one of its
foremost institutions of higher learning will continue to prosper and
serve with excellence as we enter the new century.

However, we would not want to hide the special satisfaction
caused by the fact that the new vice-chancellor at our premier university is a woman and black. South Africans tonight joyously celebrate this affirmation of the quality of our diversity and the strength
of our unity.

On a personal note: the pride we all share is amplified for me by
my special personal relationship with your new vice-chancellor.
Mamphela is a daughter and friend to me, and you will understand
my special pride and joy.

Dr Ramphele's assumption of this high and prestigious office
writes a significant chapter in our society's transformation, and so it
may be appropriate to reflect on the important concept of transformation.

Our political transition paved the way for the still greater task of
transforming social institutions in order to build the new society of
which we speak and dream. Some of our universities took the lead
in articulating the concept of institutional transformation, and are

seeking to give it content. So it is not surprising that university transformation remains such a visible and topical aspect of our changing society.

Institutional transformation requires the changing of structures. What we celebrate tonight does, however, remind us that the quality of an institution and the efficacy of change go beyond structure and form. The quality and calibre of the people who are involved and who give leadership are decisive for how well and how excellently the transformed institution is equipped to serve its social purpose.

Universities are essential in the preparation of highly skilled leadership throughout society. Our country desperately needs its universities to perform that function. Our development depends on our having skilled people in leadership positions. Selfish and self-serving individualism is not what we are seeking to promote; but we also cannot evade individual responsibility for achieving excellence. We do know that many South Africans battle against great odds; that many have to study, teach and research under conditions that are far from ideal. Transformation, however, also includes making the most of the limited opportunities available. It can never mean suspending the striving for quality and excellence until ideal conditions are achieved.

Dr Ramphele and others like her are powerful role models in this regard. They exemplify struggle against adversity combined with personal responsibility for self-development. Tonight we can savour the fruits of that individual responsibility.

One sometimes gets the impression that the nation-wide debate and struggle over university transformation concentrate too much on governance and governance structures.

Both the values we hold dear and the effective functioning of institutions require that all sectors of the university should be properly represented in structures taking decisions that affect them.

We do, however, also need to hear with equal urgency the debates on other aspects of change. At the heart of efforts to transform universities are issues of curriculum. The nation would be heartened to see teachers and students come together to explore such questions as: how we ensure quality education while broadening access in a situation of limited resources; how we harness modern communications and information technology in higher education; what is to be done to ensure an accelerated output of quality graduates in science and technology; how universities can contribute to general literacy and numeracy in our country; what are the research tasks of the universities given the changed national needs and priorities.

The University of Cape Town has long occupied a leadership position in science and higher education. And it has been well served by its leaders. The impact of its immediate past vice-chancellor, Dr Stuart Saunders, on higher education will be felt far into the future. It is a tribute to the institution that it could select from within its own ranks a successor of equal excellence.

The process of selection also showed the university in an exemplary light. The process – which we all could follow – was inclusive and respectful of the rights of all its constituent parts; it was, moreover, marked by an integrity and dignity which did the institution proud. Universities are social communities and collegial associations but they are also, and essentially so, institutions of specialised expertise. By finding a balance between inclusive consultation and participation on the one hand, and the maintenance of respect for specialised competencies on the other, such an institution safeguards its integrity and retains the confidence of the larger public.

Allow me to conclude by extending our congratulations and warmest best wishes to Dr Ramphele on this marvellous achievement. She must know how proud we all are. We wish her well, confident that she will continue to serve with the excellence to which we have become accustomed.

And we wish the University of Cape Town well. May it grow from strength to strength. May it continue to give leadership and to provide the leaders our country needs for the next century.

Africans and Afrikaans

Address on the occasion of his acceptance of an Honorary Doctorate
of Philosophy from the University of Stellenbosch, Stellenbosch,
25 October 1996.

As the Rector has noted in his address of commendation, quite a few
honorary awards have been bestowed upon me by reason of my
present and previous offices. Understandably, therefore, people may
suspect that speaking some words of appreciation on such occasions
tends in the course of time to become a mere gesture of courtesy. I
want to assure you, however, that I am deeply touched every time,
not merely by the honour done to me, but above all by the warm
affection towards me that such acts speak of so eloquently. Tonight is
no exception; and I thank you.

It would be disingenuous of me to pretend that I was not deeply
aware of the special historical symbolism of this occasion. From the
ranks of this university's alumni came each of the prime ministers
who governed white-dominated South Africa in the era between the
two Bothas. This university was the leading intellectual home of
Afrikaner nationalism. It was from this university that apartheid
received a great deal of its theoretical justification.

This institution has left its unmistakable imprint on our country's
troubled history – a history whose scars still show.

Tonight you are receiving me with hospitality and warmth as the
head of state of a democratic South Africa. Tonight this one-time
cradle of Afrikaner nationalism and white domination is honouring
a person who for decades was looked upon as an arch-enemy of that
same order. Tonight an institution that sought to give theoretical justification to racial separation and discrimination is conferring an
honorary degree on someone who has spent very nearly a lifetime
fighting for nonracism.

This occasion says much more about South Africa and South
Africans than about the individual to whom the degree is being
awarded. This occasion is testimony to the fact that we South

266

Africans have struck out on the road of building a joint future, that we are in the process of breaking down the divisive bulwarks of the past and building up a new nation – united in all its rich diversity. And for that I thank you from the bottom of my heart.

On this road of change and transformation an enormous amount remains to be done – in the country in general and certainly also here at the University of Stellenbosch in particular. What the situation requires of us, on the one hand, is to give due recognition for such changes as have taken place; on the other hand, it also requires us to acknowledge that both the rate and the scope of change still leave quite a lot to be desired.

With your leave I am going to misuse a little this occasion of the conferment of an honorary degree by saying a few words about some aspects of the matter.

Last week saw an event of the greatest significance that originated right here in Stellenbosch. This was when the Stellenbosch Presbytery of the Dutch Reformed Church confessed before the Truth and Reconciliation Commission a collective share in the systematic injustice of our past. Neither the message this conveyed, nor the impact this will make on the process of reconciliation, is to be underestimated.

The perception which many have that the Afrikaner community is the unilateral recipient in the process of reconciliation will be powerfully countered by acts such as that of the Stellenbosch Presbytery. One cannot but wish that Afrikaners over a wider front will engage in reconciliatory dialogue with fellow South Africans in the same way.

No one is asking for Afrikaners to be reviled; nor does anyone desire Afrikaners to humiliate themselves collectively in public. What no one can deny, however, is that apartheid committed a terrible injustice to this country and its inhabitants, and that this was something in which Afrikaners had a central and substantial part.

The Stellenbosch Presbytery, in doing what it did, demonstrated greatness of spirit – and it did so, not acting in a state of humiliation, but acting in a spirit of humility! It is this kind of meekness and generosity of spirit which makes us receptive to our common humanity, and enables us to clasp hands each with the other and face the future together, aware of our fallibility and intent therefore on avoiding any repetition of such injustice.

What the Stellenbosch Presbytery did reminds us also of a narrow but significant current in the history of the Afrikaners and of this university which is often quite lost sight of and, indeed, passed over in silence. After all, is it not from this same University of Stellenbosch that there arose courageous voices of warning against and opposition to the doctrine of apartheid? Voices such as those of a BB Keet, a Ben Marais, a Johan Degenaar, an André Hugo, an André du Toit, and others as well? In the affirmation of that current within your history lies the greatest hope, not only for yourselves, but for the whole of South Africa.

It is also in that kind of Afrikaans voice – a voice that is open to the rest of society, a voice that reaches out to the rest of society – that the case for Afrikaans's role and place as a scholarly and scientific medium can be most rewardingly presented.

My position on and attitude to Afrikaans have been expressed so often that surely there is no need to repeat them here. In common with all languages, no doubt, Afrikaans has to allot the credit or blame for its particular history of growth to the power relations in society. For all that, the fact of the matter is that Afrikaans is highly developed as a scholarly and scientific language. And as the Commission for Higher Education also mentions in its report: Afrikaans as a language of scholarship and science is a national resource.

The real issue therefore is not the extermination or preservation of Afrikaans as an academic medium. Rather, the question is this: amongst ourselves, how are we to negotiate a dispensation for the South African university system that meets the following three criteria? Firstly, that a milieu should be created and maintained for Afrikaans to continue growing as a language of scholarship and science. At the same time, that non-speakers of Afrikaans should not be unjustly deprived of access within the system. And moreover, that the use and development of no single language medium should – either intentionally or unintentionally – be made the basis for the furtherance of racial, ethnic or narrowly cultural separation.

Let me put it to you simply and bluntly: within a system comprising more than 20 universities, surely it must be possible to reach an accommodation to the effect that there will be at least one university whose main tasks will include that of seeing to the sustained development of Afrikaans as an academic medium.

How that institution is to accommodate languages other than Afrikaans is one of the details that can be settled through a process of negotiation. If we could manage to resolve the major political conflicts through negotiation, then surely the country's men and women of learning need not view a matter of this nature as posing some insuperable obstacle.

If those who care for Afrikaans conducted this dialogue in the spirit of openness and with the generosity of mind which we spoke of earlier, the case for Afrikaans would be that much stronger. By the same token, the whole situation would become that much easier for those of us who are willing to try and oblige the advocates of Afrikaans.

I would like to close with a quotation from a poem by Breyten Breytenbach in which he uses the word 'Afrikaans' in the broad sense of 'characteristic of Africa'. The poem, in the form of a letter to Afrikanerdom, dates from the dark years of apartheid:

> net die hoop dan, barse broer,
> dat jy wat te klein was om op te neem
> tog iewers in ons groot land nog opneembaar is.
> my broer, my dor, verlate broer:
> iets wens dat mens weer in jou groei,
> dat alles groots, Afrikaans gaan word
> en jy ook in mensbruin mense bloei.
>
> [Just hoping then, harsh brother,
> that you who've been too small to be absorbed
> yet are absorbable still somewhere in our vast land.
> My brother, my arid and forsaken brother,
> a wish: for human nature to grow back in you,
> for everything to come out grand and African,
> for you to flower in humanly brown humans, too.]

In the time since the writing of this Breytenbach poem, there has been many a change in South Africa. It still remains my wish, though, that we will all be absorbed together in this vast land. And that Afrikaans institutions and Afrikaans people will never again be surly and standoffish and apart but, rather, that they will be an interwoven part of what we are newly creating.

It is in the knowledge that this University has a large part to play in making that wish come true, that I accept the honour of being made an alumnus of the University of Stellenbosch.

Education for a Winning Nation

Speech at the Damelin Business College, Johannesburg,
13 February 1997.

It is indeed an honour to have been invited to address this graduation ceremony. Due to your hard work I have the privilege of sharing the joy of your deserved success and the warm glow of your achievements.

Some of you may have decided to study to enhance your skills in your various spheres of work; others to equip yourselves to seek jobs. Whatever the reasons, in doing so you have decided to contribute to our country's prosperity. The more effective and productive you become at work, and the more you become employable through education, the more the country benefits.

In this era of stiff international competition we have to become productive and competitive if we are to prosper as a nation. An expanding pool of skilled labour in our country will also attract both domestic and foreign investment.

Being with you tonight is a way of reaffirming government's commitment to education. That commitment is based on the knowledge that without human resource development, there can be no serious reconstruction and development of South Africa.

Our youth is our future. Whether our country will rise from the ashes of apartheid to become one of the world's success stories will to a large extent depend on what we invest in educating and training our youth.

Government has prioritised education. We have invested millions of rands in the past two-and-a-half years: building, renovating and extending schools; promoting a culture of learning and teaching; providing financial aid for needy students; establishing youth colleges; and redistributing educational resources to attain equity. Very high on our agenda is the upgrading of science and technology education, one of the greatest casualties of apartheid's neglect.

We have had significant support from the private sector in improving access to education and enhancing its quality, especially in poor rural communities. There is a growing acceptance by the private sector as well as community development organisations that government alone cannot overcome the legacy of deprivation of educational resources and facilities.

This understanding is reflected in the thriving of learning institutions like Damelin and others throughout the country. Through them, those of us who could not secure a tertiary business degree are able to access affordable and job-related education and acquire skills essential in today's world of work. The certificates you receive today will open up job opportunities. The knowledge you have gained will strengthen the enterprises and organisations you work for.

Such institutions are critical in our overall human resource development strategy. The 400 000 jobs a year that will be created through the implementation of the Macro-Economic Framework strategy will need skilled patriots to occupy them.

In conclusion, may I urge our graduates here to regard the achievements we are marking tonight not as the end, but rather as the beginning of a continuous process of learning. We are in an age in which revolutionary technological change will continuously transform the workplace and drastically alter the factors that determine success or failure, victory or defeat, and even survival of enterprises.

As your parents, brothers, sisters and leaders we are proud of you. The challenge before you is to go and use the education and skills you have acquired to make South Africa a winning nation. I am sure I also speak on behalf of your teachers in saying that we are confident that you have all it takes to make a positive contribution to the prosperity and growth of our economy, and to help build a better life for all South Africans.

Custodians of Tradition, Agents of Renewal

Speech on the installation of Professor Colin Bundy as
Vice-Chancellor, University of the Witwatersrand,
Johannesburg, 25 March 1998.

Universities are at the same time custodians of tradition and agents central to renewal. They are charged by society with safekeeping the fount of knowledge gained by generations past, while ever exploring new horizons of science and learning. As individual institutions the great universities are those built on a solid record of achievement and custom, while constantly exploring, creating and adapting to the new.

The appointment and installation of a vice-chancellor always point to that crucial intersection of tradition and renewal in the life of a university.

I am here tonight in the first place as an alumnus of the University of the Witwatersrand. I am therefore one who has shared in the institution's tradition, and may be counted in some small way to be part of it.

It gives me immense pleasure and pride to participate in the formal installation of the university's new academic leader, a scholar and administrator who, I have no doubt, will lead the university along exciting new paths while jealously safeguarding the great traditions of university life.

This evening brings many memories from the past and many hopes for the future. I remember my own days as a student and I honour some of my fellows who studied, debated and agitated on this campus. Their names are legend: Joe Slovo, Ismail Meer, Harold Wolpe, JN Singh, William Nkomo and Ruth First. They count amongst those who set forth a message and an ethos in direct contrast to the fear, oppression and subservience which legislation of the time sought to impose and inculcate. They represent one of the proud strands in the tradition of Wits, a strand which the university will undoubtedly seek to build upon as it grapples with its role in the development of a new kind of South African society.

We are greatly privileged to have as the new vice-chancellor an eminent historian, one who was part of an important renewal of South African historiography. A historian of that calibre needs no reminding that all our universities have much in their history and tradition that the present generation will look back upon with less than pride. However, dwelling on the shortcomings of the past is not the object of being aware of that history – rather, it is changing the present and making the future.

Wits and some other South African universities cherished and courageously defended their autonomy against the onslaught by the apartheid government. No history of the defence of freedoms in this country can be complete without reference to the principled stands by these universities who bravely insisted on their right to decide who and what would be taught and who would teach.

Today in looking back we may note that in spite of these noble stands, our universities too often compromised and acquiesced in the legislative strictures and dominant social practices of the day. But to acknowledge that is not to deny the proud tradition of university autonomy which we must nurture as we transform and reshape our higher education system. That tradition of open debate, enquiry and challenge remains fundamental to the life of a university and indeed of a country, now as much as then.

Periods of fundamental social and political change always highlight, and make explicit, relations and linkages which in other times are more assumed and implicit. The social obligations accompanying rights are often more pronounced in such times of transformation. Such is the case now. There are heavy social responsibilities placed on the university by its claimed right to decide who and what shall be taught and who shall teach.

To exercise that right without constant reference to the history of exclusion of the majority from the organs and opportunities of teaching and learning would be to court a dangerous and eventually self-destructive decadence in our intellectual life.

To insist on the right to decide what shall be taught without acknowledging our society's grave developmental needs would be a form of systemic autism rather than creative autonomy.

The slightest form and measure of comfort that any of us might have had from our history of division and discrimination make all of us jointly responsible for the redress of that past.

The legacy of apartheid education places an enormous responsibility on universities. The sins of our fathers visit us in the underprepared

273

generation of learners we have to guide and shape to be the creative and productive future of our country. The challenge is to be caring, responsible and innovative; and to be truly South African in our practice and approach, being neither patronising nor claiming of entitlement.

The university has the further responsibility to be a place which provides opportunities for lifelong learning, not only to graduates but also to those who never had the opportunity to attend an institution of higher learning. Wits once, under particular historical conditions, proudly claimed to be an 'open university'. Today it is lifelong learning which will mark the open nature of the great university, its access policies and programmes, and the quality of learning it engenders in its students.

Professor Bundy, we congratulate you on your assumption of the leadership of a South African institution with a proud tradition. We wish you well with the great task of leading that institution along the paths of renewal as we enter the new millennium, as our country and continent seek regeneration.

You have taught and worked at universities abroad; you came home to teach at one of our established historically white institutions; you were one of those top-class academics who joined an emerging younger historically black institution in order to become part of the exciting project of transformation there.

Few academic leaders in the country can be better equipped with that combination of being steeped in tradition and experienced in charting new terrain.

Welcome to Wits.

7
CULTURE

HOMECOMING

MIRIAM MAKEBA

When I left home, I never intended not to go back home. Many things about exile are painful. When I received the telegram saying that my mother had died, it was very painful. I had to come back to South Africa. I tried, but my passport was revoked. I could not go home.

I finally went back home in 1990 when Nelson Mandela came out of jail. He was going to be in Sweden, in Stockholm, to visit Oliver Tambo, the President of the ANC in exile, who was ill. I was in Spain, and I flew to Stockholm just in time to meet them. We talked for two hours, and Mr Mandela said how wonderful it was when the prisoners heard our records from their cells, recalling that our music sounded to them like freedom.

Then he said: 'Now you must come home!' And I said: 'How can I go home? I am a banned person.' My name was still in the computer, I thought. But the government had said everyone could come back. Nelson Mandela said I must come home.

Eventually, I received a temporary visa, and went home in 1990 for six days. It was just so incredible. I didn't believe that I was going home after so long. I never slept on the plane. I pinched myself. Am I really going home?

I didn't know how to feel. I was crying, I was happy, but also very sad. There were hundreds of people to meet me at the airport, with my family, or what was left of it.

When we arrived, an official said: 'Can I have your passport?' Why do they want my passport? In my mind, I said: 'I'm going straight to jail.' They took me away, but when I got to where they were taking me there were all these lights, and microphones, and people, and there were South African artists.

I took a deep breath. A very lovely singer, Brenda Fassie, sang the national anthem, and we all sang it, and we all cried. There were interviews from all the world press that were there. I was home.

But I was not really home. After going to my brother's house, I went to the cemetery, to my mother's grave, to ask her forgiveness that I had not been there at home when she died.

Even in exile, although I could not come home, I was always in South Africa. Physically I was far away from home, but emotionally, mentally, and otherwise I was always home. So, when people ask me now: 'How did you feel when you went back home. Wasn't it difficult after 30 years?' I say: 'No, in my mind, I've always been there.' I never forgot the language, the culture.

In 1991, I did two concerts in South Africa, which were wonderful, packed to the brim, like a revival. It was my first time singing for my people in 31 years. I didn't have to explain myself! Everybody understood. It was like a beautiful revival, and I just had to cry all night. I decided I had to stay and I gathered my rags and moved back. It's wonderful to be back home; there's no place like it.

When I came back home, many things had changed. Most of our leaders were out of jail, and we could move about, more or less. We were about to vote, if they let us. But in all honesty, for our people, nothing much was truly different. Life was still as hard as ever, if not more so. People had no housing; there were so many squatter camps; our children had no proper schools, no books; not enough hospitals, none of the basic things. So it would be an uphill battle, even if we won the elections: we'll have the flag, but not the money.

I was never politically involved. People always think I'm political, but I'm not. I just speak the truth. When I say we have been oppressed, I'm not lying. It's the truth. I'm glad I've been vindicated, in a way. I could have been in Parliament, but I'm not a politician. I'm a singer. I love to sing. That's what makes me happy.

Of course, I have had some remarkable experiences singing politically. Singing at the birth of the Organisation of African Unity in 1963, meeting all the presidents, the men who led their countries to independence; that was, for me, something. Here I was, coming from nowhere, and singing to all these important people. And then there was the birthday salute to US President John F Kennedy in 1961, where I was the only foreign artist among the big giants of America paying tribute to him.

Before the first democratic elections, I learned that I was being advanced as a possible ANC candidate for Parliament. When they asked me, I said I was very honoured, of course, but I told them that if I did anything, it was to be in my own way, with my music. Mr Mandela told me: 'You have been our ambassador, and you must continue to raise our voice in the world.' That meant more to me than any vote. Politicians come and go, you know, but music is forever.

We have culture, and we have cultures. Under apartheid, our cultures were divided, but we could never give in to the apartheid idea of tribalism. As a child of Xhosa and Swazi parents, I cannot subscribe to any tribal divisions. I'm a South African. I don't know what else I can be. In my experience, there are no tribes fighting each other. It was hurtful to read the international newspapers saying that the story in South Africa was a tribal fight.

There was greed. There was killing. But we always had hope. When you give up hope, you may as well lay down and die. I always said, maybe one day I'll go home, and I did. I never expected anything, but still some of my dreams came true. We have to thank the people at home who stood up to everything, and also the international community for raising their voices. And now we must say: Don't abandon us. This is only the beginning!

I would like us to learn things from other cultures, to sing songs from other cultures. It's wonderful. It opens up your thinking and everything else. But it should never happen to the detriment of your own. Still, we are all part of the same cultural mix.

For those of us who were artists in exile, we have had very strange careers. When you function in other nations, and you don't have the backing of your own country, it can get very difficult.

But our South African culture can produce surprising results. Take the song, 'Pata Pata', which I wrote and sang in 1956 as a dance tune for the musical venues in Sophiatown and elsewhere. A simple song, made for dancing, it didn't mean anything. Certainly, it was not political. In America, in 1967, I recorded the song again and it became a hit, but the same song was recorded in France in 1977, and in Senegal in 1998, with similar results. People, all over the world, respond. In 2000, I recorded the song again, but the song remains the same. As we have seen with so many of our artists, there is something about the South African style that works.

So, if things go well, you should see a lot coming out of South Africa, because there's a lot of talent: in theatre, in music, in dance, in painting and sculpture. These people, who have been suppressed for so long, have so much to say.

We just don't seem to want to stop. How long have we been singing 'Unify us, don't divide us'? We try to be positive in our music, as in our other arts; all of us are trying. I've always sung about real things, and now I'm saying *Masakhane* – we've been through all of that, let's work together.

A lot has changed. We are only a few years old as a new democracy, but we feel that our leaders had done their best. It's been hard. There has been a lot of pain, but people are trying hard to move on.

For the millennium, for the new century, I went to Robben Island. We sang for many people. The big thing, however, was for our former president, Nelson Mandela, to light the candle at midnight. That was really the big thing. We were there to keep the people busy before midnight. It was cold. They put up a tent in the middle of nowhere. There was no light on that island. It was very dark. I felt very strange there, like it was not a happy place to be. But we were there for Nelson Mandela to light the candle at midnight.

In 2000 President Thabo Mbeki made me South Africa's cultural ambassador. 'I am not a diplomat,' I said, 'I am a singer.' Yes, I have travelled the world. I'm never in one place for very long. It's just that I love to sing. One of the very few times I'm happy is when I'm singing. When people say I sang well, that's when I'm satisfied. So, I asked myself, how can a singer be an ambassador? How can an artist be a politician? Sometimes, however, it is the artists who can speak to all the people through their art. Sometimes, as Nelson Mandela has said, our poetry, art, and music make a difference in the lives of our people.

Where has the time gone? Time has been funny to me. I was an 'old' woman in terms of my Xhosa culture when I was 36. When I became a grandmother for the first time, my city friends asked me: 'Why do you let your daughter's children call you 'granny'? It makes you sound old!' I told them: 'But I am their granny!' But even today I feel young, and the make-up technicians keep me looking youthful! When I first heard the name 'Mama Africa' I didn't like it, because it made me sound so old, and big! But now that I am old, and have grown round, I suppose I should accept the honour gracefully. I am certainly grateful, because Africa is my wonderful home.

On my album, *Homeland*, I chose songs about love. Each one of them is about love – of one's country, one's continent, the love of children in the world, opening up your heart to them. The theme of that album was really love. The song 'In Time': 'In time we get older, in time we get mellow/I never ever changed my mind about the things I wanted in my life/I've been through changes like everyone else/My heart's been broken, put on the shelf/but now the light shines and the wounded heart will heal in time/God always answers one's prayer, his guiding light is love/No matter how hard we fall, his guiding light is love.'

But I also wanted to sing about *Masakhane*, a plea to all the people to come together, to work together. So, the first song on the album was called 'Masakhane': 'You help me I help you. Together we'll be all right.' And in the song I say I've been around the world telling the story of my country and my people and in that journey a lot of people listened and raised their voices against injustices. Those voices helped bring us where we are. I also say thank you to our children for the part they played. I say thank you to our mothers for their nurturing and their prayers. I say thank you to our traditional healers for their part, but most of all I say thank you to our leaders who are gracious and have taught us how to be tolerant: who tell us that while we may never forget, we must forgive. And so *Masakhane*: let's build together.

The lyrics of that song, 'Masakhane', also tell about our people in exile, going around the world, pleading the cause of our land and our people. Many of those people were artists, singers, and poets. Their voices, as the song goes, helped us to move on. We thank them. All of this cultural creativity, with its freedom and power of expression, helped us to move on. In the spirit of *Masakhane*, working together, our artists, singers, poets, and healers have supported our political leaders in learning how to forgive, but never to forget.

Nelson Mandela's speeches in this chapter tell this story: Our art, culture, and heritage help us remember. We must remember where we have come from. Though we may never forget, we have forgiven. Let us now join hands and work together for a better future.

ARTS OF UNDERSTANDING

BILL COSBY

All nations and all of the peoples of the world are united behind the idea that culture, indeed, what we do to validate our common humanity through our creative expressions in the arts, is at the core of the good and beautiful life. We all strive to enhance the quality of life we have, and that our children and our children's children shall have after we are no longer here. It matters not what our national, racial or regional differences are; we are all prone to acculturate ourselves toward using the arts to help us understand ourselves more fully and act as a motivating force in our daily lives. We engage in the arts to bring spiritual uplift to our physical presence in the world.

As I survey the communities around the world, I am made aware of the fact that cultural stability in a nation – that is, showing how people perceive the role of the arts to be and how they function in society – adds measurably to how a people see themselves in world history. Culture, that all-encompassing endeavour that brings people in direct contact with their unseen souls and allows them to vent the creative expression of the mind, keeps us alive and well even when the body is abused and tormented by the ills of society.

President Nelson Mandela, perhaps more than any other living person, has stood as a world cultural icon for more than five decades. He nobly endured the harsh punishment of imprisonment on Robben Island in his native South Africa in the dark days of apartheid. He refused to let down his guard and abandon his own cultural aspirations to return to his beloved people and chant the songs of freedom with those who awaited his release. His hopes for his own personal freedom and that of his people were deeply grounded in his religious faith and in the solidarity of international cultural communities from around the globe. Indeed, the arts strengthened his own creative will to survive imprisonment. It is for this reason that we look upon President Nelson Mandela as an icon of culture in the nascent years of the rebuilding of cultural

282

bridges between all of the races and peoples of the Republic of South Africa.

No one seems better qualified to lead the South African movement to cultural diversity and soulful regeneration than President Mandela. His prophetic voice of reason can best be understood by the nation practising his shared belief that South Africa be made whole in its cultural aspirations by inculcating a new spirit of creativity in the minds of all of its citizens. He suggests that this be done by the empowerment of the people through creative programmes that use education and literacy as learning stations to ensure cultural diversity. He has boldly noted that the creative, performing and visual arts are the most common and the most notable vehicles through which constructive cultural engagement can take place. We trust the arts to inform us of our inner urges. They present us with a keen insight as to who we are as well as who we wish to become. The arts bring relief to our desires to soar both physically and spiritually beyond our earthly plane. They articulate, through various media, the echoes of freedom and our desire to be at peace with one another in a most common way.

The rich tradition of artistry in South Africa, dating from the days of beautiful prehistoric rock paintings in the Kalahari Desert, is a living legacy to the longevity of the arts and testimony to the role they have played in the lives of the peoples in this part of the world over the ages. This legacy is one that all of the people of South Africa should be proud of and should work to uphold in the lineage of both ancient and current history.

In his comprehensive pronouncement on the 'Efficacy of Culture', President Mandela has addressed a series of issues that move beyond the heritable sensibilities of the peoples of the Republic of South Africa alone and thus provide a blueprint for the successful undertaking and understanding of world culture. By speaking about the various components of his own cultural experiences, President Mandela has made available to the world a personal and prophetic view of how a nation once torn apart with racial strife and arrogantly exhibiting a lack of human understanding towards its majority race, should and can rise to the occasion and achieve greatness through cultural diversity.

While President Mandela has looked cautiously with a critical and discerning eye on the 'destructive and violent legacy of apartheid' in South Africa he, like Frantz Fanon, a fellow warrior in the fight against colonial rule and human deprivation, has made clear his stance on the subject of reconciliation and democratic aspirations of all of the peoples of his great nation. He has done so by affirming his unequivocal faith in the people to rise to the occasion and divest themselves of the hatred of the past and use the arts to help heal the wounds in contemporary society. He has notably suggested that the arts should serve South Africa in the same manner that they served African Americans in the periods of slavery and racial segregation in the United States.

My people sang the Negro spiritual – 'There is a balm in Gilead, to make the wounded whole'– at a time when oppression abounded over the black race. In like manner, many of the peoples of South Africa, particularly those of multi-layered ethnicity, all of whom have known the true meaning of the oppressive hand of apartheid in their native land, look to the day when the violent experiences and fears of the past can be contained by the affirmation of their full humanity through creative expressions in the arts. President Mandela has reminded his people that it was the arts, those noble expressions of the human spirit that are communicated through literature, dance, song, film, drama, painting and sculpture, among the many other such creative means, that helped articulate the sufferings of his people that were heard around the globe. Well-wishers from many nations responded to the laments of the oppressed peoples of South Africa and offered their help. They also heard the songs of freedom sung by helpless hundreds of black mothers wailing for their children wantonly killed in the streets of Sharpeville and Soweto.

Through consummate expressions of freedom and goodwill in the arts, particularly those valiant expressions set forth in music, dance and poetry, South African artists of all races have presented their skilful talents to sympathetic audiences from around the globe. It was in the period of apartheid that their voices became the cry for freedom and helped break down the infamous system of oppression in the land. Those noble souls, many of whom were not welcomed back to their homeland, were exiled in countries where the war on apartheid received a more sympathetic voice. Miriam Makeba, the revered laureate for the songs of South Africa, indelibly sang songs of freedom in America and around the world to sympathetic audiences, as did others in the cadre of freedom fighters. The bite of the pen in the writings of novelists, playwrights and poets too numerous to mention here awakened the consciousness of many unsuspecting supporters who helped finance the freedom movement back in South Africa. The men and women who held important positions of power in sports in South Africa also joined in the cry for freedom as they abstained from participating in international sports events. Their cry of *Amandla!*, along with the voices of concerned artists from around the globe, helped bring down the walls of apartheid in South Africa. Among the many who assisted, there was an even larger number who participated in human rights movements beyond the continent of Africa, Today, President Nelson Mandela rightfully praises the many artists and patrons of the arts who worked tirelessly year after year to keep hope alive, often against the odds, that freedom for all of the peoples of South Africa was imminent. Nelson Mandela kept the faith and was victorious.

The diversity shown in the arts when the peoples of many nations joined hands to help bring down the walls of apartheid in South Africa can and must continue to serve as a model for what is wished to be achieved in the arts in the years ahead. It is imperative that the divisions seen along cultural lines that have plagued many nations be abandoned in the pursuit of cultural tolerance and reconciliation. Our nations have experienced the unhealthy pains of cultural division that do not always showcase the arts as viable instruments for change and cultural growth. President Mandela eloquently addressed the subject of cultural differences and how they should work to enhance the creative prowess of a nation, not hinder it, in his address entitled 'One City, Many Cultures' in Cape Town on 1 March 1999.

In his assessment of the terrible harm caused by the legacies of colonial rule in South Africa and the distasteful pain of apartheid, President Mandela pleaded for tolerance, forgiveness and a new spirit of cultural reconciliation in order to help unite the people in their move to a newly found cultural freedom. He has noted that the time is at hand for all of the people of his nation to begin to catch up and learn vigorously the patterns of culture that move beyond race, gender and ethnicity.

In many ways, President Mandela's assessment of the failures of the educational system in South Africa to move beyond a Eurocentric base is no different from what African Americans have experienced in their pursuit of a more inclusive form of education and cultural diversity. His eloquent plea for cultural diversity in South Africa embraces 'Muslim and Jew, Christian and Hindu, coloured, African, Indian and white'. This is the most complete formula for cultural diversity one can find in the global community.

His mandate to journalists and practitioners, and those who advocate for a free press, is that they too have a salient role to play in helping the nation move quickly to recover the 'silenced histories' of so many people whose personal and communal identities were lost due to unkind exploits of countless numbers of individuals who acted and followed blindly the will of an indifferent and inhumane form of government.

What is certain to me upon reading President Mandela's speeches on culture in this chapter is that here is a man who stands as a watchman, towering over his nation, a man whose gift of wisdom and human understanding is uncommon in our time. It is in the redefinition of cultural compensation that President Mandela believes that repair can come to the torn elements of society. Needless to say, few politicians in our lifetime believe, as does he, that the deep societal wounds of despair that are manifested through hunger, disease, war and poverty, can be remedied by the sanctioning of culture as the most eloquent expression of our full humanity.

History has taught us that we learn the rudiments of our very existence through culture. What we make with the various media in the arts and what we say with words inform those who experience our artistry, denoting who we are and what our cultural aspirations are. Museums, libraries and research institutions have been the major places and purveyors of culture. They indelibly imprint young and old minds alike; thus the reminder to those who are in charge at these institutions that the tyranny of racism and the lingering elements of derisive imaging so commonly practised over decades of apartheid in South Africa is a painful cultural construct that must be recognised and removed from the annals of education and culture.

President Mandela's plea for the accurate representation of the histories and culture of all of the peoples of South Africa is one that he believes cannot wait for another generation before a just and humane resolution is found. The reconstruction of theories of cultural largess in a democratic South Africa is what President Mandela seeks and he notes that it is to the benefit of all that no one group of people feels entitled to define another's cultural position. Perhaps more than any other place in South Africa, Robben Island epitomises the place to which no one wishes to return except to see the progress of the nation as it moves in time to erase its factual history; a tranquil island that at one time, in the dismal days of mistrust and racial hatred, was a place where lepers and later political prisoners were expected to be deprived of their will to live. Nelson Mandela, the prisoner who later became President Mandela, defeated the plan of the prison system. He survived and he is victorious.

In the early years after his imprisonment on Robben Island, Nelson Mandela became a world symbol standing for right and justice, as did Mahatma Gandhi in India and Martin Luther King, Jr in the Civil Rights Movement in America. My knowledge of the work of the African National Congress and the tireless efforts of people such as Nelson

Mandela, Oliver Tambo and others of equally dedicated persuasions and of Robben Island in the days of apartheid, was limited to what I saw on television and read in the American press for many years. Only in recent times have we in America been made aware of the partial truth of how our two countries, the United States and the Republic of South Africa, patterned their laws of repression of peoples of colour in their efforts to dehumanise the people of African ancestry in both nations. Now that we are in possession of greater truths about our similar histories and our cultural alliances, it is my sincere hope that African Americans and the peoples of African ancestry in South Africa will use every tool of invention available to them to create the proper dialogue that encourages the common bond of human understanding, love and friendship between themselves in the years ahead.

No one has more eloquently and more factually presented the model of excellence to which we should aspire in our pursuit of a colourless humanity in which culture takes the high road than has President Nelson Mandela, champion for the human rights of all people. My visit to South Africa in 1997 allowed me the chance to meet President Nelson Mandela, the man whose passionate spirit for freedom and justice in the world overshadowed all of the expectations I had for any one human being. I am richer in spirit and in truth for having stood in his presence.

Finally, I wish to end this brief cultural look at President Nelson Mandela, that magnificent tower of knowledge, wisdom and culture, on a lighter note, one befitting my own profession in entertainment. During my visit to the continent of Africa, I decided to exercise the knowledge I had gained from reading history books, watching films and television, and listening to the radio from the perspective of an African American. I asked several of the people I met to tell me about their own Tarzan, the one I had been introduced to in America in the popular media. I asked, 'Have you seen him? Have you seen his son?' Everyone I asked looked startled. Some repeated the word 'Tarzan' as if they did not know about whom I was speaking. I too was startled and somewhat amazed that they hadn't seen Tarzan, an African hero in America. I told them that Tarzan had a son. He should be about 65 and the only white man who would answer to the name Boy. I began thinking: 'Did we see too much television and watch too many films about Tarzan in America? After all, wasn't Tarzan from Africa? Why didn't enlightened Africans know about him?' Cultural differences, I suppose – or better still, cultural efficaciousness, black on white.

The Efficacy of Culture

Statement at the opening of the Cultural Development Congress,
Civic Theatre, Johannesburg,
25 April 1993.

Before the messages of condolence have even stopped pouring in to console us on the assassination of our beloved Comrade Chris Hani, we have now been dealt another blow with the loss of our beloved national chairman, my brother and friend, Oliver Tambo. Please stand for a moment of silence as we salute him.

At this time I can only say that I am bereft because I have lost my dearest brother and lifelong friend. We grieve deeply for his family and for the terrible loss to this country. Our strategist has left us as we approach the goals he set for us, but his spirit is embodied in all our work.

Oliver Tambo believed in the efficacy of culture to make us whole and to give us a richer quality of life. The ANC's policies on the arts and culture stemmed to a large extent from his vision, understanding and initiative. ANC choirs internationally, the Amandla Cultural Ensemble, the Solomon Mahlangu Freedom College, and even the ANC logo emerged from his inspiration.

During this coming week you will be involved in deliberations to examine and explore the cultural possibilities in a democratic South Africa, which is yet in embryo. Your task will be to look at ways in which this torn country can be reconstructed in part through the rich threads of culture.

Through the destructive and violent legacy of apartheid, where the sanctity of life has no meaning, we have inherited the culture of death and destruction. To the white minority regime, torture, detention, carnage and massacre were the principal weapons used to keep it in power. Dispossession and displacement, grief and anger have become the accepted hallmarks of our existence.

It is our hope and fervent belief that the universal language of culture will show us ways in which to transform and heal the consciousness of all our people. Let it be said here that throughout these long years of bitter struggle our compatriots have sustained an amazing degree of humanity. Their courage and tolerance, and their resilience have been, in themselves, attributes derived from the culture of liberation.

During the worst years of repression, when all avenues of legitimate protest were closed by emergency legislation, it was the arts that articulated the plight and the democratic aspirations of our people. This affirmation was demonstrated through drama, dance, literature, song, film, paintings and sculpture that defined the silence that apartheid sought to impose. The secret of apartheid was revealed universally, and severely condemned by the world at large. It was the cultural boycott that became one of the most effective weapons in isolating racist South Africa.

We thank the international cultural community for their solidarity, and for the pressures that they exercised, sometimes at great personal loss. It is also a fact that during those long years many of our own artists were trained and nurtured abroad through the offices of some of you here. We believe that the links that were forged during the period of enforced exile and imprisonment will continue to serve as a source of mutual inspiration for all of us in the future.

Perhaps one of the greatest challenges facing any nation in transition is to move from protest, defiance and resistance to building and reconstruction. Similarly, in our own case, we have to move from slogans and rhetoric to constructive and concrete programmes that will actually engage our beleaguered people, black and white.

We are fortunate in the diversity of our nation, and it is through cultural cross-fertilisation that we can transcend the differences that apartheid has sought to exploit. We must empower our people through programmes of education and literacy through the vehicle of culture, so that we can all begin to share and understand our richness and diversity. We must also encourage the return to centre stage of all those powerful indigenous arts that were usurped by metropolitan cultures.

The ANC's department of arts and culture, during its many years in exile, has institutionalised a mode of cultural consultation in its broadest sense, beginning with CASA in Amsterdam, followed by the Gaborone Culture & Resistance Conference to Zabalaza in London. We were building stepping stones to today's conference.

The ANC does not own or territorialise culture: creativity has no fences or boundaries and expression is free. All of South Africa is part of this building process, as are you, our foreign representatives of the world at large. Use this conference to help us and encourage us.

We too will die but that which we collectively contribute to our national cultural identity will live forever beyond us. We say to this conference, begin today! Bridge the chasm, use tolerance and compassion, be inclusive not exclusive, build dignity and pride, encourage freedom of expression to create a civil society for unity and peace. We remain confident that a democratic, nonracial and nonsexist state will be established in South Africa sooner rather than later. Our demand is for an election date now and for the establishment of the TEC to ensure joint control of the security forces.

We are already on the road to free and independent broadcasting, and all our other institutions, including cultural institutions, must follow suit.

Our Music, Dance, and Poetry

Statement at a concert organised by the Irish
Anti-Apartheid Movement, Dublin,
1 July 1990.

It is with boundless joy that we are amongst you this evening. We bring you warm and fraternal greetings from the African National Congress. We bring you warm greetings from the mass democratic movement and indeed our entire embattled people. Our President, Comrade Oliver Tambo, sends his best regards.

We are more than pleased to be with you, members of our enlarged family. For almost 30 years, the Irish anti-apartheid movement has been a consistent and staunch partner of our people in the struggle against the infamous system of apartheid. Your pioneering role has immensely contributed to the international indignation that so many harbour towards apartheid. Thanks to your tireless efforts today the entire world is united behind our struggle. Thanks to your sterling contribution the apartheid system cannot survive another day longer.

Our common struggle has reached an advanced and decisive stage. The hour of destiny has dawned. The day is not far when our dream of a united, democratic, nonracial and nonsexist South Africa shall be turned into reality. We sue for a democratic order wherein our people will be united in their diversity. Bound together by their common destiny, there will be neither white nor black, but just South Africans, free and proud. Proud to be members of the human family. Proud to be free, at last, but free.

To reach there we must stand firm and continue with the struggle. The new situation in our country has compelled new responsibilities upon our movement. We are the agency for democracy and peace. To be able to successfully accomplish this, our historic mission, we need both political and material support. To end apartheid, we must keep sanctions and all other forms of pressure in place. To find a just and lasting peace, our movement is in need of funds and other forms of assistance. Our youth are in need of training so that they too could one day be able participants in the reconstruction of their own country. On all these we are fully convinced that we can continue to rely on your ever-ready assistance.

To the artists, singers and entertainers we extend our warmest thanks. The Irish anti-apartheid movement has been a world leader in the cultural boycott of apartheid; your best writers and creative people have shunned making money out of apartheid; some of your best sportsmen and women have refused to go to South Africa. We salute these people, as we salute you tonight.

Soon, we shall gather in a free South Africa with our music, our dance, and with our poetry resounding throughout the world with the simple message: *Amandla!*

One City, Many Cultures

Speech at the opening of 'One City, Many Cultures,'
Cape Town, 1 March 1999.

I am very pleased and honoured to be given a small role in the much-needed and overdue initiative that is being launched here today.

Although the perpetrators of the recent acts of terrorism in Cape Town will be brought to book, all of us must be concerned at how their actions have caused tension and even hatred amongst people who have shared this city for hundreds of years.

Cape Town, more than any other city in South Africa, has been home to people from different cultures for a long, long time. The many people who know Cape Town as their home can trace their ancestries from across the world. Muslim and Jew, Christian and Hindu, coloured, African, Indian and white; all these and others have brought to the Cape a part of the soul of many peoples and cultures in many parts of the world.

That diversity was a valuable asset to those who shared a common vision in striving to defeat apartheid and replace it with a South Africa that belongs to all who live in it. Yet this city, like the rest of South Africa, continues to show the traces of deep divisions.

One reason lies in the Group Areas Act, which divided our communities so effectively that we became strangers to each other. Ask anyone from District Six or Sophiatown and they will recall their close familiarity with each other's lifestyles before apartheid divided us.

The Truth and Reconciliation Commission has helped open the way to the long journey from our terrible past to reconciliation. For us as individuals that journey means coming to terms with the effects that our enforced separation had on our attitudes to each other. It means working to repair the torn fabric of our society.

Another reason for this lack of tolerance lies in a problem that is not peculiar to this country. Part of the legacy of colonialism is the dominance of the history, language, culture and religion of the

293

colonial powers. We know many details of European royalty but how many of us can tell the story of Hintsa or Tuan Guru to our children? How many can recount the epic resistance to the occupation and invasion of the Cape? How many know how the Malays came to the Cape and the Indians to Natal?

Few of us know how we came to be the nation we are. Even those who feel slighted by others' ignorance of themselves are in turn often guilty of stereotyping others. We have seen recently how easily ignorance about each other can turn to demonisation and isolation of one another; how easily hostility towards a community or religion can be awakened even by false claims that others are acting in their name.

Colonialism and apartheid have left a sharply polarised society. Until we reduce the wide gaps between the educated and the illiterate, the sheltered and the homeless, the very rich and the poor, we will continue to be deeply divided.

Every day South Africans are together helping to reduce that gap through job creation, providing services and investing in our human resources. But the rebirth of our nation also requires a slow learning process in which we come to identify the values we share as a nation and respect those of others.

A part of that process is the recovery of the silenced histories of our different communities. Government is helping through the transformation of our museums and changes in the teaching of history in our schools. But all of us need to play a part, however small. In that context the One City, Many Cultures initiative is very welcome. The journalists have recognised a problem in their city and they have begun to take action, as professionals, to help address its causes.

Rather than the superficial treatment of the all-important matters of love, marriage, childbirth, prayer, initiation and death to which we have become accustomed, especially when it concerns those outside the dominant culture, readers are being given a new insight into the lives of others. They are being given a confirmation that fundamentally we all have the same needs and aspirations.

Through this initiative Cape Town is being helped to build unity from our diversity.

As one who was guest of your city for 26 years and who has since then spent much of my time here, I urge all the people of Cape Town to support the One City, Many Cultures initiative. And I encourage you all to sign the pledge that will add strength to the campaign.

The Heritage of Robben Island

Address on Heritage Day, Robben Island,
24 September 1997.

Few occasions could awaken such a mixture of emotions as today's, or illuminate so sharply the changes of recent years. Fewer still could bring to such sharp focus the challenges ahead.

It is a great joy for me that we can all come as free South Africans – with our friends – to Robben Island; and even more that we are gathered to celebrate our joint heritage as a nation, to acknowledge this heritage in the context of our commitment to democracy, tolerance and human rights.

In affirming a joint heritage in this place we are reminded that our noble ideals were spurred on even more by their long denial, that today's unity is a triumph over yesterday's division and conflict.

The memory of the political prisoners confined on this island and in other prisons reminds us that these ideals must have concrete content if they are to have real meaning. They must bring secure protection under the law, access to justice, clean water, adequate health care and shelter. They must entrench the conditions in which one can participate in building our collective democratic future, speak one's own language, have pride in one's culture and one's heritage.

In seeking to ground our heritage in these ideals we are striking out in a new direction.

During colonial and apartheid times our museums and monuments reflected the experiences and political ideals of a minority to the exclusion of others. Most people had little or no say in the depiction of their history in textbooks, libraries, or research institutions. The demeaning portrayal of black people in particular – that is African, Indian and coloured people – is painful to recall.

Of our museums all but a handful – three per cent – represented the kind of heritage which glorified mainly white and colonial history.

And even the small glimpse of black history in the others was largely fixed in the grip of racist and other stereotypes.

Unfortunately, we have to acknowledge that the redressing of this situation has barely begun. Having excluded and marginalised most of our people, is it surprising that our museums and national monuments are often seen as alien spaces? How many have gone to see one of our monuments? In other countries such places throng with citizens.

Our cultural institutions cannot stand apart from our Constitution and our Bill of Rights. Within the context of our fight for a democratic South Africa and the entrenchment of human rights can we afford exhibitions in our museums depicting any of our people as lesser human beings, sometimes in natural history museums usually reserved for the depiction of animals? Can we continue to tolerate our ancestors being shown as people locked in time? Such degrading forms of representation inhibit our children's appreciation of the value and strength of our democracy, of tolerance and of human rights. They demean the victims and warp the minds of the perpetrators.

Through the apartheid years, people responded to the denial and distortion of their heritage with their own affirmation – as indeed Afrikaners had done in an earlier period. They celebrated their heritage outside of the country's museums and monuments: in song and in ceremony; in festivals and carnivals; in the selling of their own wares and in buying items associated with their heritage; by working the history of their communities into everyday artifacts, as the women of Hlabisa weave their stories into beer baskets.

With democracy we have the opportunity to ensure that our institutions reflect history in a way that respects the heritage of all our citizens. Government has taken up the challenge. Our museums and the heritage sector as a whole are being restructured. Community consultation, effective use of limited resources, and accessibility are our guiding principles as we seek to redress the imbalances.

The recently established Legacy Project will promote a fuller representation of our nation's heritage through new monuments and heritage sites. This will ensure that we have national monuments that live in our people's hearts. When our museums and monuments preserve the whole of our diverse heritage, when they are inviting to the public and interact with the changes all around them, then they will strengthen our attachment to human rights, mutual respect and democracy, and help prevent these ever again being violated.

Robben Island is a vital part of South Africa's collective heritage. *Siqithini*, the Island – a place of pain and banishment for centuries and now of triumph – presents us with the rich challenge of heritage. Its future has been the subject of intense and wide-ranging debate.

How do we look at the histories of different people who lived here, through various ages: lepers, prisoners, jailers all together; leaders of resistance not only from South Africa but from as far afield as Namibia and the Indonesian Archipelago? How do we give expression to these diverse histories as a collective heritage?

How do we reflect the fact that the people of South Africa as a whole, together with the international community, turned one of the world's most notorious symbols of racist oppression into a worldwide icon of the universality of human rights, of hope, peace and reconciliation. How do we represent the tradition of intense political and academic education that the Island has come to symbolise?

These and many other important issues are canvassed in the 200 or more submissions received on the future of the Island, and they will be given full consideration.

I am confident that we will together find a way to combine the many dimensions of the Island, and that we will do so in a manner that recognises above all its pre-eminent character as a symbol of the victory of the human spirit over political oppression, and of reconciliation over enforced division. In this way we will help strengthen the ethos of heritage as a binding force rather than a divisive one, as a force for truth rather than an artificial construct to satisfy all and sundry.

When Cabinet decided that Robben Island should be developed as a national monument and national museum, it set in motion its redevelopment as a cultural and conservation showcase for South Africa's democracy, which will also maximise its educational potential.

In the short time since January this year, when the Department of Arts, Culture, Science and Technology took over responsibility for the Island, great progress has been made in this direction. We thank Professor Andre Odendaal and the interim administration for their sterling work, and we are certain that their experience and expertise will continue to stand us in good stead.

Today, a second phase of the Island's redevelopment begins. We wish the new Council well in the challenging task with which they have been entrusted.

This ceremony confirms for us that the struggle for human dignity and freedom – throughout the world, and in particular in South Africa – is an ongoing one. It challenges us to ensure that future generations of South Africans can claim the heritage of a nation that has eradicated the legacy of grinding poverty that our generation inherited for most of its people; the heritage of a nation that has deracialised all spheres of social life and secured the dignity of all its diverse communities.

Let us recommit ourselves to the ideals in our Constitution, ideals which were shaped in the struggles here on Robben Island and in the greater prison that was apartheid South Africa.

May this monument and the museum strengthen our resolve that never again shall this land see the oppression of one by another, nor the suppression of any community's heritage.

In conclusion, it now gives me great pleasure to formally open the new Robben Island Museum, the first major new heritage institution of democratic South Africa.

The 1820 Settlers Monument

Speech at the rededication of the 1820 Settlers Monument,
Grahamstown, 16 May 1996.

There are monuments which stand as mute pointers to a fixed and ever-receding past. Devoid of life, they have little meaning outside the history books and the minds of learned people. This national monument is not of that kind. If it were it would not have found the resources to recover from the devastation if suffered two years ago and improve itself in the rebuilding.

There are monuments which are dedicated to commemorating the past in a way which nurtures a particular tradition of our land, contributing to its vitality and growth. Such living monuments make a contribution to our society and enrich the life of our nation. But they may also exclude others. The 1820 Settlers Monument, perhaps, started its life in that way.

There are monuments which open the past to scrutiny, recalling it in order to illuminate it and transform it into part of our living and changing society, and merging the tradition from which they emerged with the rich diversity of South Africa's cultures. Such monuments, if they are successful, are a beacon for the future of all our people as much as a memory of the past.

Because this monument has set itself the goal of belonging to this last category, and because it has so forcefully identified with change and the reconstruction of our country, it is a great honour for me to share in its re-dedication today.

Pawns in a larger game, the 1820 Settlers came to this part of Africa at the behest of an imperial power seeking to use its own poor and unemployed in a bid to advance conquest and imperial ambitions. Though their own impulse to freedom rendered them largely unsuitable for that task, they were nevertheless caught up on the wrong side of history, unable or unwilling to acknowledge as equals those into whose homeland they had been implanted.

The founders of the monument two decades ago sought to redeem that limitation, without denying it, by dedicating the monument to the universal application of the ideals which the English Settlers cherished for themselves. Today, our country a democracy, and our people masters of their own destiny, we are re-dedicating the monument to the universality of those ideals at a time when we are working together to make them a reality for all.

Clearly, great strides have been taken in broadening the scope of the monument's activities and towards turning it into a national resource centre for the arts and culture. By providing the infrastructure for the National Arts Festival and the school festivals, through the many cultural projects and teacher training and development which it makes possible, the monument is making a significant contribution to our nation's cultural life and the education of its people.

The plans for a National Festival of Science and Technology are most encouraging. Apartheid's education system and the exploitation of science for repressive purposes have, for most of South Africa's youth, robbed science and technology of the excitement and the attraction which it should have. Popularising science and demonstrating the capacity of technology to help us meet the challenges of improving the quality of life will enrich South African cultural and intellectual life.

These and other plans give reason for confidence that the monument will rise to the challenge we all face, turning our goals into reality. In particular, the far-reaching aim of making this national resource one which all our diverse cultures feel to be truly their own will require hard work. But it is a task we must accomplish.

The coming of age of our democracy is also the recognition that national unity and reconciliation live in the hearts of our people rather than in law. The new patriotism is a force that propels us towards a vital and unifying national culture which respects, promotes and celebrates our diversity.

To the extent that this monument succeeds in achieving its goals, it will help us all to realise the broader vision of a new South Africa. In rededicating this restored and improved building, we are reaffirming the purposes for which it was built: 'That all might have life and have it more abundantly.'

I therefore have the pleasure of unveiling the plaque commemorating the restoration and re-opening of this monument.

Sporting Excellence

Speech on the occasion of the President's Sports Awards,
Tuynhuys, 16 May 1995.

I am honoured to share with you one of South Africa's most prestigious annual sports occasions.

Tonight's function has a special significance. For the first time, decorations are being awarded under the banner of democracy. Hand in hand with our political transition, a broader vision of a nonracial, free and vigorous sports community is coming into being. In this process there is a clear message, that we can play and recreate together as South Africans in a country to which we all owe undivided allegiance.

The dawn of this new era was not achieved by political organisations alone. The great majority of our sports people, of every colour, recognised clearly that the abnormal practices of apartheid severely handicapped their development and stature, at home and abroad.

Allow me to take this opportunity to commend you all for your contribution towards this new beginning, the new flag, the new symbols, the new anthems and the new sporting ethos.

On behalf of the government, and indeed all South Africans, I am delighted to welcome the recipients of the decorations, their friends and family members.

As pioneering sports persons, and as administrators and coaches, you have demonstrated dedication to sport, excellence, and an ability to humble yourselves even under the most challenging of circumstances.

These qualities will ensure your continuing contribution to sport and earn you the lasting respect of your country. South Africa remembers with pride the magnanimity in defeat which Elana Meyer demonstrated in Barcelona, when she proclaimed with her vanquisher the sanctity of the Olympic principle that participation is more important than winning. Mind you, we expect you, Elana, to reverse that dictum next year, even if for a moment!

The country expects much of its sporting figures, not only in the field of sport. You have much to give to the process of reconciliation and nation building. Sport, and the example and influence of leading athletes, can make an impact in tackling some of our serious social problems. These include the restoration of the culture of teaching and learning in our schools, and the reintegration of the so-called marginalised youth into the mainstream of society. Likewise with the problems of violence and drug abuse.

The Olympic Truce to be observed during the 1996 Games eloquently demonstrates the positive influence that sport can make. I heartily welcome the central themes of these Games: global peace; strengthening of family ties; and general upliftment of young people. I know the message will touch a chord in all our hearts!

A partnership of all sectors of society is busy transforming our society in order to address the legacy of apartheid. Achieving the sports goals we have set for ourselves will depend on close teamwork between government and the sport world. On its part, government is committed to the creation of an ideal climate for sport to thrive, within the constraints of our budget, recognition and development.

With the acceptance of democratic South Africa into international sport and the achievements of our teams and individuals, we have developed a new spirited patriotism. Our national teams now enjoy the support of all South Africans.

This is the spirit with which our nation will be approaching the coming World Rugby Cup – both in fulfilling the honour of hosting this prestigious event, and giving our support, in our millions, to our magnificent 15.

This new and fresh approach amongst our people has enhanced the Government of National Unity's efforts to build a new South African nation. It is an approach that should be rewarded with an acceleration of the movement towards the day when all our teams shall be truly representative of our people.

I am confident that tonight's awards will encourage the recipients to build on their successful sports careers and continue to serve our country as the role models and ambassadors that they are.

I wish to congratulate all these deserving men and women for the successes they have scored, sometimes under circumstances that were not encouraging.

Attainments in sport depend much on the support of family,

friends and community. On this occasion we should remember them and thank them for what they have given.

On behalf of the people of South Africa, I now wish to reward our sports persons, administrators and officials for their outstanding achievements during 1993 and 1994.

Africa's Champions

Speech at the Football Banquet, Pretoria,
1 March 1996.

South Africa had dared to expect much of the African Cup of
Nations. We felt we would acquit ourselves well. We believed our
administrators would do a good job. We anticipated that the display
of sporting skill by leading players from all over Africa would enthuse
the fans and win new supporters for soccer. And we expected that
our national team would give of its best and make a respectable mark
in its first continental challenge.

But as the tournament unfolded we experienced something beyond our wildest expectations. The final was breathtaking in its
excitement, and it unleashed an outpouring of national pride and
joyful unity.

And so we are gathered here tonight to celebrate one of South
Africa's most resounding sporting successes. Our national football
team has made South Africa's dreams come true against all odds.

We pay tribute to you for the determination with which you rose
to the challenge and drew on hidden strengths to beat much higher-
rated teams. You did our country proud! And you consolidated the
place of soccer as South Africa's most popular sport. Your conduct on
and off the sports field and the team-building spirit have been inspiring. Like our rugby players and cricketers you have helped bring our
people together as never before.

I also want to pay tribute to Orlando Pirates Football Club for
being the first team from Southern Africa to win the prestigious
Africa Champions Cup. Your victory was a forerunner of what was
to come!

Our sportspeople are truly amongst the pioneers of the new South
Africa, nation builders and promoters of reconciliation *par excellence*.
Our footballers have demonstrated once more that these are not the
exclusive responsibility of government and political organisations. Sport

304

has the power to overcome old divisions and create the bond of common aspirations.

I would like to thank my colleague Minister Tshwete and his Department of Sport and Recreation for their sterling work in support of the African Cup of Nations tournament and, before that, the Rugby World Cup. Their financial and organisational assistance was critical to the success of these events.

Praise must also go to the President of the Confederation of African Football, Mr Issa Hayatou, for his tireless efforts to ensure South Africa's admission to international football; to Mr Solomon Morewa for bringing the African Cup of Nations tournament to South Africa; to Clive Barker for instilling confidence into the squad; and to all South Africans for their marvellous support.

The world class performances by both teams present tonight have put South African football on the world map. They have also turned the players into exemplary ambassadors for our country.

With the national and international status of our sportspeople come greater responsibilities. Literally thousands of our young people are flocking to the stadiums and many more are being drawn by you to become football supporters. They see you as role models, and I am confident that in you they will continue to have worthy examples: both as players and as administrators of this popular sporting discipline.

We look forward eagerly to future contests in which South Africa vies with nations of the world for excellence in football and other sports. We know beyond doubt that whatever the final score, our teams will do our nation proud.

We are grateful for your contribution to the new patriotism that is bearing our country towards its goal of being a truly nonracial democracy.

Let all of us dedicate ourselves to make sport truly accessible to all our people, inspired by your achievements and by the warmth with which all the people of South Africa have taken you into their hearts.

May I once more humbly say:

Congratulations to Africa's Champions!

Congratulations to South Africa!

Free Press

Selection from an address to the International Federation
of Newspaper Publishers, Prague,
26 May 1992.

Permit me to express my profound appreciation of the invitation
extended to me by the International Federation of Newspaper
Publishers to address this important assembly. I consider it a great
honour that your organisation has asked me to share our views with
you on this occasion. I recognise that this is an honour bestowed not
on me personally, but on the movement which I have been associated
with all of my adult life.

Your conference takes place in the context of a rapidly changing
world. During this century, which has witnessed upheavals and trans-
formations of daunting proportions, the present decade will be
recorded as a period of intense change that has swept away institutions of long standing and is inaugurating a new age of democracy,
social justice and freedom. Our own country, South Africa, is also
caught up in the throes of a process of transformation which has
continental proportions.

The media, and especially the oldest component of the mass
media, the newspapers, have played their role in assisting the birth of
this emergence of this democratic order.

It is an irony that in a world in which massive illiteracy still enslaves
millions, not least in our own country, the printed word nonetheless
carries great weight. An awesome and grave responsibility therefore
devolves on the owners of media and publishers. It is a responsibility I
know you take very seriously. Three outstanding South African journalists, the late Percy Qoboza, Donald Woods and Anthony Heard,
have been recipients of your prestigious Golden Pen Award.

Your Federation so honoured them because of the contribution
they individually made to the struggle for freedom of expression in
South Africa. During the darkest days of apartheid and repression, the
International Federation of Newspaper Publishers was amongst the

many international bodies that lent their voices to those of millions in South Africa demanding freedom of the press. We remain in your debt for that support.

A South African novelist once compared 'truth' to a powerful wrestler. No matter how hard its adversary, 'falsehood', may try to overwhelm it, truth refuses to yield. And even when falsehood thinks it has overpowered truth, truth will gather new strength and cast off falsehood.

Truth has great power; yet it is also extremely elusive. No single person, no body of opinion, no political doctrine, no religious doctrine can claim a monopoly on truth. Truth can be arrived at only through the untrammelled contest among differing opinions, in which as many points of view as possible are given a fair and equal hearing. It has therefore always been our contention that laws and mores that repress freedom of expression are a disservice to society. We would also insist that these are devices that are employed by falsehood. Freedom of expression, of which freedom of the press and other media is a crucial aspect, is one of those core values of democracy that has always been a central plank of the ANC's political platform. This was inevitable because a number of the pioneers of the black press were amongst the founders of the ANC. In this context I recall the name of the first President of the ANC, Dr John Langalibalele Dube, a distinguished educator who founded Ohlange Institute and the newspaper *Ilanga lase Natal*. There was also that giant among African men of letters, Solomon Plaatje, the founder of *Koeranta eaBatswana*. No less committed a journalist and publisher was the Reverend Dr WB Rubusana, a distinguished writer and translator, the founder of *Izwi Labantu*.

With such antecedents, the ANC was, from its birth in 1912, firmly devoted to securing the right of the citizen to express whatever opinion he/she subscribed to as long as the exercise of that right did not harm others.

South Africa is indeed a land of ironies. In 1912, when the ANC was founded, there was a great diversity of media voices in our country. That is now a thing of the past. In 1912 there existed at least two weekly newspapers in the Xhosa language, published and owned by African companies. There was at least one Tswana language weekly, owned by a co-operative of African business interests. At the same time there were at least two Zulu language newspapers, similarly owned and published by African companies.

In 1913, the ANC was able to establish its own newspaper, *Abantu-Batho* (The People). With the exception of *Imvo*, formerly *Imvo Zabantsundu* (Black Opinion) and *Ilanga lase Natal,* every one of these African newspapers has disappeared. Both *Imvo* and *Ilanga* are no longer under African ownership, having been acquired by the powerful media giants that dominate the print media in South Africa.

The false impression is sometimes created that the demise of the black-owned newspapers was purely the outcome of market forces. The hard facts of the matter are that successive white minority governments have since 1910 steadily undermined and destroyed the legal property rights of the disenfranchised majority of South Africans.

It was the brutal application of racist law that deprived the African community of the economic capacity to build and sustain any autonomous institutions of value. By 1950, virtually every venture made by black South Africans to gain a foothold in publishing had come to naught. We should also not forget that the outright banning of publications played no small part in this.

The reality is that today, three large conglomerates, drawn exclusively from the white racial group, dominate the print media of our country. This, as you may well imagine, has produced an alarming degree of conformism in the South African print media. With the exception of one daily, *The Sowetan*, the senior editorial staffs of all South Africa's daily newspapers are cast from the same racial mould. They are all white, they are all male, they are all from a middle class background and tend to share a very similar life experience. The same, unfortunately, holds true for the mass circulation weeklies – again with a few exceptions.

The ANC has no objection in principle to editors with such a profile. What is disturbing, however, and in our view, harmful, is the threat of one-dimensionality this poses for the media of our country as a whole. It is clearly unacceptable that a country whose population is overwhelmingly black, 85 per cent of the total, is serviced by media whose principal players have no knowledge of the life experience of that majority.

. . .

Freedom of the press is amongst the oldest and most valued of the freedoms for which so many South Africans have given their lives. Among them we are proud to recall the names of two courageous ANC militants, Joe Gqabi and Ruth First, the tenth anniversary of whose assassination we are marking this year.

Joe Gqabi was a skilled journalist who served a twelve-year prison term on Robben Island. In 1982 he was assassinated in Harare, the capital of Zimbabwe, by persons in the hire of the South African Intelligence Services.

Ruth First was an outstanding investigative journalist and academic. She was murdered with a parcel bomb in her offices at the Eduardo Mondlane University in Maputo, Mozambique, by agents of the Directorate of Military Intelligence of the South African Defence Force.

These were journalists in the tradition of the founders of the ANC whom I have already mentioned. It would be a slight to their memory and their pioneering work if by our actions we proved unworthy of their sacrifice.

I cannot overemphasise the value we place on a free, independent and outspoken press in the democratic South Africa we hope to build. This task will be even more important given the legacy of information manipulation and distortion employed by the National Party's faithful servants, the South African Broadcasting Corporation.

Such a free press will temper the appetite of any government to amass power at the expense of the citizen. A free press will be the vigilant watchdog of the South African public against the temptation to abuse power. This is all the more reason why the press in South Africa, including its ownership, should reflect the composition and varied viewpoints of all our people.

The African National Congress reiterates its commitment to the attainment of freedom of the press in South Africa as a democratic objective of intrinsic value.

The tide in the annals of all countries and peoples ebbs and flows. Even when it appears we have sustained reverses it would be foolish to despair. South Africa is experiencing the terrible birth pangs occasioned by a democracy struggling to be born. If we are to secure the life of the mother and her child, we dare not fail.

In closing, permit me to quote the words of that democratic journalist, Thomas Paine: 'These are the times that try men's souls. The summer soldier and the sunshine patriot will, in this crisis, shrink from the service of their country; but he that stands by it now, deserves the love and thanks of man and woman. Tyranny, like hell, is not easily conquered; yet we have this consolation with us, that the harder the conflict, the more glorious the triumph.'

8
RELIGION

RELIGIOUS FREEDOM

DESMOND TUTU

Soon after his release in 1990 Nelson Mandela visited our Anglican Episcopal Synod, our quarterly such meeting of all the bishops of the Church of the Province of Southern Africa, which included bishops from Lesotho, Swaziland, Mozambique, Namibia and St Helena Island, as well as the Republic of South Africa. We were all thrilled that he had accepted to come and we were meeting in a church conference centre in Jabavu, Soweto. He was gracious and elegant in a dark suit (he still wore suits conventionally!), and was generous in his comments about what the prison chaplains' services meant to all the inmates on Robben Island and by extension at all the other maximum security prisons of our land. He was quite funny because he did say that the prisoners tended to be thoroughly ecumenical, and that they would attend the church services no matter what the chaplain's denomination turned out to be. They were ready as prisoners to do or endure anything that saved them even briefly from their humdrum, tedious prison existence. They were not too fussy and even sometimes attended services conducted by Muslim and Hindu religious leaders. They were happy to be interfaith adherents if it got them out of their cells.

More seriously though, he paid a very warm tribute to what the Church had done in our country's history. He, like many of our political leaders, was indebted to the Church which had provided blacks with a sound education in its church schools and colleges. Had it not been for the Church's involvement, and had things depended only on the government, then many of them would have either had no education at all or would have had to be content with an inferior brew available in the few government institutions set aside for blacks. As it happens, very, very few would have had the opportunity of a tertiary education had there been no University of Fort Hare. Indeed, many of Africa's leaders would have had no tertiary education to speak of, as several from the then

Rhodesia and other African countries obtained their university degrees at Fort Hare. And Fort Hare was founded by the Presbyterian Church. Whilst their secondary schools and teacher training institutions were of uneven quality, by and large they were outstanding institutions staffed by dedicated and inspiring individuals who left an indelible mark on many of their charges. It was at his first school that his teacher decided Rolihlahla would be a mouthful and gave him the 'Christian' name of Nelson.

He was thankful for that crucial role in the development of our people. He was aware as well that much of the medical care our people received, especially in the rural areas, was provided by church hospitals and clinics with deeply committed Christian doctors and nurses working conscientiously with devotion to care for those who needed this ministry.

He was, however, particularly concerned to express appreciation for the Church's role in the anti-apartheid struggle, seeking to help establish a new dispensation that would be just, democratic and free where each person would enjoy the inalienable rights to which each is entitled. He had been closely associated with persons such as Trevor Huddleston, who had made a name for himself in opposing the demolition of Sophiatown and who was there in Kliptown in 1955 when the Freedom Charter was signed. He would have thought of people like Michael Scott and his UN appearances regarding South West Africa and who had highlighted the plight of squatters in Orlando, or Ambrose Reeves, the doughty Bishop of Johannesburg who became *persona non grata* to the apartheid government through his opposition to Bantu Education and his exposé regarding the Sharpeville massacre of 21 March 1960, or Archbishops Geoffrey Clayton and Joost de Blank, who were not exactly the blue-eyed boys of the government and the white community.

He would in his tribute have been lauding the outstanding work of the South African Council of Churches, which provided legal defence for those appearing in political trials and gave support to the families of detainees and political prisoners. It provided accommodation in its Cape Town Cowley House for relatives visiting prisoners on Robben Island, giving transport to bring them to and from the ferry going to the Island. And he was full of praise for those who had not been silent but had been quite vociferous in their condemnation of the vicious system – the Beyers Naudes, the Archbishop Hurleys, the Peter Storeys, the Johan Heynses, the Nico Smiths, the David Boschs, the Allan Boesaks, the Frank Chikanes, the Sam Butis, the Bongani Fincas (and later the Mvume Dandalas and the Njongonkulu Ndunganes).

Subsequently at other venues we were visited by Mosiuoa 'Terror' Lekota when he was Premier of the Free State, and Tokyo Sexwale when he was Premier of Gauteng. They too were warm in their plaudits. Terror said people should not be surprised that they in the ANC were so committed to forgiveness and reconciliation. He asked why we seemed surprised. It was all quite easy to explain – it was the influence of the Church and its teaching. They were almost all products of the schools and institutions of higher learning that owed their existence to the churches and most of them were committed and devout members of one or other Christian denomination and the central tenets of their faith were important to them. They might not always carry their faith as it were on their sleeves, but they had been deeply influenced by those teachings and it showed in their commitment to forgiveness and reconciliation rather than demanding retribution and revenge.

Madiba's own passion for equality and democracy as well as the enjoyment of inalienable rights for all must to a very considerable extent have been lit by the biblical teaching of the infinite worth of everyone because of being created in the image of God. It had nothing to do with extrinsic attributes or circumstances such as ethnicity, skin colour or social standing. It was a universal phenomenon, and this dignity, freedom and equality of all were things which he was wanting to fight and live for, but if necessary, he would be prepared to die for.

His opposition to injustice, racism and oppression were thus not just political and ideological but in a very real sense deeply religious as well. The obverse to this was a passion for freedom, nonracialism and righteousness which would come to be enshrined in our magnificent Constitution that ensures that that legacy will live forever.

He was tempered in the fire of adversity. All that he endured in the times when he was the elusive Black Pimpernel with hardly a family life to speak of and the 27 years of incarceration, were important in the making of the man. It gave him a new depth, helped him to be more understanding of the foibles of others, to be more generous, more tolerant, more magnanimous and it gave him an unassailable credibility and integrity and so he could be as he was when he emerged from prison, willing to extend a hand of friendship to his former adversaries and be generous when they were vanquished. He lived out the understanding that an enemy is a friend waiting to be made, and so could have his white former gaoler attend his Presidential inauguration as a VIP guest; and have Dr Percy Yutar, who was the prosecutor in the Rivonia Trial when he was sentenced to life imprisonment, the Dr Yutar who had wanted the death sentence, come to lunch with him at the Presidency; and could visit the widow of Dr Verwoerd, the high priest and architect of apartheid, for tea when she was not able to come to the Presidency. The former terrorist could have those who used to think of him as public enemy number one eating out of his hand.

He awed everyone as a spectacular embodiment of magnanimity and forgiveness and he saved our land from the bloodbath that most had predicted would be our lot in resolving the problem of apartheid's vicious oppression of the vast majority of our motherland's population. Suffering can embitter, but it can also ennoble, and God blessed us richly when the latter happened in Madiba's case.

He grew in moral stature as he grew in attributes of tolerance. He could try to see the other person's point of view and thus would be so ready to make concessions and to be on the look-out for the compromise that could often help to pull the chestnuts out of the fire. Bishop Stanley Mogoba, when still Presiding Bishop of the Methodist Church, and I convened a meeting between him and Dr Mangosuthu Buthelezi at the Lutheran Kempton Park Centre to try to resolve the problem posed by the Inkatha Freedom Party's threat to boycott the general elections, which meant only one thing – more blood-letting in the devastated, conflict-ridden KwaZulu-Natal region. I was amazed at the number of points Madiba was willing to concede and acquiesce in the demands of Dr Buthelezi. He was, however, unable to persuade the IFP leader to agree to a date for the elections. This readiness to compromise did not mean that he was spineless. He could get quite angry, and walked out of Codesa after the Boipatong massacre, which he said could have been prevented had Mr FW de Klerk heeded the warnings the ANC had given and if Mr De Klerk had shown he cared about black lives as much as he did about white lives. The point being made, though, is that he was tolerant, almost to a fault, of different points of view.

He learned that a leader ultimately exists for the sake of the led. It was not something to do with self-aggrandisement. It was the best form of altruism. That is an attribute not too obvious among many leaders, who seem to be where they are for what they can get out of it. The led are quick to sense when one is there for them and not around to manipulate or to exploit them. That is one reason why Madiba has captured their hearts and their devotion. In scriptural terms, he is the good shepherd ready to lay down his life for them. Of course he had said he was willing to die for the cause – now it was that he was ready to be a spendthrift, a prodigal, on their behalf. He has left people half his age panting in his wake with the rigour of his punishing schedule. But it is a matter of honour for him. Even after retiring and long past 80 years of age when everybody would say he had earned a well-deserved rest, he keeps at it, using his charm and persuasive skills to extract huge donations from the private sector helping to build schools and clinics especially in the impoverished rural areas. It is almost as if he really can't stop himself. He has always got to be there for others. That is a wonderful part of the legacy he will leave for others to emulate.

He has been scrupulous to ensure that he demonstrated a profound respect for all the faiths to be found in our country. After he was elected by Parliament as our first democratically elected President on 9 May 1994, on that Friday he went to a mosque and on the following day attended a synagogue and on the Sunday attended a large inter-denominational service at the FNB Stadium in Soweto. At his inauguration on 10 May prayers were offered by Muslim, Jewish, Hindu and Christian ministers. This spirit of tolerance is now enshrined in the custom that Parliament starts each day with a period of quiet to allow each person to use as is consistent with his or her faith or lack of it. It replaces the way things were done in the old, all-white Parliament when Christian prayers were the order of the day despite the fact that a few members were Jewish. The respect for and sensitivity to the things others hold dear is a precious part of the legacy that this great man leaves us and is a tremendous contribution to the kind of future we want to see, particularly at this time when religious fundamentalisms of all kinds and fanaticism threaten to destroy global peace and harmony. We have been helped to celebrate our rich diversity and to exult in being truly the rainbow people of God, diverse ethnically, culturally, linguistically and religiously but clinging to one another in our passionate love for this land which was saved from a bloody conflagration by the application of the precious religious concepts of forgiveness and reconciliation in place of the dreaded retribution and revenge.

This appreciation for our diversity and a deep reverence for the innate dignity and worth of others has been shown too in his abhorrence of male chauvinism and his advocacy of the equality of the sexes as grounded in the principle of interdependence and complementarity. He has been almost obsessed in ensuring that women are given the respect due to them and been quite determined in appointing them to the Cabinet and as Deputy Ministers. The two Houses of Parliament have been presided over by women, the National Assembly from the moment a democratic dispensation was in place.

It has been wonderful to see such an outstanding embodiment of impeccable integrity and truthfulness in public life. It has come as a breath of fresh air, utterly consistent with his passion to be a leader for the sake of the led and a spendthrift with himself on their behalf. There has been a splendid consistency about his life so that he was able to lay down his tools when others are so bent on staying on as presidents. It seems true that the ones whom the people would have loved to see continue their tenure are the ones who step down too readily, while those who are not so popular, whom the people would wish to see relinquish their positions as quickly as possible, turn out to be the ones who are not so eager to go, playing ducks and drakes with their constitutions and worse. Julius Nyerere, Joachim Chissano and Madiba are amongst the foremost among the reluctant rulers who could have gone on for at least one more term, and the people would have loved it so.

Madiba has been loyal to a fault, often with some detriment to himself and possibly to his country. Note his refusal to jettison President Castro and Colonel Gaddafi. The objects of his loyalty might be questionable but the attribute is an admirable virtue, not to be a fair-weather friend. And also admirable has been his penchant to speak the truth almost always in love as when he spoke about HIV/Aids and the strange policies of our government, or his acerbic comments about President Bush and Prime Minister Tony Blair concerning the unnecessary war against Iraq. How the world needs people of integrity and uprightness.

We have been richly blessed in him. Anyone else at the helm of affairs in the difficult days of the delicate transition from repression to democracy would have steered us on to the rocks, the bloodbath that so many had grimly predicted to be our lot would almost certainly have overwhelmed us. Mercifully for us, it was this man – now widely acclaimed as standing head and shoulders above all statesmen and world leaders, revered as an icon of forgiveness and reconciliation – through whom we were spared a comprehensive disaster. He has given us firm foundations, whose bricks are magnanimity and generosity, forgiveness and reconciliation; leadership that is altruistic and not self-serving for its own aggrandisement, ready to step down before being pushed; that prizes highly freedom of religion and conscience and respects all faiths and has a passion for integrity and honesty and respect for the inherent dignity of every person.

The South Africa he has helped to bring to birth will survive and continue so utterly improbably to be a source of hope for others who have to deal with conflict and its aftermath.

318

Religious Diversity

Response to the 1994 Peace Lecture of the World Conference
on Religion and Peace (South African Chapter),
7 August 1994.

It is not the easiest thing in the world to respond to any Peace Lecture.
But to respond to one by as accomplished a peace warrior as the
People's Bishop is a daunting task.

I hope that I speak on behalf of all those assembled here in thanking
Archbishop Desmond Tutu for his inspiring and thought-provoking
remarks. The ideas were so clearly espoused, so simply and honestly
articulated that there is effectively nothing to add. These are qualities
which earned him the most passionate hatred by those who defend
injustice, and at the same time the loving embrace of the poor and
downtrodden.

Nevertheless, we are called upon to partake in this discourse.

You have chosen the most relevant theme for the times in which
we live: 'Let us celebrate our diversity'.

From the point of view of the shocking images that we see on our
television screens these are words not easily uttered. In a world in
which there is a prevalent tendency to see diversity as a curse, an omen
for self-destruction, yours were candid and encouraging remarks. For
you reminded us once more that diversity can be a source of common strength, the pool whence we should deepen our sense of
humanity.

But, alas, we have seen intolerance of diversity precipitating im-
plosions that have rent nations apart in Africa, Europe, the Americas
and Asia.

Often, when we are struck by these images, we tend to rationalise
about who might be right or wrong. However, there cannot be any
conceivable instance where justice can be associated with pogroms
and genocide.

So we dare ask the questions: Why is it that in this day and age,
human beings still butcher one another simply because they dared to

belong to different religions, to speak different tongues, or belong to different races? Are human beings inherently evil? What infuses individuals with the ego and ambition to so clamour for power that genocide assumes the mantle of means that justify coveted ends?

These are difficult questions, which if wrongly examined, can lead one to lose faith in fellow human beings. And there is where we would go wrong.

Firstly, because to lose faith in fellow humans is, as the Archbishop would correctly point out, to lose faith in God and in the purpose of life itself. Secondly, it is erroneous to attribute to the human character a universal trait it does not possess – that of being either inherently evil or inherently humane.

I would venture to say that there is something inherently good in all human beings, deriving from, among other things, the attribute of social consciousness that we all possess. And, yes, there is also something inherently bad in all of us, flesh and blood as we are, with the attendant desire to perpetuate and pamper the self.

From this premise arises the challenge to order our lives and mould our mores in such a way that the good in all of us takes precedence. In other words, we are not passive and hapless souls waiting for manna or the plague from on high. All of us have a role to play in shaping society.

We South Africans are fortunate in having had the leadership – political, religious and otherwise – that helped us approach our problems in a manner that obviated the worst possible scenarios. From the beginning of the century and before then, men and women of wisdom challenged our version of oppression and repression with an antidote of equality and nonracialism.

In this sense, the worst in human beings as represented by the ideology and practice of apartheid helped bring out the best in its opponents.

While we can justifiably say that the African National Congress has been at the head of this political movement, we all derive pride from the fact that these qualities owe their origins and guidance also from the teachings of all religious faiths. Mahatma Gandhi, Abdullah Abdurahman, Reverend Rubusana and Father Trevor Huddleston – to quote a few religious leaders – all contributed to the school of thought that guided our liberation movement.

They helped us to see the struggle as one against a system and not a racial group. They helped instil resistance fighters with the morality to seek reconciliation even in the worst of times. Our religious establishment was able to do this because it was an active part of the struggle.

And so, we have turned back from the abyss because the pressure of principled struggle backed by the message of reconciliation finally prevailed. Even during our difficult transition, with its violence and other schemes of sabotage, reason finally carried the day. We dare call this a miracle, an achievement that we should protect with all the strength that we have.

Yet, we would be wrong to assert that we are altogether out of the woods. Dealing with the legacy of apartheid will take years and even decades. The challenge is how to consolidate this fledgling democracy and make it flourish!

The formality of a Constitution and legislation is an important part of this: statutes that should protect diversity and tolerance – be it racial, ethnic, religious or political. This, however, needs to be deepened into a national culture encompassing all the people. Changes in attitudes – in communities, in the home, at the workplace and within ourselves as individuals – is crucial for our small miracle to fully come of its own.

Among the most crucial tasks in transforming society is to change the terrible conditions to which the majority are relegated. It requires concrete, realistic and realisable programmes to bring about social justice. Our Reconstruction and Development Programme is meant precisely to attain these goals. Economic growth and equity, urban and rural renewal, and rebuilding of the social fabric of all communities are among its central objectives.

We have already made progress in implementing some of the initial projects in this broader programme: free health care for children under six years of age and pregnant mothers, starting the building of houses, intensifying the electrification project and so on. But there are many lessons to be learnt.

Among others, how to gear the whole state structure, including the civil service, for this mammoth task; how to actively involve communities and their political, social and religious organisations in the process of formulating projects and their implementation; the need to speed up formation of transitional local government structures; and many more. We will soon be making important announcements with regard to many of these issues.

I wish, however, to emphasise the role of the religious community in reconstruction and development. On the one hand, we view it as only natural that the partnership against apartheid should mature into one for the betterment of the life of all South Africans, especially the poor. On the other hand, your prophetic voice is crucial in reinforcing the moral fibre of the new democratic state – be it in the application of human rights statutes or the integrity of its financial and other practices.

In other words, the new democracy needs you: as an active participant in its consolidation, as a critical watchdog and as a crucial part of its spiritual guide. To us, the individual religious groups and the inter-faith movement that South Africa has forged over the years, will always be our source of strength.

This is how we should celebrate our diversity:

Allow our variety of cultures, races, religions and languages to inform the total richness that is our rainbow nation.

Ensure that this multiplicity is harnessed for our mutual benefit as South Africans.

This also requires maximum sensitivity on the part of both the government and civil society. For, unlike with many other issues, diversity in areas of culture does not lend itself to cold rational calculation and the equation of numbers. The correct balance has to be struck all the time.

We are confident that your prophecy will help lift our nation to greater and greater heights. And that together, as partners, we will continue to celebrate our diversity in joint efforts to accomplish the historic mission of South Africa today: reconciliation and reconstruction.

Religious Heritage

Selection from a lecture, 'Renewal and Renaissance:
Towards a New World Order,' Oxford Centre for Islamic Studies,
Oxford, 11 July 1997.

When the Prophet Muhammad sent his oppressed followers to the African Christian King Negus of Abyssinia for safety, and they received his protection, was that not an example of tolerance and co-operation to be emulated today? Is that not a profound pointer to the role that religion can play, and the spiritual leadership it can provide in bringing about the social renewal on our continent and in the world?

Africa's history has been profoundly shaped also by the interplay between three great religious traditions – Islam, Christianity and African traditional religions. As it faces the new millennium, the conduct of this religious heritage may very well again be decisive in determining how Africa meets the challenges of the future.

As in the new global order, no country, region or continent can any longer operate in isolation from the rest of the world. No social movement in any country or continent can isolate itself from similar movements co-existing with it. This would apply to religion as much as anything else living in a society.

The way in which these three great religions of Africa interact and co-operate with one another could have a profound bearing on the social space we create for the rebirth of our continent. The relationship of Islam and Christianity to one another and of those two to African traditional religion, may be pertinent aspects of this process. How Islam (and Christianity, for that matter) relates to African traditional religion presents a particular challenge to its followers all over Africa. It represents a call to Muslims to harness the more inclusive strands in their own theological heritage in order to contribute to a more humane Africa, acknowledging the humanity of those traditions that are unique to the continent.

As with other aspects of its heritage, African traditional religion is increasingly recognised for its contribution to the world. No longer seen as despised superstition which had to be superseded by superior forms of belief, today its enrichment of humanity's spiritual heritage is acknowledged. The spirit of *Ubuntu* – that profound African sense that we are human only through the humanity of other human beings – is not a parochial phenomenon, but has added globally to our common search for a better world.

The nature of interaction between the strands of our religious heritage could help lay solid foundations for the establishment of a world order based on mutual respect, partnership and equity. On a continent battling the scourge of underdevelopment, Aids, ecological disaster and poverty, competition amongst religions will be utterly misplaced. Tolerance and co-operation, on the other hand, will give the moral leadership so gravely needed.

If I may conclude with one more reference to the experience of our own country during the struggle against apartheid. The strength of inter-religious solidarity in action against apartheid, rather than mere harmony or co-existence, was critical in bringing that evil system to an end. This approach, rather than verbally competing claims, enabled each tradition to bring its best forward and place it at the service of all. I am confident that the religions of our continent will walk a similar path in the reconstruction and renewal of our continent. And in that way we shall play our full role in the creation of the new world order.

Methodist Christians

Address to the annual conference of the
Methodist Church, Umtata,
18 September 1994.

It is indeed a great honour for me to bring my personal greetings to one of the most significant Christian communities in our land.

My joy at being in this conference is multiplied many-fold by the fact that this is for me also a personal homecoming, both in the physical and spiritual sense. The environs of Umtata are not only my humble origins. It is here that my spiritual association with this great church started. And I cannot overemphasise the role that the Methodist Church has played in my own life.

Your church has a proud record of commitment to the development of Africa's sons and daughters in more areas than one. The great institutions of learning which spread from the Reverend William Shaw's 'Chain of Mission Stations' in this region shaped the minds and characters of generations of our people as well as many of our present leaders.

Although the dark night of apartheid sought to obliterate many of these institutions, the impact of their academic and moral teachings could not be trampled on. We who passed through them will not forget the excellent standards of teaching and the spiritual values which were imparted to us.

It is therefore heartening to learn that Methodism is returning to this great tradition with the rehabilitation of Healdtown, your new John Wesley School in Pinetown, the use of Indaleni for community development, the return to Kilnerton and the hundreds of pre-schools you have established. All these and other endeavours vividly demonstrate the fact that the religious community in our country is not only a spiritual and moral force. It is also an important social institution, contributing to the development and wellbeing of the people as a whole.

The sense of social responsibility that the religious community has always upheld found expression in your immense contribution to the efforts to rid our country of the scourge of racism and apartheid. When pronouncements and actions against the powers-that-be meant persecution and even death, you dared to stand up to the tyrants.

In the founding and evolution of the African National Congress, the religious community played a central role. We refer here to leaders such as Calata, Mahabane and Mapikela as well as Abdullah Abdurahman and Mahatma Gandhi.

Especially while political leaders were in prison and in exile, bodies like the South African Council of Churches and its member churches resisted racial bigotry and held out a vision of a different, transformed South Africa. Methodist leaders were prominent among the prophets who refused to bow to the false god of apartheid. Your ministers also visited us in prison and cared for our families. Some of you were banned. Your Presiding Bishop himself shared imprisonment with us for some years on Robben Island. This you did, not as outsiders to the cause of democracy, but as part of society and eminent prophets of the teachings of your faith.

It is fitting that this conference is taking place in this particular chamber, after the advent of democracy in our country. The Methodist Church was the only church to be declared an illegal organisation under apartheid, and for ten long years you were forbidden to operate in the Transkei bantustan. It is in this very chamber that this banning order was promulgated.

One cannot overemphasise the contribution that the religious community made particularly in ensuring that our transition achieves the desired result. The spirit of reconciliation and the goodwill within the nation can, to a great measure, be attributed to the moral and spiritual interventions of the religious community.

Now that a major part of the journey towards democracy has been traversed, new and more difficult tasks lie ahead of us. For, political democracy will be empty and meaningless if the misery of the majority of the people is not addressed.

The Church, like all other institutions of civil society, must help all South Africans to rise to the challenge of freedom. As South Africa moves from resistance to reconstruction and from confrontation to reconciliation, the energy that was once dedicated to breaking apartheid must be harnessed to the task of building the nation.

Our programme of Reconstruction and Development is designed

to unite sound economics with true compassion and justice so that all the people of this land may share in its resources. But this programme cannot succeed unless people who have been repressed by years of subjugation are motivated to participate in building their future.

We are encouraged that in the South African religious community the Government of National Unity has an experienced, morally upright and reliable partner. With its long history of involvement in development projects and widespread infrastructure, the Church is strategically placed to empower our people to take hold of their freedom and work together to transform their conditions. This should include paying particular attention to millions of children and youth who need to be specially nurtured, so as to restore their dignity and afford them opportunities to make a constructive contribution to society.

The Church, with its message of forgiveness, has a special role to play in national reconciliation. After so much suffering and injustice the instinct for revenge is a natural one. But the transition we are going through shows that those who suffered under apartheid are prepared to bury the past. At the same time, those who enjoyed the fruits of unjust privilege must be helped to find a new spirit of sharing. Your message and example can enable that to happen.

The Truth and Reconciliation Commission is an important instrument, not only in dealing with past wrongs, but also in freeing all of us to move with a clean conscience into the future.

The objective of this commission is neither vengeance nor retribution. We have to forgive the past but at the same time ensure that the dignity of the victims is restored, and their plight properly addressed. We are confident that the conclusions that this commission will come to will contribute not only to reconciliation, but also to reconstruction and development.

In the end, reconciliation is a spiritual process which requires more than just a legal framework. It has to happen in the hearts and minds of people. Indeed, no institution is better placed to assist this process than the thousands of religious congregations which gather every week all over the land and among all communities.

This will also form an important part of the process to cast the demon of crime and violence out of our social life. The government is determined to use all the means in our power to eradicate this problem. However, this requires co-operation between communities and the security agencies. Again, the religious community has a central role to play in ensuring that this happens.

South Africa now has a democratic government representative of, and accountable to, all the people. By your fearless commitment to truth and justice the Methodist Church and other religious bodies helped realise this. But all governments, no matter how democratic, need constructive criticism and advice. I ask you to continue to play your prophetic role, always seeking to hold the nation and all its leaders to the highest standards of integrity and service.

One of the critical issues in this regard is the disparity, within society as a whole, between the lowest and the highest social echelons. To address this problem requires comprehensive measures to develop our human resources. It also demands bold action on the part of the leadership in the public sector, the private sector and organs of civil society, including religious institutions.

I am confident that, with the support of the Methodist Church and the religious fraternity as a whole, our nation will reach the mountain tops of its collective desires.

I am mindful that the great hymn which is now part of our national anthem was first sung long ago at the ordination of a Methodist minister. I join you in that humble prayer: *Nkosi Sikelela iAfrika!*

Ethiopian Christians

Speech to the Free Ethiopian Church of Southern Africa,
Potchefstroom, 14 December 1992.

I am greatly honoured by your invitation to me to share in the centenary celebration of the Free Ethiopian Church of Southern Africa.

The centenary of the Ethiopian Church should have been celebrated throughout the length and the breadth of our country because it touches all the African people irrespective of their denomination or political outlook. The Free Ethiopian Church of Southern Africa is the only surviving institution that is in the hands of the African people. This is a remarkable feature for which we have to give credit to the leaders of this church throughout the difficult years of final dispossession of our people. Indeed our people were not dispossessed only of their land and cattle but also of their pride, their dignity and their institutions. In celebrating this century you have disproved the lie that the African people cannot run their own institutions.

The links between the Ethiopian Church and the ANC and the struggle for national liberation in general go back to the 1870s when the products of missionary education observed and recorded that, as they put it, colonialism is a one-teated cow that only feeds the whites. They soon made a very incisive observation that the sons of the missionaries were now filling the various magistracies that were arising as a result of the rapid African land dispossession from the 1880s onwards.

The role that the missionaries played in the accelerated African dispossession of the late nineteenth century called for a response from the African people in general and African religious leaders in particular. The response took a political form on the one hand and a theological form on the other. On the political front various provincial African political associations and newspapers mushroomed in the last 30 years of the nineteenth century. On the theological front African clergymen sought to free themselves from the fetters of white missionaries by establishing African Independent Churches. One of the most celebrated breakaways was that of Nehemiah Tile who founded the Thembu Church in the Transkei in 1884.

The process of founding African Independent Churches, though covering all parts of South Africa by the late 1880s, could not be described as a movement until the Ethiopian Movement came into being and increased the anxiety of the various colonial governments in South Africa. The Ethiopian Movement was more than a religious movement. Though its fundamental basis was the African interpretation of the scripture it went well beyond the churches it had helped produce.

Fundamental tenets of the Ethiopian Movement were self-worth, self-reliance and freedom. These tenets drew the advocates of Ethiopianism, like a magnet, to the growing political movement. That political movement was to culminate in the formation of the ANC in 1912. It is in this sense that in the ANC we trace the seeds of the formation of our organisation to the Ethiopian Movement of the 1890s.

Zionist Christians

Speech at the Zionist Christian Church
Easter Conference, Moria,
20 April 1992.

Reading from the 'Lamentations of Jeremiah', Chapter 5:

Remember, O Lord, what is come upon us:
consider, and behold our reproach,
Our land is turned over to strangers, our homes to foreigners,
We are orphans and fatherless, our Mothers are as widows,
We have to pay for our water; and our wood is sold unto us,
Our necks are under the yoke of oppression, we labour, and we
    have no rest.

Khotsong Masione! Peace unto you! *Uxolo Mazayoni!*
Permit me to thank you for your kind invitation to attend your
Easter Conference here at the holy city of Moria. Moria, a tabernacle
erected by the Zionist Christian Church as a site of annual pilgrim-
age and renewal! I am honoured that you have invited me on this
occasion to pay my respects to the leadership and the members of
this mighty church on the sub-continent. Since my release from
prison, I have attempted to find a time suitable to both myself and
His Grace, Bishop Lekganyane, so that we could confer about our
common aspirations and the challenges facing our nation in these
trying times.

My coming here today is a long-awaited moment. I come to the
Holy City of Moria as a pilgrim, with other pilgrims, senior members of the African National Congress, as a mark of respect and as an
act of communion.

I present Cyril Ramaphosa, Secretary-General of the ANC;
Thomas Nkobi, our Treasurer-General; Joe Nhlanhla, a member of
the National Executive Committee of the ANC, and others.

We bring to your gathering heartfelt greetings from the entire

331

membership of the ANC. *Khotso e be le lena!* May peace be with you!

We have joined you this Easter in an act of solidarity, and in an act of worship. We have come, like all the other pilgrims, to join in an act of renewal and rededication. The festival of Easter, which is so closely linked with the festival of the Passover, marks the rebirth of the resurrected Messiah, who without arms, without soldiers, without police and covert special forces, without hit squads or bands of vigilantes, overcame the mightiest state during his time.

This great festival of rejoicing marks the victory of the forces of life over death, of hope over despair. As we bow our heads in prayerful worship this day, our minds cannot but dwell on the evil of violence that today stalks our land. We cannot but call to mind the cries of mothers violated, brutalised and outraged by armed foreign mercenaries and killers in our midst.

As we lower our heads in supplication to the Lord of Hosts, the blood-curdling battle cries of armed men, sweeping through a township like a swarm of locusts in a maize field, ring in our ears, and we know that in some home, this night shall be a night for mourning.

We pray with you for the blessings of peace! We pray with you for the blessings of love! We pray with you for the blessings of freedom! We pray with you for the blessings of reconciliation among all the people of South Africa!

Khotso e be le lena! May peace be with you!

When Bishop Engenas Lekganyane founded this church in 1910 that occasion represented an important act of the oppressed to resist the theology of submission. It was an act of self-assertion on the part of a people who were expected to remain unheard and unseen while they ministered to the needs of others.

In its own way, the Zionist Christian Church was expressing what we of the ANC, two years later, tried to assert and have fought to entrench as the basis of the politics of our country. That principle, so eloquently simple but yet so profound, has moved thousands through the ages to strive for a better world. We restate it today for emphasis: The brother and sisterhood of all human beings, and the common fatherhood of God Almighty!

It is that simple truth we have inscribed in our political programme, the Freedom Charter, that South Africa belongs to all who live in it, black and white! It is because of our devotion to, our fervent belief in, and our tenacious refusal to give up that principle that many of us have suffered persecution. It is because we stood firm that we have been compelled to go into exile. It is because we would not bend in the face of state intimidation that we have been condemned to banishment; to torture; to imprisonment; and even to the gallows.

Yes! We affirm it and we shall proclaim it from the mountain tops that all people – be they black or white, be they brown or yellow, be they rich or poor, be they wise or fools – are created in the image of the Creator and are his children!

Those who dare to cast out from the human family people of a darker hue with their racism; those who exclude from the sight of God's grace people who profess another faith with their religious intolerance; those who wish to keep their fellow countrymen away from God's bounty with forced removals; those who have driven away from the altar of God people whom He has chosen to make different, commit an ugly sin! The sin called APARTHEID.

We of the African National Congress, its leadership and its membership, shall sooner break the laws and defy the fanciful wishes of mortal men when we know that in so doing we are being obedient to God. And in obedience to God we declare that all South Africans – be they Christians, Muslims, Jews Hindus, Buddhists – have an equal and untrammelled right to worship God as they see fit. No government should have the right to prescribe religious observance for the citizens of this country.

The ZCC is part of that rich tapestry of experience, culture and lifestyle that make up all our people today. Both as a church and as individual members you have lent your efforts to bring justice to our land. We applaud in particular your role in the trade union movement in pursuance of workers' rights. The struggles of our people for land and against apartheid-inspired land robbery – the forced removals – would be poorer were it not for the contribution of congregants of this church. We acclaim also the role played by ZCC businesspeople, who in the teeth of the discriminatory policies of the Pretoria government ran successful enterprises providing jobs and trade in far-flung villages.

The bond between you and the ANC is even clearer when we consider that many members of our organisation belong to the Zionist Christian Church. Among them, Peter Mokaba and Ngoako Ramatlhodi, who are with us today, grew up and have become what they are in the struggle in great measure inspired by your teachings.

Many others have fallen in the struggle. Many have been subjected to terms in jail. But their spirit remains with the people.

Khotsong Masione! Peace be with you!

This great institution, the ZCC, owes much to the person of Bishop Edward Lekganyane, whose tireless efforts have made it the largest church on the Southern African sub-continent. We also salute you for further strengthening the church and maintaining its commitment to the oppressed and the poor.

Those who are denied their just claims to the land of their birth, come to you for solace. Those condemned to the low wages and denied their rights as the creators of wealth look to you for spiritual leadership. Those cast out into the darkness and bitter loneliness of poverty and deprivation lean on you for sustenance. Those whose homes and families have been destroyed so that the ugly designs of racial oppression may be realised have come to you for comfort. Those who are denied a voice in governing of their country because they are black turn to you for inspiration.

You have engendered high standards of morality and discipline in an era characterised by racism, poverty and imposed powerlessness. It is because of these qualities, embodied in this mighty church, that year after year millions gather at Moria for this act of spiritual renewal.

On behalf of the African National Congress, we have come here in all humility to break bread and worship with you, to join you in this sacrament of spiritual rejuvenation.

Khotso e be le lena! May peace be with you!

Since 1986 the ANC took it upon itself to search for a path to peace in our troubled land. From jail, from exile, from the underground hideouts inside South Africa, we extended a hand of peace to the South African government. For four long years, like Pharaoh of old, the South African government spurned it and refused to listen to the plea: 'Let my people go!'

In spite of this, in spite of the continuing arrest, detention, torture, imprisonment, shooting, killing and execution of those who opposed apartheid, we would not give up. We continued to press forward. We kept up the pressure for peace – through struggles, through sanctions, through boycotts – through every means we could muster until we have now reached a stage where we can all say there is a real possibility to solve our problems by negotiations.

The convening of Codesa was like the parting of the waters, opening the way to the promised land of freedom beyond. It was a great victory for the people of South Africa, black and white. We hope that the waters will not return before we have crossed to the promised land of democracy.

Progress in these talks shall depend on the willingness of those in power to share it during the transition to democracy. We must move as speedily as possible to an elected Constituent Assembly which can draw up a new constitution which all South Africans can be proud of. Our brothers and sisters, deprived of South African citizenship because of apartheid, must have it restored forthwith!

These and many other principles can be agreed upon without further delay, provided there is willingness on the part of those who hold power to reach a speedy conclusion.

The role your church can play is more crucial in these difficult times. The violence that is wrecking our country, tearing our communities apart from places far and wide, is a scourge that must be ended now! On the Witwatersrand, in Natal, in the Eastern Transvaal we have been driven from our homes.

In Cape Town, Groblersdal and other areas we have lost loved ones in senseless taxi wars. The murders, beatings, the shameful assaults on women and mayhem visited upon our people in Phola Park and other squatter camps fill our hearts with sorrow. On the trains we lose lives every day at the hands of merciless killers who attack with no motive and melt away, immune from arrest and prosecution. The Trust Feed incident, now before the courts, where the police murdered mothers and babies in their sleep, demonstrates the depravity to which the country could descend.

This violence robs us all of our humanity. It is the main obstacle to a truly democratic South Africa. We appeal to you all to pray and work for peace. The violence must be ended and those who fuel it must be brought to justice. We cannot afford to fail! For success we ask you all to remember us in your prayers.

Uxolo Mazayoni! Khotsong Masione! May peace be with you!

I wish to close on a note of hope. May this Easter bring with it the blessings of our risen Messiah and may His love shine upon you all.

Muslim Peace

Message to the Muslim Community,
12 March 1993.

I have always been particularly attached to the Muslim greeting – I thus greet you in the name of Peace.

Peace remains foremost in the minds of every community as we witness continuance of killings and the growing crime rate.

I am sure that throughout the world joy-filled homes will be marking this Eid ul Fitr with fervent prayers for world peace.

I hope your prayers for peace and justice to prevail in this troubled land are answered. I trust that your sacrifice and discipline during the fast will stand this nation in good stead.

It is on festive days like these that our minds turn to ponder the universality of humanity and the plight of those who have been excluded and denied. The Koranic injunction to rededicate ourselves to the resolute fight against any and all forms of injustice, tyranny and oppression is universal and strikes responsive chords in the hearts of people of all faiths.

Let us make this the last Eid ul Fitr that we have to celebrate under a system that has systematically trampled on our rights and our human dignity.

Let us make this the Eid ul Fitr of Hope – where the less privileged, unemployed and poverty-stricken can also look forward to sharing the bountiful fortunes of this land.

On behalf of the National Executive Committee of the ANC and its entire membership I wish you all *Eid Mubarak* and may you have a joyous day.

Muslim Renewal

Speech at an Intercultural Eid Celebration,
Johannesburg, 30 January 1998.

I join you today filled with admiration for the communities who for
the past month have fasted from sunrise to sunset. Such sacrifice as
that of Ramadan promotes spiritual growth. It demonstrates the
power of self-discipline; nurtures feeling for those who are starving;
and provides an opportunity for renewal.

It begins, too, to explain the make-up of people like Shaykh
Matura, from whose *kramat* on Robben Island as prisoners we drew
deep inspiration and spiritual strength when our country was going
through its darkest times.

That contact with Islam through the *kramat* and the regular visits by
Imam Bassier also had their lighter moments. We noticed that the
prisoner assigned to clean the *kramat* had grown very fat, while
prisoners in general lost weight; it was only later that we discovered
that he had in fact been eating the biryani and samoosas which
visitors had left behind.

Shaykh Matura also reflects the deep roots of Islam in the history
of South Africa; as do those brought to the Cape as political exiles or
slaves, starting with Shaykh Yusuf, freedom fighter and leader from
the Indonesian islands, and many of those brought to our Eastern
shores as indentured labour from India and Zanzibar to work the
sugarfields of Natal. These threads and others have left indelible
marks on the South African landscape.

Our country can proudly claim Muslims as brothers and sisters,
compatriots, freedom fighters and leaders, revered by our nation. They
have written their names on the roll of honour with blood, sweat and
tears.

As we celebrate the day of Eid, as we harvest the benefits of
Ramadan, and as we reflect on how Islam has enriched our nation
and how our nation in turn has embraced the Muslim community

as its own, we can only feel saddened that ignorance and prejudice about Islam and Muslims in Africa and beyond are still used to fuel tensions.

And, yet, although religions are still too often misused in this way, they have a profound power to unite and generate respect for others. It is my belief that Muslims can, by harnessing the more inclusive strands in their own heritage, make a particular contribution to a more humane Africa.

Africa has made Islam its own, from the very beginning when the African Christian King Negus of Abyssinia gave protection to the followers of Prophet Muhammad. That example of respect and co-operation points to the role religion can play, and spiritual leadership can provide, in contributing to the social renewal of our continent.

Now that South Africa is free, the ties which the Islamic community has always had with other parts of our continent can flourish and enrich our nation without restraint or distortion. They are part of our common African heritage.

During the apartheid years Muslims rose to the call to unite in struggle against oppression. Here in this area of Johannesburg we witnessed resistance to the Group Areas Act which will live in the annals of history.

Victory in our struggle, with the support of the international community, has won for all South Africans the right to govern themselves. It has also brought a Constitution that guarantees the equality of all religions and gives them full protection.

Now we face a new and even more difficult struggle. In the first years of our freedom we have, as a nation, made a good start. Yet all of us in every community do also know that there is much more still to be done. The call now is for each of us to ask ourselves: Are we doing all we can to help build the country of our dreams; to use the opportunities where we have them to create jobs and sustained growth; to ensure as law-abiding citizens that criminals find no refuge in our midst; to take an active part in improving the areas in which we live?

I know that Muslim organisations in South Africa will continue their sterling humanitarian work, transcending the divisions which were imposed upon us. In this way they are helping to heal our social fabric torn by apartheid's long and destructive history.

I am sure today's Eid celebration and the inspiration of Ramadan will reinforce what is known in Arabic as *Sumud*, everlasting moral strength, in order to create a better life for all, more especially for the poor.

May you continue to experience the benevolence of God in your journey of renewal of the heart and mind. May your strong call to serve humanity, on this Day of Eid, be answered, in yourselves and in others.

Hindu Light

Speech at the Diwali Celebration, Durban City Hall,
Durban, 3 November 1991.

Diwali brings back for me memories of days on Robben Island. Regularly at this time of year when our Hindu friends the world over were preparing to celebrate the Festival of Lights we would be visited by Hindu priests. I recall Mr Govender from Cape Town and Mr Padyachee from Pretoria. They would come and offer prayers with us and bring with them parcels of sweetmeats. The authorities were insistent that these parcels were only for believers in the Hindu faith. Through our struggles we were able to challenge the authorities on this narrow conception and we insisted that all the embracing philosophies that Hinduism is based on extended a hand to all of humanity. In this way I and my fellow comrades such as Wilton Mkwayi, Ahmed Kathrada, Ismail Ebrahim and many more joined Billy Nair, Mac Maharaj, Issoo Chiba, George Naicker and others in collectively marking this important celebration in the Hindu calendar and also enjoying the offerings that were prepared at this time

It humbles me to be associated with a festival that goes back over 5000 years. I also feel privileged and proud that our country is blessed with so much diversity and richness of cultures and traditions.

The Festival of Diwali and the history and significance that is a part of the festival carries innumerable lessons for us all and I can refer to only a few.

We have been engaged in the battle against the forces of darkness along lines similar to the Hindu scriptures. The policies of apartheid and its creator, the National Party, have inflicted serious damage on the country and its people. Notwithstanding some apologies for this crime against humanity, this party now wants to project itself as the defenders of the peace and the guardians of democracy. Today, it is this party which wants to woo the Indian people into its ranks.

But let us remind ourselves of the historical role that the Indian community has played in resisting every form of discrimination, inequality and oppression. From the time of Gandhi, who enabled this community to create the first democratic political organisation in Africa by creating the Natal Indian Congress in 1894, this community has displayed consistent political wisdom and courage. From the first mass actions during the passive resistance campaigns of 1913 to the total rejection of the Asiatic Land Tenure and Indians Representation Act in 1946 to the gallant Defiance Campaign of 1952 and the defeat of the Nationalist Party's plan to repatriate Indians in the 1950s, the Indians have demonstrated their oneness with all other oppressed South Africans.

But this tradition continued even during the worst years of repression when the leadership of the Congresses were forced into jail, exile or silence; they still refused to accept the National Party-chosen South African Indian Council in 1962. This rejection was demonstrated time and again during the SAIC elections of 1981, during the Tri-Cameral elections of 1984 and during the elections of Management Committees and Local Affairs Committees during the eighties. Generation after generation have been the proud bearers of the mantle of Gandhi and defenders of the rich political culture that Satyagraha introduced into the politics of this country.

This I can vouch for from my own personal development. I and my generation of political activists owe a great debt to the Gandhian tradition of passive resistance. It was this spirit which moved us in 1949 to formulate the programme of action of the African National Congress Youth League. It is this spirit which inspired us to launch the Defiance Campaign of 1952.

It is this unity in action ushered into our history by the Dadoo-Xuma-Naicker Pact in 1947 which consolidated a political relationship and tradition which has endured the trials of many decades since. This is the substance of the Congress tradition: an unmovable commitment to nonracialism, to unity in action and to safeguarding the interests of every section of the oppressed community. It is these years which created a comradeship among Yusuf Dadoo, Monty Naicker, Bram Fischer, Oliver Tambo, Jimmy La Guma and many others.

We are poised to see through our long battle the forces of truth, enlightenment and democracy triumph. But this is not going to come easily. It is still a battle. This past weekend in Durban we were part of creating a Patriotic Front which is intended to bring us all together to make one big push against the forces of darkness that we have been confronting and struggling against for so long.

Justice, truth, integrity, humility, freedom, are values that the Hindu scriptures like the scriptures of most other religions espouse. In the ANC we have built on these values and through the contribution of the people in 1955 we drew up the Freedom Charter which has acted as a beacon for us in our struggle for nonracial democracy in South Africa. We have worked hard to build unity among all the people of this country and for us to come together to build a peaceful, tolerant and prosperous country. The ANC has been and will continue to be a home for all freedom-loving people not least of all our Indian brothers and sisters. We are committed to building bridges and helping to embrace all of humanity under one umbrella and move forward in strength and confidence to a better future. We believe that this is not different from what Hindu scriptures have also been saying.

At this time of Diwali and as I light this sacred lamp I am aware of how this lamp symbolises the triumph of enlightenment over blind faith, prosperity over poverty, knowledge over ignorance, good health and wellbeing over disease and ill-health, freedom over bondage.

In our struggle we will be celebrating this triumph together. But we have a difficult road to walk before we can claim that victory for us all in this country. The Indian community has always supported the cause of freedom. Now more than ever before it will have to become more visible and in that way recognised and acknowledged.

I am told by learned Hindu scholars that as we light the lamp and also pray to the Goddess Lakshmi, we need to remember that from our position of wellbeing and prosperity that there are many who are less fortunate and deprived and that we will have to work together to formulate ways of helping to respond to the grinding poverty and desperation in the country.

At this time we also remember leaders and persons who gave their lives for the cause of freedom. Now as we remember Swami Dayanand who was poisoned for his convictions for a free and independent India and who died on Diwali day, we remember the many brave persons in our struggle who gave their lives for the cause of freedom. We remember Krish Rabillal, Ahmed Timol, Solomon Mahlangu and thousands of others. Those lamps went out and in their place thousands more lamps were lit for there to be freedom and peace in our land.

Friends, I feel deeply honoured to be with you at this time of Diwali. I will always remember this festival which we religiously marked for many years on Robben Island. In our struggle in this country there are many lessons that can be drawn from the festival and the epic, the *Ramayana*, which is closely associated with the festival. We are on the verge of entering a new era in this country. We have to light lamps of thanksgiving for enlightenment as we go forward into the future in peace and hope and prosperity.

Amandla!

Mahatma Gandhi

Speech at the opening of the Gandhi Hall, Lenasia,
27 September 1992.

I regard it as a privilege and great honour to be present with you today on this historic occasion, when we once again pay a deserving tribute to the memory of MK Gandhi. He served his apprenticeship in South Africa for 21 years and then as the Mahatma liberated, through mass action, India from her imperialist bondage. Gandhiji was a South African and his memory deserves to be cherished now and in the post-apartheid era.

The Gandhian philosophy of peace, tolerance and non-violence began in South Africa as a powerful instrument of social change. In the twentieth century this weapon was effectively used by India to liberate her people. Martin Luther King used it to combat racism in the United States.

South Africa has a legacy of racism and violence perpetuated by decades of apartheid rule. If the Mahatma was here today he would tell us that the root cause of the violence in our country is apartheid. He would have warned us not to allow the philosophy of divide and rule to sow seeds of division in our midst but to unite and restore human freedom to all South Africans.

I think that it is absolutely necessary to spell out here today what the Mahatma has meant to South Africa and to the rest of the world. And we must never lose sight of the fact that the Gandhian philosophy may be a key to human survival in the twenty-first century.

The African National Congress has spearheaded the path to lasting peace in this country. Our initiative to negotiate with the government and the suspension of our armed struggle arose out of our desire to bring about an end to the systemic violence that apartheid created, indeed, to bring an end to the racial division apartheid implanted upon us.

We can say that our decision to negotiate created new avenues for unifying our people of every race, colour or creed. The formation of the Patriotic Front is one case in point. Gandhiji would have acknowledged that the time we are in is difficult and dangerous and he would have pressed us to continue and to ensure that our liberation when it is finally achieved is not tentative but a lasting legacy to peace, democracy and unity.

The Gandhi Hall of the Seva Samaj must become a focal point for the development of a nonracial, nonsexist South Africa. And if it does so, then it will be worthy of the name of Mahatma Gandhi. It will be worthy of the name of those who followed in the footsteps of Gandhi in the 1946 passive resistance, in the 1952 Defiance Campaign, the Congress of the People's rally and the birth of the Freedom Charter in 1955. It will be worthy of the rise of the United Democratic Front and the Mass Democratic Movement, steps in our history which resulted in the unbanning of the liberation movements and the release of political prisoners.

To the officials of the Hindu Seva Samaj, I humbly say that you have a great democratic heritage, which you must uphold with the rest of South Africa. You must enter the new era of freedom not only proud of your past, but proud of the present.

I remember the Gandhi Hall in Fox Street. This was the venue where freedom was taught. The teachers included Dr AB Xuma, Yusuf Dadoo and Monty Naicker, who gave us the 1947 Freedom Pact.

After the historic Freedom Charter was drawn up in Kliptown it was read for the first time in the Gandhi Hall. Apartheid took away the old Gandhi Hall, and the people have given us this new symbol of peace and with it the remembrance of a man who changed the pattern of thinking in the twenty-first century about race and class.

Yesterday, the ANC and the SA government agreed to renew negotiations. We have established that we, the ANC, want to have freedom for all in this country at all costs, but I hasten to add not at any price. Political prisoners have been used as hostages for too long, the question of weapons of death has been addressed in part, and the hostels which have been the centres of the low-intensity warfare waged against our communities are to be fenced off and phased out.

We will continue to talk and press forward towards an Interim Government of National Unity and a Constituent Assembly which must be elected by all South Africans. Gandhi pledged 21 years of his life to the development of nonracialism and democracy in our country. It is our duty to ensure that we not only remember his deeds but that we emulate and uphold them.

A united, nonracial, nonsexist and democratic South Africa will become the jewel of this planet. We face a bright future notwithstanding the horrors of apartheid and its violence. We are dedicated to a negotiated settlement and to lasting peace. We call on all those present and those not present to reject apartheid and its past and present supporters. Your place and mine is in the democratic camp to which the Mahatma belonged.

Attaining our liberation cannot be an easy and smooth task. We shall obtain it through our collective efforts. May the new Gandhi Hall serve all the people of South Africa and may it serve the cause of peace, justice and reconciliation.

With these thoughts, I have the great pleasure of declaring this Hall named after the Mahatma formally opened.

Jewish Tradition and Justice

Address at the opening of the 37th Congress of the
South African Jewish Board of Deputies, Johannesburg,
21 August 1993.

I consider it a privilege to have been invited to make this keynote address to this congress. In the 81 years of the life of our movement, this is the first occasion on which the President of the ANC has been asked to address a national congress of the Jewish community.

It is an index of the changes we have achieved during the first few years of this decade that the various South African communities are beginning to find each other and are striving towards a national consensus. A consensus not cobbled together through shoddy compromises, but rather one based on a recognition of a shared commitment to this country and a future founded on justice.

It is not uncommon these days to hear the plea that we should bury the past and focus our attention on the future. While we can all agree that the past should not be permitted to become a burden that impairs the ability of our country and its people to move forward, it would be extremely short-sighted to dismiss it and try to forget it as if it only had one single, brutal dimension. Your own experience of the Holocaust teaches that one must learn from the past, not ignore it.

Casting our eyes back over the nine decades of this century it is clear that our South African past is as rich in the striving for justice as it is in the suppression of justice. It is as inspiring in the fight for democratic norms as it is depressing in the violation of those norms. South Africa's history abounds in heroes and heroines who have stood up for freedom as it abounds in persons who have sought to crush it.

The danger in trying to forget the past is that we may relegate to our collective amnesia the unequal contest between freedom and domination that has been the motor of our country's history for all of this century. It is to that unequal contest that I wish to address my remarks tonight.

Our national experience as South Africans is dominated by conflict. The three centuries of contact between the peoples of Africa, Europe and Asia on these shores have for too long been regarded as purely negative, as an object lesson in the incompatibility of peoples from different races, religions and cultures. Yet, when viewed from another perspective, conflict can be a creative force through which the latent potential of a society is released. Perhaps because our shared past looks different from the perspective of most members of this audience we find it necessary to recount it as my comrades and I have experienced it.

It was the refusal of the then colonial government of Britain to listen to the entreaties of a nonracial group of petitioners who travelled to London in 1909 that led to the formation of the African National Congress. For three successive decades, until the 1940s, we continued to seek a dialogue with successive white South African governments around the grievances of the majority of South Africans who were born black.

By the mid-1940s, the decade during which I entered politics in earnest, it had become clear that nothing would change except at the instance of massive pressure from below. It is a matter of record that our peaceful mass protests – strikes, stay-at-homes, defiance campaigns, demonstrations, marches and boycotts – were then, as they continue to be, met with brute force and armed repression. It was this studied refusal to respond to our reasonable demands for redress that compelled us, like many other people before us, to take up the armed struggle more than three decades ago.

The possibilities for a peaceful transition to democracy, which everyone, including those who repressed us, say they welcome, became real because of, and through, conflict. South Africa stands on the threshold of democratic transformation today because there were women and men who refused to submit to the blandishments and bullying of tyranny.

It is important for our future that there is an understanding that it is struggle rather than submission that is the creative force; that it is the proverbial 'troublemakers' rather than the silent conformists who are responsible for human progress; that it is those who resist oppression who make freedom a realisable possibility.

The struggle for national liberation and democracy in South Africa has never been a racial affair, though it has indeed always been integrally related to the overthrow of racism and racial oppression.

From that early group of petitioners to London – which included WP Schreiner (one of whose descendants today serves with distinction in the ranks of the ANC); Dr Abdullah Abdurahman, the famous Muslim physician; John Tengo Jabavu, the father of African journalism; J Lenders and others – down to the present day, it has been a struggle waged by South Africans of all colours, races, faiths and classes.

That is a legacy we shall always uphold.

For many thousands it entailed immense sacrifices – imprisonment, exile, underground activity, the destruction of family life, injuries and death. Every racial group, every faith, every ethnic and language community in our country has contributed its quota to the roll call of martyrs, heroes and heroines. In honouring those who fell in the struggle for freedom we honour no single group, defined by race, region, religion or colour. We honour the daughters and sons of our country, South Africa.

South Africans of Jewish descent have historically been disproportionately represented among our white compatriots in the liberation struggle. The names of Emil 'Solly' Sachs, Bennie Weinbren, Max Gordon and Ray Alexander are indelibly inscribed in the history of the South African labour movement because of the contribution they made to it. Among the champions of the rightless we shall always count Senator Leslie Rubin, Sam Kahn, Helen Suzman and Ruth First, all of whom employed their talents in the pursuance of justice.

I want to take this opportunity also to make special mention of some of the other outstanding leaders and figures from the Jewish community who have been in the forefront of the struggle for human rights. All South Africans owe much to the example set by Mr Gerald Leissner, the President of the South African Jewish Board of Deputies, Mr Mervyn Smith, its current Chairman, and Professor Michael Katz, its past president. Members of the legal profession cannot forget the name of Advocate Maisels, an outstanding civil liberties lawyer who had a very distinguished career at the Bar.

Many black South Africans are indebted to Jewish philanthropists who assisted them when opportunities in education, the professions and business were largely closed to them because of racist laws and practices. I would like to believe that this and future generations from your community will build on these firm foundations by fully committing themselves to the future of our country.

We in the African National Congress are well aware that the tasks ahead are many and difficult. To make our dream of a united, democratic, nonracial, nonsexist South Africa real is an immense challenge. Yet we look forward to the future with confidence and hope, because we know that the people of this country, all the people of South Africa, are possessed of many talents, skills and an infinite resourcefulness.

Even while the majority of our people are denied equal opportunities in education and work, much positive development has occurred in South Africa. In a number of fields – from transport to mining, in the universities and in the application of science and technology to life – our country stands poised to play its part in the modern world. What we must now do is to make good the enormous lag caused by the ravages of apartheid.

It is in this respect that I wish to appeal to the Jewish community in particular. Yours is a community that has a deserved reputation for being well educated and for the skills it possesses – professional, commercial and industrial. I believe those skills can and should be used both to help the development of the country and to mount programmes, using your own knowledge and skills, to contribute to the development of those who have been denied fair opportunities. The international community has begun to invest in our education and training.

I believe that co-operation, commitment and imagination could ensure that more programmes for larger numbers of people can be established. The Jewish community must find a role for itself in such activity.

Events in our country sometimes challenge the sort of confidence I am expressing in our future. The seemingly unending spiral of violence, the soaring crime rate, the decline of South Africa's economy are all real and very palpable threats to any future we might hope to build. There are, too, the fears of a community that is relatively small, and is a minority within a minority. We cannot minimise these fears and must address them in all seriousness.

Yet, I must sound a word of warning against the temptation to cast oneself in the role of a victim, even when this is unwarranted. It is important that we retain some perspective in relation to these matters. At present, most black communities in South Africa feel the scourge of violence and crime more keenly than any white community. The killings on trains have been confined exclusively to black commuter traffic. The sense of insecurity that grips some white residential areas is far more intense in the African townships of the East Rand, the Natal Midlands and Southern Natal.

I say this not to belittle what our white compatriots have suffered from crime and violence. But it does underscore that black South Africa has an even greater interest and sense of urgency in reducing the crime rate and finding peaceful ways of settling differences.

There can no longer be any doubt that some of the political violence has been encouraged by *agents provocateurs*, and that many of these have been planted for that very purpose by agents of the white minority state. The violence is frequently presented as 'black on black' violence; it is ascribed to ethnic conflicts and petty political rivalries. While elements of all these are manifest, the root cause of the violence, we have no doubt, is elements within the state's security services who are determined to thwart the advent of democracy.

We firmly believe that concerted action involving the police, the communities and the structures of the National Peace Accord, including international monitors, can reduce and finally end the violence. Peace will not come about by magic. It requires people of goodwill who must help to produce a more tolerant society where at least some swords will be beaten into ploughshares.

It also requires a police force that has credibility and that enjoys the confidence of the people. It requires a government that will make available resources to the peace structures and eschew bombastic law-and-order rhetoric.

We in the ANC are determined to do all we can to stop the killing.

A little over a week ago we were shocked to read the remarks of Mr Ben Yehuda, the vice-president of the Jewish Agency in Israel. In an interview with the Agence France Presse, Mr Ben Yehuda warned that catastrophe awaited South Africa's Jewish community as there was little doubt that the forthcoming general elections, planned for April 1994, will result in a black majority government.

I want to state in the most unequivocal terms that the African National Congress has stood firm against anti-Semitism as it has stood firmly against all other forms of racism. It is our belief that all citizens should be protected against all forms of racism, including anti-Semitism. Our track record on this score is there for anyone to examine! As a lawyer, I know there will be difficulties and problems of definition in law and interpretation of law. But these, we are confident, are issues that a Bill of Rights will and can address.

As democrats, we support basic civil liberties for all citizens, the separation of church and state, which necessarily entails the freedom of religious observance and non-observance. As long ago as 1955 we committed ourselves to the right of religious communities to establish and maintain their own places of worship, their own communal organisations and their own private schools provided there was no racial discrimination involved.

The suggestion that an ANC-led government could ever indulge in or connive at anti-Semitism is a scandalous slander inspired either by sheer ignorance or malice!

We were pleased to learn of the repudiation of Mr Ben Yehuda's sentiments by the South African Jewish Board of Deputies. That episode is now, hopefully, past.

The ANC's relations with the Palestinian Liberation Organisation have been a matter of concern for many Jews, not only here but also in other parts of the world. It was an issue we discussed when I recently met the American Jewish Committee.

As a movement we recognise the legitimacy of Palestinian nationalism just as we recognise the legitimacy of Zionism as a Jewish nationalism. We insist on the right of the State of Israel to exist within secure borders but with equal vigour support the Palestinian right to national self-determination. We are gratified to see that new possibilities of resolving the issue through negotiation have arisen since the election of a new government in Israel. We would wish to encourage that process, and if we have the opportunity, to assist.

The ANC, in common with the international community, was extremely unhappy about the military cooperation between the State of Israel and the apartheid regime in South Africa. The refusal of Israel, over many years, to honour its international obligations to isolate the apartheid regime did influence our attitude towards that government.

However, as my distinguished predecessor and colleague, the late Oliver Tambo, stated in Lusaka in 1989, we ask you, in your relationship with the ANC, to focus on our shared goals in South Africa. As South Africans we should avoid being drawn into conflicts and tensions arising from the agendas of others beyond our shores.

Democracy, respect for democratic norms, the rule of law, and an entrenched Bill of Rights are the surest guarantee of the security and wellbeing of the Jewish and every other minority community in

South Africa. The demography of our country dictates that democracy inevitably entails a government led by the black majority.

I would like to end my remarks with a special appeal, addressed particularly to those among you who may sometimes feel the waves of despondency engulfing you when you contemplate the fraught transition our country is passing through.

There is much that we have achieved. Five years ago many of my comrades and I were in prison with very little prospect of being released. Five years ago the African National Congress was an illegal organisation, whose name was spoken in whispers in secret meetings. Five years ago thousands of our compatriots were in exile, some with fading memories of a homeland they left decades ago.

There is every reason to be optimistic!

This is not the time to beat a retreat. The future of our country beckons us all to rise to the challenge of building. South Africa needs all its people, black and white; young and old; Christian, Muslim, Hindu or Jewish. There is a place for all of us provided we have the courage to work together to build that common future.

World Religions

Speech at the Parliament for the World's Religions,
Cape Town, December 1999.

Unfortunately, I must tell a story, which in gatherings of this nature I have told more than a hundred times, because that story puts in context some of the remarks that have been made here about one individual. This is when I spent a holiday in the Bahamas in 1993. I met some tourists – a man and a wife – as I was taking a walk and the man stopped and said: 'Mr Mandela.'

I said: 'Many people mistake me for that chap.'

And he said: 'Would I be entitled to take you for that chap?'

I said: 'You'd be doing what many people are doing.'

He then turned to his beloved wife and said: 'Darling, Mr Mandela.'

She was totally unimpressed. She said: 'What is he famous for?'

And the husband in his embarrassment dropped his voice and said: 'Mr Mandela, Mr Mandela.'

And the woman insisted: 'I asked what is he famous for?' And before the husband answered she turned to me and said: 'What are you famous for?'

I couldn't answer the question.

But there is another incident nearer by, at home, when a five-year-old lady – I was told by security that she was at the gate – and I said: 'Let her come in.'

And then security said: 'She is very cheeky'

I said: 'Precisely for that reason let her come in.'

And indeed she was quite a lady because she just stormed into my lounge without knocking, did not greet me and the first remark was: 'How old are you?'

I said: 'Well, I can't remember, but I was born long, long ago.'

She said: 'Two years ago?'

I said: 'No, much longer than that.'

She suddenly changed the topic and said: 'Why did you go to jail?'

I said: 'Well, I didn't go to jail because I liked. Some people sent me there.'

'Who?'

I said: 'Some people did not like me.'

And she said: 'How long did you remain there?'

I said: 'Now I can't remember.'

'Two years?'

I said: 'No, more than that.'

Then she says: 'You are a stupid old man, aren't you?' And having made that devastating attack, she sat down with me and joked with me as if she had paid me a compliment.

Well, I hope at the end of my speech if you feel that I have not risen to expectations, you will be more diplomatic than that young lady.

The truth of the old African proverb that we are people through other people is tonight very evocatively being demonstrated by this gathering of so many people from all parts of the world. This coming together here in this southernmost city on the African continent of representatives from such a wide range of the faiths of the world symbolises the acknowledgement of our mutual interdependence and common humanity. It is to me a humbling experience to be part of this moving expression and reaffirmation of the nobility of the human spirit. This century has seen enough of destruction, injustice, strife and division, suffering and pain and of our capacity to be massively inhuman the one to the other. There is sufficient cause for being cynical about human life and about humanity. This gathering at the close of our century serves to counter despair and cynicism and calls us to a recognition and reaffirmation of that which is great and generous and caring in the human spirit. We are being reminded in the words of the psalm that we were indeed created a little lower than the angels and crowned with glory and honour.

I accept with humility and great appreciation the honours that you have thought fit to bestow on an old man in the years of his retirement. If nothing else, it demonstrates that old age still intimidates people into paying respect and homage.

I accept these awards not merely on my behalf. I do so in recognition of the three persons after whom the awards are named and in celebration of what they stood for. I wish through the receipt of these awards to identify with those values which they represented so powerfully in their respective lives and works – a commitment to peace, non-violence and dialogue.

I also dedicate these awards to those millions and millions of ordinary unsung men and women all over the world who throughout this century courageously refused to bow to the baser instincts of our nature and to live their lives in pursuit of peace, tolerance, and respect for differences.

Even in the closing decade of the century, we have witnessed how internecine strife degenerated into genocide with former neighbours participating in the slaughter of each other. This century, unfortunately, had too many leaders attempting to exploit communal differences for their own political ends. In most instances, it was the resolve and the determination of ordinary citizens to resist this recourse to destructive sectarianism that saved our world from even more instances of genocide and violent conflict. It is them – the decent, general citizenry – who we salute at the close of the century that has had its share of war and strife. We have had men who were so arrogant that they wanted to conquer the world and turn human beings into their slaves. But the people always put an end to such men and women. Alexander the Great thought he could conquer the world. Caesar also had the same ambitions. Napoleon almost succeeded in laying the whole of Europe at his feet. And during our time, there emerged Hitler who did exactly the same thing. But it was the ordinary people, not kings and generals; it was the ordinary people, some of whom were not known in their own villages, who put an end to those tyrants – to those dictators. And it is for that reason that the real leaders of the world are those who for 24 hours a day think in terms of the poorest of the poor. It is those men and women who know that poverty is the single most dangerous threat to society in the world today.

In our country, my generation is the product of religious education. We grew up at a time when the government of this country owed its duty only to whites: a minority of less than 15 per cent. They took no interest whatsoever in our education. It was religious institutions – whether Christian, Muslim, Hindu or Jewish – in the context of our country, they are the people who bought land, who built schools, who equipped them, who employed teachers, and paid them. Without the Church, without religious institutions, I would never have been here today. It was for that reason, that when I was ready to go to the United States on the first of this month, an engagement which had been arranged for quite some time, when my comrade Ebrahim told me about this occasion, I said I would change my whole itinerary so I would have the opportunity to appear here.

But I must also add that I do appreciate the importance of religion. Apart from the background that I've given you, you'd have to have been in a South African jail under apartheid, where you can see the cruelty of human beings to others in their naked form. But it was again religious institutions, Hindus, Muslims, leaders of the Jewish faith, Christians, it was they who gave us the hope that one day we would come out. We would return. And in prisons, the religious institutions raised funds for our children who were arrested in thousands and thrown into jail.

And many when they left prison had a high level of education because of the support we got from religious institutions. And that is why we so respect religious institutions and we try as much as we can to read the literature which outlines the fundamental principles of human behaviour, like the Bhagavad Gita, the Koran, the Bible and other important religious documents. And I say this so that you should understand that the propaganda that has been made, for example about the liberation movement in this country, it is completely untrue. Because religion was one of the motivating factors in everything that we did.

In some respects, the turn of the century is an arbitrary happening in the cycle of human life where there is always change from one day to the other. In other respects, it provides us with the symbolic opportunity to take stock of the substance of our lives and of what lies ahead.

As we approach the twenty-first century, we cannot but be starkly aware that we stand at a crossroads in our history. That the general citizenry to which we referred – those women, men and children who merely desire and have an inalienable right to lead a decent life – continue to suffer deprivation and poverty. The world is still marked by massive inequality. In too many parts of the world warfare and violent conflict still reign. The powerful dominate at the expense of the poor and the vulnerable. The symbolic turn of the century calls us to a commitment to make the coming century one in which these and other issues of human development are fundamentally addressed. We shall have to reach deep into the wells of our human faith as we approach the new century. No less than in any other period of history, religion will have a crucial role to play in guiding and inspiring humanity to meet the enormous challenges that we face. In our South African society, we have identified a crucial need for our efforts at material and social development and new construction to be matched and accompanied by what is called an RDP of the soul – a moral reconstruction and development programme. That is no less true of our entire world.

The world is undergoing a profound redefinition of values and modes of perception. The globalisation of the world economy and the outstanding advances of communications technology have drawn all of us together into a smaller world. Those technical advances might, however, also have contributed to a growing confusion of values as people seek to find their localised places in that globalised world. The escalation of poverty in a world that is at the same time marked by such opulence and excessive wealth, the suffering and marginalisation of vulnerable groups at a time when the concepts of democracy and equality are supposed to have become universal, the growing degradation of the environment often caused by the greed of industrial development, these are but some of the contradictions that at heart are moral and ethical questions. And on the level of personal life, as the world supposedly becomes smaller, the loneliness of individual human beings across the globe increases.

Religion, like all other aspects of human lives, of course faces its own challenges. We have seen how religion at times provided the basis and even gave legitimisation to violent expressions of intolerance and conflict. Tragically, religion sometimes seemed to have lost its ability to hold people to good values and to inspire in them those articles and approaches that transcend narrow and immediate considerations. Religious leaders, institutions and adherents now once more need to draw upon those critical resources that have made religion such a central part of human life throughout the ages. Few other dimensions of human life reach such a massive following as the religious. Its roots are in every nook and cranny of society where political leaders and the economically powerful have no sway. The religions and faiths of our world are pondered over and listened to. Hence the importance to once again draw on those forces of spirituality and innate goodness.

No government or social agency can on its own meet the enormous challenges of development of our age. Partnerships are required across the broad range of society. In drawing upon its spiritual and communal resources, religion can be a powerful partner in such causes as meeting the challenges of poverty, alienation, the abuse of women and children, and the destructive disregard for our natural environment.

We read into your honouring our country with your presence an acknowledgement of the achievement of the nation and we trust that our struggle might have contributed in a small way to other people in the world.

We commend the Parliament for the World's Religions for its immense role in making different communities see that the common ground is greater and more enduring than the differences that divide. It is in that spirit that we can approach the dawn of the new century with some hope that it will indeed be a better one for all of the people of the world.

9
HEALTH

HEALTH FOR ALL

OLIVE SHISANA

I feel honoured to have been the first woman director-general and first Director-General of Health in the Mandela post-apartheid government. I drew great inspiration from a man I admired throughout the time I was in exile in the mid-seventies and continue to do so today. He is a man with a crystal clear vision, commitment to removing inequities and ensuring fairness, a man with compassion and care. It is these qualities that continue to inspire me to direct my energies to helping him achieve his dreams. Last year, I agreed to join his Foundation's Advisory Board on HIV/Aids, where I participate in a number of activities aimed at tackling the HIV/Aids epidemic. In my current portfolio, as Executive Director of Social Aspects of HIV/Aids and Health at the Human Sciences Research Council, I continue to conduct research to support the work he does on HIV/Aids.

Nelson Mandela's government inherited one of the most inequitable health care systems in the world. Yet under the inspiring leadership of the new president, remarkable strides were made to bring to life the ANC's election promise of 'health for all'. The apartheid health system was divided along racial, ethnic, old provincial and local lines, as well as between the public and private health sectors. So inequitable was the public-private sector divide that the private health sector, which served about 20 per cent of the population (mainly whites), consumed the same amount of resources as the public health sector, which served 80 per cent of the population. In 1991, the national infant mortality rate was 54 deaths per 100 000 live births, and yet among Africans the figure was between 94 and 124 infant deaths per 100 000.

Before health for all could be delivered, the health department had to be transformed from 14 fragmented departments into one national department and nine provincial departments. To do this, strategic management teams were created in each province with the assistance of the then Minister of Health, Dr Nkosazana Dlamini Zuma and myself, as her special advisor. These teams comprised both progressive people who came with the new government and civil servants from the old apartheid government. The new civil servants shared Mandela's vision of removing inequities in access to health care. The old civil servants brought the skills of managing the financial, human and physical resources. Both new and old era civil servants had to learn to work together. They took their cue from Mandela's broad vision of equity in access to health care, poverty alleviation and improvement of the quality of life, as well as his commitment to reconciliation.

As a result of the Mandela government, South Africa now has one national health system that is focused on access to health care for all, regardless of race or ethnic group. Health services now reach people in urban and rural areas. But there are still major challenges to ensure quality health services, availability of medicines and supplies, ensuring all children are immunised. In addition, the progression of HIV/Aids and the high prevalence of tuberculosis have complicated the transformation process, and may even reverse some of the advances the Mandela government made.

In his very first state of the nation address, Mandela announced that there would be free health care for pregnant women and children under the age of six years, where the need arose. He immediately backed his policy with an injection of additional money, amounting to R680 million per year, into the public health sector and declared that the programme had to be operational within the first 100 days of his presidency. The announcement took health workers by surprise and was greeted with disbelief, because they were ill-prepared to implement the programme. Soon after the announcement, Dr Dlamini Zuma and I toured the provinces to give guidance on how to translate this new policy into action. We took this opportunity to facilitate the creation of nine provincial departments of health, which were nonexistent yet crucial for the successful implementation of the programme.

With the support and motivation of a president with such vision, compassion and energy, health workers were mobilised at national, provincial and local levels to implement the programme. Needless to say, in many areas there were not enough clinics, staff, medication and other supplies to ensure complete delivery under this programme. But so infectious was Mandela's commitment to providing health care to those in need that health workers made sure the programme was implemented to the best of their ability with the increased financial resources allocated.

The response was overwhelming. Clinics and hospitals were sudden-ly flooded with patients coming for antenatal care, family planning, and paediatric services. No longer did the patients worry about not having the R8 required to pay for the services. Now their concern was getting through the long queues. No longer did they have to worry about having to prove they were poor, a process that had required a magistrate's dec-laration before they could access the services of a district surgeon.

However, nurses used this as an opportunity to demand more money on the grounds that their workloads had increased in the first year of the Mandela presidency. Since unions and government had to jointly agree on salary increases in the Central Bargaining Chamber, the concerns of nurses, who were not members of the unions, could not be addressed immediately. Realising that they would not receive any pay increase out-side of the normal cycle of negotiation, some nurses decided to go on strike in 1995.

This strike was a baptism of fire that tested the ability of the Mandela government to resolve conflict. I remember going to a television studio with the then MEC for Health in Gauteng, Amos Masondo, and facing a barrage of questions from the presenter and strike leaders. Armed only with the official position of government of 'no salary increases outside the negotiation cycle', we urged nurses to join unions in the Central Bargaining Chamber and bargain for better salaries through those struc-tures. Needless to say, some nurses continued to strike. Worried about the possible loss of patients' lives, the Mandela government called in the Defence Force to ensure the provision of health care to patients. Nurses were asked to return to work, and most heeded the call. Those who refused, particularly in the Eastern Cape where the strike was wide-spread, were discharged from the public service and had to reapply for their jobs.

Thus, the Mandela government demonstrated that the lives and rights of patients could not be sacrificed for better salaries and that problems had to be dealt with through the right channels. Indeed later, the gov-ernment, through negotiation with the unions, was able to grant large salary increases to all health workers. This was accompanied by a new negotiated policy that workers involved in the provision of essential serv-ices could not strike.

While pregnant women and children under the age of six now had access to free health care, there were still a number of poor people who could not afford health care. Thus, in 1996, Dr Dlamini Zuma intro-duced a policy of free universal access to a package of primary health care for all South Africans in the public health sector. Again, the response was overwhelming. When I went to launch the policy at the Zola clinic in Soweto in April 1996, an old man came to thank us for helping him to use the clinic for free. He showed us a wound and said that, without this new policy, he would have had to wait until pension day to get money to attend the clinic. In short, the barrier to health care for the poor was removed.

Mandela also allocated additional funds to build clinics where there were none and to upgrade those that were dilapidated. The aim was to ensure that every South African should live within a five-kilometre radius of a health care facility. To achieve such a goal in a relatively short time was nearly impossible within the rule-bound and rigid confines of the bureaucratic civil service. Determined to deliver on this project, we devised means to fast-track the process by appointing consultants to produce several clinic models and then consulting communities on these plans. By doing so, it was possible for the government, with community and private sector support, to build 500 clinics between 1994 and 1998. This gave an additional five million people access to health care who under apartheid had had no such access. In addition, 249 clinics had major upgrading, 2 298 clinics had minor upgrading and new equipment, 124 new visiting points for mobile services were established and 215 new mobile clinic vehicles were purchased. Mandela himself opened many of the clinics to personally deliver to communities the promises he had made in his first state of the nation address. Since leaving office, he has continued to work with the private sector to ensure that more clinics are built in under-served areas.

But fast-tracking the building of clinics was done at a political cost. The Auditor-General found that tender procedures had been flouted and political opponents misinterpreted this as corruption. But Mandela did not shy away from supporting the Department of Health, arguing that a distinction must be made between corrupt practices, which he abhors, and circumventing the rules to accelerate service delivery. He suggested that the rules should be amended to ensure that delivery took place. For us, as managers and health workers, it was a relief to know that we had the solid support of the President for doing our work. After the staff testified before the Parliamentary Portfolio Committee on Finance, it became clear that there had been no corruption and Parliament thus authorised the expenditure.

Mandela's support for his staff was extraordinary. The National Party (NP) called on him to fire Zuma and me on 20 March 1996. Mandela responded by calling those members of his Cabinet from the NP and the party's spokesperson on health in Parliament on 5 June 1996 to a meeting at his house to clarify their request and invited Zuma and me. Former President FW de Klerk then complained that the health department had, with Zuma's and my intervention, unfairly awarded a contract on health informatics to an ANC ally in India. But the company awarded the tender was in Oman and not India. In addition, I did not participate in the tender committees that adjudicated the tenders, as they claimed. Mandela then asked the NP to publicly withdraw its statement before he retired for the night. Through the successful mediation of NP Cabinet minister Roelf Meyer between the NP spokesperson in Parliament, Willem Odendaal, and me, the NP retracted the statement. I called the President, just before 9 pm, to inform him that the press statement had been finalised and agreed to by Odendaal. He then asked whether I was satisfied with the statement and when I said yes, he said he could then go to bed. Mandela's support meant a lot and strengthened our commitment to reverse the effects of apartheid.

Mandela also announced, within the first 100 days of his presidency, that a programme to supplement the nutrition of primary school children must be introduced to alleviate hunger in school children. The programme encompassed feeding children at school, parasite control and nutritional education. So enthusiastic were the Health and Education Departments in meeting the challenge that they, and more than 53 000 community members, fed 4.9 million children in more than 14 200 schools between 1994 and 1997.

However, there was very little management expertise in the black areas to implement such a massive programme and many staff were unable to operate within allocated budgets, creating accounting problems. Indeed, an independent evaluation recommended that the programme be transformed to target only needy schools and that the operational management systems be improved. Consultants to build capacity in management and financial controls were then appointed to assist the provincial and national government departments. This step significantly improved delivery. The programme was later changed to an integrated nutrition programme that included food gardens and nutrition education to increase household food security.

Within two years of his release from prison, Mandela showed his commitment to tackle a disease he thought threatened future generations of people in South Africa. He gave a speech in Nasrec, Gauteng at the launch of the National Convention on Aids in South Africa (Nacosa) in

October 1992. In this speech, Mandela shaped the post-apartheid government's broad policy and plan on HIV/Aids, namely to address conditions that increase vulnerability to HIV, such as poverty, overcrowding, the migratory labour system and single-sex dwellings. He also indicated the importance of treating sexually transmitted infections, advocated for increased information, education and communication aimed at raising awareness of the HIV epidemic, ending stigma and encouraging condom use. In short, he urged the country to rapidly implement prevention programmes within an enabling environment.

In giving this speech, Mandela was keenly aware of the major historical, social and political factors that increased vulnerability of South Africans to HIV infections. He pointed out how the apartheid migratory labour system and poverty had increased people's vulnerability to HIV infections. He pointed out that African families were fractured because the migratory labour system caused men to leave their homes and stay in single-sex hostels. Informal settlements mushroomed around the mines as sex workers put up homes to ply their trade. Many families lived in overcrowded homes because of poverty and lack of adequate housing. He raised the problem of the low socio-economic status of women in our country, which prevented them from demanding from partners to wear condoms to prevent HIV.

When Mandela became President, his government immediately doubled the Aids budget from R21 million in 1993/4 financial year to R42 million, and increased it further by 1996/97 financial year to R70 million, and then to R80 million in 1997/98 – a four-fold increase. His government implemented nearly all of the key issues he raised in the Nasrec speech.

Condom procurement and distribution were increased from around five million in 1994 to 140 million in 1997. By 2003, 90 per cent of youths and adults said they could get a condom when they needed it, mainly from their local clinics. By 1998, more than 10 000 secondary school teachers were trained in life skills and ready to start educating the youth. The Department of Health provided in-service training of syndromic management of sexually transmitted diseases to over 450 clinicians and managers. This method of treating sexually transmitted diseases is effective in preventing HIV infections. Mandela also pushed for the speedy delivery of housing, knowing that the lack of adequate housing made people vulnerable to HIV.

One of the major contributions of Mandela's government to the struggle against HIV/Aids involved pushing access to affordable drugs to the forefront of the agenda of the international public health and trade communities. In 1997, the Department of Health drafted the Medicines and Related Substances Control Amendment Bill to allow parallel importation of drugs and permit compulsory licensing to enable South Africa to obtain affordable drugs and also be able to produce them locally. The drugs of interest were antiretroviral therapy and other drugs on the essential drug programme. The bill aimed to permit South African pharmaceutical companies to manufacture low-cost generic versions of proprietary drugs produced and sold by pharmaceutical companies from industrialised countries.

This move unleashed the anger of the multinational pharmaceutical industry. Forty pharmaceutical companies took the South African government to court to pressure them to remove the sections related to parallel importation and compulsory licensing, a case they later lost. They also sought the assistance of the US government and found it in Vice President Al Gore, who threatened to implement sanctions against South Africa. Activists raised their concerns with him and Gore eventually withdrew his demand for South Africa to remove the 'offending' clauses in the legislation.

Despite international pressure, Mandela signed the Medicines and Related Substances Control Amendment Act into law. The Mandela government also took the issue of affordable access to drugs to the World Health Assembly, where the debate focused on public health interests versus private profits obtained from the sale of drugs. It became a battle of intellectual property versus access to drugs for the poor.

The World Health Assembly of 1999 passed the resolution that would give primacy of public health over commercial interests. Later, US President Bill Clinton signed an Executive Order that encouraged Sub-Saharan countries to use the options in the Trade and Related Aspects of Intellectual Property (Trips) agreement to import or use compulsory licensing to gain access to drugs for HIV/Aids-related illnesses. These were major victories for the Mandela government.

At an event to mark World Aids Day in 1994, Mandela reiterated his concern about this epidemic: 'The campaign against Aids is the task of all of us, young and old, government and community organisations, religious and traditional institutions, cultural and sporting bodies. Aids knows no custom. It knows no colour. It knows no boundaries. We have to work together wherever we are to preserve our nation, our continent and humanity as a whole. ... As government, we will continue to take active part in Aids-awareness initiatives. We will continue to allocate as much resources as government can afford to combat this epidemic. However, success in this campaign will depend on the input of all sectors of society.'

Mandela continues to be committed to fighting HIV/Aids. Since he left government, he has created an HIV/Aids Programme under his Nelson Mandela Foundation. Through the foundation, he has mobilised traditional leaders in the North West, Limpopo and Eastern Cape to join in the struggle against HIV/Aids. He has funded a pilot programme, jointly with the South African Medical Association, to make antiretroviral therapy accessible to the needy. He has also spent an inordinate amount of time nationally and internationally advocating for prevention of HIV among the youth, increased access to antiretroviral therapy and appropriate infant feeding to prevent mother-to-child transmission of HIV, and has advocated for increased access to antiretroviral therapy for those for whom it is medically indicated. He has waged a campaign of care and compassion for those living with HIV/Aids, emphasising adherence to human rights principles and the removal of stigma for those living with the disease. His towering stature and resolve to deal with HIV/Aids is the force behind the work of health workers, activists, donors, scientists and the international community.

Last year, he commissioned the study I led at the Human Sciences Research Council to conduct the largest-ever national study to investigate HIV prevalence, behavioural and socio-cultural determinants and the impact of mass media on HIV in South Africa. The study found that 4.5 million South Africans were living with HIV/Aids; that is, 11.4 per cent of the household population aged two years and older were living with the virus. He personally launched the results to the public on 5 December 2002.

The legacy of apartheid will take centuries to address. Blacks still have the highest rates of tuberculosis, sexually transmitted infections, HIV and Aids and many other communicable diseases. Simply put, they die prematurely from preventable diseases. But the Mandela-era government transformed the health care system to make it more equitable, resourced it and created a sustainable infrastructure. It remained true to the primary health care philosophy. It has made health care accessible to millions through the free health care programme to pregnant women and children less than six years old, the policy on universal access to health care, clinic building and upgrading programme and primary school nutrition programme.

Much of what happened in the first five years of the post-apartheid

370

government would not have materialised if Mandela had not been committed to ensuring delivery against all odds, along with his ability to temper progress with realism and encourage patience from the masses. However, it was clear that the problems of the previous four decades could not be wiped out immediately. Mandela frequently reminded deprived South Africans that, even though there was progress in delivering extension of primary health care to all, 'we know this is only a start of a task that will take us many years'. His ability to celebrate the success and simultaneously temper the expectation with realism was key to maintaining stability in the country.

Health and Human Rights

Speech at the Nelson Mandela Award for
Health and Human Rights ceremony, Cape Town,
6 March 1995.

I am extremely glad that we can all be together, here in South Africa, for this year's Health and Human Rights Award.

I feel most honoured to welcome you, the Board of Trustees of the Kaiser Family Foundation, on your first visit to a democratic South Africa. For us, as I know it is for you, it is a great joy to be able to state that the South African government has made universal access to primary health care a priority. We all share in the pride of knowing that amongst the very first actions of the democratic government was the initiation of two successful programmes in the field of health. Over four million school children are being fed each day and there is free health care for pregnant mothers and young children.

Access to clean water, adequate food, housing, employment and sanitation play a decisive role in determining the health status of a population and this government is committed to providing these over time. While effective changes in health service provision will improve access to health care, long-term improvements in the health of our people hinge on tangible improvements in living conditions.

The Government of National Unity is in the process of ensuring that spending is shifted towards addressing the most pressing needs, as spelt out in the Reconstruction and Development Programme.

The Ministry of Health has presented a five-year health spending plan that will target the health of pregnant women, mothers and children; building and staffing clinics in under-served areas; and retaining more nurses in clinical and primary care skills.

These strategies are designed to promote health, prevent diseases and treat in the community those diseases that commonly result in hospitalisation.

This enormous challenge can be met only by a partnership of all social structures in the very broad field of health.

On the part of government it means pursuing the commitment to shift priorities towards basic needs. And it means continuing the process of consultation with all role players which has marked the development of health policy thus far.

On the part of communities it means being ready to take responsibility for their own primary health care, something which will be greatly enhanced by our first democratic local government elections later this year.

On the part of health workers and organisations it means bringing their particular skills, experience and resources to bear in finding solutions to problems created by our history of division and inequality. It means being ready to find ways of reconciling particular interests with the broader national interest of ensuring affordable primary health care for all.

The Henry J Kaiser Family Foundation can be proud of its record as a partner in this process. Its programme in this country, initiated in 1988, has helped South Africans in the task of establishing a more equitable national health system. Its work has been mainly directed at improving health care for the most disadvantaged sectors of the population, with a particular focus on communities in rural areas and peri-urban informal settlements.

Through the National Progressive Primary Health Care Network, the Health System Trust and other initiatives, the Foundation has contributed substantially to preparing the ground for implementation of the new government's health plans.

This record exemplifies the contribution which private donors can make to the task of addressing the legacy of apartheid. It is believed by some that aid from private American foundations will now fall markedly because of a belief that their role must be taken over by government and bilateral donors.

This would be a mistake. Government cannot do everything alone. Private donors and non-governmental organisations have a vital contribution to make within the framework of the national Reconstruction and Development Programme. They can often play a distinctive role in kick-starting important processes; assisting innovation by demonstrating alternative approaches; and capacity building in order ultimately to make government more effective. This is amply demonstrated by the contribution which the Foundation has made to the cause of health in both the United States and South Africa.

I am proud to be associated with an award which honours the

accomplishment of individuals whose life's work gives expression to the goal of good quality health care, a basic right of every citizen.

The Nelson Mandela Award for Health and Human Rights is given annually to an American and a South African. In so doing, it underlines the linkages and historical parallels between our countries. We have much to learn from one another, and the award gives meaning to a process of shared experience and mutual learning.

It is my great pleasure to announce that the winners of the 1995 Nelson Mandela Award for Health and Human Rights are Ms Charlotte Webb Collins and Ms Mankuba Ramalepe. I would like to congratulate them sincerely on their achievement.

They exemplify the values celebrated by this award. Not only have they devoted many years to the service of the poor and disadvantaged, and done so in a way that gives full recognition to how firmly health is rooted in socio-economic conditions. Still more, they have helped to empower individuals and communities to access health resources and to become active partners in health care.

Theirs is an example in the spirit of renewal and reconstruction which puts the involvement of communities in their own upliftment at the heart of change.

May this award inspire others to follow their path!

And may the Kaiser Family Foundation long be a partner in the reconstruction and development of our country!

Public Health

Speech accepting the American Public Health Association
Presidential Citation, Pretoria,
14 October 1997.

I am deeply honoured to receive this citation. That is because it comes from an association of men and women who are dedicated to the public health and wellbeing of their nation, an organisation that also cares for the health of people across the world.

I would like to use this opportunity to express our appreciation to members of the American Public Health Association, as part of the international community of public health workers, for their solidarity with our struggle for freedom.

Your support was essential to our victory, which is also your victory. We thank you from the bottom of our hearts.

As we face our new challenges we are strengthened by the knowledge that we have your continuing support. Freedom for South and Southern Africa has brought the opportunity at last to address the basic needs of our people. It allows us not only to attend to immediate health needs but also to begin to eradicate the legacy of poverty and inequity that is the greatest threat to our public health.

Achieving these goals will take us many years. But we have made a start and we face the future with confidence. We do so because the people of South Africa have united to put the conflict of the past behind them and to work together for a better life for all, especially the poor.

It is this achievement of our whole nation I do know that you are celebrating by the honour you are awarding me; and I humbly accept it in their name.

May your award, and our acceptance of it, strengthen the continuing partnership of public health workers in South Africa and the United States, in Africa and across the globe, for health, social justice, human rights and peace.

Community Health

Speech at the opening of the
Embo Community Health Care Centre, Embo,
29 May 1998.

It is a great pleasure to return to Embo. I have come to see with my own eyes what has been achieved by a community that did not wait for government to bring improvements.

When I visited Embo in 1995, we discussed the serious lack of health facilities. I learnt that people had to go more than 100 kilometres to Prince Mshiyeni Memorial Hospital for treatment. I heard how many people grew more ill and even succumbed to illness because of this distance and lack of money for transport. We resolved then that we would tackle the problem head-on.

Today, we meet again, on the hill where Tilongo and Sikhukhukhu united to join Bambata.

Today we are here to witness a new kind of unity amongst our people, a partnership between government, South African Breweries, the Embo Masakhane Development Committee and the community.

Today, the Embo Community Health Centre stands as a proud landmark shoulder to shoulder with the Ngilanyoni and Nhlazuka Mountains.

The patients who are already visiting the centre are only the first of many, many people who will benefit from the health care it brings.

This facility, built under the leadership of Amakhosi Asembo, will serve all the people of this region, from all tribal areas around it, irrespective of political affiliation.

The population of more than a quarter of a million of Umbumbulu and surroundings have for years suffered from inadequate health facilities. All of them must find comfort here. All must feel welcome. Deliveries will take place here. The children of Embo will be born here in Embo; and the children of Umbumbulu will be born here in Umbumbulu!

The building of this clinic was a part of our national effort to bring health services to the people. Five hundred new clinics have been built since 1994 bringing access to health care for five million people. Over 130 of those are in KwaZulu-Natal. Never have so many clinics been built within such a short space of time in both urban and rural areas.

Government could not have achieved this on its own. It is a product of the spirit of *Masakhane*. The building of this health centre has shown what can be achieved when we work together. It shows us that development, skills training and job opportunities walk hand-in-hand with peace and stability. Without peace, stability and respect for the law there can be no development.

It is with great sadness that I have learnt of murders taking place in Umbumbulu, Margate, KwaMaphumulo and other areas over the past few months.

I make a plea to all *Amakhosi* and political leaders to work together to create peace. The leadership of KwaZulu-Natal can take great pride in the progress they have brought together for peace. Let us not allow political violence to return to this province.

I want to convey my unequivocal support for the peace initiatives in this province. I urge *Amakhosi* to utilise their influence to strengthen peace. I urge *Amakhosi* to avoid being used or drawn into the political contest.

I would also like to take this opportunity to encourage the Premier, Dr Ben Ngubane, the Minister of Economic Affairs, Jacob Zuma, and their colleagues to speed up the peace process. No opportunity should be left for the forces of violence to derail the process. Let us not allow our people to be discouraged by those who seek to take us back to war talk and political intolerance.

This peace process has the support and blessings of both my leaders, President Thabo Mbeki of the ANC and President Mangosuthu Buthelezi of the IFP. The working relationship between the IFP and the ANC in government remains remarkable at both national and provincial levels. Let us therefore not send one message at leadership level and another one at a grassroot level.

I want the people of KwaZulu-Natal to heed the advice and the call for peace made on numerous occasions by His Majesty King Zwelithini. For, he has made this call for people of KwaZulu to respect each other, tolerate each other's views and to fight together against our common enemies, which are poverty, unemployment, ignorance, disease and other ills. Let us make the vision of the founder of the Zulu nation a proud reality in our times. Let us commit ourselves to embrace peace and work for social upliftment of our people. And to you, Your Majesty, we thank you for your unwavering leadership.

But today we are here to celebrate. We celebrate because development has begun to flow to Umbumbulu. Delivery is occurring here as it is in other rural areas, amongst our people who were neglected for so many years by the former government. As you are celebrating the expansion of primary health care today, others across the country have reason to celebrate the connection of electricity or telephone services, clean water supplies or improvements to their roads.

Of course, even as we rejoice, we know this is only the start of a task that will take us many years. But the foundations have been laid and today we have seen how we can build when we join hands.

So we must pay tribute to all those who have made this project a resounding success: *Amakhosi*, the Embo Masakhane Development Committee and the community.

We pay tribute to Mr Meyer Kahn, Mr Dunbar Buckhall and the entire South African Breweries. Without their massive financial support of over R3 million this health centre would still be a dream in the minds of the Embo community. Just as important is SAB's spirit of goodwill that has led them to help improve the lives of many communities, in projects such as Mawele High School in Msinga and others in this province as well as many other provinces.

Lastly I must thank the province and the department of health for ensuring that this facility was completed.

As this clinic was built, so should it be officially opened, as a collective effort it is therefore right that I should be joined in this ceremony by representatives of all the partners in this project: *Amakhosi*; the Development Committee; and government at national and provincial level.

Mkhize, Khabazela Kamavovo Gcwabe Kazihlandla, Ngunezi!

A Clinic for Nobody

Speech at the opening of the 350th clinic built since South Africa's
first democratic election, ga-Nobody, Limpopo Province,
20 September 1997.

I am deeply grateful to be invited here today to join you in celebrating this milestone in our long journey towards a better life. When our new government was elected in 1994, we all entered our democracy full of hope and determination to build a new South Africa.

With our freedom won, we faced the challenge of using our limited resources to provide the majority of our people with adequate housing, education and health services. These things are regarded as basic human needs anywhere in the world and yet most of our people had been denied them.

This province was one of the worst affected by the policies of apartheid. It was treated mainly as a source of cheap labour for urban areas; it was neglected and deprived of resources. It was turned into one of the poorest parts of South Africa.

Because there were very few hospitals and clinics, only those with money and who were healthy enough could travel the long distances to get proper medical help. This was the situation of millions of South Africans across the country.

One of the most important steps the government has taken to deal with this crisis in our nation's health was to introduce free universal primary health care. Since April last year, for the first time in our history, basic health care has become available to everybody without cost.

And to make that health care easily accessible, especially to the poor, we launched the clinic-building programme so that there would be a clinic within walking distance – five kilometres – of every household.

Primary health care uses measures for both prevention and cure, like immunisation, family planning and health education. But in order for these programmes to work we also need to make sure that communities have adequate shelter, employment, sanitation and clean water supply. Poverty and lack of essential services are the greatest threat to our nation's health.

As a nation we have made progress in this regard since 1994. Government's programmes for housing, electrification, school-feeding and water supply are already improving the lives and the health of millions. But this is only the start. While bulk water supply and electricity have been extended to some areas in Mankweng, and while projects to create new jobs are taking shape, this area, like most others in our country, has much to catch up.

So we all need to work together to speed up the delivery. The government appreciates that people have been patient, and much hard work will still be needed. Our goals will take years to achieve and success requires communities to take active roles in their own upliftment.

It is all of you, through your civics, police forums, co-operatives and other development bodies, who are going to make the difference. But with your co-operation and your creative ideas we can build those classrooms, fix those roads, attract investment for more jobs and light up all our communities with electricity.

The fast-track building of clinics is one way in which government, the private sector and communities are working together for the common goal of improving people's lives.

It is because of this partnership that an average of five clinics are now being built each week and we are approaching a total of 400 new clinics.

It is this spirit of *Masakhane* that has brought direct access to affordable quality health care to more than 8.5 million people.

Today we are gathered at the 350th clinic built in South Africa since April 1994. We are amongst a population of 17 000 people from neighbouring villages who can all walk to the clinic. We are in a community that now enjoys mother- and child-care services, family-planning and psychiatric services, and which can get treatment for chronic conditions and communicable diseases.

Together with the other clinics in Mankweng, Nobody is an investment in our future. I would like to use this occasion to thank all the nursing staff, the doctors and others who make this clinic and other clinics work. They are truly helping to build our nation.

This achievement is an inspiration as we intensify the building and upgrading of health and educational facilities for many, many more people in this area, in the Northern Province and across our land.

The foundation for a better life has been laid. Forward ever!

[In earlier times, when Africans travelled from the North to get to town on a donkey cart, they had to rest on their way back home in the area in which this clinic is situated. Legend has it that this area was by then haunted by the ghost of its former owner, a white man who told the Africans that he wanted 'Nobody to come sleep on my land'. From then on, this area was called ga-Nobody (pronounced GA-NNO-PO-TRI). Minister of Health press statement, 18 September 1997.]

For the Health of All

Speech at the opening of Sangoni Clinic, Sangoni,
10 July 1998.

Today I have the special pleasure of being part of a celebration that
is especially close to my heart. Many of you here today will not know
this, but I was born within walking distance from where we are
today. Every visit here brings back special memories.

Having grown up in this area, I know first hand the deprivation
caused by apartheid and the former corrupt homeland leaders in this
province. I have seen for many years how people were deprived of
the most basic amenities: food, shelter, proper education, health care,
employment. Many had to travel huge distances to find jobs, creating unhealthy situations here at home, because healthy breadwinners
had to leave to find work.

Since our first democratic election in 1994, government, together
with its partners in the private sector, in non-governmental organisations
and in communities has been working hard to correct the imbalances.
We have seen massive programmes for housing, electrification, school
feeding schemes and water supply getting under way. Already clean
water has been made available to about two million people, electricity
to about two million homes and telephones to one million homes.

With regards to health services, much restructuring had to take
place because in the past the hospitals catered mainly for a minority
of South Africa's population. This is why there was such a strain on
facilities and resources when health services were opened to all.

The emphasis on primary health care which government has
introduced will help reduce the strain on hospitals. The clinic building programme aims at having a clinic within walking distance of
every household. Already, 500 new clinics have been built since
1994, bringing access to health care to another five million people.

Just recently we laid the foundation stone for the Umtata Academic
Hospital. It will improve the level of care for people in this region,

attracting specialists and academics. Sangoni clinic will be a referral clinic to the Umtata hospital. Like other primary health clinics, it will help lay the foundations for building a healthy nation. The clinic improvements will benefit the community and the better working conditions will help the doctors, nurses and other health workers.

This clinic is a product of the spirit of *Masakhane*. The Sangoni Masakhane project is based on the recognition that all agencies and individuals have a part to play in maintaining and improving the health of our people.

A special tribute should go to the combined efforts of the Eastern Cape Department of Health and Welfare, Eastern Cape Department of Public Works, the Eastern Cape Department of Water Affairs and Forestry, the Independent Development Trust (IDT) and the community. In particular, we honour the contribution of Siemens. By their funding of this project, and by contracting a local company for the building, Siemens have shown they are genuinely interested in the reconstruction and development of our country.

Dr Doring, I thank you for the generous sponsorship towards uplifting this community. I can assure you that we look forward to strengthening the relationship between Germany and South Africa and that Siemens is an essential link in the chain, through initiatives such as this one. As a leading supplier of technology in medical engineering, Siemens is an excellent partner for government and the community. I congratulate them on the successful completion of the new Sangoni Clinic.

It is precisely this kind of partnership of all sectors of our society that has been laying the foundations for a better life all over South Africa. We know that we have made only a start – many more people still wait for the most basic of services. The government appreciates that people have been patient and that much hard work will still be needed. Our goals will take years to achieve and success requires that we all pull together. It requires that communities are active in their own upliftment; that the private sector makes development part of its business; and that government facilitates this process with infrastructure and resources.

Siemens, along with other businesses who have joined hands with government and communities to provide clinics and schools across our country, are giving real meaning to reconciliation. Their efforts deserve wider recognition, and we urge others to follow their example.

Now that this facility has been completed, it is up to the community to take advantage of it and to nurture the health of all those who live in the area.

Kick Polio Out of Africa

Speech at the launch of the 'Kick Polio out of Africa' Campaign,
2 August 1996.

Africa is renowned for its beauty, its rich natural heritage and prolific resources – but equally, the image of its suffering children haunts the conscience of our continent and the world.

The legacy of our colonial past, lack of resources and the devastation of war have rendered our children especially vulnerable to disease.

Co-operation between nations across the world coupled with scientific advancement have made the global control of certain diseases possible. One of the great achievements of our generation is the eradication of smallpox from the world.

The World Summit on Child Survival in September 1990 defined as one of its goals the eradication of poliomyelitis by the year 2000. The 'Kick Polio out of Africa' campaign is going to help achieve this goal and I am deeply privileged to be a part of it.

In April last year, on World Health Day, I called on South Africa to join the initiative towards a 'World without Polio by the Year 2000'. The response was phenomenal. Thanks to the efforts of our own dedicated health workers and those belonging to regional and international organisations, many thousands of children all over South Africa were given the polio vaccine.

In Africa as a whole the incidents of polio in children have decreased from more than 4000 in 1990 to less than 1000 in 1993. The dedication of volunteers all over Africa as well as the tireless efforts of international organisations and external partners in this regard are to be highly commended.

But our aim is not merely to reduce the numbers afflicted – it is to eliminate the disease completely. No country can be safe from this disease until the whole world is rid of it. For it can cross borders with ease. We should therefore take to heart the call by the Organisation for African Unity Summit last month for all African countries to urgently address the problem of polio and give their support to actions aimed at eradicating this disease from our continent.

Dr Samba [Regional Director of the World Health Organisation] is to be congratulated on the formation of this Committee for a Polio Free Africa, composed of such distinguished persons. Their role will be critical in securing co-operation from governments in the campaign to kick polio out of Africa.

Mass immunisation campaigns have started in many African countries this year. With the help of our partners, the World Health Organisation, Unicef, Rotary International, USAid, the Centre for Disease Control and Prevention and the government of Japan, we hope to reach 50 million children with the vaccine this year.

But we do know that the immunisation campaign will not reach everyone this year. The children who have not been immunised will remain susceptible to the disease – even in areas where cases of polio have not been seen for some time. And so to give meaning to the noble work being done by health workers in all our countries, we must attack the disease from all fronts. Every rural parent should be able to recognise the warning signs in the form of weakness in the limbs of a child. They should be able to gain access to medical resources to treat their children, and be able to prevent the disease from endangering their other children.

We are calling on the continent's football players to bring their enormous influence to this campaign. Only unified efforts which galvanise whole societies towards these goals will succeed in kicking this virus, that looks so much like a football, out of Africa and, eventually, out of the world.

It was a partnership between international organisations, governments, the private sector and communities that enabled us to eradicate smallpox from the world. Let that achievement inspire us all to redouble our efforts in this campaign.

The Polio-Free Africa Committee will be taking this message across our continent, even to its remotest corners. The momentum of this year's campaign must be multiplied next year and the following year, until we have reached every child in Africa – until we can safely say we have kicked polio out of Africa forever.

The Gift of Hearing

Speech at the Baragwanath Hearing Aid Project,
Soweto, 23 May 1997.

One of the wonders of the modern age is that we can overcome many of the obstacles that nature and misfortune impose on us. If we all co-operate to use the technology that is available, then there is little that can stop us.

Today we are putting the spotlight on a problem that afflicts millions of South Africans. Our Department of Health tells us that one out of every 25 South Africans is profoundly deaf or extremely hard of hearing.

All of you who have hearing difficulties know that it does put barriers in the way of developing and using your talents for the benefit of your community and society. For many it can mean a special kind of loneliness.

A hearing aid can provide a key to many opportunities.

I would like to tell you that I also wear hearing aids, just as you do. These little instruments made a big difference to my life. Wherever I go, they help me to listen better, to understand better.

I would like to encourage you to wear your hearing aids, as they will help you, especially to learn. Learning is your future and it is the future of our country. Use this opportunity to help yourselves and your nation.

It needs discipline to use a hearing aid. And to get the improvements in communication that make it possible requires the understanding, expertise, love and dedication of many people: family, friends, members of the community, teachers, and health professionals.

I would like to take this opportunity to extend a particular word of thanks to the audiology department of the Baragwanath Hospital for their splendid work to make this project a success. Thank you also to Siemens for their valuable contribution of the hearing aids. And we are grateful to Republic Hearing Instruments for their efforts to co-ordinate the contribution of all the other companies and service providers.

Today we also think of the many, many more people who need such devices, but who cannot get them because of the cost. This is especially so in a country like ours which is emerging from a past in which the health needs of most people were shamefully neglected.

The challenge we must all take – government, the hearing aid industry, and professionals – is to ensure that these hearing aids are within the reach of all those in need of them.

This partnership of innovation and service delivery should include those who have hearing difficulties themselves. We as users can play an important role in guiding the engineers and scientists to make the technology even more effective.

We do know that if all of us work together then we will create more and better opportunities, especially among children from black communities. Let us join hands: young and old, those with no hearing difficulties together with the deaf and the hard of hearing.

Together we can make a difference. Together we can remove barriers to full participation in the new nation we are building.

Aids: For Whom the Bell Tolls

Speech to the National Conference on Aids, NASREC,
23 October 1992.

When I was asked to open this conference some months ago, I felt
greatly honoured by the invitation and at the same time, greatly
humbled by the enormity of this problem facing our own country
and many other countries. My mind was sharply focused on the
words in Hemingway's novel that:

> man is not an island
> he is not an entity unto himself . . .
> therefore ask not for whom the bell tolls
> it tolls for thee.

The reality of the Aids epidemic worldwide is that it is not merely a
medical condition, it is a disease with socio-medical implications.

In South Africa, this problem challenges the entire socio-economic
fabric of our society and poses a threat to future generations.
Statistics indicate that those forced to live in poor socio-economic
conditions are the highest at risk in our population.

As at 30 June this year, 1 316 cases of Aids were recorded, and the
majority of these were recorded in Natal, with the highest incidences
of Aids countrywide being recorded in the urban areas. Apartheid's
legacy has played a great role in this factor, particularly in the black
communities where overcrowding in homes does not provide for
privacy within the family; where lack of housing and the creation of
informal settlements as well as the lack of recreation facilities make
the black community even more susceptible to the sex-related virus.
Single-sex hostels lead to the disintegration of family units in rural
areas and hostel dwellers are forced to have casual relationships since
they cannot live with their families.

Another startling statistic is the incidence of Aids in young children.

Most children born with the Aids virus die before they reach their second birthday. The fact that the virus attacks the most economically active age group in our population is also an issue worthy of discussion.

The serious consequences of inadequate health care facilities nationally, as well as the fact that there is limited access to the health facilities which treat sexually transmitted diseases, is a matter which this conference must pay serious attention to.

Women are the most seriously affected by the Aids virus. They are the poorest people in our country due to the lack of education and work opportunities. The position of women in our society forces them into a situation where they are unable to protect themselves or an unborn infant against the virus. Many women find it very difficult to insist that their partners wear condoms due to the socialisation of both men and women on the issue of sex.

Our most potent weapon against this virus is education. We have, perhaps, for some time allowed ourselves to believe that like other epidemics it will come and go; that the great advances of our time in science and technology will offer us appropriate quick intervention.

The key to our success is our own collective effort. The time for rhetorical arguments and victim blaming has passed. Now is the time for action. What we know about this disease already is enough to enable us to put in place comprehensive and appropriate intervention strategies. We already know that Aids has no cure and no vaccine despite the intensive research efforts. Therefore, prevention remains for us the strategy we must employ.

We do have a problem with the efforts being made by the South African government in that the efforts by the government to introduce preventative measures are viewed with suspicion and as a ploy to control the population. This government does not have the credibility to convince the majority of black South Africans to change their sexual behaviour.

Our first thought must be the protection of our people against this disease, and therefore it is necessary that we adopt a broad front approach to the problem. All sectors of our community must become engaged in this battle and resources available from the government must be distributed to our communities. This problem does not allow anyone the luxury of political bias or hearts-and-minds-winning exercises. We need to set up a structure at national, regional and local level which goes beyond health workers and the government.

Aids exposes an aspect of our lives that we are most loath to discuss openly, but it also touches on religious and cultural sensitivities. We must be sensitive to these, yet be bold to explore all avenues that will ensure that our message is not only received but well received. The only sure way of achieving this is by involving all of us in our home, our institutions, organisations, places of worship and work.

I believe that a central component of our intervention strategy must be to strengthen the capacity of our people individually and collectively to recognise, understand and act decisively against this scourge.

Let us ensure that everybody understands that a successful fight against Aids is not a success only for individuals, but for families, communities and indeed for our country as a whole.

In this regard I wish to make a special appeal to the government, the business community and other formations to, as a matter of urgency, make resources available for a speedy implementation of the recommendations that will come from this convention. I have already said that education is our most potent medicine against this virus – we need to bring home to parents, church leaders, political organisations and all other organs of civil society that stigmatisation of Aids victims does not solve the problem. The victims of Aids are victims of the illnesses in our society and we need to proceed from that basis.

Many of us find it difficult to talk about sex to our children, but nature's truth is that unless we guide the youth towards safer sex, the alternative is playing into the hands of a killer disease. In this regard I wish to endorse the idea of an Aids charter which will educate and activate our population, as well as entrench the rights of Aids victims. We have an obligation to move decisively to remove all those obstacles which limit our capacity to deal effectively with this scourge. Do we really have any justification for perpetuating such practices as the migrant labour system, single-sex hostels, which not only destroy family life, but certainly limit our capacity to establish stable self-reliant communities that can be the core of a dynamic society able to cope with this and other problems? Is it not time we address the problem of illiteracy, poverty and empower our womenfolk – all crucial factors for an effective intervention strategy?

Very few, if any, diseases better illustrate the truth in the dictum 'prevention is better than cure'.

Lastly, Aids definitely has profound direct micro- and macroeconomic impacts. In the years ahead, as we face the process of national reconstruction, we shall need the best possible performance of our national economy. Let us therefore act now to ensure that our efforts at nation building and democratic transformation will not be frustrated.

Aids: A Task for Us All

Message on World Aids Day,
1 December 1994.

On 1 December, South Africa and the international community mark World Aids Day. The fact that we can now observe this day as a democratic country gives us the rare opportunity to co-operate as a nation in addressing this most pressing problem. It is estimated that in some parts of our country, already one out of ten people are infected with the Aids virus. And the epidemic is spreading rapidly. Young people, in particular, face the highest risk.

It is appropriate that this year's theme for World Aids Day is 'The Family and Aids'. For, it is in the family that the values required to combat this plague can be popularised. Mutual trust and support, particularly between parents and children, is crucial in spreading awareness about Aids, and preventing it. Above all, we need to work together in eradicating the legacy of apartheid, including homelessness, illiteracy, the lack of health facilities, the migrant labour system and bad living conditions – all of which have created fertile ground for the spread of Aids.

But public awareness around Aids is needed today, not tomorrow. The challenge of today, to youth and adults alike, is to make lifestyle choices which help to combat this epidemic.

World Aids Day also brings to the fore the message of tolerance and support. As individuals and as a nation, we need to treat relatives, friends and other compatriots who are infected, with compassion. This applies more so to orphans and infected children.

The campaign against Aids is the task of all of us – young and old, government and community organisations, religious and traditional institutions, cultural and sporting bodies. Aids knows no custom. It knows no colour. It knows no boundaries. We have to work together wherever we are to preserve our nation, our continent and humanity as a whole.

As government, we will continue to take an active part in Aids-

392

awareness initiatives. We will continue to allocate as much resources as government can afford to combat this epidemic. However, success in this campaign will depend on the input of all sectors of society.

Now is the time to work together to combat Aids.

Aids: Shared Rights, Shared Responsibilities

Message on World Aids Day,
1 December 1995.

On 1 December, South Africa and the international community mark World Aids Day. Throughout the world, people use this day to reaffirm their commitment and dedication to stemming the further spread of this pandemic and to providing care and support to those already infected or affected by the Aids virus. South Africans join the world community on this day through a range of special events that are organised throughout the country.

This year's theme for World Aids Day is 'Shared Rights, Shared Responsibilities'. As South Africans we are able to identify closely with this theme as we have recently ensured that all people share political rights, and share the responsibility of governing. Aids poses a major threat to the reconstruction process underway. It is estimated that approximately two million South Africans are already infected with the Aids virus, and approximately 10 000 people have already progressed to Aids. In the past five years we have experienced a ten-fold increase in HIV infection in the population. Most affected are youth, women and migrant workers. Factors such as the status of women in society, child abuse, migrant labour, unemployment, lack of housing, illiteracy, sexual prejudice, discrimination in the work-place and other settings have contributed, and continue to contribute to the rapid spread of the virus in South Africa.

We need to ensure that we provide the supportive environment to afford people the capacity to protect themselves through increasing access to condoms, drugs for sexually transmitted diseases, access to health care and testing and counselling facilities. At all times we must speak out against the stigma, blame, shame and denial that has thus far been associated with this epidemic. Through our actions let us demonstrate that as a country we are in the forefront of protecting the rights of people with HIV and acting on our responsibilities to stem the epidemic and ensure a caring and supportive environment.

I urge all South Africans to participate actively in the special events being held throughout the country – wear a red ribbon as a symbol of your solidarity and support us as we take on the challenge posed by this new threat. Let us ensure that by 1 December 1996, we are facing a very different South Africa – one where all citizens are able to protect themselves from infection, where people with HIV/Aids are given all possible support so that we may all share the benefits of our newly found freedom.

Now is the time to work together to combat Aids.

Aids: A New Struggle

Speech at the World Economic Forum Session on Aids,
Davos, 3 February 1997.

I feel greatly honoured to be invited to address you today on a matter
that so deeply affects the whole world. Although HIV/Aids has been
with us through the 1980s and 90s, it is a problem whose solution
continues to elude us. We have made progress in understanding the
epidemic. But we are still unable to contain its spread.

The Aids pandemic is getting worse at a rate that makes a collective global effort imperative. When the history of our time is written,
it will record the collective efforts of societies responding to a threat
that has put in the balance the future of whole nations. Future generations will judge us on the adequacy of our response.

In many ways South Africa's past – as that of most colonial societies – remains with us today, not least in the social dimensions of the
unfolding Aids epidemic. The poor, the vulnerable, the unschooled,
the socially marginalised, the women and the children, those who
bear the burden of colonial legacy – these are the sectors of society
which bear the burden of Aids. We are concerned at the discrimination and stigmatisation directed at people living with this virus and,
in many instances, their families as well. Beyond the enormous suffering of individuals and families, South Africans are beginning to
understand the cost in every sphere of society, observing with growing
dismay its impact on the efforts of our new democracy to achieve the
goals of reconstruction and development.

South Africa is confident that it is making headway in implementing its macroeconomic strategy for growth, employment and redistribution. All the signs point to a sound trend of economic fundamentals; to our being on track; and to a national consensus on policy that
will see us reach our targets of economic growth and job creation. Our
own development takes place within, and is boosted by, the framework of increasingly integrated development across Southern Africa

as our region acts to fulfill a long-cherished dream of co-operation for peace and prosperity. And yet, while South and Southern Africa can take pride in these achievements, we do know that the great and urgent needs of our people would be more easily met were it not for diseases like Aids.

It is anticipated that if current trends continue then Aids will cost South Africa one per cent of our GDP by the year 2005; and that up to three-quarters of our health budget will be consumed by direct health costs relating to HIV/Aids. Even creative low-cost alternatives to hospital care will leave us with a significant impact on our health care budget.

Though the details may vary from country to country, this experience is one we share with the world. No country can avoid this disease. The challenge is to seek ways to minimise its effects, to prepare for its impact and to co-operate for long-term solutions.

How will we address child mortality rates which are set to increase threefold in Africa?

With 6 000 new infections occurring every day throughout the world; with 22 million men, women and children infected; with six million people estimated to have died; and with nine million children under the age of 15 having lost their mothers to Aids, there can be no doubt that humanity faces a major challenge.

The severity of the economic impact of the disease is directly related to the fact that most infected persons are in the peak productive and reproductive age groups. Aids kills those on whom society relies to grow the crops, work in the mines and factories, run the schools and hospitals and govern nations and countries, thus increasing the number of dependent persons. It creates new pockets of poverty when parents and breadwinners die and children leave school earlier to support the remaining children.

The epidemic is fuelled by other evils which afflict our world – open conflict and low-intensity war cause population movements and social dislocation which promote the spread of infection.

With cruel irony, even our achievements in improving communication networks and transportation systems, and the building of regional economic blocs, influence the attitudes and behavior patterns of people in ways that sometimes accelerate the spread of the disease.

These are well-known facts. If we recall them now it is to underline the scale and the multifaceted nature of the problem. The health sector cannot meet this challenge on its own. Nor can government.

All sectors and all spheres of society have to be involved as equal partners. We have to join hands to develop programmes and share information and research that will halt the spread of this disease and help develop support networks for those who are affected.

By 1985 the global community had recognised the need for a multi-sectoral response and had endorsed a structure to support such an expanded response by all countries. The Joint United Nations Programmes, UNAids, recognises that, in the longer term, it will be community development, employment and wealth creation, literacy programmes, promotion of equality between men and women and the protection of human rights which will address the underlying conditions and the consequences.

In general the responses by individual countries to date have fallen short of what is needed. In some cases political commitment has been lacking, in others resources have been limited. Frequently even essential services are non-existent.

Conscious of our own need to put the effort to combat Aids on a higher plane, South Africa's National Aids Programme has made the call for 'A New Struggle'.

The vision which fuelled our struggle for freedom; the deployment of energies and resources; the unity and commitment to common goals – all these are needed if we are to bring Aids under control.

South Africans achieved victory in their struggle for freedom, thanks to the solidarity of the international community and its commitment to justice. As the freedom of each nation is interdependent with that of others, so too is the health and wellbeing of their peoples. Nowhere is this more true than in the case of Aids.

The challenge of Aids can be overcome if we work together as a global community. Let us join hands in a caring partnership for health and prosperity as we enter the new millennium.

Aids: Breaking the Silence

Keynote Address at a rally on World Aids Day,
Mtubatuba, 1 December 1998.

We have come to Mtubatuba for World Aids Day because this province
and this area have been hard hit by this deadly virus. We have come here
as Partners Against Aids, to express our solidarity and support. We have
come to accept the help of the government and the people of KwaZulu-
Natal in making our nation understand what this disease really means.

Aids is one of those problems that are beyond the capacity of any
one community, or any province, to solve on its own – or even any
one nation alone.

To win we must join hands in a partnership against Aids, and also
work with other nations as part of the international community. We
need the help of organisations like the United Nations and it is
therefore a special pleasure to welcome Dr Piot, the Director of
UNAids, who has come to share this day with us.

Although Aids has been a part of our lives for 15 years or more,
we have kept silent about its true presence in our midst. We have too
often spoken of it as if it was someone else's problem.

We had hoped that today, before this rally, we could visit a community that has been badly affected by Aids, and pay our respects to
those whose lives were taken by the disease. We want our communities to be able to say to our country: Come and witness the reality of
Aids; see the devastation in our community; see the fresh graves; see
the courage of those who live with the infection and of the children
who have lost their parents.

We must remove the silence that leads companies to say to a newspaper: 'We want to put an advertisement in your paper, but it must
not be near anything about Aids.' It is the silence that leads us, when
we see all the signs in our friend's face, to speak of anything else,
rather than ask, 'Do you have Aids? How can we help?' It is the
silence that hangs over our cemeteries when we bury loved ones

knowing they died of Aids, but not speaking of it. It is the silence that is letting this disease sweep through our country, adding 1 500 people each day to more than three million already infected. It isolates those who need our support and help. It threatens to undermine our efforts to grow our economy and build a better life for all our people.

It is time to break the silence. That is why we are here today as political leaders, following the lead given by Deputy President Thabo Mbeki.

We are grateful to a province that has the courage to declare that it has a high rate of infection. We admire the brave men, women and children who are with us today to say: We are the human face of Aids – we are breaking the silence! If we are to succeed then all of us must follow these examples and take responsibility for dealing with this problem.

Though we are doing all we can to search for a cure for Aids, it has not yet been found and therefore prevention is the key to turning the tide. Because this disease is so new, and because it spreads mainly through sex, prevention requires of us that we speak of it in a way that our traditions, our cultures and our religions provide little guidance for.

We must repeat over and over again our appeal to young people to abstain from sex as long as possible. If you do decide to engage in sex, then use a condom. We must repeat over and over again our appeal to all men and women to be faithful to one another, but otherwise to use condoms.

It is possible for any of us to be infected for eight years without knowing it, and therefore to pass on the infection to others without knowing it. We appeal to all sexually active people who have not been tested, to have the test for the virus and if you are infected to openly seek the support of the community.

But we do know that we can only make this call upon those who have been affected if the community accepts its responsibility to give support to people living with HIV/Aids. All of us, in our communities, in our educational institutions, in our workplaces, in our media, in our financial institutions, our places of worship and recreation must work to eradicate the discrimination that denies support and dignity to those who need it. As traditional leaders and people of influence in our communities, provinces and nation, let us set an example.

South Africans have overcome obstacles which others thought were insurmountable, because we joined hands to work for the good of all rather than remaining divided by less important things. Just as we defied the prophets of doom who foresaw endless conflict in our land, we can defeat this terrible disease by all of us accepting responsibility for prevention of infection and for care of those who have been affected.

In October we launched a Partnership Against Aids, and declared our united resolve to save the nation. Since then much has happened, but all of us need to ask ourselves: Are we doing enough to lend strength to the partnership on which our future depends? What are we doing as teachers and parents? As business people, big and small? As employers and workers?

The young people, who are our future, are most at risk. We rely on their capacity for vision and on the courage that has been shown by people living with HIV/Aids to give our nation the lead it needs to rise to this challenge.

Together we can succeed. On this World Aids Day let us make a pledge. Let us do everything possible to prevent ourselves and our partners from getting infected. Let us build the Partnership Against Aids so that it unites every community and sector of our society into a force for change. Let us break the silence by speaking openly and publicly about Aids, and by bringing an end to discrimination against those living with Aids. Let us care for those living with HIV/Aids and the orphans, and give them support, with love and compassion.

And let us say that we will wear the Red Ribbon today, and every day, in remembrance of those who have died and in solidarity with those who are infected. Let us wear it as a sign of our commitment to this pledge.

Aids: From Rhetoric to Action

Closing Address at the 13th International Aids Conference,
Durban, 14 July 2000.

To have been asked to deliver the closing address at this conference, which in a very literal sense concerns itself with matters of life and death, weighs heavily upon me for the gravity of the responsibility placed on one.

No disrespect is intended towards the many other occasions where one has been privileged to speak, if I say that this is the one event where every word uttered, every gesture made, has to be measured against the effect it can and will have on the lives of millions of concrete, real human beings all over this continent and planet. This is not an academic conference. This is, as I understand it, a gathering of human beings concerned about turning around one of the greatest threats humankind has faced, and certainly the greatest after the end of the great wars of the previous century.

It is never my custom to use words lightly. If 27 years in prison have done anything to us, it was to use the silence of solitude to make us understand how precious words are and how real speech is in its impact upon the way people live or die.

If by way of introduction I stress the importance of the way we speak, it is also because so much unnecessary attention around this conference had been directed towards a dispute that is unintentionally distracting from the real life-and-death issues we are confronted with as a country, a region, a continent and a world.

I do not know nearly enough about science and its methodologies or about the politics of science and scientific practice to even wish to start contributing to the debate that has been raging on the perimeters of this conference. I am, however, old enough and have gone through sufficient conflicts and disputes in my lifetime to know that in all disputes a point is arrived at where no party, no matter how right or wrong it might have been at the start of that dispute, will any longer be totally in the right or totally in the wrong. Such a point, I believe, has been reached in this debate.

The president of this country is a man of great intellect who takes scientific thinking very seriously and he leads a government that I know to be committed to those principles of science and reason. The scientific community of this country, I also know, holds dearly to the principle of freedom of scientific enquiry, unencumbered by undue political interference in and direction of science.

Now, however, the ordinary people of the continent and the world – and particularly the poor who on our continent will again carry a disproportionate burden of this scourge – would, if anybody cared to ask their opinions, wish that the dispute about the primacy of politics or science be put on the back burner and that we proceed to address the needs and concerns of those suffering and dying. And this can only be done in partnership.

I come from a long tradition of collective leadership, consultative decision making and joint action towards the common good. We have overcome much that many thought insurmountable through an adherence to those practices. In the face of the grave threat posed by HIV/Aids, we have to rise above our differences and combine our efforts to save our people. History will judge us harshly if we fail to do so now, and right now.

Let us not equivocate: a tragedy of unprecedented proportions is unfolding in Africa. Aids today in Africa is claiming more lives than the sum total of all wars, famines and floods, and the ravages of such deadly diseases as malaria. It is devastating families and communities; overwhelming and depleting health care services; and robbing schools of both students and teachers. Business has suffered, or will suffer, losses of personnel, productivity and profits; economic growth is being undermined and scarce development resources have to be diverted to deal with the consequences of the pandemic.

HIV/Aids is having a devastating impact on families, communities, societies and economies. Decades have been chopped from life expectancy and young child mortality is expected to more than double in the most severely affected countries of Africa. Aids is clearly a disaster, effectively wiping out the development gains of the past decades and sabotaging the future.

Earlier this week we were shocked to learn that within South Africa one in two, that is half, of our young people will die of Aids. The most frightening thing is that all of these infections which statistics tell us about, and the attendant human suffering, could have been, can be, prevented.

Something must be done as a matter of the greatest urgency. And with nearly two decades of dealing with the epidemic, we now do have some experience of what works. The experience in a number of countries has taught that HIV infection can be prevented through investing in information and life skills development for young people. Promoting abstinence, safe sex and the use of condoms and ensuring the early treatment of sexually transmitted diseases are some of the steps needed and about which there can be no dispute. Ensuring that people, especially the young, have access to voluntary and confidential HIV counselling and testing services and introducing measures to reduce mother-to-child transmission have been proven to be essential in the fight against Aids. We have recognised the importance of addressing the stigmatisation and discrimination, and of providing safe and supportive environments for people affected by HIV/Aids.

The experiences of Uganda, Senegal and Thailand have shown that serious investments in and mobilisation around these actions make a real difference. Stigma and discrimination can be stopped; new infections can be prevented; and the capacity of families and communities to care for people living with HIV and Aids can be enhanced.

It is not, I must add, as if the South African government has not moved significantly on many of these areas. It was the First Deputy President in my government that oversaw and drove the initiatives in this regard, and as the President continues to place this issue on top of the national and continental agenda. He will with me be the first to concede that much more remains to be done. I do not doubt for one moment that he will proceed to tackle this task with the resolve and dedication he is known for.

The challenge is to move from rhetoric to action, and action at an unprecedented intensity and scale. There is a need for us to focus on what we know works. We need to break the silence, banish stigma and discrimation, and ensure total inclusiveness within the struggle against Aids. We need bold initiatives to prevent new infections among young people, and large-scale actions to prevent mother-to-child transmission, and at the same time we need to continue the international effort of searching for appropriate vaccines. We need to aggressively treat opportunistic infections. We need to work with families and communities to care for children and young people to protect them from violence and abuse, and to ensure that they grow up in a safe and supportive environment.

For this there is need for us to be focused, to be strategic, and to mobilise all of our resources and alliances, and to sustain the effort until this war is won. We need, and there is increasing evidence of, African resolve to fight this war. Others will not save us if we do not primarily commit ourselves. Let us, however, not underestimate the resources required to conduct this battle. Partnership with the international community is vital. A constant theme in all our messages has been that in this interdependent and globalised world we have indeed again become the keepers of our brother and sister. That cannot be more graphically the case than in the common fight against HIV/Aids.

As one small contribution to the great combined effort that is required, I have instructed my Foundation to explore in consultation with others the best way in which we can be involved in the battle against this terrible scourge ravaging our continent and world.

I thank all of you most sincerely for your involvement in that struggle. Let us combine our efforts to ensure a future for our children. The challenge is no less.

Aids: Confronting the Crisis

Address to the Cosatu Executive Committee,
25 July 2001.

Whenever we talk about HIV/Aids the word 'crisis' immediately comes to mind. In many ways this has served to deaden our thoughts about just how big a crisis HIV/Aids indeed is. It is like the message on cigarette packs: we are told that smoking will kill us, yet we continue to smoke.

Perhaps we need to remind ourselves just how big the Aids crisis really is:

Status of HIV/Aids in South Africa:
– 4.7 million or 13 per cent of the world's 37 million HIV-infected people live in South Africa;
– 250 000 people in South Africa die of Aids-related diseases each year;
– there are at least 250 000 orphans because of Aids deaths;
– anywhere between 50 000 and 100 000 children (under the age of sixteen) are the heads of households;
– infection rates are still unacceptably high, anywhere between 13 and 25 per cent.

We also need to ask ourselves why HIV infection rates continue to spiral, in spite of the numerous efforts and the millions of rand being spent to educate people about the disease. Many of these efforts are of high quality, and those implementing those programmes are people of integrity.

In a recent survey commissioned by the Nelson Mandela Foundation and the Children's Fund, it was found that:

– HIV/Aids awareness programmes are not reaching all South Africans. There are many barriers, including cultural, linguistic and geographic.

- Awareness, where it occurs, does not necessarily translate into behaviour changes.
- There continues to be huge mistrust of the message and the medium. It was found that only 1 per cent of South Africans 'listen' to the media, whether it emanates from government or NGOs.
- 46 per cent of South Africans said they had learnt nothing about HIV/Aids during the last year.

If we evaluate the various awareness programmes, I am sure that we will find all kinds of technical reasons for their apparent inability, when taken cumulatively, to make any real impact on people's attitudes towards HIV/Aids. Yes, the existing programmes can be strengthened, and the Nelson Mandela Foundation intends helping many of the organisations fighting the spread of the disease.

My own belief is that the anti-Aids message is not succeeding because of one major obstacle: stigmatisation. There is still a huge sense of shame attached to the disease. Those who become HIV-positive are often seen as simply promiscuous, when in fact the truth is far more complex. How many individuals have infected their partners because they are afraid to acknowledge to themselves that they are HIV-positive, or cannot speak about their infection for fear of alienating their loved ones?

There are also so many myths about how HIV is spread. There are people who believe that the disease can be contracted by simply being in the same room as someone who is HIV-positive. This results in a culture of secrecy and denial. It inhibits voluntary testing on a nationwide scale. This is the only way we can really establish the true extent of the disease, its geographic patterns, and its age and gender distribution.

Furthermore, the refusal or inability to speak openly about the disease, especially in our rural areas and among other traditional societies and religious groups, makes it difficult to develop effective education campaigns.

The time has come for South Africans to make a concerted effort to fight the stigmatisation of those who are HIV-positive, those who are dying of Aids. And it is time for South Africans to stop saying that it is someone else's responsibility to combat this illness. It is the responsibility of every South African. Of course, this process of developing 'champions' of a cause requires catalysts, individuals who influence the opinions of others.

It should start with each member of the *Amakhosi* talking frankly to his people, it should extend to Members of Parliament devoting the first ten per cent of every speech to this topic, to every doctor talking to their patients during each consultation. Every trade union leader, every shop steward, every employer, every lawyer should, during the course of their daily work, ask: what can we do to help stop the spread of HIV?

This country should develop an army of anti-Aids campaigners; they should regard Aids as an enemy against which our country is at war. They should fight this war every day, from the shop floor, from offices, on sports fields and in classrooms.

Perhaps we can make a start here today: how many commanders of this anti-Aids army will come forward from the leaders of the trade union movement? You need to be bold and vociferous. We cannot just rely on political leaders, on billboards and TV adverts to spread the message. It should be spread by word of mouth, from comrade to comrade, from worker to worker, until we have defeated this dreadful enemy called Aids.

Say to people: Aids is not a curse that we must deny, it is an illness that can be defeated. Resisting the continued stigmatisation of HIV-positive people is not only a compassionate act, it is practical and pragmatic.

10
CHILDREN

TANGIBLE CARE

GRAÇA MACHEL

I come from a culture in which, traditionally, children are seen as both our present and our future, so I have always believed it is our responsibility as adults to give children futures worth having. I have often been shocked and angered to see how shamefully we have failed in this responsibility.

Children are precious gifts, which adults everywhere have a duty to protect. Political leaders make promises about the protection of children, but the important thing is that they should fulfil those promises. We have been making beautiful speeches, trading phrases, and making noble promises, only to fail in the execution.

After the first children's summit of 1990, the rights of children became quite high on the international agenda. There is much more awareness today than there has been in the past. But more importantly, there is some progress that can be measured. It is limited, but there is progress. We can see what has been happening in dealing with malnutrition, in expanding education, and in other areas. In some countries, the situation of children has improved tremendously. So, we can observe a momentum. What I believe is extremely important, however, is to strengthen the political will – the will that political leaders have to actually mean what they say. They have to allocate human resources to make things happen, to allocate financial and material resources for the wellbeing of children.

Nelson Mandela, without any doubt, always means what he says. As President of South Africa, he certainly meant it when he said that the wellbeing of children was a national priority. The speeches in this chapter recall Nelson Mandela's commitment to caring for children, not merely by making promises, but by establishing programmes that weave children into the social fabric of a caring, responsible nation.

Subsequently, in the ongoing work of the Nelson Mandela Children's

411

Fund, as well as in other initiatives, we have been able to see the results of this tangible care. Sharing his concern, and sharing his work, I can only mention here some of the critical issues we are addressing on behalf of our children not only within South Africa but also in the larger world.

We are all challenged by the fact that millions across the globe live in impoverished and insecure conditions that prevent them from exercising the rights that have been proclaimed to be universal. This is especially and shockingly true of children. Although the problems are especially acute in the developing world, it is not only in the developing world that children are afflicted by the violence of poverty. The problem is a global one.

We stand at the beginning of the twenty-first century, a time filled with great promise and yet great misery for children. This is an era of amazing technological innovation, where we have dramatically advanced our global interactions and communication abilities. It is an era during which the world has accumulated huge amounts of knowledge, even if we do not always use it with wisdom. It is a time of extraordinary scientific advances where illness and diseases that were once fatal are now preventable. It is also a time of enormous wealth within and among nations, where the global economy generates $30 trillion. Truly then, we live in a world, and in a time, which should be full of hope and promise for our children.

Yet, in these amazing times, when one looks more broadly at the condition of children one sees the justification of speaking of the violence of poverty: 600 million children in the world live in absolute poverty on less than one dollar a day. The 'silent emergency' of malnutrition and preventable disease kills 12 million children each year. Nearly 4 000 children die each day due to lack of vaccinations. Instead of being in the classroom, over 70 million children between 10 and 14 years of age are employed in child labour. Millions of children have no home or family.

Today we are also becoming aware of the devastating impact that HIV/Aids has on children. All too often we think of this mainly as an adult problem. I must acknowledge that I myself have only recently understood the extent to which children are affected: in Sub-Saharan Africa, it is estimated that 13 million children have lost their mothers or both parents to Aids. Every five minutes, an African youngster between the ages of 15 and 25 is infected with HIV. And the epidemic is spreading with frightening rapidity in many parts of Asia, Eastern Europe, and the Caribbean, with a devastating impact on children, families, communities, and nations throughout the world.

These are only a few of many statistics that paint a terrible picture of the lives that millions of children live. But they are statistics that, I believe, should motivate all of us. They are statistics that make me impatient for change, and frustrated with the lack of progress we have made in improving the lives of children despite the many promises made by adults and leaders of all kind.

In Africa our own national budgets often do not prioritise the basic needs of children. Yet increasing budget allocations for health, education, and water and sanitation would help overcome poverty, improve human development, and help promote peace and security. It is a sad fact that many African countries, particularly those in conflict, spend more on their defence budgets than on basic social services. Why is it that we can mobilise vast resources to fund wars, but we cannot mobilise adequate funds to protect children throughout the world?

Millions of children have died as a result of armed conflict in the last decade alone, while countless millions more have been left physically and emotionally disabled by horrific conflicts where children have been deliberate targets. Power and greed can never be an excuse for sacrificing children. In tolerating the scourge of war against children, every one of us becomes complicit in the violence and harm inflicted upon them.

It is unfortunate that adults, on many occasions, put children in situations where they have no option for survival other than to pick up arms. I have to stress here that the responsibility is that of adults, not of children. But of course it is true that sometimes they have to try to do something in order to survive and then the only chance they have is to pick up arms. That is why I call on the responsibility of adults for never allowing a child to be in that situation. It is our responsibility, not theirs.

In some countries, conflicts have raged for so long that children have grown into adults without ever knowing peace. I have spoken to a child who was raped by soldiers when she was just nine years old. I have witnessed the anguish of a mother who saw her children blown to pieces by landmines in their fields, just when she believed they had made it home safely after the war. I have listened to children who were forced to watch while their families were brutally slaughtered. I have heard the bitter remorse of 15-year-old ex-soldiers mourning their lost childhood and innocence, and I have been chilled listening to children who have been so manipulated by adults and so corrupted by their experiences of conflict that they could not recognise the evil of which they had been a part.

These are the stories behind the news, the statistics, the reports that give figures of such magnitude that they often hide the impact of these horrors on each child, each family, each community. Here are some figures: 2 million children were killed and 4.5 million were wounded in wars during the 1990s. Still more were left homeless, orphaned, and traumatised. Increasing numbers of children under 16, an estimated 300 000, become involved in armed conflict as child soldiers.

I have learned that despite being targets in contemporary armed conflicts, despite the brutality shown towards them and the failure of adults to nurture and protect them, children are both our reason to eliminate the worst aspects of armed conflict and our best hope of succeeding in that charge. In a disparate world, children are a unifying force capable of bringing us all together in support of a common ethic.

Above all else, this process has strengthened my conviction that we must do anything and everything to protect children, to give them priority and a better future. We must listen to this call to action, a call to embrace a new morality that puts children where they belong – at the heart of all agendas. Protecting children from the impact of armed conflict is everyone's responsibility – governments, international organisations and every element of civil society.

The challenge for all of us is to ask what we can do to make a difference. And then we must take that action, no matter how large or how small. For our children have a right to peace.

The future of our children lies in many ways in leadership and the choices that leaders make. Governments must be held accountable for their leadership in putting the wellbeing of children at the centre of all national and international agendas and decision making. But commitment and action cannot be left to government leaders alone; each of us, in our professional capacities and in our personal lives, must take action. We must embrace a number of social, economic, and political measures that promote the rights and wellbeing of children and break down the linkages between poverty, discrimination, and violence. As individuals, organisations, governments and societies, we must ensure that resources are available to address inequities within nations and internationally. We must promote and build partnerships between industrialised and developing countries and between governments and peoples.

I think all of us will acknowledge that at times it is not easy to speak about the suffering of children without feeling tempted to despair. What leads us in this direction is an apparent discrepancy between our principles and our practice where children are concerned. After all, the modern world economy has the capacity to produce more than enough to meet its needs. And the international community has developed an unprecedented array of institutions, policies and declarations that pro-

414

claim the rights of children and other vulnerable groups. There is a host of conventions, treaties and other instruments that guarantee those rights and entrench them.

And yet in many respects the situation of children has worsened. This is not to ignore or devalue the significant advances and improvements that have been made. Nor is it a counsel of despair. But we cannot escape the contradiction between what, as an international community, we have proclaimed ought to happen and the preventable wrongs that happen in reality. It is for that reason that we are led to speak of a moral crisis in humanity.

Recent events have shown us that we are a single, interdependent world. But the burden of any world crisis falls most heavily on the developing countries and on their peoples. And everything that we have learnt tells us that it is the children who will be feeling the harshest and the most permanent effects. Can we therefore claim in all earnestness to love our children – the children of the North and the South – if we do not give the most serious attention to preventing a world that has more than enough resources from dividing ever more deeply between rich and poor?

What is required is a determined, concerted and sustained action by the nations of the world in a partnership of industrialised and developing countries. In the interests of our children, we need both national and international initiatives. We need the global institutions to release the capacity and the resources they have by making them available to national institutions to operate.

We can't say that only national organisations can make a difference. Global institutions like the IMF, the World Bank and others, have more and more to respond to the challenge of being not only heard but also seen to be releasing resources to make programmes at the national level work.

Children do not live in the abstract. They live in a country; they live in a province; they live in a district; they live in a place. From global institutions to local community-based organisations, we all have a responsibility. So it is important that national governments, religious groups, civil-society organisations, workers' unions – and everyone – concentrate their efforts in making the lives of children better.

In the end, the whole of society is not only going to benefit, but it is actually going to change if we concentrate on children. The challenge for each of us is to move from rhetoric to action. We must realise that behind every statistic is the face and the life of a child – someone's daughter or brother or grandchild. We all have opportunities to effect change in the lives of children in South Africa and throughout the world.

A Fabric of Care

Speech at his 80th birthday party, Kruger National Park,
16 July 1998.

Birthdays are a time to celebrate our lives and families and today I
would like us to do just that. We should celebrate the strength and
courage that helps us through unhappiness and pain. We should
celebrate the continued support, compassion and care of our friends,
families and communities.

Our communities and our families are still experiencing apartheid's destruction of our social fabric. There are between 50 000 and
80 000 young people in one or other form of foster care in South
Africa. In most cases these are informal foster care placements with
a grandmother or other relative. Considering the scale of our needs
in South Africa, we need many, many more foster homes.

Our country's first democratically elected government has put the
interests of our children amongst its highest priorities.

On my 77th birthday, we launched the Inter-Ministerial Committee on Young People at Risk to transform the child and youth
care system. This transformation process is now well under way and
includes many changes to the foster care service in South Africa.
Pilot projects with non-governmental organisations in the field of
family preservation and new foster care approaches have proved to
be extremely effective. They will be repeated in many of the provinces, starting from this year.

The communities, families, foster families and young people involved in these projects have shown courage, strength and great
commitment in demonstrating that South African communities do
understand the responsibility we all have for each other. Other initiatives such as the Children in Distress project in Pietermaritzburg
and foster care projects run by child and welfare societies are also
proving to be extremely positive.

Minimum standards for foster care within the new framework and principles are to be developed within 1998 in a partnership between foster parents, foster children, the national Department of Welfare, NGOs and a foster care forum.

No single institution, including government, is capable of meeting the enormous needs of these children. Without adequate care they will not fulfil their potential and their much-needed contribution to social development in South Africa will be hampered. If we have any hope for their future, we all need to become involved in tackling the problem of children in need of a home and a family to love and care for them, now rather than later.

Together government, non-governmental organisations, the private sector, communities and individuals must act together to boost community-based forms of foster care which include an understanding of the child and his or her family.

As we celebrate the family today, we must all commit ourselves to ensuring that all our youngsters can experience a sense of family each day. Today is also about our efforts to keep our children within their families and within their communities, or re-integrating them within their families and communities as soon as we are able.

Our country's wellbeing depends on the wellbeing of our communities and of our children. We cannot build our country without building our communities and developing our children.

So, today we are paying homage to all foster families who have demonstrated their courage and strength by opening their hearts and homes to share all that they have in fostering children who have no other place to go.

As today is my 80th birthday, I also want to pay a special tribute to the elderly, many of whom are much older than me, who care for the young in South Africa. I know how much your wisdom and love is needed for nation building and child development. I want to assure you that the Ministry of Welfare is exploring ways in which we can strengthen and support you.

To those who foster a child in South Africa, whether informally as a relative or through the child and youth care system: I want you to know that you have made a big difference. This is truly a realisation of the spirit of *Ubuntu* – that profound African sense that each of us is human through the humanity of other human beings. As we face the struggle of HIV/Aids and other life-threatening illnesses in South Africa, we will need many thousands more like you.

I wish to express a special thank you to all the participants – the foster families, the foster children, the sponsors and the organisers who have made today possible. You have made me proud to have met such giving people. You have given me a great gift. All of you here today are participants in this building process. These splendid celebrations are the product of the kind of partnership we need. It shows what can be achieved.

Let us together build communities and families in which our children and youth, especially those who are most troubled, can belong. Let us build a country in which our children and youth can meet their need for mastering new skills, in which our children and youth can learn to care for and respect others so that one day they, too, will build a family, a community and a country which is well and strong.

To all the children in South Africa who hurt inside, to those who care for them each day, and to their families and communities, we say that together we will continue to conquer the mountains in front of us, and we will triumph.

International Children's Day

Statement on International Children's Day,
1 June 1994.

Today, 1 June, is International Children's Day. I wish to take this opportunity to reiterate the commitment of the South African government to a comprehensive programme to ensure that children of our country grow up secure in family life, enjoying all the rights and privileges they deserve. We recommit ourselves to the UN Declaration on the Rights of the Child.

In order to realise these objectives, the government has already set in motion mechanisms to implement various programmes that we announced at the opening of the last parliamentary session. These include:

- Free medical care in state hospitals and clinics for children under six years of age. A decision has been taken that this should come into effect immediately where mechanisms have been put in place, and it will apply to all cases where such a need exists.
- A nutritional feeding scheme in primary schools. The relevant ministry is already identifying the areas most in need for the urgent implementation of this measure.
- The Departments of Justice and Welfare will soon announce a detailed programme to empty our jails of children and to provide alternative care centres.
- Legislation to introduce free and quality education for all children will be introduced at the next parliamentary session.

Among the measures that are also under urgent consideration are the conditions of street children, and ways in which the government can contribute to alleviate and finally eradicate their plight. Further, legislation on the eradication of child abuse and child labour will be processed with deliberate speed.

On this day, we also extend our solidarity with children through-out the world whose lives are ravaged by the scourges of hunger, war and ignorance. We commit ourselves to contribute, to the best of our ability, to the international efforts aimed at resolving these problems.

The South African government's approach to the question of children's social and political rights derives from the basic principle that to value our children is to value our future.

A Society's Soul

Speech at the launch of the Nelson Mandela Chilren's Fund, Pretoria, 8 May 1995.

There can be no keener revelation of a society's soul than the way in which it treats its children. We come from a past in which the lives of our children were assaulted and devastated in countless ways. It would be no exaggeration to speak of a national abuse of a generation by a society which it should have been able to trust.

As we set about building a new South Africa, one of our highest priorities must therefore be our children. The vision of a new society that guides us should already be manifest in the steps we take to address the wrong done to our youth and to prepare for their future. Our actions and policies, and the institutions we create, should be eloquent with care, respect and love.

This is essentially a national task. The primary responsibility is that of government, institutions and organised sectors of civil society. But at the same time we are, all of us, as individuals, called upon to give direction and impetus to the changes that must come. Our actions should declare, in a practical and exemplary way, the importance and the urgency of the matter.

This was the thought to which I wished to give effect by initiating the establishment of the Nelson Mandela Children's Fund. The Fund provides a way in which people, including myself, could make their own direct contribution to alleviating the plight of young people in need.

The first celebration in a democratic South Africa of the anniversary of 16 June 1976 was an appropriate date for the announcement of the Fund. It evoked the suffering of children in the past and the legacy of deprivation to be addressed. Equally, it served to imprint upon the character of the Fund a recognition of the potential embodied in the youth of our country. They rose to the challenge of history by assuming a responsibility for their own future and for that of their country, beyond their years.

The Children's Fund therefore has a special importance. It includes, but goes far beyond, the immediate relief it will give to young people deprived of what should be their right: amongst other things, a home, formal education, freedom from detention. It is concerned, too, with helping open opportunities that have been denied, as well as developing the potential in our young people to play a major role in the reconstruction and development of our country. More than this, it has the potential to make a seminal contribution to the efforts of institutions concerned with children, the private sector and government.

From this follow certain requirements concerning the nature of the Fund and its activities. It means that it should be an example to all our institutions and organisations in how it conducts its affairs, in its integrity, its probity and openness. The distinguished character of its trustees and management leaves no room for doubt that this will be so. It means that the Fund should work together with other institutions dedicated to relieving the plight of disadvantaged children. It will join in the partnership that cuts across all social sectors, which is carrying us forward in the grand enterprise of transforming our society. It means that the projects and institutions that the Fund assists should exemplify the characteristics needed for the reconstruction and development of our country.

The Fund will deploy its resources to facilitate initiatives by young people or communities that are ready to shoulder responsibility for their own improvement and upliftment. Lasting improvement, and not only immediate relief, will be a guiding objective. The work supported by the Fund should foster the spirit of co-operation, mutual respect and consultation as well as openness and prudent use of resources.

The needs which have to be addressed are great. The number of young people who live under seriously deprived socio-economic circumstances in our country is shockingly high. Youth unemployment, homelessness, lack of formal education – these are all measured in millions.

All this means that if the Children's Fund is to make a significant contribution to addressing these needs, it must be as well endowed as possible, both financially and in terms of the support it enjoys. A firm foundation has already been laid, and I would like to use this opportunity to thank all those who brought us to this point.

The initial donors gave substance to the idea. The management and trustees have given of their time and experience to endow the Fund with the legal form and the administrative capacity to set it on course. Many people have worked hard and with imagination to prepare this splendid occasion. To all of you, to everyone who has taken the trouble to be with us tonight, and to the young people of South Africa, whose need and whose promise is our driving force, may I express my sincere and heartfelt thanks.

On all of you who are here, there rests a double challenge. As distinguished individuals and representatives of corporate bodies, you have the capacity to build the financial resources of the Fund. Your standing in society gives you considerable influence that you can lend to this enterprise. I would urge you most sincerely and passionately to be unstinting in your assistance in both regards.

You will be setting in motion a process that draws in many more individuals, corporations and aid agencies, both South African and international.

You will be sending a powerful message to government, the private sector and institutions, that the plight of our young people and their future should receive the nation's urgent attention.

You will be setting a compelling example which in the end will help to ensure the happiness and welfare of all our children.

A Quest for a Better Future

Statement at a media conference on the launch of the
Nelson Mandela Children's Fund, Pretoria,
8 May 1995.

Last year, at the commemoration of 16 June, South Africa Youth Day, I made a pledge to contribute R150 000 of my salary per year to a children's trust fund named after the President. I emphasised then that this amount would be paid on an annual basis even if there was a cut in the President's salary.

A cheque was presented the same afternoon to Senator Sam Motsuenyane, President of the African Bank. Today, almost a year later, I will take the opportunity to present this year's amount.

It is not my task on this occasion to detail the evolution of the Fund over the past 11 months. As you can see, I am flanked by men and women of great repute, who possess a wealth of experience on these matters. I will therefore leave the elaboration of issues relevant to the Fund in their capable hands. Suffice it here to underscore some important matters of principle.

The purpose of the Nelson Mandela Children's Fund is to help inspire new efforts and strengthen existing ones aimed at alleviating conditions of South African young people in dire need. Our primary focus is on youth under the age of 30 years who are homeless, who have not had the privilege of formal education or who are in detention.

I view it personally as one of the greatest tragedies of our nation's history that young people who would otherwise have been developing their talents to the full, and making a valuable contribution to society, are, by dint primarily of the system of apartheid, living a life of hermits and outcasts.

Like all of us, they deserve a better social and family environment to fulfil their dreams. They deserve, and indeed desire, to live a normal life as upright citizens. They are justified in expecting of the new, democratic order, meaningful assistance in the quest for a better future.

Though this tragic situation plays itself out to varying degrees in all communities, black children – African, coloured and Indian – are worse off. We all have a responsibility to contribute in eradicating the wretched existence of what is in fact a significant segment of the nation's future.

In taking the first steps towards setting up this Children's Fund, we knew we were making only a humble contribution to a task that devolves on the nation as a whole – be it government, the private sector and indeed local communities and individual citizens.

The Trust Fund is therefore not an isolated initiative, but one in a rich alliance of structures which have taken it upon themselves to make a practical contribution to the future of disadvantaged youth. Neither is it an act of charity; nor the self-serving gesture of distant and condescending philanthropists. At the core of the Fund's approach is to help these young people to help themselves.

Over the past months, we have had a wave of responses far exceeding our most optimistic forecasts. Today, the Fund has in its accounts just over R1.9 million in donations by companies and individual businesspersons, governments and private citizens both in South Africa and further afield. We would wish to single out those contributors who have pledged to donate at least R150 000 on a yearly basis for five years and more. Others have offered facilities and other resources. Today is our unique opportunity to formally say: thank you most profoundly to all the donors! We acknowledge the material sacrifice tempered by compassion for a good cause.

In formally launching the Nelson Mandela Children's Fund this evening, we shall also be launching a more systematic and people-centred fund-raising drive. I should repeat: all donations – large and small – are welcome.

We shall also be starting to process applications in accordance with the principles outlined in the brochure. Such allocations will essentially be from the annual income that the Fund derives from investment so as to ensure that it can operate on a sustainable basis. Needless to say, the trustees and management will ensure the highest moral principles, professionalism, inclusivity, non-partisanship, non-sexism and nonracialism in the operation of the Fund.

For the trustees and management, and for me personally, this is a joyous day in the life of the Fund; a dream come true. But it is only the beginning of a hard slog in a difficult, but challenging and fulfilling, endeavour. Perhaps the only appropriate words on this occasion are: let's get down to work!

A New Alliance

Speech at the launch of the Friends of the
Nelson Mandela Children's Fund, New York,
23 October 1995.

Tonight marks a special and very exciting moment in the life of our
Children's Fund. Assembled here are distinguished Americans and
South Africans brought together by a commitment to a noble cause:
the plight of South Africa's youth and how to alleviate it. It would
be improper to select some for special mention. But I cannot contain my pleasure at being in the company especially of the American
members of the Board of Directors of the Friends of our Fund: David
Dinkins, Wayne Fredericks, Leon Higginbotham, Rodney Wagner,
Bernard Watson and Mark Weinberg. I wish to thank you and all the
friends assembled here for replying to our call.

This evening's events are a spectacular declaration that a new
alliance is in the building. Eminent Americans are once more reaching out across the oceans to join hands with South Africans. They are
doing so, so that they can work together to address the needs of
young people whose lives have been devastated by apartheid.

I am very proud to be associated with so generous a development, and I would like to express my heartfelt appreciation at being
able to share in the first major event of the Friends of the Children's
Fund.

The Fund was initiated in South Africa in order to lend urgency to
the task of addressing the wrong done to our youth and to help them
prepare for the future. It is this humble wish which motivated me to
launch the fund and pledge over one-third of my salary to the Fund.

For me personally, it is one of the cruellest facets of South Africa's
history that tens of thousands of young people who could otherwise
have been developing their talents to the full and making a valuable
contribution to society are living a life on the margins of society,
mainly because of the legacy of apartheid.

In building a new South Africa our children must be one of our

426

highest priorities. They are the foundation on which our future is being built.

The Fund is a small but proud member of a partnership that unites all sectors of our society in pursuit of a noble ideal. Today, that partnership is being born across boundaries. It is finding expression in the Friends of the Children's Fund here in the United States. It provides a way in which individuals, corporations and other institutions can make their own direct contribution to helping those of our young people most seriously in need.

I would like to express my sincere thanks to those who have worked to get the Friends started; to those whose support made this evening's event possible; and to those whose pledges have set an example – such as Denzel Washington – which I hope will be emulated by many others.

Every measure of support that comes through the Friends will lend added impetus to our own efforts. For the needs which have to be addressed are great indeed.

The response to the initiative in South Africa has surpassed expectations. And we are convinced that the same will happen here.

This is as it should be.

The children of South Africa deserve no less.

Consensus for Children

Speech at the launch of the
Friends of the Nelson Mandela Children's Fund, London,
12 July 1996.

Early tomorrow morning I will be leaving Britain. Over the past five days I and my colleagues have been privileged to engage with the government and people of Britain in a way that we had never dreamed of.

We had expected to be well received. But the goodwill and warmth we have experienced on this visit has been beyond our wildest expectations. It has been quite overwhelming and deeply humbling. I will cherish the memories of my encounters with the people of this great country. Wherever we went we felt the commitment in government and in every sphere of society to build strong relations between our countries. I will be able to tell my people that in Britain we have true friends, partners in making a reality of the vision of a better life for all.

What was clear in all our encounters was that the welcome we received grew from two things: a shared commitment to the goals of freedom and justice; and an appreciation of the way in which South Africans have so speedily put behind them the division and conflict engendered by the apartheid system. People are moved by the spectacle of former enemies joining hands to work for the important things they share, rather than remain divided because of the lesser things about which they disagree.

This is something that moves me too. Time and again ordinary South Africans have proved to be far in advance of the politicians in reaching out to each other and building a new society based on equality and mutual respect. It is this powerful impulse towards unity and peace which has given the government the strength to chart a clear and firm path of reconstruction and development.

We do not underestimate the problems we face. On the contrary, we recognise their enormity, but we are nevertheless confident that

South Africans have the capacity and the will to deal with them. Our confidence grows out of the readiness of all major role-players to join hands and find solutions, putting long-term interests above short-term considerations: be it in the implementation of the government's macroeconomic strategy, in defining labour relations and labour market policies, or in dealing with crime.

Broad partnerships which harness our nation's resources are the key to achieving our goals, because they give each and every person the opportunity to be part of bringing about change.

One area of consensus which binds South Africans is the concern for their children. We have recently launched a National Programme of Action for Children in which government is working hand in hand with its social partners to make the interests of the child paramount and give them first call on society's resources.

A small part of the alliance for children's needs is the Children's Fund, the British chapter of which we are launching today. Tonight therefore marks a special and very exciting moment in the development of our Children's Fund.

Assembled here are distinguished members of British society and South Africans, joined in their commitment to alleviate the plight of South Africa's youth. It would be improper to select some for special mention, but I cannot contain my pleasure at being in the company of so many old friends and the members of the board of directors of the Friends of our Fund registered here in the United Kingdom. I wish to thank you all assembled here, for replying to our call.

This is a new alliance in the making. Eminent people from this land are again reaching out across the oceans to join hands with the rainbow nation that is now South Africa. The antagonisms of centuries gone by are transforming into a partnership for the future. I am very proud to be associated with so generous and so noble a development.

The Children's Fund was initiated in South Africa in order to lend urgency to the task of addressing the wrong done to our youth and to help them prepare for the future. It is this humble wish which motivated me to launch the Fund and pledge over one-third of my salary to it for five years. It was also a way of making a personal commitment to the World Declaration on the Survival, Protection and Development of the Child.

For me personally, it is one of the cruellest facets of South Africa's history that so many young people are living a life on the margins of the society. In building a new South Africa, our children must be one of our highest priorities. They are the foundation on which our future is being built.

The Fund is all about opening the doors of opportunity and releasing the potential of our young people. Our main aim is to strengthen their capacity to engage positively and successfully in every aspect of life.

SOS Children's Village

Speech at the official opening of the
Cape Town SOS Children's Village, Cape Town,
25 May 1996.

The children of South Africa have assumed a responsibility beyond their years, both in the freeing of our country and in building its future. This SOS Badge of Honour in Gold really belongs to them, and to all those who have joined hands to ensure that the children of the future have a better life than themselves. It is on their behalf that I humbly accept the award.

I am also greatly honoured to accept the jersey presented to me by our young football star. As some of you may know, I am a keen collector of jerseys and I shall certainly treasure this one.

It is a great pleasure to join you in celebrating the opening of another worthy project for the benefit of our country's children. I would especially like to thank Mr [Helmut] Kutin, President of SOS-Kinderdorf International, for making the long journey from Austria to be with us today. Your personal attention to the plight of our country's children is greatly appreciated.

The plight of South Africa's children is also of concern to me, personally. Our children have borne the brunt of apartheid's ravaging deprivation. Most were robbed of their right to a decent education, adequate health care, stable family lives – and sometimes of their entire childhood. And this applies to the majority of children. The graver circumstances of those who are homeless, destitute or orphaned without any love or care, are deeply distressing. Soon after my release from prison I visited the Ennerdale and Mamelodi SOS Villages, where I was warmly welcomed by the children. I found that these children now had a home, a mother and a safe, secure place in which to live.

During a recent visit to South Africa by Queen Noor of Jordan I learned from her of the inspiring world-wide work of the organisation. Its holistic and nurturing approach reflects the vision and ideals of the South Africa we are building.

Democracy has brought us the opportunity to make a reality of this vision. It means that our country has a government that puts the needs of people first. And it means that our friends in the international community who share our democratic ideals, like SOS-International, are now able to join hands with us in addressing these needs.

Our government is extremely pleased to work with you in providing a permanent home for the orphaned and abandoned children of South Africa. We deeply appreciate the decision of SOS-International to invest R60 million in its work for children in South Africa.

Your work is a shining example of the kind of partnership on which the achievement of all our goals depends. The tasks we face, great though they are, can be achieved when government is able to work together with every sector of society – non-governmental organisations, the private sector, international funders, and the community.

Democratic local authorities, to be established for the very first time in this province in next week's local elections, will give local communities a new voice, and strengthen the relationship between the Children's Villages and the communities in which they are located. We are encouraged by your approach to also making the villages serve as resource centres and models for communities.

Of great importance, too, is the fact that you are not only meeting the immediate needs of your children, but also creating opportunities for them to develop into self-sufficient, dynamic adults who will contribute to their fullest potential to the development of our country.

For all these reasons, we welcome your efforts to provide more beautiful children's projects across the country, such as this one. I encourage you to have one in each of our provinces as a symbol of hope and peace for children in need of love and security all over South Africa.

As your next project is to be in Umtata, I hope I am permitted to be an occasional visitor. It will be near my childhood home, from where I take my strength and which holds fond memories. I look forward to watching this new project grow for the benefit of that region's children.

It is my hope that within this community a culture of understanding, acceptance and love can be nurtured. Let this Children's Village be an example of tolerance and reconciliation so that we, as adults, can learn from these children.

I would like to end by saying to each young person here today that I love you very much. You are the future of South Africa. The hope of our rainbow nation.

Programme of Action for Children

Speech at the launch of the National Programme of Action for
Children and Report on Child Poverty, Pretoria,
31 May 1996.

Today is an important milestone for our nation and its children.
Building on the steps that government has already taken, the
National Programme of Action for Children will give concrete
meaning to the call by the 1990 World Summit for Children to give
children's essential needs a first call on society's resources.

It will give practical expression to the obligations which South
Africa assumed by ratifying the UN Convention on the Rights of
the Child on 16 June last year. It will make a reality of the injunction in our new Constitution to make the best interests of the child
paramount.

To reach this point has required the co-operation of several ministries, departments and organisations. They have worked hand-in-
hand with our international partners, in particular Unicef and the
Nordic countries, whose support we deeply appreciate.

I would like to take this opportunity to commend all those
involved for their dedication to our children and the spirit of partnership that has informed their work. Congratulations! You have created a sound framework to guide us in one of the most important
challenges facing our nation.

Our children are our nation's future. Prospects for development are
seriously undermined by the kind of large-scale deprivation of children that South Africa has experienced. On the other hand investing
in their health, nutrition and education not only improves our children's quality of life – the gains reverberate into future generations.

Having a specific integrated programme to ensure the survival, protection and development of South Africa's children is therefore a vital
element in building an economically dynamic and healthy nation.
Children can be our spearhead for attacking poverty, reinforcing
human rights, and accelerating economic growth and development.

Such a programme will also help alleviate the urgent plight of the children of today, the principal victims of yesterday's neglect of the majority of South Africa's people. The report commissioned by our RDP Office starkly details the dreadful legacy of that neglect. Its grim statistics should jolt us into renewed determination to act.

We have the resources, if we use them wisely, to change the situation. There is no reason for our society to allow one out of every eight children born to die before their fifth birthday, and a quarter of those that survive to grow up physically stunted. It should not continue to be the case that more than half of rural South Africans live over five kilometres from a medical facility. The extent of illiteracy amongst adults and emotional disturbance amongst young children must not be part of our future.

In response to this legacy, many of the government's priority programmes were strongly child-focused, including the RDP's Presidential Lead Projects. The National Programme of Action for Children consolidates this focus within a single, comprehensive programme central to national development. It sets national goals which establish priorities and specific targets to guide the efforts of ministries and provincial authorities, in collaboration with civil society organisations, local authorities, communities and individuals concerned for children.

This is a programme for practical and achievable action. South Africa has the accumulated knowledge, the technologies, and the communications capacities to protect the normal growth and development of almost all children at relatively low cost. Reducing malnutrition, disease, and illiteracy is therefore among the most achievable as well as the most fundamental of development's challenges.

In launching comprehensive and long-term programmes, sight is sometimes lost of immediate needs and particular problems. It is not the intention that the launch of this programme should be at the expense of any children anywhere, nor of the organisations which played so important a role when government neglected our children. On the contrary, such a programme should involve steps to deal with existing problems and to assist the organisations to adapt their roles to present needs.

Tackling the needs of children calls for a comprehensive approach that affects all areas of policy, legislation and practice. It will mean that departments and offices of government at all levels should co-operate and join hands with non-government organisations and all sectors of society.

For example, for a child to learn properly requires a conducive environment: warmth and light at home and school; good health; reliable transport to school; a secure and stable family life and parental involvement in schooling.

Throughout government and civil society, therefore, there has to be awareness of the needs of children in all the activities contributing to the building of a new society, and co-ordination of those activities in the interest of children.

The national programme of action sets out the priorities and the framework to help us realise our goals for children. The challenge now is to put the programme into action. That brings at least three major tasks.

Firstly, we must find the ways to unleash the power and wisdom of all South Africans in this endeavour. The national programme will only bring real change when it is taken up at provincial, district and community level programmes of action. I am very pleased that as we launch the framework for the national programme, the provinces are launching their own programmes within this framework.

Secondly, we need to refine the estimates of the programme's costs and mobilise the funds needed from within government, from civil society and the international aid community.

Finally, effective implementation requires a reliable monitoring and information system to measure progress and identify further needs. The report being presented today provides an important baseline from which we can measure progress. The needs, the targets and the progress should be known not just to decision makers, but to ordinary people throughout South Africa. In that way they too can help in mobilising resources, rejoice in progress and successes, and urge more action when it is needed. Improving the welfare of our children should become as much a part of the new patriotism as success on the sporting field and progress in overcoming the divisions of the past.

Each of these steps show that government alone cannot achieve the goals of the world summit, or implement the Convention on the Rights of the Child, or make a reality of the vision for children in our new Constitution. Each and every South African has a role to play, a specific responsibility to become part of the revolution for children.

As we celebrate International Children's Day tomorrow, there is no better time to commit ourselves – individually and collectively – to the task of building a better future for our children.

Global Partnership for Children

Statement on Building a Global Partnership for Children,
Johannesburg, 6 May 2000.

Graça and I are proud to be here today with our esteemed friend Carol
Bellamy, the Executive Director of the United Nations Children's
Fund [Unicef], to announce our commitment to work closely with
her and her respected organisation on a cause we hold most dear to
our hearts – the rights of the children and adolescents of this world
to live safe from violence and exploitation free of poverty and discrimination and to grow healthy and strong.

Here in my beloved country where people once divided by
apartheid now work together in the name of justice, Graça and I
pledge our energies to building a global partnership for children of
leaders from every sector and every calling who share a dogged
determination to change the way the world sees our children and the
way the world treats our children.

Our purpose is to get specific commitments from these leaders
and specific results. We will be insistent on a gracious 'yes' but unyielding as we make phone calls, write letters, provide consultations
and make speeches on behalf of children – pressing a wide circle of
leaders from business, civil society and governments to rethink what
they do every day to better the lives of children. And whatever it is
they do today, we will coax them to do more tomorrow.

We will urge these leaders to take their turn in reaching out to a
wider circle still, inviting, cajoling, carrying each other along in an
unprecedented international movement, a collective global force that
will herald the rights of children and act to ensure them.

This global partnership will be guided in its work by the Convention on the Rights of the Child, that luminous living document
that enshrines the rights of every child without exception to a life of
dignity and self-fulfilment.

We are not seeking – nor will we accept – vague promises. We will challenge enlightened government leaders to join us and turn their words into deeds, enforce the laws, enact the policies and search out the excluded children – the girl child, the poor child, the one little one with disabilities, the one from the wrong tribe, wrong caste – and find the ways to embrace them.

We will ask innovators in the business world to put their unique abilities to work for children. Use distribution networks that deliver cola drinks to the most remote towns, and get textbooks and vaccines there first. Share profits, share talent, share advertising space – all in the name of children.

We will call upon leaders in academia, the media and other sectors to join with us to ensure that the world honours its obligation to children. Be ever vigilant; hold governments accountable; struggle for peace and justice. Do not let up for a moment, for there is no circumstance in which the neglect or abuse of children can ever be tolerated.

And to all who would be leaders we will issue the challenge that, if met, will speak louder than any document: reach out to children and adolescents themselves, involve them, engage them and listen to what they have to say. Make certain that the global partnership for children includes children.

This new partnership for children builds on the promises made nearly a decade ago at the World Summit for Children, when national leaders from every part of the world made a solemn commitment to ensure the wellbeing of all societies by giving high priority to the rights of children to their survival and to their development. Those leaders pledged to act together in international cooperation as well as in their respective countries to enhance child health and pre-natal care, to promote optimal child growth and development, to work toward strengthening the role and status of women and to mount a global attack on poverty.

In the ensuing years some objectives – but far from all – of that noble agenda have come to pass. Now at the dawn of the twenty-first century we have a unique opportunity to fulfil the remaining commitments of the World Summit for Children – while simultaneously tackling new and emerging problems including poverty, HIV/Aids and the scourge of armed conflict.

In this world in which we have the means to cure many of the cancers that only a decade ago were considered lethal, surely we are able to vaccinate all children against child-killing diseases. In this world of such abundance surely we can find the means to assure that no child will go hungry, no pregnant woman will be too weak to survive childbirth, and that every one of the nearly 6 million children who will die next year because of malnutrition will be saved.

Surely in a world where communication technologies let some children exchange messages across oceans in seconds, we can provide every child with a basic education of the very best quality. In this world of such invention there can be no excuse for not ensuring that all our children will have the knowledge and skills for success and the capabilities to work with others to reach their full potential and transform their society.

Surely when children and adolescents in every part of the world can name their favourite soft drink, running shoe or sports, we are able to ensure that they will have access to the information they need to stay healthy. In a world that so often decries the apathy of its youth we can open our arms for the millions of adolescents eager to contribute their new ideas and bounding enthusiasm. And surely we can stand by the commitments that nearly every government in the world has made to children in signing the Convention on the Rights of the Child.

Governments remain the primary actors in addressing such challenges – and indeed in playing a leading role in all development cooperation while involving the poor and the young themselves as full participants.

But now amid growing economic interdependence among nations we see a new global reality with additional protagonists, including non-governmental organisations, grassroots groups, private enterprise, the business community and other diverse elements of civil society.

These new actors possess both the knowledge and the resources to make a difference. Thus their involvement in a global partnership for children is not only desirable, it is vital. The task before us is to bring them together.

But time is short – for if we do not act now in concert, the brush-fire crises that are proliferating around the world may yet become an uncontrollable conflagration.

Graça and I hope that we can act as catalysts in helping to persuade leaders of government and civil society at every level to recognise that if we want a more just, equitable and thriving world we need to invest in children now.

This must include efforts that take full account of the immense peril that HIV/Aids and armed conflict pose to every aspect of child survival and the recognition that global poverty, which has already consigned some three billion people to living on less than $2 a day – half of them children – is not only a moral outrage but a profound political and economic threat to the whole world. The knowledge, the resources and the strategies all exist to make this a better world for all children – and Graça and I are convinced that if we start now we can build a truly global alliance to bring it about.

To dear Ms Bellamy, to Unicef and to the children of the world, we say, you have our word to help.

To our friends and colleagues, we say, expect our call.

11

HEROES

A SELF–EFFACING
HERO

AHMED KATHRADA

I have known Nelson Mandela for more than 50 years, the half-century over which this remarkable man has emerged all the more clearly as a heroic statesman not only in South African but also in world affairs. And, as the speeches in the pages to come may suggest, it is a heroism that was and remains the expression in large measure of a generous, self-effacing view of the collective efforts of others, a keenness to recognise greatness and achievement elsewhere and apportion credit accordingly, to play his part as one among many and to consider the interests of the many in playing his singular part.

Of course, he is mortal, and his humanity is as complex and even at times as contradictory as any other man's. The Mandela mythology has often not done justice to the real Madiba. Yet it is his virtues more than any kind of imperiousness that has made it difficult for people to see him as anything less than a flawless hero.

I have written before about the challenge of seeing the man more clearly as he is, a man who has more charisma and charm and more of a commanding presence than one's next-door neighbour, yet whose saint-like qualities of forbearance and generosity and tolerance do not make him a saint. He has his weaknesses and failings.

On the occasion of his 80th birthday, I penned a biographical essay in which I tried to express the sum of the human Mandela by describing what I believe to be an uncommon amalgam of the peasant and the aristocrat; the quintessential democrat who nonetheless possesses something of the autocrat; the traditionalist who is also an innovator; a man who is at once proud but also simple; soft and tenacious; determinedly obstinate and flexible; vain and shy; cool and impatient.

My sense of these things, of the true character of this twentieth-century hero, derives from an always respectful, sometimes difficult and frustrating, but enduringly rewarding relationship that spans my life. I was a

443

schoolboy, 11 years his junior, when we first met. I had got into politics at a young age, and it was through my association with two students, Ismail Meer and JN Singh, both studying law at Wits University, that I met Mandela. He was their fellow student, and friend.

This was the mid-1940s, and there weren't many black students or professional people then, and the few one did encounter – it was rare – were looked on with awe as role models and leaders. This was certainly the case with Nelson Mandela.

I began to see more of him from 1947 when Ismail Meer returned to Natal at the completion of his studies (by law, it was not possible for him to remain in Johannesburg). About a year earlier, Meer had asked me to move into his central city flat. His intention was that I should become the formal occupant after his departure. That flat – which is still there today, in Market Street, and still in my name – became the meeting place for a core of politically active people, black and white. There was nowhere else to meet in a town that was, for all intents and purposes, for white people only. While the flat became the centre of exciting politics, I, because of my youth and inexperience, was more of an interested and curious observer than a participant.

As time went on, though, I grew to know Mandela better, and we became closer. The virtually unique qualities of Mandela, Meer and Singh were their ability to make me feel part of them. They never treated me condescendingly, although I was much younger.

We had our political differences. I was in the Young Communist League and Mandela was prominent in the ANC Youth League. We became close, but he was an extreme nationalist – though not a racialist – who did not believe in co-operation with any non-African organisations, and was anti-communist. He certainly sympathised with the Indian passive resistance of 1946, but as far as co-operation was concerned, he adhered to the Youth League view.

This strategic schism was to provide a telling insight into the way of Madiba, and it emerged over the Witwatersrand political strike of 1950, organised jointly by the ANC, the Communist Party and the Transvaal Indian Congress. The ANC Youth League, though, opposed it, arguing that it would detract from the ANC's own programme of civil disobedience, formulated in the wake of the leadership change in 1949, when, under pressure from the Youth League, the organisation became more radical. It got ugly. The Youth League went as far as disrupting meetings. On one occasion, Mandela himself actually pulled one of the Indian Congress leaders, Yusuf Cachalia, from a public platform.

Tensions were running high, and it was in this charged atmosphere that I bumped into Madiba one day in Commissioner Street. After the usual pleasantries, we got talking about preparations for the strike, and our discussion became fairly heated, until, with the youthful arrogance of a 21-year-old, I challenged him to a public debate at a venue of his choice, with the rejoinder: 'I'll beat you!' He got quite angry, and we parted. I thought that was the end of it, but it wasn't.

The strike was successful, though 18 people were killed and political tensions escalated. As a result, the National Executive of the ANC called a meeting with the national executives of the Indian Congress and the Communist Party – then just on the eve of being banned. I was there, but as a helper, on the sidelines, minding the door and so on. There I was when, to my shock, Mandela stood up and complained about my disrespect towards him. I expected my friends to defend me, but they didn't. Instead, Ismail Meer appealed to him not to take this 'hot-headed youngster' seriously. It was a tense moment, but he relented. And that was it.

In prison, years later, we teased each other about this. But what the incident revealed to me at the time was that he was a man who was not afraid to express himself forcefully whatever the circumstances, yet he could listen to and accept views that differed from his own.

This was true also of his engagement with Marxist thinking, which, in his early Youth League days, was anathema, a foreign notion that was not what Africa needed or wanted. In 1951, I spent almost a year abroad, mostly at the World Federation of Democratic Youth headquarters in Budapest. I made it my mission in life to encourage black activists to think in Marxist terms, so I began sending a lot of literature back to him, and others. Of course, he was already mixing with communists like Joe Slovo and his wife Ruth First, Yusuf Dadoo and Moses Kotane, among others.

I remember in prison, much to our shame, discovering that veteran communists knew less than he did about Marx and Engels. That was typical of him. It did not make him a communist, but if something was important to know about, he made it his business to master it.

Much has been made of the impact, the maturing influence, of the prison years, and especially Madiba's years on Robben Island, on the measured political leader who emerged so powerfully in 1990. And this is true to an extent. But it risks being over-stated. People have to be reminded that Mandela was already a significant and influential leader before the Rivonia Trial. He was the Youth League president, then the president of the ANC in the Transvaal, and, by virtue of that, the first deputy president, nationally, of the ANC. He was also National Volunteer in Chief of the Defiance Campaign. And his qualities as a leader, the rare insights that sometimes gave rise to unexpected decisions, and the foresight, are evident in events from the 1950s. The pace with which his thinking changed can be gauged from his willingness to conduct the Defiance Campaign jointly with the Indian Congress. This was in 1952, barely two years after his public hostility over the strike of 1950.

In the early years of the decade, nearly 10 years before the 1961 launch of the armed struggle, it was Madiba who asked Walter Sisulu, whom he regarded as his senior and closest colleague and confidant, to visit Communist China – which had just a few years before, in 1949, overthrown the forces of Chiang Kai-Shek – to discuss the idea of an armed struggle in South Africa, and the possibility of securing arms from China.

As it happens, they advised against it, warning that without considerable practical and political preparation it would be premature. The fact is, he was focusing on strategies that few others were even considering yet. In strategic matters, as the 1950s wore on, his strengthening association with Moses Kotane, the General Secretary of the Communist Party, and Yusuf Dadoo, leader of the Indian Congress and chairman of the Communist Party, was very significant.

Mandela's singular and persuasive view of things was revealed in other ways. In 1958 – Madiba was a practising attorney by then – he was the defence lawyer in a case, and I had occasion one day to visit the court to discuss something with him. Though I wasn't there for long, I would, in the next few days, remember something rather important from this brief visit.

The very next Saturday – and it was typical for Saturdays – we had a bit of a party in the flat. At the end of the evening, I had gone downstairs with some friends – I was going to drive them home – when I noticed a man sitting on the opposite pavement. I asked him what he was waiting for, and it turned out he was waiting for a bus. It was far too late and there were no buses running at that hour, and just as I was telling him this, it suddenly struck me I had seen him before: he was the prosecutor in the trial in which Madiba was acting.

It is terrible to say so now, but we thought to ourselves, this man is probably a Nat, let's destroy him. So I offered him a lift, and he accepted. We asked if he wanted another drink, and he said he did. But then he added: 'What I'd really like is a black woman.' Well, we saw our opportunity. We said we'd arrange it, but what we had in mind was arranging a photographer, too.

We persuaded a woman to play along, assuring her we would not allow anything to happen, and raced over to the *Sunday Express*, where the night editor was very excited about the story. The prosecutor was very drunk by now, but we got our picture, and then took him home. First thing the next morning, I went out to Orlando to tell Mandela about our coup. I didn't expect what he had to say.

'Agreed, he is a prosecutor,' Madiba said, 'and he may even be a Nat. But he's a good chap, as a prosecutor.' It turned out that this man had shown some understanding for the accused in the trial, and that had made an impression on Madiba. Joe Slovo and Harold Wolpe, both lawyers, agreed with him. So, with Slovo, I went back to the *Sunday Express* and asked them to destroy the pictures, which they did.

I was, of course, disappointed that we were not able to destroy this man. But, in retrospect, and thanks to the maturity of Mandela, Slovo and Wolpe, we did not. Their advice was correct. This kind of response to individuals comes up over and again in the records of Mandela's dealings with people: his magnanimity, and his willingness to see each individual in his or her own right.

In a quite amusing way, I discovered to my cost how he sometimes misjudged circumstances. He was very flashy in the 1950s, and always wore magnificent suits made by a Commissioner Street tailor by the name of Kahn, who also, as it happens, was the tailor patronised by the Oppenheimers. He had had Kahn embroider a beautiful ANC emblem on the breast pocket of one of his blazers, and I was very impressed by it. I asked him about it once, and he quite airily recommended I pay a visit to Mr Kahn and have one made for myself. I did, to my peril, because it was very expensive. I did not have the means to be as flashy as he was.

It was a likeable vanity, though when he was on the run from the security police in the early 1960s, this quality was a distinct drawback: he absolutely refused to shave off his beard, which he was very proud of. There was nothing we could do to convince him.

In political matters, though, he was unhesitatingly selfless. I witnessed this as a fellow accused in the three big trials of the 1950s and 1960s, the Defiance Campaign trial, the marathon Treason Trial and, finally, the Rivonia Trial. It was especially true of the last.

From the time of our arrest, the police and prison warders kept drumming it into our heads that we were going to hang. Mandela, of course, had been sentenced earlier to five years, and only joined us as Accused No 1 after the end of our initial 90-day detention. This coincided with our first meeting with Bram Fischer and our legal team, and it was at this meeting that our lawyers told us to prepare for the worst.

During these consultations, Madiba put forward the argument that because we were fighting the case as a political trial it would be an anti-climax if we were to lodge an appeal, even if we were sentenced to death. He reasoned that for the sake of the people, for their morale, and the success of the struggle, we could not allow the case to end with an anti-climax. This, he insisted, was the correct political stand, but he urged us also to bear in mind that the judges at that time would never acquit us on appeal.

This was not an easy decision to take, but we accepted it after much anguished discussion. Madiba remained unshakeably committed to this despite our legal team's warning that we should prepare for the worst. And that commitment, which we all approved and accepted, shines from his monumental statement from the dock: 'During my lifetime I have dedicated myself to this struggle of the African people. I have fought against white domination, and I have fought against black domination. I have cherished the ideal of a democratic and free society in which all persons live together in harmony and with equal opportunities. It is an ideal which I hope to live for and to achieve. But if needs be, it is an ideal for which I am prepared to die.' This statement stands as a memorable beacon in our history.

There followed the long years of imprisonment, years in which those of us who were with him witnessed time and again his courage, foresight and wisdom. He would accept no special treatment, and though his leadership was respected he counted in his lot with the rest of us.

Of course, balancing the instincts of the leader with the dictates of the democratic will has sometimes tested both his personal resolve and his commitment to the cause. A notable illustration of this was the occasion while we were on Robben Island when Chief Kaizer Matanzima, then Transkei's bantustan leader, and Madiba's nephew, intimated his wish to visit Mandela. Mandela's loyalty is extraordinary. To get him to change his view of a friend is virtually impossible. He will insist, like a good lawyer, on seeing proof of a failure, a wrong-doing, before he will consider turning his back on someone.

Matanzima had overseen the burial of Mandela's mother, and Madiba wanted to see him. But he knew it would not be popular, so he put it up for debate. It must have been disappointing to him, as most of us – and ANC prisoners in the communal cell, too – opposed it. And that he accepted, as much as he wanted to see Matanzima. This is typical of how he was, and how he remains.

Of course, this democratic habit of mind had its disadvantages. Newspapers were hard to come by in prison, but they were occasionally smuggled in. And we had a system, to get the news out to other prisoners, of transcribing reports by hand so that they could be surreptitiously disseminated. There was a small group who would do the transcribing, and, of course, Madiba wanted to help. But the very first report he did came straight back to us with a rather pointed message. The writing, we were told, was very beautiful, very symmetrical, but unfortunately illegible. So we had to tell him, Madiba, your help is appreciated, but you are just increasing our workload! And, of course, he accepted that.

Nothing, though, would dissuade him from doing his fair share of the chores in prison, the cleaning, and so on. And once, when there was a 'flu epidemic, and he and just a few other newcomers were the only ones not afflicted, he joined them every morning in taking out our toilet buckets, cleaning them and putting them in the sun to dry. He never made a fuss about these things. It was a reflection of his sense of the collective interest.

Ironically, this was probably never as starkly revealed as it was when he acted entirely on his own in an initiative that contributed enormously to changing the face of South African politics. It was a major departure – not from policy, since policy was always that even the armed struggle was aimed at bringing the enemy to the negotiating table. But it was a major departure that he chose to act alone, without any consultation whatsoever.

This situation arose when, after 18 years on Robben Island, five of the seven Rivonia Trialists were transferred to Pollsmoor. For some reason they left Govan Mbeki and Elias Motsoaledi on the Island. But the rest of us – Madiba, Sisulu, Raymond Mhlaba, Andrew Mlangeni and I – went over to the mainland.

Then, in 1986, Mandela was taken away and kept alone, away from us. Instinctively, we wanted to protest, but he told us – not in these words – Cool it, chaps. As new developments came to light, it became clear that Madiba had made up his mind it was time to take the initiative in talking to the enemy.

Of course, he expected opposition from us, and did not want it. He wanted to present us with a *fait accompli*. And when he was eventually allowed to see us, one by one, two of the four agreed with him. Walter hesitated, and I was entirely against. Madiba, of course, was right.

When the news spread that Madiba had been isolated from the four of us, first at Pollsmoor (from 1986 until 1988) and then at Victor Verster prison near Franschhoek from 1988 to 1990, it gave rise to rumours, both in the country and abroad. Some within South Africa went as far as suggesting that he was selling out, and cautioned against visiting him.

But in response to an enquiry from the ANC leadership in exile, Madiba explained that all he was trying to do was to persuade the enemy to start talking to the leadership in exile. Through this, and other smuggled messages to the leadership abroad, and the underground leadership in South Africa, the air was cleared, and Madiba was given the go-ahead.

The fact is that he had foreseen the moment, the possibilities, and must have known others had not. And so, understanding what it meant – not for him, or not him alone, but the people – he acted alone. It was the masterstroke of a visionary, and it changed everything.

It was, you might say, a truly heroic impulse.

Steve Biko

Address at the commemoration of the twentieth anniversary
of Steve Biko's death, East London,
12 September 1997.

We are gathered here to pay homage to one of the greatest sons of our nation, Stephen Bantu Biko. His hope in life, and his life of hope, are captured by his resounding words: 'In time, we shall be in a position to bestow on South Africa the greatest possible gift – a more human face.'

And so we are assembled here to pledge our commitment to that ideal: the hope of a giant bequeathed to our land by a region that has down the centuries spawned men and women of outstanding qualities, leaders who have proved themselves in the most testing conditions. It has nurtured a tradition of uncompromising struggle unbroken from the days of Hintsa; through Enoch Sontonga, Vuyisile Mini, Matthew Goniwe, Fort Calata, Sparrow Mkhonto; to Griffiths and Victoria Mxenge – to name but a few. Many of them were butchered with a cold disregard for life by agents of a doomed regime.

Today's occasion speaks of our resolve to preserve the memories of our heroes and heroines; to keep alive the flame of patriotism which burnt in the hearts and minds of the like of Steve Biko; to redeem the pledge to give a more human face to a society for centuries trampled upon by the jackboot of inhumanity.

In eulogies to the departed, the words of the living sometimes bear little relation to reality. Yet, what has been said about Steve Biko, what passed through the walls of Robben Island and other prisons along our political grapevine, has stood the test of time. That he was indeed a great man who stood head and shoulders above his peers is borne out not only by the testimony of those who knew him and worked with him, but also by the fruits of his endeavours.

History called upon Steve Biko at a time when the political pulse of our people had been rendered faint by banning, imprisonment, exile, murder and banishment. Repression had swept the country

451

clear of all visible organisation of the people. But at each turn of history, apartheid was bound to spawn resistance; it was destined to bring to life the forces that would guarantee its death.

It is the dictate of history to bring to the fore the kind of leaders who seize the moment, who cohere with the wishes and aspirations of the oppressed. Such was Steve Biko, a fitting product of his time, a proud representative of the re-awakening of a people.

It was a time when the tide of Africa's valiant struggle and her liberation, lapping at our own borders, was consolidating black pride across the world and firing the determination of all those who were oppressed to take their destiny into their own hands.

It is also the fate of leadership to be misunderstood; for historians, academics, writers and journalists to reflect great lives according to their own subjective canon. This is all the more evident in a country where the interpreters have a much greater pool of resources to publish views regarding the quest for dignity and nationhood.

From the start, Black Consciousness articulated itself as 'an attitude of mind, a way of life'. In various forms and under various labels, before then and after, this attitude of mind and way of life have coursed through the veins of all the motive forces of struggle; they have fired the determination of leaders and the masses alike.

The driving thrust of Black Consciousness was to forge pride and unity amongst all the oppressed, to foil the strategy of divide-and-rule, to engender pride amongst the mass of our people and confidence in their ability to throw off their oppression.

And for its part the ANC from the first years of the 1970s welcomed Black Consciousness as part of the genuine forces of the revolution. It understood that it was helping give organisational form to the popular upsurge of all the oppressed groups of our society. Above all, the liberation movement asserted that, in struggle – in mass action, underground organisation, armed actions and international mobilisation – the people would most readily develop consciousness of their proud being, of their equality with everyone else, of their capacity to make history.

It is both natural and a matter of proud record that the overwhelming majority of young fighters who cut their teeth and shaped part of their political being in the Black Consciousness Movement are today leaders in their own right in national and provincial government, in the public service, in the judiciary and in the security and intelligence structures of the democratic government. They are to be found in the professions, in business, in the trade union movement and other structures of civil society – strategically placed to make their mark on the new order being born.

The attitude of mind and way of life that Biko and his comrades called for are needed today in abundance. They are relevant as we define our being as an African nation on the African continent. They are pertinent in our drive to ward off the temptation to become clones of other people.

A new attitude of mind and way of life are required in our efforts to change the human condition. But they can only thrive if we succeed in that common effort to build a better life. They are required as we strive to bring all power into the hands of the people; as we seek to shape a new media that appreciates the conditions and aspirations of the majority; as we change the structure of ownership of wealth; as we build a new ethos in our ideals, and yet at the same time, in the specificity of our own concrete conditions.

While Steve Biko espoused, inspired, and promoted black pride, he never made blackness a fetish. At the end of the day, as he himself pointed out, accepting one's blackness is a critical starting point: an important foundation for engaging in struggle. Today, it must be a foundation for reconstruction and development, for a common human effort to end war, poverty, ignorance and disease.

One of the greatest legacies of the struggle that Biko waged – and for which he died – was the explosion of pride among the victims of apartheid. The value that Black Consciousness placed on culture reverberated across our land, in our prisons, and amongst the communities in exile. Our people, who were once enjoined to look to Europe and America for creative sustenance, turned their eyes to Africa.

I speak of culture and creativity because, like truth, they are enduring. It is then a happy coincidence of history that Steve Biko is honoured with a statue, sculpted in bronze by Naomi Jacobson, whom one can say is his distant home-girl. It also gives a certain kind of joy that the financial cost of creating the statue was footed by people in the creative field, including Denzel Washington, Kevin Kline and Richard Attenborough, who will be remembered for the film on Biko, *Cry Freedom*. Another contributor is Peter Gabriel, whose song 'Biko' helped keep the flame of anti-apartheid solidarity alive. This collaboration of British and American artists bears eloquent witness to Steve Biko's internationalism.

In speaking about 'a more human face', Steve Biko was rejecting the brutality of men who behaved as if possessed, in their defence of injustice. It is these brutes that he faced without flinching, and the true story of his last moments we are only now starting to fathom.

As the Truth and Reconciliation Commission inches its way towards this truth, we are all bound to agonise over the price in terms of justice that the victims have to pay. But we can draw solace from the conviction that the half-truths of a lowly interrogator cannot and should not hide the culpability of the commanders and the political leaders who gave the orders. For we do know that what they desperately sought to get from him was his contact with the leadership of the liberation movement. In time, the truth will out!

In those difficult hours 20 years ago, the slings and arrows of outrageous fortune robbed a nation of a gifted young man whose contribution to our cause would have been even more immense. But our commitment to the unity that Steve Biko stood for will continue to guide us as we join hands in practical action to redress the legacy of oppression.

It means working together, government in each sphere and all sectors from society, in bringing prosperity to the province, the country and the continent which spawned him. It means all of us helping to take South Africa across the threshold of greatness on which it stands. That will be achieved by each of us respecting ourselves first and foremost, and in turn respecting the humanity in each one of us. It means an attitude of mind and a way of life that appreciates the joy in the honest labour of creating a new society.

In time, we must bestow on South Africa the greatest gift – a more humane society.

We are confident that by forging a new and prosperous nation, we are continuing the fight in which Steve Biko paid the supreme sacrifice.

We hope that by unveiling this statue, renaming the bridge and declaring his Ginsberg house a national monument, we are making our own humble contribution to immortalising his life.

Ruth First

Address at the Ruth First Tenth Anniversary
Commemoration Trust, Cape Town,
17 August 1992.

Ten years ago today, while I was in Pollsmoor Prison, I felt shattered and terribly alone when I received the news that Ruth First had been assassinated. My grief was all the more poignant because I knew both of the men injured in the same blast.

In my mind's eye I saw Pallo Jordan as I had last seen him when, during 1948, I spent a few days in his home. Similarly, I could see Comrade Braganza talking intensely to me when we met during my stay in Morocco in 1962.

But most clearly I could see Ruth: Ruth engaged in intense debate while we were at Wits University together; who uncompromisingly broke with the privilege of her wealthy background; who readily crossed the racial barrier that so few whites were, or still are, able to cross; a woman whose passion and compassion enabled others, including those from liberal and conservative perspectives, to play their part.

It is a small consolation that her memory lives beyond the grave, that her freedom of spirit infuses many committed to an open society, rigorous intellectual thought, courage and principled action.

Ruth spent her life in the service of the people of Southern Africa. She went to prison for her beliefs. She was murdered because of her acute political acumen combined with her resolute refusal to abandon her principles. Her life, and her death, remains a beacon to all who love liberty.

Many of you here today also knew Ruth personally, and will pay fitting tribute to her. But for us the assassination of Ruth First was not only a personal tragedy of immense proportions. It was part of a pattern of the systematic elimination of leading opponents of apartheid. Ten years later this commemoration is most appropriate, because it is only now that information is beginning to come out about the death squads and the crimes committed in defence of apartheid.

Our country cries out for peace. But this will be difficult to achieve until there is a recognition of the real causes of the violence, and the disbanding of those forces at the centre of what is in reality a low intensity war against the people.

The violence destroying the very fabric of our society has distinct patterns.

Firstly, there is random terror where anyone, irrespective of political affiliation or ethnic origin, can be a victim. This occurs through train massacres, attacks on taxi passengers, revellers in taverns, etc.

Secondly, within this random terror, there is the clear pattern of assassination of lower and middle leadership of the mass democratic movement. And this includes those members of the communities working within the peace structures to bring an end to violence. Such assassinations serve to deliberately fuel tensions and generate patterns of revenge killings.

Thirdly, there is the systematic assassination of leading political figures, including Ruth First, Joe Gqabi, Matthew Goniwe, David Webster and Griffiths and Victoria Mxenge, to name but a few.

And through all these layers runs a consistent thread: the South African security forces who, until now, have been placed above the law. A gathering such as this should not only pay tribute to those we have lost, but should also focus on how to bring to public knowledge what happened, and what structures still exist, so that the violence can be brought to an end.

The rampant lawlessness can be seen in the systematic torture – by such means as beatings, electric shocks and the use of hoods to suffocate prisoners – as well as the continued occurrence of deaths in police custody.

We are asked to believe that the Boipatong tapes were erased by mistake. But if this is true, the reflection of police incompetence is simply beyond belief. If we accept the argument that the tapes were erased through over-recording, we also have to accept that the police did not know how to use their equipment, did not know they did not know, and were completely unaware that they did not have tape recordings of daily routine calls. If we accept this version of how the tapes were erased, we also have to accept a complete lack of accountability, internal reporting or any system within the police force.

Among the revelations we need to pay attention to is that which places former Law and Order Minister Adrian Vlok as chairing a State Security Council meeting which spoke of 'removing Goniwe from society'. We need to relentlessly pursue information on the role of General Van der Westhuizen, not only in relation to the Goniwe murder but also more generally, especially given his involvement in a recent bid to assassinate Dirk Coetzee in London.

This is but the tip of the iceberg, and already government ministers are clamouring for a general amnesty. While we do not in principle oppose a general amnesty, such a matter is the province of an interim government. This minority government cannot pardon itself. Furthermore, integral to an amnesty is full revelation of past crimes and who committed them. This is not for the purpose of revenge, but to ensure that we do not carry such festering sores with us into the future.

A cleansing process is not simply the granting of pardons. Moreover, endeavours to equate the criminal activities carried out in defence of apartheid with the actions of those who fought to rid our country of this terrible scourge are not helpful. The actions of the French resistance were never comparable to the actions of the occupying German army.

The way forward requires cool heads and iron discipline. We welcome the proposed investigation into the SADF, SA Police, KwaZulu Police, Umkhonto we Sizwe, Apla and others proposed by the Secretary-General of the United Nations, Mr Boutros Boutros-Ghali. This investigation into all these forces is to be conducted by Judge Goldstone, and we will afford his commission every assistance.

Flowing from Mr [Cyrus] Vance's visit, the Security Council is meeting today to consider what the next steps should be. There has been a very sympathetic hearing of our request for international monitors to be permanently based in South Africa, and we await a final decision in this regard.

But the most urgent task facing us is to bring all the security forces under a central command structure, and for control to be placed in the hands of a multi-party commission.

All of this is necessary so that we can end the bloodletting, and move forward to peace and democracy in South Africa. Let us all play our part.

The memory of Ruth First and countless others who died that we may be free lives in our hearts. They will never be forgotten.

Bram Fischer

Speech at the first Bram Fischer Memorial Lecture,
Market Theatre, Johannesburg,
9 June 1995.

Many thousands are grateful to the Legal Resources Centre for taking the initiative in establishing a Bram Fischer Memorial Lecture. I
thank you for asking me to deliver the first. I am confident that
there will be Bram Fischer Memorial Lectures for as long as South
Africans yearn for freedom in a nonracial democratic South Africa.

Bram Fischer was a great advocate and a great patriot. The lectures
that will follow this inaugural lecture will provide opportunities for
lawyers and others to address fundamental issues relating to law and
society with which Bram Fischer was deeply concerned, and which
are also concerns of the Legal Resources Centre. But as this is the first
Bram Fischer Lecture I have chosen to talk about the man rather than
the law.

The last time that I saw Bram Fischer was on Robben Island about
two weeks after we had been sentenced to life imprisonment. It was
in June 1964. He came with our attorney Joel Joffe, to see how we
had settled in and whether or not we stood by our decision not to
appeal. I was restrained by the Major from hugging him. Though he
was strongly of the view that we should appeal, he resigned himself
to our decision. He and Joel wanted to know how we were being
treated and we told them. I then asked Bram about Molly, his wife.
No sooner had I pronounced Molly's name than Bram stood up,
excused himself and abruptly walked out of the room. A few minutes later he returned, once again composed, and resumed the conversation but without answering my question. On our way back to
the cells the Major asked me whether I considered Bram Fischer's
behaviour strange. I said yes it had been. He told me that Molly had
died in a car accident the previous week.

We were devastated by the news. Molly was a wonderful woman,
generous and unselfish, utterly without prejudice. She had supported

Bram in more ways than it was possible to know. She had been a wife, colleague and a comrade.

The refusal to talk about Molly and what had happened was typical of Bram's character. He was a stoic, a man who never burdened his friends with his own pain and troubles. He had come to advise us and to express concern for our predicament; he did not want to become the focus of our concern.

Bram was a courageous man who followed the most difficult course any person could choose to follow. He challenged his own people because he felt that what they were doing was morally wrong. As an Afrikaner whose conscience forced him to reject his own heritage and be ostracised by his own people, he showed a level of courage and sacrifice that was in a class by itself. I fought only against injustice, not against my own people.

Shortly after his arrest that led to him being sentenced to life imprisonment, Bram Fischer was asked whether his sacrifice of family and legal practice, being hunted as an outlaw and the inevitable harsh punishment that was to follow, was worth the gains of leading the underground struggle for less than a year. He was offended by the question. He replied sharply: 'Did you ask Nelson Mandela, Walter Sisulu, Govan Mbeki or Kathy Kathrada or any others that have already suffered this punishment? If not, why do you ask me?'

I waited for over 70 years to cast my first vote. I chose to do it near the grave of John Dube, the first President of the ANC, the African patriot that had helped found the organisation in 1912. I voted not only for myself alone but for many who took part in our struggle. I felt that with me when I voted were Oliver Tambo, Chris Hani, Chief Albert Luthuli and Bram Fischer. I felt that Josiah Gumede, GM Naicker, Dr Abdullah Abdurahman, Lilian Ngoyi, Helen Joseph, Yusuf Dadoo, Moses Kotane, Steve Biko and many others were there. I felt that each one of them held my hand that made the cross, helped me to fold the ballot paper and push it into the ballot box.

Even his political opponents would agree with us, his comrades, that Bram Fischer could have become prime minister or the chief justice of South Africa if he had chosen to follow the narrow path of Afrikaner nationalism. He chose instead the long and hard road to freedom not only for himself but for all of us. He chose the road that had to pass through the jail. He travelled it with courage and dignity. He served as an example to many who followed him.

Many have asked what in his early life led Bram to choose

between the privileges offered to him by the system and the imprisonment and the harsh condemnation that he knew he would suffer.

His grandfather, Abraham Fischer, was a close confidant of President Steyn of the Orange Free State at the turn of the century and particularly during the Anglo-Boer War. He became Prime Minister of the Orange River Colony when the bitter pill of defeat had to be swallowed. Leadership was needed to help rebuild the country and heal the ravages of war. His grandfather offered that leadership. His father, Percy Uhlrig Fischer, in his youth, was more militant than his grandfather. He identified himself with Hertzog's brand of Afrikaner nationalism and even organised an ambulance service to help those who in 1914 rebelled against Louis Botha's South African Party government.

Some of the burgers of the Orange Free State did not want to go to war against Germany at the invitation of the British Empire but chose to take part in the war on the other side, from which they hoped the Afrikaner people might gain their freedom. As a member of the Bar, Bram's father defended many of the Boer rebels and often expressed his disgust at the South African judges who, he said, had sold their souls to the *rooinekke* and sentenced burgers to prison.

When South African judges sent our comrades to prison for five, ten or at times 15 years for comparatively less serious offences, Bram would relate how his father had threatened to burn his counsel's robes when a burger was sentenced to three years' imprisonment.

Bram also spoke about how members of his family visited General De Wet and other rebels in prison. Although he was less than eight years of age he was taken along to such visits by his father or mother. His father's actions cost him and his family dearly. His support for the rebel cause offended against prevailing values of the time and his practice as an advocate suffered. The family was compelled for financial reasons to live away from Bloemfontein on a farm. His mother sold flowers at the station to supplement their income. Like many of our people do now, she had to get up at 4 o'clock in the morning to manage the home and her other responsibilities.

With that background he could not but have become an Afrikaner nationalist, as we became African nationalists 30 years later as a result of our oppression by whites. Both of us changed. Both of us rejected the notion that our political rights were to be determined by the colour of our skins. We embraced each other as comrades, as brothers, to fight for freedom for all in South Africa, to put an end to racism and exploitation.

In November 1965 Bram was arrested. In March 1966 he explained from the dock how that change came about. He spoke about growing up as a young boy on a farm where he felt no different from the two young Africans who were his constant companions and playmates. Later, in the city at school and at university, there were only masters and servants, not friends across the colour line. Under that influence he came to believe in segregation. He was attracted to the Bloemfontein Joint Council of Europeans and Africans, a body devoted largely to trying to induce the authorities to provide proper but separate amenities for Africans. He still believed in segregation. He found it difficult to touch the hand of a black man in friendship.

At Grey College his history teacher, Leo Marquard, had an important influence on his life, and broadened his vision. After matriculating he went to the University of Cape Town for a year but returned to Bloemfontein in order to give himself a better chance of gaining a Rhodes Scholarship to Oxford. He could reconcile his anti-imperialism with the acceptance of a scholarship named after this arch-imperialist. After all, his father's Afrikaner nationalism had not been blunted by his having studied at Cambridge.

In 1929 the National Union of South African Students – Nusas – was formed. A mock parliament was established. Political parties reflecting those who participated in the all-white Parliament of South Africa were established. Bram Fischer championed the cause of Afrikaner nationalism. He was elected the first prime minister of the student body. The ordained path to climb high in political office had been well and truly made. But a new vision for South Africa was beginning to take shape in his mind.

At about this time he drove an old ANC leader home to the west of Johannesburg. He tried to persuade him that friction between the races would only be avoided if they were kept apart. According to Bram, the old ANC leader didn't see it that way. He mentioned this incident at his own trial. What the old ANC leader said to him was this:

> If you place the races of one country in two camps and cut off contact between them, those in each camp will begin to forget that those in the other are ordinary human beings, that each lives and laughs the same way, that each experiences joy or sorrow, pride or humiliation for the same reasons. Thereby each becomes suspicious of the other and each eventually fears the other, which is the basis of all racism.

461

Bram came to believe in this himself, and having done so commit-ted himself without reservation to the struggle for a society which acknowledged this. There are still a small number of our people within South Africa who may cling to notions of living in inde-pendent homelands but the vast majority have accepted the validity of the words of that old ANC leader. I would urge the rest to follow that majority. Their own culture and heritage will not be compro-mised when they accept unreservedly that we are one country and that we should all constantly strive to become one nation.

Bram's studies at Oxford, his travels in Europe and especially in Germany and the Soviet Union, brought home to him the ideolog-ical divide between Nazism and socialism. The super-race ideology of the former struck him as no different from white racism in South Africa. Yet, it was not an experience that led him to join the Communist Party in South Africa. He returned from his travels to take up practice as an advocate, and it was only years later that he joined the Communist Party. He was apparently influenced by peo-ple such as JB Marks, Moses Kotane and Yusuf Dadoo, and by the fact that with the exception of a small number of religious leaders, communists were the only ones amongst the whites who seemed unreservedly to accept blacks as equals.

In 1935 Bram became a member of the Johannesburg Bar. In 1937 he married Molly Krige, a niece of Ouma Smuts. He became famil-iar with the life of the oppressed through his involvement in the South African Institute of Race Relations, the Joint Council of Europeans and Africans and, more particularly, the Alexandra Health Committee. Bram and Molly served on the district committee of the Communist Party. Molly was almost elected to the Johannesburg City Council as a communist, a feat later to be achieved by Hilda Watts, the wife of Rusty Bernstein, our co-accused in the Rivonia Trial. He recalled the successes of the forces of the Soviet Union against Nazism, and how at that time attitudes to the Communist Party were different, and how it was able to find favour among the white voters of South Africa. It was only later, with the combination of the Cold War propaganda and the beating of the tribal drum by the Nationalists, that most whites viewed the Communist Party with hatred. They also believed that by branding anyone who took part in the freedom struggle as a communist they would discredit our movement.

In 1946 the district committee of the Communist Party identified itself with the plight of the black miners who had gone on a so-called 'illegal' strike against the Chamber of Mines. Although Bram was absent when the decision was taken, in a characteristic act of solidarity he accepted legal responsibility and was convicted.

Bram's commitment to the struggle helped to change many of us in the ANC from being Africanists to believers in a nonracial democracy. The declaration in the Freedom Charter of 1955 that South Africa belongs to all, both black and white, was inspired by many people of all races who had identified themselves with our struggle. Amongst them none were held in higher esteem than Bram and Molly Fischer.

Bram often acted as our legal adviser and defended us in Court. In cases in which he could not appear or thought it advisable for other reasons not to do so, he asked other leaders of the Bar to act for us. Harold Hanson, Isie Maisels, Walter Pollak, Rex Welsh, HC Nicholas, Vernon Berrangé, John Coaker, Sydney Kentridge, Tony O'Dowd, Chris Plewman and many others did so. All had the greatest respect for Bram. Because of this they often acted on our behalf without a fee.

They acted for us when we were charged in the Defiance Campaign trial, when attempts were made to remove us from the roll of professional organisations, and when we were tried on charges of high treason from the end of 1956 to the beginning of 1961. Bram's painstaking work on the law and above all his understanding of the vital political issues of those days played a crucial part in the defence, which led to our acquittal.

His integrity and reputation as a great South African of Afrikaner stock was of vital importance to our magistrates and judges. The magistrate who tried Ismail Meer, JN Singh and me on charges arising out of my having sat on the wrong seat on the tram, when the conductor referred to me as their 'kaffir friend', was overawed by Bram's presence and hastily acquitted us.

But the dark clouds were beginning to gather. Our acquittal in the treason trial was a pyrrhic victory. Our organisation had been declared unlawful a year earlier. The whole leadership including those of us on trial were detained in terms of the emergency regulations. Our attempts to continue the struggle by peaceful means were increasingly frustrated.

Bram, like many of us, reluctantly came to the conclusion that the state's institutionalised violence against the majority of the people of

South Africa, and more particularly the liberation movement, left us with no option other than to turn to armed struggle. Prompted by his humanity, he supported the decision that violence was to be confined to attacks on the symbols of apartheid and that great care should be taken that there should be no loss of lives.

During this period he remained in close contact with the underground leadership of the African National Congress and its military wing Umkhonto we Sizwe, which accepted political violence for the liberation.

When our leaders were arrested at Rivonia, our families and friends feared that the hysteria created by the government propaganda machine was likely to lead to death sentences being imposed on us. Naturally, they turned to Bram for guidance in relation to our defence. He did not want to be part of the defence team at the trial, although he was willing to appear in Court on the day that we would be charged and argue for the time that we would require to prepare our case. He had personal knowledge of the decisions which had been taken to turn to the armed struggle and had been party to such decisions. He felt that with such knowledge he could not act as our counsel. But he could not tell our families and lawyers what his reasons were. Joel Joffe, our attorney, and Arthur Chaskalson and George Bizos, our counsel, assumed that he would lead the defence. They put tremendous pressure on him by using the argument that there was no other advocate in the country who could say that we had done nothing more than what his people, the Afrikaners, had done in 1914, and that despite the loss of life in that rebellion, there were no death sentences; that if people were to die there would never be reconciliation between black and white in South Africa.

Bram knew then that he was at risk, and that he might soon find himself in the dock. He ultimately agreed to lead the defence team and persuaded Vernon Berrangé to join it. His knowledge that the leaders with whom he had been in contact – Walter Sisulu, Govan Mbeki and myself – were not going to put in issue what we had done or the decisions that had been taken, probably helped him to resolve the conflict within himself. We, unlike Joel, Arthur and George, knew why he was reluctant to appear at the trial. We did not press him to do so, and we admired his courage when he accepted the brief.

He helped to formulate the nature of our defence. The prosecution expected us to try to avoid responsibility for our actions. However, we became the accusers, and right at the start, when asked to plead we said that it was the government that was responsible for the state of affairs in the country and that it was the government that should be in the dock. We maintained this position throughout the trial in our evidence and in the cross-examination of witnesses.

His carefully prepared logical argument led to the quashing of the indictment against us. This helped to change the atmosphere which had been created by government propaganda, and led to both internal and international campaigns calling for our release.

When the trial proper started he spent many hours with us in Pretoria Prison, helping us to prepare the statements that we were to make from the dock and to prepare the statements from which comrades Walter Sisulu, Govan Mbeki and others were to be led. He led comrade Walter carefully, with compassion and great understanding. As a result, a confident Walter Sisulu was able to put down the overzealous prosecutor who not only wanted to convict us but also to discredit us. We have always felt that Bram's strategic planning of our defence, the support that we received from freedom-loving people in South Africa, and the unanimous call by the United Nations to release us saved our lives.

After Bram had visited us on Robben Island I wrote to him on behalf of myself and my co-accused to express our condolences on Molly's death. I was assured that it would be posted. Apparently, it was not, for I have since learned that he did not receive the letter. I deeply regret that he died without knowing what our feelings were and what we had said in the letter. Not long after his visit to Robben Island he was arrested and charged with furthering the objects of communism. He was admitted to bail to enable him to appear in a case before the Privy Council in England. He had promised to come back to face trial. He did so despite pressure put on him by our comrades who were in England, to forego his bail and go into exile.

He returned and attended his trial in which he was the first accused. One day he did not arrive at Court. Instead he sent a letter to his counsel, Harold Hanson, which was read out in Court. He wrote:

> By the time this reaches you I shall be a long way from Johannesburg and shall absent myself from the remainder of the trial. But I shall still be in the country to which I said I would return when I was granted bail. I wish you to inform the Court that my absence, though deliberate, is not intended in any way to be disrespectful. Nor is it prompted

by any fear of the punishment which might be inflicted on me. Indeed I realise fully that my eventual punishment may be increased by my present conduct. ...

My decision was made only because I believe that it is the duty of every true opponent of this Government to remain in this country and to oppose its monstrous policy of apartheid with every means in his power. That is what I shall do for as long as I can. ...

There are already over 2 500 political prisoners in our prisons. These men and women are not criminals but the staunchest opponents of apartheid. ...

If by my fight I can encourage even some people to think about, to understand and to abandon the policies they now so blindly follow, I shall not regret any punishment I may incur. ...

I can no longer serve justice in the way I have attempted to do during the past thirty years. I can do it only in the way I have now chosen.

He wrote a further letter in less than two weeks, prompted by the overhasty action of his colleagues at the Bar. He said:

I have been following the Press and have seen the reports of a decision in terms of which it is said that the Johannesburg Bar Council intends applying to Court in order to have my name struck off the roll of advocates. I assume that the sole reason for the decision is that I deliberately absented myself from my trial and estreated my bail.

The principle upon which I rely is a simple one, firmly established in South African legal tradition. Since the days of the South African War, if not since the Jameson Raid, it has been recognised that political offences, committed because of a belief in the overriding moral validity of a political principle, do not in themselves justify the disbarring of a person from practising the profession of the law. Presumably this is because it is assumed that the commission of such offences has no bearing on the professional integrity of the person concerned.

When an advocate does what I have done, his conduct is not determined by any disrespect for the law nor because he hopes to benefit personally by any 'offence' he may commit. On the contrary, it requires an act of will to overcome his deeply rooted respect of legality, and he takes the step only when he feels that, whatever the consequences to himself, his political conscience no longer permits him to do otherwise. He does it not because of a desire to be immoral, but because to act otherwise would, for him, be immoral.

Bram was underground for almost a year. When he was ultimately arrested and brought to trial he was sentenced to life imprisonment. In his speech from the dock on 28 March 1966 he said that apartheid had been in existence before the advent of the Nationalist government in 1948. The Afrikaners had isolated themselves from contact with black people. The policy had been intensified during the previous 15 years and the Afrikaners were being blamed for all the evils and actions of apartheid. This had led to a deep-rooted antagonism to the Afrikaner. All the wisdom of the leadership and the influence of the Congress leaders who had been silenced and imprisoned would now be needed in order to bring about a reconciliation. He said that he felt that there was an additional duty cast on him, so that at least one Afrikaner should publicly identify himself with the plight of the people. We can do no better than remember Bram's own words:

> It was to keep faith with all those dispossessed by apartheid that I broke my undertaking to the Court, that I separated myself from my family, pretended that I was someone else, and accepted the life of a fugitive. I owed it to the political prisoners, to the banished, to the silenced and to those under house arrest not to remain a spectator, but to act. I knew what they expected of me, and I did it. I felt responsible not to those who are indifferent to the sufferings of others, but to those who are concerned. I knew that by valuing above all their judgement, I would be condemned by people who are content to see themselves as respectable and loyal citizens. I do not regret any such condemnation that may follow me.

Bram was condemned to life imprisonment. The conditions under which he was held were intended to deny his human dignity by every means his gaolers could imagine. He was not even allowed to attend the funeral service of his only son Paul, the wedding of his daughter Ilse, nor to hold in his arms any of her or her sister Ruth's children, his grandchildren. His gaolers did all they could to break Bram's spirit, to warn others who might join in the struggle of what was to be in store for them. Their meanness continued almost to the end when a terminally ill Bram Fischer was allowed to go to the home of his brother Paul in Bloemfontein, but still a prisoner, isolated from all except close members of his family. When I heard that Bram was terminally ill, I repeatedly asked Jimmy Kruger, the then Minister of Justice, to be allowed to see him. Kruger found reasons why I should not. They not only feared Bram and what he stood for, they were afraid to release his body for proper burial; they were afraid to release his ashes to his family.

They failed. The contribution of Bram Fischer will live on. Had

he been alive a year ago to celebrate with us the freedom we gained
for all South Africans he would have been well pleased. The acceptance by the vast majority of his fellow Afrikaners of a nonracial and
democratic South Africa would have been a realisation of what he
had fought for, for the better part of his life. Bram wanted a better
South Africa for all; a South Africa where there is not only political
freedom but housing and health services, education and cultural
development and a more just distribution of the wealth of the country among all of its people.

Please forgive me for quoting myself from the last chapter of my
book, *Long Walk to Freedom*, where I said:

> The policy of apartheid created a deep and lasting wound in my coun-
> try and my people. All of us will spend many years if not generations
> recovering from that profound hurt but the dictates of oppression and
> brutality had another unintended effect, and that was it produced the
> Oliver Tambos, the Walter Sisulus, the Chief Luthulis, the Yusuf Dadoos,
> the Bram Fischers, the Robert Sobukwes of our time – men of such
> extraordinary courage, wisdom and generosity that their like may never
> be known again. Perhaps it requires such depth of oppression to create
> such heights of character. My country is rich in the minerals and gems
> that lie beneath its soil but I have always known that its greatest wealth
> is its people, finer and truer than minerals and diamonds.

In any history written of our country two Afrikaner names will be
always remembered. Happily one is still with us, dear comrade Beyers
Naudé. The other is Bram Fischer. The people of South Africa will
never forget him. He was among the first bright beacons that attracted millions of our young people to fervently believe in a nonracial
democracy in our country.

Bram Fischer was a son of the soil. His spirit lives on!

Chris Hani (1)

Address to the nation on the assassination of Chris Hani,
10 April 1993.

Today, an unforgivable crime has been committed. The calculated, cold-blooded murder of Chris Hani is not just a crime against a dearly beloved son of our soil. It is a crime against all the people of our country. A man of passion, of unsurpassed courage, has been cut down in the prime of his life.

Chris Hani is known to all of us, loved by millions, hated only by those who fear the truth. We say to all South Africans, black and white, that day of truth will dawn.

Chris spent his life fighting for freedom, democracy and justice. It was this passion for liberty that persuaded him, at an early age, to commit himself fully to the African National Congress and the South African Communist Party.

Chris Hani knew from personal experience the pain of deprivation and social inequality. An erudite scholar who could have chosen a less arduous path, he nonetheless selflessly chose the often thankless task of being a freedom fighter. He shared the trials and tribulations of three decades of exile. During that time he served the cause of the liberation movement with distinction, earning the respect and love of millions in our country.

His death demands that we pursue that cause with even greater determination.

We appeal to every religious service over this Easter Holiday to commemorate Chris Hani's life and what he stood for. Let Wednesday 14 April be a day on which, wherever we are, we hold memorial services in honour of one of the greatest freedom fighters this country has ever known.

We are a nation deeply wounded by callous, uncaring men who plot such heinous crimes with impunity. The cries of our nation are heard from old men who bury their sons and daughters, wives who weep for their husbands, communities who endlessly bury young and old, infants and pregnant women.

This killing must stop.

Chris Hani championed the cause of peace, trudging to every corner of South Africa calling for a spirit of tolerance among all our people.

We are a nation in mourning. Our pain and anger is real. Yet, we must not permit ourselves to be provoked by those who seek to deny us the very freedom Chris Hani gave his life for. Let us respond with dignity and in a disciplined fashion. Let us observe April 14 in dignified memorial services and in accordance with the decisions of our leadership.

The date of Comrade Chris Hani's funeral will be announced after full consultations with the family. We shall lay to rest the mortal remains of Comrade Chris Hani in a manner befitting a hero of our people. No one will desecrate his memory by rash and irresponsible actions.

At this moment of unbounded grief for the whole country, our deepest sympathies go to Chris's wife, Limpho, the children and the rest of the family. The ANC dips its banner in salute to this outstanding son of Africa.

Chris Hani (2)

Televised address to the nation on the assassination
of Chris Hani, 13 April 1993

Tonight I am reaching out to every single South African, black and white, from the very depths of my being. A white man, full of prejudice and hate, came to our country and committed a deed so foul that our whole nation now teeters on the brink of disaster. A white woman, of Afrikaner origin, risked her life so that we may know, and bring to justice, this assassin.

The cold-blooded murder of Chris Hani has sent shock waves throughout the country and the world. Our grief and anger is tearing us apart. What has happened is a national tragedy that has touched millions of people, across the political and colour divide. Our shared grief and legitimate anger will find expression in nationwide commemorations that coincide with the funeral service.

Tomorrow, in many towns and villages, there will be memorial services to pay homage to one of the greatest revolutionaries this country has ever known. Every service will open a Memorial Book for Freedom, in which all who want peace and democracy pledge their commitment.

Now is the time for all South Africans to stand together against those who, from any quarter, wish to destroy what Chris Hani gave his life for – the freedom of all of us. Now is the time for our white compatriots, from whom messages of condolence continue to pour in, to reach out with an understanding of the grievous loss to our nation, to join in the memorial services and the funeral commemorations. Now is the time for the police to act with sensitivity and restraint, to be real community policemen and women who serve the population as a whole. There must be no further loss of life at this tragic time.

This is a watershed moment for all of us. Our decisions and actions will determine whether we use our pain, our grief and our outrage to move forward to what is the only lasting solution for our country – an elected government of the people, by the people and for the people. We must not let the men who worship war, and who lust after blood, precipitate actions that will plunge our country into another Angola.

Chris Hani was a soldier. He believed in iron discipline. He carried out instructions to the letter. He practised what he preached. Any lack of discipline is trampling on the values that Chris Hani stood for. Those who commit such acts serve only the interests of the assassins, and desecrate his memory.

When we, as one people, act together decisively, with discipline and determination, nothing can stop us.

Let us honour this soldier for peace in a fitting manner. Let us rededicate ourselves to bringing about the democracy he fought for all his life; democracy that will bring real, tangible changes in the lives of the working people, the poor, the jobless, the landless.

Chris Hani is irreplaceable in the heart of our nation and people. When he first returned to South Africa after three decades in exile, he said: 'I have lived with death most of my life. I want to live in a free South Africa even if I have to lay down my life for it.'

The body of Chris Hani will lie in state at the FNB Stadium, Soweto, from 12 noon on Sunday 18 April until the start of the vigil at 6 pm. The funeral service will commence at 9 am on Monday, 19 April. The cortege will leave for Boksburg Cemetery, where the burial is scheduled for 1 pm.

These funeral services and rallies must be conducted with dignity. We will give disciplined expression to our emotions at our pickets, prayer meetings and gatherings, in our homes, our churches and our schools. We will not be provoked into any rash actions. We are a nation in mourning.

To the youth of South Africa we have a special message: you have lost a great hero. You have repeatedly shown that your love of freedom is greater than that most precious gift, life itself. But you are the leaders of tomorrow. Your country, your people, your organisation need you to act with wisdom. A particular responsibility rests on your shoulders.

We pay tribute to all our people for the courage and restraint they have shown in the face of such extreme provocation. We are sure this same indomitable spirit will carry us through the difficult days ahead.

Chris Hani has made the supreme sacrifice. The greatest tribute we can pay to his life's work is to ensure that we win freedom for all our people.

Helen Joseph

Speech at the funeral service of Helen Joseph,
St Mary's Cathedral, Johannesburg,
7 January 1993.

I am immensely honoured to speak at the funeral of my friend, my sister and comrade Helen Joseph. In the past two weeks since Helen died, I have heard people remembering her in many ways. Some spoke of her courage and her commitment to our struggle, of her humane and kind personality, her fierce battle against apartheid and her tireless campaign for the emancipation of women.

Many of her friends spoke of her influence as a very shrewd politician in various organisations. Helen had touched so many lives in the garment workers union, Fedsaw [Federation of South African Women], COD [Congress of Democrats], the UDF, and the ANC.

I cannot but agree that the things people remember are all true of her remarkable life.

Helen Joseph taught us many lessons and I wish to recount these to you today.

Helen believed that unity in action was the key element to our passage to liberation. She took a very broad view of the nature of the course that we should take in uniting the South African people. Her own political involvement was shaped by her experience working with Solly Sachs in the garment workers union. It was here that she encountered the triple oppression suffered by South African women and the added repression that the pass laws brought to bear on the majority of black South Africans.

Helen's response to the pass laws was that they affected African men and women directly and oppressed all South Africans who were forced either to carry a pass or to watch others being persecuted.

Together with women such as Lilian Ngoyi, Francis Baard, Ray Simons, Rahima Moosa, Amina Cachalia, Albertina Sisulu, Ruth Mompati, Dora Tamana and Ama Naidoo and many others, a Federation of South African Women was formed. Fedsaw was way ahead of the thinking of even the ANC at the time, because it brought together women of all races, classes and religious affiliation with the aim to challenge the pass laws as a united force. The slogan 'You strike a woman you strike a rock' was born out of this period.

Helen Joseph was central to the strategic thinking and the action that would unite 20 000 women in a march on the Union Buildings in Pretoria. She had the unique ability to pick up on the most burning issues and translate those into a programme of mass action.

Helen challenged the paternalism of our society and left a legacy that the struggle for the emancipation of women had to be side-by-side with the struggle to liberate the people of South Africa. She believed that the two processes were inseparable.

Helen also believed that whilst the government of South Africa relied on white people to keep it in power by denying black people the right to vote, white South Africans could not be left uncontested and that they needed to be consistently challenged to accept the responsibility of democracy and human rights, to acknowledge the equality of all the people in South Africa and to respect the inalienable right of every South African to vote for the political party of their own choice. This is a lesson that all South Africans must take with us as we go into a year which must be decisive.

She recounted to me once that Lilian Ngoyi had challenged her to organise amongst the white people and not only work with black women and their problems. She took up this challenge and intensified her involvement in the Congress of Democrats. To her, apartheid was evil and her boundless energy went into fighting it.

Helen Joseph had a profound influence on the student movement in South Africa. Many Nusas activists sought her advice and she was very pleased when Sasco [South African Students Congress] finally emerged. She transferred her skills onto others easily and recognised the contributions that young people had to make. To her a united student movement would be able to address the problems of this sector much more effectively than a splintered dismembered one.

One of the lessons I have personally learned from Helen is that her profile as an international and national leader did not detract from her commitment to maintaining contact with her grassroots constituency. She showed deep concern for her comrades as human beings and became actively involved in the struggles they encountered. Helen did not forget the political prisoners and together with others campaigned for the release of all political prisoners.

For many of us Christmas Day was more special because Helen chose to celebrate it by remembering her friends in prisons throughout this country. She wrote to me once about the DPSC [Detainees Parents Support Committee] and her friend David Webster and their work to fight for the rights of detainees and their release. She did not have any children of her own, but there are many here today who can lay legitimate claim to being her children.

Helen had the gift of working with people she did not agree with politically. It is well known that Helen was not a committed Marxist and she was not a member of the SACP, but she worked with people who were because she was a democrat and believed in the freedom of political choice. During the Treason Trial, which lasted from 1956 to 1961, our speeches in court would condemn British imperialism, American neo-imperialism, Dutch, French and Belgian imperialism. When Helen was cross-examined and asked what she thought about British imperialism, she answered that there was no such thing because the British had spread out to bring civilisation to all the countries they went to.

Helen was a South African revolutionary, but a lady of the British Empire. A contradiction in the eyes of many, but to Helen her own reality. She did not fear to contradict and be contradicted; she feared only the loss of her dignity as a human being and the loss of dignity forced upon others. That is why she fought apartheid so fearlessly and paid the price with banning orders and house arrests which spanned a 20-year period.

During the 1960 state of emergency our lawyers withdrew from the Treason Trial in protest and Duma Nokwe and I undertook to take the statements from the trialists. Helen answered all the questions I put to her very regally and very correctly – all except one. I asked her how old she was and she immediately stiffened and asked me what that had to do with the case. I considered this a very natural question to ask. She told me that she would tell me later confidentially. I had no idea that my sister and comrade and fellow freedom fighter would not reveal her age publicly. This was Helen Joseph, a woman of contrast and courage, a woman we can truly regard as a figure which has helped to shape our destiny and an indelible part of our history.

She worked for a nonracial, united and democratic South Africa She died trusting that we would all deliver this to our country. I salute *Isitwalandwe* Helen Joseph. [*Isitwalandwe* (or *Isitwalandwe-Seaparankoe*), which literally means 'the one who wears the plumes of the rare bird', is the highest honour awarded by the African National Congress to those who have made an outstanding contribution to the struggle for liberation.]

In closing I would also wish to pay tribute to Sina Mlambo, Helen's close companion for the past ten years, and thank her for taking care of Helen. I also wish to pass our condolences to Helen's relatives, Clive and Jeremy Fennell, who are with us today.

Malibongwe.

Trevor Huddleston

Speech at a memorial service for
Father Trevor Huddleston, Johannesburg,
5 May 1998.

All who encountered Father Huddleston in the closing years of our struggle will know of his longing to see a free South Africa before he died; and his impatience with mere speeches that would exasperate him to exclaim: 'Words, words, words – I am sick of words!'

It is therefore with special humility that I join in his commemoration to convey the sense of loss we feel, as a nation, at Father Huddleston's death, and our abiding gratitude that the vagaries of history brought him to our land. I do so in the knowledge that I am speaking of one who touched the hearts of millions of South Africans.

Although he disparaged empty words, this man of action, who also lived a deeply contemplative life, inspired the world to action through his eloquent denunciation of our condition and the realities of forced removal and Bantu Education. This was no contradiction, but part of the strength and variety of his character.

In the same way he combined a gentle compassion for the victims of injustice with uncompromising hostility to the oppressor. His unyielding challenge to church and state was combined with absolute discipline towards his order, even when that discipline took him, as it then seemed, far from the scene of the struggle with which he had identified.

His courage was not only of the kind which is needed to choose difficult and unpopular paths. He was also fearless where others might shrink from personal and physical danger, as I myself had occasion to witness.

He was one of those rare people, good men and women who make the world the theatre of their operations in pursuit of freedom and justice.

He did so not in any abstract and distant way. His sacrifices for our

477

freedom and his unceasing efforts to build the international campaign of solidarity with our cause were not those of a distant benefactor. They told of a fellow human sharing dangers and deprivations as well as aspirations. They told of our capacity, on the basis of our common humanity, to touch one another's hearts across the social divides and across the oceans.

In Father Huddleston we see exemplified in the most concrete way the contribution that religion has made to our liberation. Whenever the noble ideals and values of religion have been joined with practical action to realise them, it has strengthened us and at the same time nurtured those ideals within the political movement. In turn, Father Huddleston often spoke of how the struggle of ordinary people for their dignity gave concrete meaning to the principles of his Christianity.

It is therefore a cause for joy that his wish that dignity should be restored to South Africans in his lifetime was granted him. We are grateful that he lived to return to our land in 1991 to open the ANC Conference as it addressed the challenges of transition. We are glad that he did see the dawn of freedom break on 27 April 1994. He saw too how the British Anti-Apartheid Movement transformed itself from a legion of freedom fighters into a corps of fellow workers for reconstruction and development. He witnessed how the international community embraced a democratic South Africa as a partner in the pursuit of international peace and development.

For us who gather in thanksgiving for his memory, the challenge has moved from the quest for liberation to the quest for transformation and the reconciliation of those whom our oppressive past set one against the other. But in this new and even more difficult struggle, the principles for which Father Huddleston fought and campaigned are as young and as relevant as they ever were. Though we have made a start in addressing the basic needs of our people, it is no easy task and one that will take many years.

As religious organisations became an indispensable part of our struggle for freedom, so too do we need them now to be actively engaged in the rebuilding of our society, strengthened by the new unity within and between religions which liberation has made possible.

As the commitment to the ideals of freedom and justice took their meaning for him through action to realise them, so will our commitment to undo the legacy of our divided past gain content through our joint efforts to address the needs of especially the poorest of our society.

We will need his readiness to join hands with people of all backgrounds and all persuasions, in pursuit of shared goals. We will need *Isitwalandwe* Trevor Huddleston's impatience with fine words that do not translate into action.

May we honour his memory in the building of a better life for all.

Walter Sisulu

Speech during the 90th birthday celebrations of Walter Sisulu,
18 May 2002.

We are highly privileged to be able to celebrate the 90th birthday of such a giant and a cornerstone of our movement.

Our movement has made its name in the history of liberation movements, not only of Africa but the entire world. For 90 years it has been fighting uncompromisingly for the liberation of our country and the emancipation of its people. Great freedom fighters – men and women of exceptional courage and commitment – have played their roles in making our movement achieve for the people as it has done. Amongst those the name of the man with whom we celebrate today stands supreme.

Walter Sisulu has lived through and witnessed the major events of the last century that shaped South Africa. What is more important, is that he was a major participant in decisively shaping and making that history.

Often in addressing younger people I make the point that what counts in life is not the mere fact that we have lived. It is what difference we have made to the lives of others that will determine the significance of the life we lead. For this, there can be no greater and more inspiring example in the history of our organisation, and hence of our country, than Walter Sisulu: a man whose every deed speaks of leadership that made the kind of difference which brought us to where we are today as a country and a people.

Actually we should not be speaking on this occasion. Walter is such a unique source of historical experience and such a rich font of information and knowledge that we should be celebrating by hearing him tell his story, and so listen to and learn about our own.

Of course, on a personal level I can tell of a relationship – a friendship and comradeship – that was profoundly formative in my life. The nature of that relationship and the spirit that informed it was such that the personal was transcended. The essence of that relationship was in how it shaped one's life as a member of our organisation. The unstinting commitment to the common good and to the service of the people completely filled the life of Walter Sisulu and deeply touched those like ourselves.

There are so many examples I can quote of the wisdom and leadership qualities of Walter. In all of those instances he demonstrated the ability to see the broader picture and to project himself way beyond the immediate considerations that others found ourselves focusing on.

The question we as a movement, and particularly our younger people, should be asking is what we learn from the life of this giant of our struggle and where it guides us to for the future.

While the circumstances and the specific nature of the challenges in our country might have changed, the task of our organisation basically remains the same: to lead the country in creating a better life for all our people, particularly the poor. The cardinal attributes of Walter Sisulu, the freedom fighter, remain as important to emulate today as it ever was the case.

The absolute selflessness with which he gave his life to the struggle is especially important to remember and hold dear as the new conditions create the temptations of self-interest and personal enrichment. Corruption, opportunism and self-serving careerism have no place in the organisation Walter Sisulu led and helped build. His discipline in service of the organisation and the people must serve as an abiding example. In everything he did or spoke, the paramount consideration was: what is best for the organisation and for the advancement of the liberation struggle?

We all respected his wisdom and leadership, more so because he was such a strong exponent of collective leadership. He knew and taught us that wisdom comes from sharing insights and listening to and learning from each other. He was a unifier, not a divider. Where others of us would speak a hasty word or act in anger, he was the patient one, seeking to heal and bring together.

We congratulate him on his birthday and thank him for having given so entirely of his life to the struggle and to our organisation. And when we talk about how entirely he has done that, we cannot forget to mention Albertina who was such an integral part of that giving in entirety. And one cannot forget the rest of their family either. Many families suffered a great deal during apartheid. Families were divided and broken up as parents or children were persecuted, killed, jailed, driven underground and into exile. The Sisulu family count among those who have suffered severely and who have given most selflessly of themselves.

As we congratulate Walter, we above all shall commit ourselves to being faithful to the example he has set as a leader, a freedom fighter and a servant of his people.

Congratulations, Walter, and best wishes for the years we have left.

Joe Slovo

Address at the funeral of Joe Slovo, Johannesburg,
15 January 1995.

We are assembled to mourn the passing of a leader, a patriot, a father, a fighter, a negotiator, an internationalist, a theoretician and an organiser. Indeed, it is the combination of all these qualities so splendidly in one individual, which made Comrade Joe Slovo the great African revolutionary that he was.

Men and women of rare qualities are few and hard to come by. And when they depart, the sense of loss is made the more profound and the more difficult to manage.

Yet we do draw comfort, Comrade Joe: from the knowledge that the greater part of the journey that was the passion of your life has been traversed; from the knowledge that you left a legacy which we shall all strive to emulate; from the knowledge, Comrade Joe, that you continue to live in each one of us through your force of example, vitality of spirit and passion for justice.

Today, as the nation bids you final farewell, we are at the same time celebrating a life lived to the full, the richness of which touched the hearts of millions and made an indelible mark on the history of our country.

When future generations look back on the 1994 breakthrough, they will be justified in saying: Uncle Joe was central in making it happen.

When the working people start enjoying, as a right, a roof over their heads, affordable medical care, quality education and a rising standard of living, they will be right to say: Comrade Joe was a chief architect who helped lay the foundation for a better life.

When those yet to be born marvel at how South Africans of our times managed a delicate transition, they will be within their right to sing, as we did during the years of armed struggle: *u'Slovo ikomando*, a commando of reconstruction and development, a warrior of peace and reconciliation, a builder *par excellence*.

Comrade Joe Slovo was one of those who taught us that individuals do not make history. Yet, in each generation there are a few individuals who are endowed with the acumen and personal bearing which enable them to direct the course of events.

Comrade Joe Slovo, *Isitwalandwe-Seaparankoe*, belonged in that category. In that sense he was a rare species, an institution. To reflect on Joe's contribution is, therefore, to retrace the evolution of South African politics in the past half-century.

Such is the life we celebrate today: a life not so much of white generosity to the black people of our country; for JS did not see himself as a white South African but as a South African. He was a full part of the democratic majority, acting together with them for a just and democratic order.

Comrade JS lived the life not merely of a theoretician, confined to the boardroom and library. He was at all stages of struggle, there at the forefront, generating ideas, and there too, in their implementation.

When, in 1934, the village of Obelkei in Lithuania bequeathed to South Africa an eight-year-old Yossel Mashel Slovo, there was no predetermined course that his life would follow. Forced to leave school at an early age because of poverty; part of the passionate political debates of that period among immigrants in Johannesburg; a poor Jewish family upbringing in the period when Nazism was rearing its ugly head – all these factors helped mould one of the greatest South African and African revolutionaries of our times.

Joe Slovo was among the few white workers who understood their class interest and sought common cause with their class brothers and sisters irrespective of race. In this sense, Comrade JS leaves the South African working class – black and white – a challenge, particularly now that the walls of racial division are finally collapsing: the time for unity has come!

The young Joe could have later chosen a lucrative life, after returning from service in the Second World War, and acquiring the opportunities accorded white veterans. He could have elected, as many in his position did, to part ways with his black colleagues as they rode into oblivion on the bicycles given them as the thankless reward for their service in the war.

But Joe Slovo was a full human being at heart. And he possessed the passion and natural intellect to see reality for what it was. He had, at the age of 16, joined the Communist Party of South Africa. To use his own words, he had decided that in his life there was only one target, and that target was to remove the racist regime and obtain power for the people. Those of us who had the honour to be closely associated with Comrade Joe know that he lived true to that dedication. He knew fully well that he would walk again and again through the valley of the shadow of death to reach the mountaintops of his desires.

I was fortunate to meet him in our younger days at Wits University. With his future wife, Ruth First, Ismail Meer, Harold Wolpe, Jules Browde, JN Singh and others, we would debate many issues well into the wee hours of the morning. His sharp intellect and incisive mind were apparent then.

But Joe was a well-rounded human being. Up to his last days, he lived life to the full. He never claimed to be a saint. He was a good organiser of enjoyable parties. He liked to eat and dress well. He had humour in abundance.

It is this passion for happiness in his life and the lives of others that we saw in his contribution to the campaigns of the working people; in court as a devastating human rights lawyer; in the underground; and in the formation of Umkhonto we Sizwe in 1961. When we were on Robben Island, we managed on a few occasions to exchange correspondence. But if there is any form of intimate contact that one could point at, it was the glowing praise from the young cadres who joined us and who had developed both politically and militarily under his guidance.

It is precisely because of his seminal contribution to the liberation struggle that Comrade JS was loved by those struggling for freedom.

Though the defenders of apartheid sought to obliterate his memory, the struggling people knew that he was an effective and skilful MK Chief of Operations; they knew that he was a loved and respected MK Chief of Staff; they knew that he planned and inspired many special operations of the people's army that shook the foundations of the apartheid establishment. They knew too that he was at the core of collectives that drafted many strategy and tactics documents of the movement.

The most central factor in his approach to struggle on any front was the understanding of the political situation, the balance of forces and thus the approaches necessary to advance that struggle. Thus he was able to appreciate changes in the objective conditions and initiate discussions on changes to the tactics to be applied.

He knew when to compromise. Yet he never compromised his

principles. He was a militant, yet a militant who knew how to plan, assess concrete situations and emerge with rational solutions to problems.

We shall forever remember Slovo as one of the embodiments of the alliance between the ANC and the SACP. Joe knew that the interests of the working class in our country were intimately bound up with those of the rest of the oppressed majority in pursuit of democracy and a better life. He knew too that for the working class to realise these interests it had to play an active role in the liberation struggle and the liberation movement.

Joe appreciated that the alliance between the ANC, the SACP and the progressive trade union movement was premised on concrete democratic and social tasks. He appreciated the need to strengthen this alliance, especially now when we are reconstructing and developing South Africa.

More than in theory, his own practical life demonstrated his profound understanding of the nature of the relationship between the ANC and the SACP: the leading role of the ANC; the principles of consultation, consensus and criticism within disciplined structures of the allies.

The advocates of racial superiority could not understand how Slovo could be part of the liberation struggle and operate under the leadership of the hapless inferiors they despised. But Joe took part in the struggle as an equal, as part of the people.

The defenders of national oppression could not understand why Slovo would seek to end the dominance of his racial 'kith and kin'. But Joe's kin was all humanity, especially the very poor.

The champions of privilege and concentration of wealth could not fathom why Slovo identified with the wretched of the earth. But Joe knew that these were the creators of wealth and they deserved their fare share.

It is the tragedy of South Africa that his humanity, pragmatism and industriousness were realised by many, particularly among the white community, only after close on to 40 years of an artificial silence imposed on him by constant banning. And it is a tragedy still that these qualities are extolled by some as if they were new.

Let it be said loud and clear today that the qualities Slovo demonstrated in abundance in the past few years were the same attributes that spurred him to struggle, the qualities that drove him to join the liberation movement and the qualities that he helped engender in these organisations.

We in the Government of National Unity know intimately what vacuum Minister Joe Slovo's departure has left in our midst. We shall miss not only his incisiveness, experience and verve. We are conscious that it is given to a few to so ably combine theory and practice, as Joe demonstrated in his portfolio.

But we know too that he has left us a legacy which will continue to guide our approach. And that is to mobilise all the role-players in any area of work for joint efforts to build a better life for all. The depth of it all is captured in the profound messages that we have received from the civics movement, mortgage-lending institutions, the construction industry, property owners' associations, the banks and many others.

Contained in all of them is the appreciation of Joe's central theme that all of us have a responsibility to ensure that the RDP succeeds. Those with resources have a crucial role to play. The government should discharge its responsibility. But, above all, ordinary people themselves should guide policy formulation and implementation. Among the last issues he was working on with a passion only typical of him was the launch of a campaign to ensure delivery of houses and services; and at the same time, to mobilise communities to pay their bonds, rents and service charges.

I wish on behalf of government to reiterate that the course Joe Slovo had charted will continue to guide us in fulfilling the housing programme. His firmness in dealing with obstacles to this pro- gramme will remain one of the central features of our work.

If we have taken the liberty to claim Comrade Joe as ours today, this merely underlines that there are those to whom he was more than just a revolutionary and a friend. There are times when our demands on him - indeed the demands of struggle – made it difficult for him to play fully the role of father and brother. There are times when his commitment and that of Ruth First – who was murdered in cold blood in 1982 – created a world apart, where full family life, as with most other revolutionaries, became an ephemeral dream.

We know, dear Helena [Dolny, Joe Slovo's wife], Shawn, Gillian, Robin [his daughters] and Rene [his sister] that you feel this pain more deeply. We cannot fully grasp the magnitude of your grief, particularly the bond that was cemented in the normal life that he could live only in the last few years, no longer a fugitive. Please be comforted by the fact that the nation shares your grief, and we shall always be at your side. Like you, our sorrow is made the more intense because we have lost not just one of our leaders; we have lost a veteran whose qualities are in many respects unequalled. He is irreplaceable.

The irony that Joe so succinctly captured, that life is after all a terminal illness, is the tragedy of the natural order that we can do nothing to change. But like him, we can so live that, when we depart, we shall have made life that much more bearable for others.

Comrade Joe, in our grief, we do remember that you enjoined us not to mourn but to celebrate the achievements you humbly helped realise. If you see tears welling in our eyes, it is because we cannot bear saying: Farewell dear comrade, dear brother, dear friend!

Oliver Tambo

Speech at the funeral of the national chairperson
of the ANC, Oliver Reginald Tambo, Johannesburg,
2 May 1993.

A great giant who strode the globe like a colossus has fallen. A mind whose thoughts have opened the doors to our liberty has ceased to function. A heart whose dreams gave hope to the despised has for ever lost its beat. The gentle voice whose measured words of reason shook the thrones of tyrants has been silenced.

Peoples of the world! Here lies before you the body of a man who is tied to me by an umbilical cord which cannot be broken.

We say he has departed. But can we allow him to depart while we live? Can we say Oliver Tambo is no more, while we walk this solid earth?

Oliver lived not because he could breathe. He lived not because blood flowed through his veins. Oliver lived not because he did all the things that all of us as ordinary men and women do. Oliver lived because he had surrendered his very being to the people. He lived because his very being embodied love, an idea, a hope, an aspiration, a vision.

While he lived, our minds would never quite formulate the thought that this man is other than what the naked eye could see. We could sense it, but never crystallise the thought that with us was one of the few people who inhabited our own human environment, who could be described as the jewel in our crown.

I say that Oliver Tambo has not died, because the ideals for which he sacrificed his life can never die. I say that Oliver Tambo has not died because the ideals of freedom, human dignity and a colour-blind respect for every individual cannot perish. I say he has not died because there are many of us who became part of his soul and there-fore willingly entered into a conspiracy with him, for the victory of his cause. While the ANC lives, Oliver Tambo cannot die! While Umkhonto we Sizwe exists, Oliver Tambo cannot die!

Oliver Tambo cannot die while his allies in the South African Communist Party and the Congress of South African Trade Unions remain loyal to the common purpose. OR cannot cease to be, while the millions of our people gather themselves into the democratic organisations that make up our own rainbow coalition.

OR cannot be consigned to the past, while those who are with us today from the rest of the world remain as they have been, opponents of the apartheid crime against humanity, proponents of the common vision of justice and peace, defenders of the right of the child, the man, the woman and the beast of the forest to live, to be free and to prosper.

We all know many who have killed in defence of oppression. But we also know that some of these have themselves been victims of oppression.

We know that black and white, across the globe – the Pole, the Greek, the Ethiopian, the Cuban, the Brazilian and the Eritrean, people of all nationalities – are all united in their opposition to apartheid and injustice. While these exist, Oliver Tambo cannot perish. Let he or she who dares, stand up and tell us that it will happen that, while humanity survives, it will come to pass that OR Tambo will cease to be.

All tyrants, whatever their colour and their shape and their garments, come today and are gone tomorrow. The people, the victims of their tyranny, live on. All tyrannical systems, whatever the name they give themselves – Nazism, colonialism, apartheid, racism are some of their names – all, without exception, come today and tomorrow are no more than a bad memory. The opponents of tyranny – the South African, Oliver Tambo; the South African, Chris Hani; the South African, Albert Luthuli; the Indian, Indira Gandhi; the Indian, Rajiv Gandhi; the Grenadian, Maurice Bishop; the Zimbabweans, Herbert Chitepo, Jason Moyo and Josiah Tongogara; the Mozambican, Samora Machel; the Swede, Olof Palme; the Americans, Martin Luther King Jr, John F Kennedy and Malcolm X; the Angolan, Agostinho Neto; the Guinean, Amilcar Cabral, the Nigerian, Murtala Mohammed; the Chilean, Salvador Allende; the Ghanaian, Kwame Nkrumah; the Egyptian, Gamal Abdel Nasser; the Motswana, Seretse Khama; the Swazi, King Sobhuza II; the woman, the man, the son, the daughter, the unknown soldier, the nameless heroes and heroines for whom no songs of praise are sung; all of them continue, still, to speak to us because they live.

Dear brother: you set yourself a task which only the brave would dare. Somewhere in the mystery of your essence, you heard the call that you must devote your life to the creation of a new South African nation. And having heard that call, you did not hesitate to act.

It may be that all of us – your dear wife, Adelaide, your children, those of us who are proud to count ourselves among your friends, your closest comrades – it may be that all of us will never be able to discover what it was in your essence which convinced you that you, and us, could, by our conscious and deliberate actions, so heal our fractured society that out of the terrible heritage, there could be born a nation.

All humanity knows what you had to do to create the conditions for all of us to reach this glorious end.

There are many who did not understand that to heal we had to lance the boil. There are many who still do not understand that the obedient silence of the enslaved is not the reward of peace which is our due. There are some who cannot comprehend that the right to rebellion against tyranny is the very guarantee of the permanence of freedom.

We demand answers from all those who have set themselves up as your critics, but still dare to call themselves democrats.

We want to know – if life itself was threatened, as apartheid threatened the very existence of those who are black, was it not imperative that everything be done to end apartheid – and if necessary by force of arms?

We want to know – if a crime against humanity was being perpetrated, as did the apartheid system, was it not necessary to ensure that the criminals were isolated and quarantined, and if necessary by the imposition of sanctions?

We want to know – if a social system was established whose central pillars were racial oppression and exploitation, such as the apartheid system was, would it not be correct that such a system be rendered unworkable and such a society ungovernable?

We want to know – when powerful, arrogant and brutal men deliberately close their ears to reason, and reply to the petitions of the dispossessed with the thunder of the guns, the crack of the whip and the rattle of the jail keys, is it not right to bring down the walls of Jericho?

Dear brother, dear friend, dear comrade: you did all this and continued to maintain tolerance for your detractors and a healthy scorn for your enemies.

Today, we stand watching the dawn of a new day. We can see that we have it in our power to remake South Africa into what you wanted it to be – free, just, prosperous, at peace with itself and with the world.

Let all who value peace say together – long live Oliver Tambo!

Let all who love freedom say together – long live Oliver Tambo!

Let all who uphold the dignity of all human beings say together – long live Oliver Tambo!

Let all who stand for friendship among the peoples say together – long live Oliver Tambo!

Let all of us who live say that while we live, the ideals for which Oliver Tambo lived, sacrificed and died will not die!

Let all of us who live, say that while we live, Oliver Tambo will not die!

May he, for his part, rest in peace. Go well, my brother, and farewell, dear friend. As you instructed, we will bring peace to our tormented land. As you directed, we will bring freedom to the oppressed and liberation to the oppressor. As you strived, we will restore the dignity of the dehumanised. As you commanded, we will defend the option of a peaceful resolution of our problems. As you prayed, we will respond to the cries of the wretched of the earth. As you loved them, we will, always, stretch out a hand of endearment to those who are your flesh and blood.

In all this, we will not fail you.

Desmond Tutu

Speech at a thanksgiving service for Archbishop Desmond Tutu,
Cape Town, 23 June 1999.

It is a true privilege and honour for me to share in this thanksgiving service for the Archbishop of Cape Town and the Primate of the Church of the Province of Southern Africa, who retires in one week's time, just ahead of his 65th birthday. I suspect that he is doing so just to set the record by retiring before I do!

I know that I speak for all of you, when I say that Archbishop Desmond Tutu has been a blessing and inspiration to countless people, here and abroad, through his ministry; his acts of compassion; his prophetic witness; and his political engagement. He has a distinguished record as a leader of his church and the ecumenical movement, and as a fearless fighter against the evil and inhuman system of apartheid. He is renowned for selfless commitment to the poor, the oppressed and downtrodden. With his colleagues he remained an effective voice of the people of South Africa when so many of their leaders were imprisoned, exiled, banned and restricted.

Desmond Tutu is esteemed the world over for his commitment to justice and peace everywhere. He is forthright in condemning corruption. As President of the All Africa Conference of Churches he missed no opportunity to speak out against human rights violations and oppressive regimes in our continent and elsewhere. The Nobel Peace Prize measures his extensive international recognition.

His most characteristic quality is his readiness to take unpopular positions without fear. Thus it was that he campaigned for sanctions against apartheid at a time when churches in South Africa were still hesitating. He speaks his mind on matters of public morality. As a result he annoyed many of the leaders of the apartheid system. Nor has he spared those that followed them – he has from time to time annoyed many of us who belong to the new order. But such independence of

493

mind – however wrong and unstrategic it may at times be – is vital to a thriving democracy.

I would therefore like to take this opportunity to thank the Archbishop for his valuable contribution to the struggle for freedom and justice. The way you accompanied our people on the long walk to freedom helped foster respect for life and for human rights, irrespective of colour, religion, gender or age.

Our new Constitution embodies and secures our collective vision of a just, nonracial, nonsexist, democratic society. Making a reality of that vision is the supreme challenge that faces us all. As long as many of our people still live in utter poverty; as long as children still live under plastic covers; as long as many of our people are still without jobs; no South African should rest and wallow in the joy of freedom.

The touchstone of our success in transforming South African society will be the extent to which we correct the imbalances and inequalities created by apartheid. The seriousness of our intent is inscribed in our macroeconomic strategy for growth, employment and redistribution. It is a framework within which all sectors of our society can join hands and, putting long-term interests above short-term considerations, achieve our goals for transformation, for reconstruction and development.

In this great partnership the religious community has a special and important role. As the churches in South Africa and abroad accompanied us in the struggle for justice and peace, so should they now accompany us in building a just and equitable society.

This is not a call for the religious community to accompany government uncritically. Uncritical support would endanger our infant democracy. On the other hand, criticism without visible action to help alleviate poverty and suffering can only serve to discredit the message of the Church. Rather, the way forward is in what some theologians have called 'critical solidarity' with government in the reconstruction and development of the country.

The track record of the religious communities, both before and after the achievement of democracy, makes us confident that in them we do indeed have strategic partners in the project of empowering our people to use their freedom to work together for a better life. In the building of our new nation, reconstruction goes hand in hand with reconciliation. We look to the Church, with its message of justice, peace, forgiveness and healing, to play a key role in helping our people, of every colour, to move from the divisions of the past to a future that is united in a commitment to correct wrongs and restore a just order.

Archbishop Tutu, with his celebration of our rainbow nation and his powerfully healing guidance of the Truth and Reconciliation Commission, is an inspiration to us all in this most crucial task of reconciling our nation. His joy in our diversity and his spirit of forgiveness are as much part of his immeasurable contribution to our nation as his passion for justice and his solidarity with the poor.

In conclusion, may I say again to the Archbishop: We are thankful for all that you have done. You were one of those who blazed the trail of the new patriotism that is abroad in our land. We wish you peace and joy in your retirement.

12
PEACE

PROMOTING PEACE AND PRACTISING DIPLOMACY

JAMES A JOSEPH

It is through the careful reading of Nelson Mandela's own words that those who meet him in these pages will come to understand why even in retirement he remains so widely revered and respected around the world. The portrait that emerges from his speeches in this section is that of: (1) A statesman who defied conventional wisdom about the relationship between power, diplomacy and the state; (2) A diplomat who in a world of technocrats, bureaucrats and other intermediaries revelled in personal diplomacy while maintaining great respect for multilateral institutions; (3) An optimist whose capacity to win over his adversaries led him to believe that international conflicts, even those of long standing, could be resolved through 'brains rather than blood'; (4) An international icon who was admired and honoured by heads of state, royal families and social elites around the world, but whose commitment to 'the poorest of the poor' never wavered; (5) An African with strong attachments to the continent and its people; and (6) A transforming leader who, like Gandhi and King, had an uncanny instinct for moving and persuading people, changing attitudes and appealing to the best in human nature.

The question future generations may well ask is, how did an elderly African leader on the southern tip of the African continent become so adept at using what is now called soft power – public diplomacy, moral messages, exemplary behaviour and respect for differences – at a time when global influence was measured largely by military might and economic muscle? Arthur Schlesinger, Jr once wrote: 'Every great power has its warrior caste.' Mandela emerged from his long incarceration at a time when the projection of state power beyond its borders had become the domain largely of the warrior caste. Yet, his standing at home and his influence abroad went far beyond the size of the military or the Gross Domestic Product of South Africa.

According to Joseph Nye of the Kennedy School of Government at

Harvard, hard power is the ability to get others to do what we want while soft power is the ability to get others to want the same thing we do. The former is based on coercion and the latter is based on attraction.

Nelson Mandela is the prototype of soft power. His influence comes from the attractiveness of his ideals, the elegance of his humanity and the power of his personal story. He reminds us that despite the prevailing dominance of hard power, international influence in the future may well depend on a moral ecology that cannot be found in hard power alone. To be sure, hard power can inflict or even prevent significant pain, but it can rarely ensure long-term compliance or goodwill.

Principled diplomacy for Mandela was not a theory. It was a way of being. In getting to know him, one is struck by the fact that his extraordinary capacity to do the right thing has more to do with his natural disposition than it has to do with public relations techniques or good 'spin doctors'. I once congratulated his communications assistant on the way in which the staff always seemed to put Mr Mandela in the right place at the right time with the right message. He looked at me in amazement and said: 'It is not us; it is Madiba himself.'

Nelson Mandela promoted peaceful co-existence in international affairs with the same moral audacity and political tenacity with which he promoted reconciliation in domestic affairs. He had no permanent enemies, only friends and those with the potential for becoming friends. He warned against the politics of vengeance and the moral pitfalls of selective national memory that focuses more on the barriers that once limited relationships rather than the potential for beginning anew.

The first time I was asked to meet with him to register my government's concern about a proposed visit to South Africa by the leader of one of the so-called pariah states, I delivered a carefully prepared *démarche*, as is the practice in such matters. He listened carefully and said: 'Tell your government that I negotiated with the representatives of the apartheid state without compromising any of my values and there is no danger of my compromising them now.' His commitment to universality in foreign affairs, and loyalty to the friends who had supported his cause when Western leaders considered the African National Congress (ANC) a terrorist organisation, often caused alarm in Washington and London, but he remained true to his word and true to his basic values.

Scholars in the realist tradition of international politics have usually raised a sceptical eye at the notion of placing ethical boundaries around diplomacy. They are the ones most likely to regard the idea of principled diplomacy as a conceptual contradiction that has no place in the *realpolitik* of the modern world. In asking not simply what is in the national interest but what is right, Nelson Mandela defied conventional wisdom, demonstrating that ethics in diplomacy is not only desirable, but also altogether feasible.

Nelson Mandela's leadership style was honed in the political culture of the African National Congress, with its emphasis on co-operative and consultative leadership, so it should be no surprise to learn from his speeches that in the international arena he sought, first, and wherever feasible, to work through multilateral organisations like the United Nations, the Non-Aligned Movement, the Organisation of African Unity and the Southern African Development Community. While he became for a time the most important spokesperson for the developing world, he sought also to be a bridge builder between rich and poor nations.

In the international arena, he was an especially important voice in efforts to maintain the nuclear non-proliferation edifice. He had special credibility in this regard because one of his first acts as President of South Africa was to dismantle South Africa's nuclear capacity. He was also a strong supporter of a ban on chemical and biological weapons, the banning of small weapons and de-mining.

It was at the regional level, especially his efforts to work through the Southern African Development Community, that we first saw Nelson Mandela's commitment to multilateralism. But it was also at the regional level that we saw the difficulty of transforming leadership from an elected head of state when he or she moves outside national boundaries. Nelson Mandela found out very early that South Africa's dominance in the region, and on the continent, caused it to face the same problem with its African neighbours that the US faces in the world. There is a natural suspicion of the intentions of the dominant power in any relationship, even when those intentions seek to serve a larger public good. The dilemma for Nelson Mandela was that if he spoke out, he ran the risk of being accused of throwing his weight around; but if he did not, he ran the risk of being accused of inaction and indifference.

This fear of big brother dominance actually robbed the region of the full potential of his leadership, but he increasingly found others, both on the continent and in other parts of the world, looking to him to help solve regional conflicts, ranging from his efforts to promote a non-violent end to the Mobutu regime in the Congo to his work for democratic evolution in Nigeria and his successful efforts to persuade Gadaffi to turn over the Libyans accused in the Lockerbie bombing. He was a champion of the notion of an African Renaissance and a new Africa, but most importantly he was a role model for a new generation of leaders who have been building new democracies and opening markets while totally ignored by a Western press obsessed with failed states, coups and inefficient governance.

Much is made of the universality of Nelson Mandela's embrace, but he was an African who took pride in his African identity as well. In his 1994 speech in Tunis, he spoke of the responsibility to restore to the African continent its dignity. He said the great giants of Africa, such as Gamal Abdel Nasser of Egypt, Kwame Nkrumah of Ghana, Patrice Lumumba of Zaire, Agostinho Neto of Angola, Samora Machel of Mozambique, WEB Du Bois and Martin Luther King of America, Marcus Garvey of Jamaica, Albert Luthuli and Oliver Tambo of South Africa, had given him reasons for hope. He also celebrated African contributions to the condition of civilisation, 'like the pyramids of Egypt, the sculptures of the ancient kingdoms of Ghana, Mali and Benin, like the temples of Ethiopia, the Zimbabwe ruins and the rock paintings of the Namib deserts'.

He argued for African solutions to African problems and was a vigorous cheerleader for President Clinton's statement to the South African Parliament that the developed world had been asking the wrong question. 'We have been asking what can we do for Africa, what can we do about Africa,' President Clinton said. 'We must now ask what can we do with Africa.' This was a clear signal that the United States had heard and understood Nelson Mandela's plea for a partnership between rich and poor nations rather than benevolent big brother dominance.

For Nelson Mandela, globalisation had its limits, but his reservations were not about the reality of economic interdependence, but about the way the game seemed to be rigged to favour the most competitive nations. As the leader of the non-aligned nations, he felt it important to point out that even when governments wanted to do the right thing, to open markets and expand the architecture of democracy, Aids, foreign debt and other impediments forced on them by globalisation made it hard to reach the 'lift-off' stage that all parties desired.

Without doubt, it is the commitment to reconciliation that stands at the core of the Mandela legacy. It influenced both his efforts to build a new democracy at home and his contribution to the resolution of conflicts in the larger world. When others doubted whether it was still possible for old enemies to beat their swords into ploughshares, he showed us how. He was a healer who understood that diversity need not divide. He was an astute observer of the human condition who believed with all his being that we diminish the preciousness and sacredness of life when we denigrate, disrespect or oppress people based on the colour of their skin or their ethnicity or culture. He never allowed himself to be seduced by the trappings of power because, like Robert Greenleaf's notion of the servant leader, his first choice was the choice to serve. Leadership is what followed.

While it is correct to emphasise Mandela's commitment to reconciliation, it would be a mistake to overlook how his notion of reconciliation also included justice. When most people think of justice, they tend to think of either retributive or distributive aspects. Mandela believed, however, that there is another understanding of justice – a restorative justice that is concerned with the restoration of broken relationships. Traditional African jurisprudence contends that the perpetrator must be given an opportunity to be reintegrated into the community he has injured by his offence. Thus, restorative justice is being served when efforts are made to work for healing, harmony, forgiveness and reconciliation.

Members of royal families, heads of state, legislative leaders, and power brokers from every corner of the globe made their way to South Africa during Nelson Mandela's presidency in hopes of getting a photo opportunity for their family albums, political campaigns, company brochures or the national press; but Nelson Mandela is probably best remembered as the champion of the underdog, the people's president who brought the races together in a country where most of the world had expected a bloodbath rather than a democracy.

The adulation he received from the world's elite was in stark contrast to Margaret Thatcher's assertion in the late eighties that Nelson Mandela was a terrorist and anyone who thought the African National Congress would someday form the government of South Africa was living in a 'cloud-cuckoo land'. I am not fully sure what this last phrase means, but it does not sound like a compliment.

Mandela's authorised biographer wrote later about Mandela's first state visit to England, when the British monarchy was so under siege that even the royals were hoping to benefit from the mystique of their regal visitor. Lady Thatcher was up front basking in Mandela's glow and beaming about the magnanimous qualities of this great leader, but it was the Queen who seemed most at home and at ease in his company. One observer commented that she had a lot in common with Mandela because they had both spent a lot of time in prison.

It is not easy for an objective observer to get beyond the icon. The myth is usually so powerful that it blurs the reality, but in this case I found the reality to be even more appealing than the myth. Consider, for example, what he had to say during the state visit to Britain when he was surrounded by hundreds of years of pomp and circumstance: 'The history of liberation heroes shows that when they come into office they interact with powerful groups; they can easily forget that they have been put in power by the poorest of the poor. They often lose their common touch, and turn against their own people.' Mandela never lost the common touch, but what about Nelson Mandela the political animal? It has been said that as a politician he made the profession seem noble. While some are inclined to portray him as almost a saint he has been known to say, 'I am no angel'. And when one considers that he survived in the political jungle for almost 50 years, it would be naïve to assume that he did not bring to his international peace-making efforts the same pragmatism he demonstrated in domestic affairs.

Anthony Sampson makes the claim that as a politician he was both pre-modern and post-modern. He was pre-modern in that he was very much a product of the older tribal tradition in which he had been brought up, of a chief accountable to his people, settling their disputes with careful courtesy, making them all feel important and representing them with a dignity and bearing that was as regal as anything we have seen in European royalty.

He was post-modern in that he had a brilliant sense of political texture and timing, a master of imagery who knew instinctively how to work the room or flatter an adversary. He was the master of the photo-op, the sound bite, the intimate handshake, the seductive smile and the disarming charm. The difference from so many other politicians is that this all comes naturally. It was not Nelson Mandela playing a role. It was simply Nelson Mandela being himself.

We tend to romanticise transforming leadership as though it is distinct from what James Macgregor Burns called transactional leadership, but Nelson Mandela represented the best of both. He could have satisfied his conscience and accomplished nothing for his constituents if he had not been willing to get his hands dirty, to negotiate, make deals and engage occasionally in compromise in order to achieve a larger public good. Nelson Mandela may not be a saint, and, as he personally reminds us, certainly no angel, but what makes him very special is that he always seems to understand the imperfections of our humanity as well as its potential. President Clinton had it right when he commented at a White House reception: 'Every time Nelson Mandela walked into a room we all felt a little bigger, we all wanted to stand up. We all wanted to cheer because on our best day we all wanted to be like him.'

Mandela's role as a transforming leader in international affairs extended to his personal relationship and standing with the leaders of the rich nations as well. But while he shared many of their public values and understood the importance of the developed nations to South Africa's developing economy, he did not hesitate to take an opposing stand on issues where he felt morally bound to speak out. He articulated a foreign policy of universality, espousing sympathetic positions to states regarded by the US and Britain, for example, as pariahs. His support for Cuba in the United Nations and elsewhere, his meetings with Gadaffi and support for the OAU resolution opposing United Nations Security Council Lockerbie sanctions on Libya all reflected his independence, while posing problems requiring deft handling within private diplomatic channels. He did not hesitate to voice his unease with the idea of an African Crisis Response Force nor his concerns about conditionalities in the Africa Growth and Economic Opportunity Act as it was making its way through the United States Congress. In short, where other heads of state might have asked first what is in our national self-interest, he was more likely to ask what is right.

Nelson Mandela's transforming role in international affairs was grounded in several ethical norms and personal traits:

- His belief in, and his ability to appeal to, people's better nature. He believes very strongly in the potential of individuals and even nation states to change. This is not the naivety of an idle dreamer, but the convictions of a man who has been involved in causing major change, both publicly and behind the scenes.
- His ability to connect with other people, even his adversaries. Scott Peck, the eminent psychiatrist, once wrote that we build community out of crisis and we build community by accident, but we do not know how to build community by design. That may be true, but there is a lot we can learn from Nelson Mandela in this regard.
- His lack of bitterness after 27 years of imprisonment. People throughout the world admired him, and saw him as evidence of the potential of the human spirit. They marvelled at his ability to forgive and were often inspired to do the same.
- His commitment to changing the practice of the adversary while maintaining respect for his or her humanity. This is what Martin Luther King called loving the enemy.

- His commitment to reconciliation as a public value and a public process. This may be his most important contribution to international affairs, and not surprisingly, it may be the most important reason for comparing him to Burns's 'transforming leader'.

In international affairs, as in domestic leadership, Nelson Mandela remains an influential statesman even when he no longer has formal authority, because his appeal has always been based on something deeper and more enduring than political position. In his last speech to the United Nations in September 1998 he spoke of quiet retirement where he would 'sit in Qunu and grow as ancient as the hills', but while the pace of the long walk may have been slowed he continues to defy the aging process he once described as 'the changing season'.

Nobel Peace Prize

Acceptance speech at the Nobel Peace Prize
Award Ceremony, Oslo, Norway,
10 December 1993.

I am indeed truly humbled to be standing here today to receive this year's Nobel Peace Prize.

I extend my heartfelt thanks to the Norwegian Nobel Committee for elevating us to the status of a Nobel Peace Prize winner.

I would also like to take this opportunity to congratulate my compatriot and fellow laureate, State President FW de Klerk, on his receipt of this high honour.

Together, we join two distinguished South Africans, the late Chief Albert Luthuli and His Grace Archbishop Desmond Tutu, to whose seminal contributions to the peaceful struggle against the evil system of apartheid you paid well-deserved tribute by awarding them the Nobel Peace Prize.

It will not be presumptuous of us if we also add, among our predecessors, the name of another outstanding Nobel Peace Prize winner, the late African-American statesman and internationalist, the Rev Martin Luther King, Jr. He, too, grappled with and died in the effort to make a contribution to the just solution of the same great issues of the day which we have had to face as South Africans.

We speak here of the challenge of the dichotomies of war and peace, violence and non-violence, racism and human dignity, oppression and repression and liberty and human rights, poverty and freedom from want.

We stand here today as nothing more than a representative of the millions of our people who dared to rise up against a social system whose very essence is war, violence, racism, oppression, repression and the impoverishment of an entire people. I am also here today as a representative of the millions of people across the globe, the anti-apartheid movement, the governments and organisations that joined with us, not to fight against South Africa as a country or any of its peoples, but to oppose an inhuman system and sue for a speedy end to the apartheid crime against humanity.

These countless human beings, both inside and outside our country, had the nobility of spirit to stand in the path of tyranny and injustice, without seeking selfish gain. They recognised that an injury to one is an injury to all and therefore acted together in defence of justice and a common human decency.

Because of their courage and persistence for many years, we can, today, even set the date when all humanity will join together to celebrate one of the outstanding human victories of our century. When that moment comes, we shall, together, rejoice in a common victory over racism, apartheid and white minority rule.

That triumph will finally bring to a close a history of five hundred years of African colonisation that began with the establishment of the Portuguese empire. Thus, it will mark a great step forward in history and also serve as a common pledge of the peoples of the world to fight racism wherever it occurs and whatever guise it assumes.

At the southern tip of the continent of Africa, a rich reward is in the making, an invaluable gift is in the preparation, for those who suffered in the name of all humanity when they sacrificed everything – for liberty, peace, human dignity and human fulfilment.

This reward will not be measured in money. Nor can it be reckoned in the collective price of the rare metals and precious stones that rest in the bowels of the African soil we tread in the footsteps of our ancestors. It will and must be measured by the happiness and welfare of the children, at once the most vulnerable citizens in any society and the greatest of our treasures.

The children must, at last, play in the open veld, no longer tortured by the pangs of hunger or ravaged by disease or threatened with the scourge of ignorance, molestation and abuse, and no longer required to engage in deeds whose gravity exceeds the demands of their tender years.

In front of this distinguished audience, we commit the new South Africa to the relentless pursuit of the purposes defined in the World Declaration on the Survival, Protection and Development of Children.

The reward of which we have spoken will and must also be measured by the happiness and welfare of the mothers and fathers of these children, who must walk the earth without fear of being robbed, killed for political or material profit, or spat upon because they are beggars. They too must be relieved of the heavy burden of despair which they carry in their hearts, born of hunger, homelessness and unemployment.

The value of that gift to all who have suffered will and must be measured by the happiness and welfare of all the people of our country, who will have torn down the inhuman walls that divide them.

These great masses will have turned their backs on the grave insult to human dignity which described some as masters and others as servants, and transformed each into a predator whose survival depended on the destruction of the other.

The value of our shared reward will and must be measured by the joyful peace which will triumph, because the common humanity that bonds both black and white into one human race, will have said to each one of us that we shall all live like the children of paradise.

Thus shall we live, because we will have created a society which recognises that all people are born equal, with each entitled in equal measure to life, liberty, prosperity, human rights and good governance. Such a society should never allow again that there should be prisoners of conscience nor that any person's human rights should be violated. Neither should it ever happen that once more the avenues to peaceful change are blocked by usurpers who seek to take power away from the people, in pursuit of their own, ignoble purposes.

In relation to these matters, we appeal to those who govern Burma that they release our fellow Nobel Peace Prize laureate, Aung San Suu Kyi, and engage her and those she represents in serious dialogue, for the benefit of all the people of Burma. We pray that those who have the power to do so will, without further delay, permit that she uses her talents and energies for the greater good of the people of her country and humanity as a whole.

Far from the rough and tumble of the politics of our own country, I would like to take this opportunity to join the Norwegian Nobel Committee and pay tribute to my joint laureate, Mr FW de Klerk. He had the courage to admit that a terrible wrong had been done to our country and people through the imposition of the system of apartheid. He had the foresight to understand and accept that all the people of South Africa must, through negotiations and as equal participants in the process, together determine what they want to make of their future.

But there are still some within our country who wrongly believe they can make a contribution to the cause of justice and peace by clinging to the shibboleths that have been proved to spell nothing but disaster. It remains our hope that these, too, will be blessed with sufficient reason to realise that history will not be denied and that the new society cannot be created by reproducing the repugnant past, however refined or enticingly repackaged.

We live with the hope that as she battles to remake herself, South Africa will be like a microcosm of the new world that is striving to be born. This must be a world of democracy and respect for human rights, a world freed from the horrors of poverty, hunger, deprivation and ignorance, relieved of the threat and the scourge of civil wars and external aggression and unburdened of the great tragedy of millions forced to become refugees.

The processes in which South Africa and Southern Africa as a whole are engaged, beckon and urge us all that we take this tide at the flood and make of this region a living example of what all people of conscience would like the world to be.

We do not believe that this Nobel Peace Prize is intended as a commendation for matters that have happened and passed. We hear the voices which say that it is an appeal from all those, throughout the universe, who sought an end to the system of apartheid.

We understand their call, that we devote what remains of our lives to the use of our country's unique and painful experience to demonstrate, in practice, that the normal condition for human existence is democracy, justice, peace, nonracism, nonsexism, prosperity for everybody, a healthy environment and equality and solidarity among the peoples.

Moved by that appeal and inspired by the eminence you have thrust upon us, we undertake that we too will do what we can to contribute to the renewal of our world so that none should, in future, be described as the wretched of the earth. Let it never be said by future generations that indifference, cynicism or selfishness made us fail to live up to the ideals of humanism which the Nobel Peace Prize encapsulates.

Let the strivings of us all prove Martin Luther King, Jr to have been correct when he said that humanity can no longer be tragically bound to the starless midnight of racism and war. Let the efforts of us all prove that he was not a mere dreamer when he spoke of the beauty of genuine brotherhood and peace being more precious than diamonds or silver or gold.

Let a new age dawn!

United Nations 1993

Statement at the United Nations, New York,
24 September 1993.

We are most grateful to the Special Committee against Apartheid and its distinguished Chairman, His Excellency Professor Ibrahim Gambari, as well as the United Nations as a whole, for enabling us to address this gathering today. We have, together, walked a very long road. We have travelled together to reach a common destination.

The common destination towards which we have been advancing defines the very reason for the existence of this world organisation. The goal we have sought to reach is the consummation of the yearning of all humankind for human dignity and human fulfilment. For that reason, we have been outraged and enraged that there could be imposed on any people the criminal system of apartheid.

Each and every one of us have felt our humanity denied by the mere existence of this system. Each and every one of us have felt brandished as sub-human by the fact that some could treat others as though they were no more than disposable garbage. In the end, there was nobody of conscience who could stand by and do nothing in the search for an end to the apartheid crime against humanity.

We are here today to convey to you, who are the representatives of the peoples of the world, the profound gratitude of the people of South Africa for your engagement, over the decades, in the common struggle to end the system of apartheid. We are deeply moved by the fact that almost from its birth, this organisation has kept on its agenda the vital question of the liquidation of the system of apartheid and white minority rule in our country.

Throughout the many years of struggle, we, as South Africans, have been greatly inspired and strengthened as you took action both severally and collectively, to escalate your offensive against apartheid rule, as the white minority regime itself took new steps in its own offensive further to entrench its illegitimate rule and draw tribute from those it had enslaved. In particular, we are most grateful for the measures that the United Nations, the OAU, the Commonwealth, the Non-Aligned Movement, the European Community and other intergovernmental organisations took to isolate apartheid South Africa. We are deeply appreciative of similar initiatives that individual countries, non-governmental organisations, local communities and even single individuals took, as part of their contribution to the common effort to deny the apartheid system all international sustenance.

This global struggle, perhaps without precedent in the inestimable number of people it united around one common issue, has helped decisively to bring us to where we are today. Finally, the apartheid regime was forced to concede that the system of white minority rule could no longer be sustained. It was forced to accept that it had to enter into negotiations with the genuine representatives of our people to arrive at a solution which, as agreed at the first sitting of the Convention for a Democratic South Africa, Codesa, would transform South Africa into a united, democratic, nonracial and nonsexist country. This and other agreements have now been translated into a specific programme that will enable our country to take a leap forward from its dark, painful and turbulent past to a glorious future, which our people will strive with all their strength to make a future of democracy, peace, stability and prosperity.

The countdown to democracy in South Africa has begun. The date for the demise of the white minority regime has been determined, agreed and set. Seven months from now, on 27 April 1994, all the people of South Africa, without discrimination on grounds of gender, race, colour or belief, will join in the historic act of electing a government of their choice. The legislation has also been passed to create the institutions of state, the statutory organs that will ensure that these elections are held and that they are free and fair.

As a consequence of the creation of these statutory instruments, we have arrived at the point where our country will no longer be governed exclusively by a white minority regime. The Transitional Executive Council, provided for in this legislation, will mark the first-ever participation by the majority of our people at governmental level in the process of determining the destiny of our country. It will be the historic precursor to the Interim Government of National Unity which will be formed after the democratic elections

512

of 27 April. The other structures now provided for in law, the Independent Electoral Commission, the Independent Media Commission and the Independent Broadcasting Authority, will themselves play their specified roles in ensuring a process of transition and a result which our people as a whole will accept as having been legitimate and therefore acceptable.

We must however warn that we are not yet out of the woods. Negotiations are continuing to agree on the Interim Constitution, according to which the country will be governed as the elected National Assembly works on the final Constitution. There will therefore be continuing need that this organisation and the world movement for a democratic South Africa as a whole sustain their focus on the transitional processes, so that everybody concerned in our country is left in no doubt about the continuing determination of the international community to help see us through to democracy.

The reality is that there are various forces within South Africa which do not accept the inevitability of the common outcome which all humanity seeks. Within our country, these forces, which seek to deny us liberty by resort to brute force, and which have already murdered and maimed people in their tens of thousands, represent a minority of the people. They derive their strength not from the people but from the fear, insecurity and destabilisation which they seek to impose through a campaign of terrorism conducted by unknown killers whose hallmark is brutality and total disregard for the value of human life.

There are other forces, which because of narrow, sectarian interests, are also opposed to genuine change. These are engaged in other actions which seek to create obstacles on the way to a smooth transition to democracy. We believe that it is critically important that these forces too should understand that the international community has the will and determination to act in concert with the majority of the people of our country to ensure that the democratic change which is long overdue is not delayed.

The apartheid system has left a swathe of disaster in its trail. We have an economy that is tottering on the brink of an even deeper depression than the one we are experiencing now. What this means practically is millions of people who have no food, no jobs and no houses. The very fabric of society is threatened by a process of disintegration, characterised by high and increasing rates of violent crime, the growth in the numbers of people so brutalised that they will kill for a pittance, and the collapse of all social norms. In addition, the absence of a legitimate state authority, enjoying the support of the majority of the people, immensely exacerbates this general crisis, emphasising the critical importance of speedy movement forward to democratic change. In sum, acting together, we must, at all costs, resist and rebuff any tendency of a slide towards another Somalia or a Bosnia, a development which would have disastrous repercussions extending far beyond the borders of South Africa.

What we have just said is not intended to alarm this august gathering. Rather, it is meant to say – now is the time to take new steps to move us forward to the common victory we have all fought for! We believe the moment has come when the United Nations Organisation and the international community as a whole should take stock of the decisive advances that have been made to create the setting for the victory of the cause of democracy in our country. We further believe that the moment has come when this same community should lay the basis for halting the slide to a socio-economic disaster in South Africa, as one of the imperatives in ensuring the very success of the democratic transformation itself.

In response to the historic advances towards democracy that have been achieved; further to give added impetus to this process; to strengthen the forces of democratic change and to help create the necessary conditions for stability and social progress, we believe the time has come when the international community should lift all economic sanctions against South Africa. We therefore extend an earnest appeal to you, the governments and peoples you represent, to take all necessary measures to end the economic sanctions you imposed and which have brought us to the point where the transition to democracy has now been enshrined in the law of our country.

We further urge that this historic step, marking a turning point in the history of the relations between South Africa and the rest of the world, should not be viewed as an act of abstention but one of engagement. Let us all treat this new reality as an opportunity and a challenge to engage with the South African situation in a way that will advance the democratic cause and create the best possible social and economic conditions for the victory of that cause.

The Special Committee against Apartheid has itself led the process of preparing the United Nations and its specialised agencies for the new reality that is the fruit of our common struggle. We trust that the UN family will therefore not delay in engaging the people of South

Africa in a new way. We trust also that the governments across the globe that have been so central in the effort to defeat the system of apartheid will do what they can to help us ensure the upliftment of our people.

A similar appeal extends to the millions of people organised in the broad non-governmental anti-apartheid movement themselves to remain involved in the continuing struggle for a democratic South Africa and to add to their programmes the extension of all-round development assistance from people to people.

We hope that both the South African and the international investor communities will also take this opportunity themselves to help regenerate the South African economy, to their mutual benefit.

As you know, our people have not yet elected a democratic government. It is therefore important that the white minority government which remains in place in our country should not be granted recognition and treated as though it were representative of all the people of South Africa. The Transitional Executive Council provides the appropriate mechanism for such interaction as should take place between ourselves and the international community in the period between now and the formation of the new government.

We should here mention that within the ambit of the diplomatic sanctions which many countries imposed, we also believe that such countries may now establish a diplomatic presence in South Africa to enhance their capacity to assist the people of our country to realise the common objectives.

This organisation also imposed special sanctions relating to arms, nuclear matters and oil. In this regard, we would like to urge that the mandatory sanctions be maintained until the new government has been formed. We would leave the issue of the oil embargo to the discretion of the committee of the General Assembly responsible for the enforcement of this particular sanction.

We would further like to request that the Security Council should begin consideration of the very important issue of what this organisation should do to assist in the process of organising for and ensuring that the forthcoming elections are indeed free and fair. This, naturally, should be accompanied by a review of the important contribution that has been made by the UN Observer Mission to South Africa, which is helping us to address the issue of political violence, to ensure that this contribution addresses adequately this continuing problem.

We cannot close without extending our congratulations to the PLO and the government of Israel for the important step forward they have taken which, hopefully, will lead to a just and lasting settlement of the Middle East question. To them and to the peoples and governments of the region as a whole, we extend the good wishes of all the people of our country and the assurance of our support for their noble effort to establish justice and peace.

We continue to hope that progress will be made towards the just resolution of the outstanding issue of Western Sahara.

Angola continues to bleed. We urge this organisation and especially the Security Council to leave no stone unturned to ensure that the killing ends and the democratic process is respected.

We are encouraged by the steps that have been taken to bring peace to Mozambique and trust that no new obstacles will emerge to deny the people of this sister country the peace, stability and prosperity which they have been denied for so long.

Our common victory against the only system to be declared a crime against humanity since the defeat of Nazism is in sight. The historic need to end this crime as speedily and peacefully as possible requires that we, the peoples of the world, should remain as united as we have been and as committed as we have been to the cause of democracy, peace, human dignity and prosperity for all the people of South Africa.

Standing among you today, we continue to be moved by the selfless solidarity you have extended to our people. We are aware that by our common actions we have sought not only the liberation of the people of South Africa but also the extension of the frontiers of democracy, nonracialism, nonsexism and human solidarity throughout the world. Understanding that, we undertake before you all that we will not rest until the noble cause which unites us all emerges triumphant and a new South Africa fully rejoins the rest of the international community as a country which we can all be proud of.

United Nations 1994

Address to the 49th Session of the
General Assembly of the United Nations, New York,
3 October 1994.

It surely must be one of the great ironies of our age that this august Assembly is addressed, for the first time in its 49 years, by a South African head of state drawn from among the African majority of what is an African country. Future generations will find it strange in the extreme that it was only so late in the twentieth century that it was possible for our delegation to take its seat in the Assembly, recognised both by our people and the nations of the world as the legitimate representative of the people of our country.

It is indeed a most welcome thing that this august organisation will mark its fiftieth anniversary next year with the apartheid system having been vanquished and consigned to the past. That historic change has come about not least because of the great efforts in which the UN engaged to ensure the suppression of the apartheid crime against humanity.

Even as it was still in the process of establishing its institutions, the United Nations was confronted by the challenge of the accession to power of the party of apartheid domination in our country. Everything this system stood for represented the very opposite of all the noble purposes for which this organisation was established.

Because apartheid reduced and undermined the credibility of the UN as an effective international instrument to end racism and secure the fundamental human rights of all people, its establishment and consolidation constituted a brazen challenge to the very existence of this organisation.

The United Nations was born out of the titanic struggle against Nazism and fascism with their pernicious doctrines and practices of racial superiority and genocide. It therefore could not stand by while, in South Africa, a similar system was being established by a government which also had the temerity to claim representation

517

within the UN. We believe that it was indeed of great importance to the universal efficacy of and respect for the Declaration on Human Rights and the UN Charter, that the United Nations should have spurned the pleas of the apartheid regime that the gross violation of human rights in South Africa was a domestic matter of no legal or legitimate concern to the world body.

We stand here today to salute the United Nations Organisation and its member states, both singly and collectively, for joining forces with the masses of our people in a common struggle that has brought about our emancipation and pushed back the frontiers of racism.

The millions of our people say thank you and thank you again that the respect for your own dignity as human beings inspired you to act to ensure the restoration of our dignity as well. We have together traversed a course which we are convinced has strengthened human solidarity in general and reinforced the bonds of friendship between our people and the nations of the world. This dates back to the early days when India put the question of racism in South Africa on your agenda, to the moment when the world community, as represented here, could adopt consensus resolutions against apartheid, with none dissenting.

It was therefore with great joy that at our inauguration to the Presidency of our Republic we received, among others, such high and distinguished officials of this organisation as the Secretary-General, the President of the General Assembly and the Chairman of the Special Committee against Apartheid.

And so we have embarked on the road to the remaking of our country, basing ourselves both on the democratic Constitution which came into force on 27 April this year and the Reconstruction and Development Programme which has become the property of all our people.

Clearly, these documents would have no life unless the people give them life. The words printed in them must inspire common owner-ship by, and common allegiance of, all our people to the process and the results which these documents intend. For this to happen, as we propagate the vision these documents contain, we must, at the same time, engage in a historic effort of redefinition of ourselves as a new nation.

Our watchwords must be justice, peace, reconciliation and nation-building in the pursuit of a democratic, nonracial and nonsexist country. In all we do, we have to ensure the healing of the wounds inflicted on all our people across the great dividing line imposed on our society by centuries of colonialism and apartheid. We must ensure that colour, race and gender become only a God-given gift to each one of us and not an indelible mark or attribute that accords a special status to any. We must work for the day when we, as South Africans, see one another and interact with one another as equal human beings and as part of one nation united, rather than torn asunder, by its diversity.

The road we shall have to travel to reach this destination will by no means be easy. All of us know how stubbornly racism can cling to the mind and how deeply it can infect the human soul. Where it is sustained by the racial ordering of the material world, as is the case in our country, that stubbornness can multiply a hundred-fold. And yet however hard the battle will be, we will not surrender. Whatever the time it will take, we will not tire. The very fact that racism degrades both the perpetrator and the victim commands that, if we are true to our commitment to protect human dignity, we fight on until victory is achieved.

We firmly believe that we, who have particular experience of the destructive and anti-human force of racism, owe it to ourselves to centre our transformation on the creation of a truly nonracial society. Because we know racism so intimately, we must stand a good chance to develop and nurture its opposite. It will perhaps come to be that we who have harboured in our country the worst example of racism since the defeat of Nazism, will make a contribution to human civilisation by ordering our affairs in such a manner that we strike an effective and lasting blow against racism everywhere.

Some of the steps that we have taken already, including the establishment of a Government of National Unity, the orderly transformation of the institutions of state and the cultivation of a national consensus on the major issues of the day, have started us off on a correct footing, with regard to continuing the processes leading to the creation of the just society we have been speaking of.

Our political emancipation has also brought into sharp focus the urgent need to engage in struggle to secure our people's freedom from want, from hunger and from ignorance. We have written this on our banners that the society we seek to create must be a people-centred society. All its institutions and its resources must be dedicated to the pursuit of a better life for all our citizens. That better life must mean an end to poverty, to joblessness, homelessness and the despair that comes of deprivation. This is an end in itself because the happiness of the human being must, in any society, be an end in itself.

At the same time, we are intensely conscious of the fact that the stability of the democratic settlement itself and the possibility actually to create a nonracial and nonsexist society, depend on our ability to change the material conditions of life of our people so that they not only have the vote, but they have bread and work as well. We therefore return to the United Nations to make the commitment that as we undertook never to rest until the system of apartheid was defeated, so do we now undertake that we cannot rest while millions of our people suffer the pain and indignity of poverty in all its forms. At the same time, we turn once more to this world body to say we are going to need your continued support to achieve the goal of the betterment of the conditions of life of the people.

We are pleased and inspired that both the Secretary-General and the specialised agencies of the UN have taken up the development challenge in South Africa with the enthusiasm that they have. We believe that it is in the common interest that we sustain the common victory that we have scored in South Africa, and take it further by achieving success not only in politics but also in the socio-economic sphere.

It is perhaps common cause among us that everywhere on our globe there is an unmistakable process leading to the entrenchment of democractic systems of government. The empowerment of the ordinary people of our world freely to determine their destiny, unhindered by tyrants and dictators, is at the very heart of the reason for the existence of this Organisation. But it is equally true that hundreds of millions of these politically empowered masses are caught in the deathly trap of poverty, unable to live life in its fullness.

Out of all this are born social conflicts which produce insecurity and instability, civil and other wars that claim many lives, millions of desperate refugees and the destruction of the little wealth that poor countries are able to accumulate. Out of this cauldron are also born tyrants, dictators and demagogues who not only take away or restrict the rights of the people but also make it impossible to do the things that must be done to bring lasting prosperity to the people.

At the same time, the reality can no longer be ignored that we live in an interdependent world which is bound together to a common destiny. The very response of the international community to the challenge of apartheid confirmed this very point that we all understood, that as long as apartheid existed in South Africa, so long would the whole of humanity feel demeaned and degraded.

The United Nations understood this very well, that racism in our country could not but feed racism in other parts of the world as well. The universal struggle against apartheid was therefore not an act of charity arising out of pity for our people, but an affirmation of our common humanity. We believe that that act of affirmation requires that this organisation should once more turn its focused and sustained attention to the basics of everything that makes for a better world for all humanity. The elaboration of a new world order must, of necessity, centre on this world body. In it we should find the appropriate forum in which we can all participate to help determine the shape of the new world.

The four elements that will need to be knit together in fashioning that new universal reality are the issues of democracy, peace, prosperity and interdependence. The great challenge of our age to the United Nations Organisation is to answer the question – given the interdependence of the nations of the world, what is it that we can and must do to ensure that democracy, peace and prosperity prevail everywhere?

We are aware of the fact that the United Nations is addressing this question in many ways. And yet there can be no gainsaying the fact that such progress as we have made has been more by stealth rather than in the bold and determined fashion which the world crisis demands. Perhaps a new and forceful initiative is required. Such an initiative should inspire all of humanity because of the seriousness of its intent. It should also have a chance to succeed because it will have been underwritten by the commitment of the masses of the people in each member country to join hands with other nations, to address together the related issues of democracy, peace and prosperity in an interdependent world.

We are aware of the fact that the dictates of *realpolitik* militate against the speedy realisation of such an initiative. But we do believe that the reality of life and the realism of policy will, at some point, bring to the fore the fact that the delay we impose on ourselves today will only serve to increase the pressure on all of us to incorporate, within what we consider possible, a sustainable vision of a common world that will rise or fall together.

Undoubtedly, to inspire greater confidence in itself among all the member nations and to reflect better the impulse towards the democratisation of international relations, the UN will have to continue looking at itself to determine what restructuring of itself it should effect. This process must, naturally, impact, among others, on the structure and functioning of the Security Council and the peace-making and peacekeeping issues raised by the Secretary-General in his Agenda for Peace.

Democratic South Africa rejoins the world community of nations determined to play its role in helping to strengthen the United Nations and to contribute what it can to the furtherance of its purposes.

Among other things, we have this morning acceded to the Covenants and Conventions adopted by this organisation, which address various matters such as Economic, Social and Cultural Rights, Civil and Political Rights, and the Elimination of All Forms of Racial Discrimination, to say nothing of our irrevocable commitment to the realisation of the objectives contained in the Universal Declaration of Human Rights.

We are determined to play our full part in all processes that address the important question of the non-proliferation and destruction of weapons of mass destruction. Our government has also decided to become a signatory to the Convention on Prohibition and Restrictions on the Use of Certain Conventional Weapons.

In a similar vein, we shall not be found wanting in the quest for sustainable development that is in keeping with the Rio Declaration on the Environment and Development, as well as Agenda 21.

Equally, our own national interest dictates that we join forces with the UN and all its member states in the common struggle to contain and end the traffic in narcotics.

Even in constitutional terms we are committed to the advancement of the objective of the emancipation of women, through the creation of a nonsexist society. Apart from anything else, we are therefore actively engaged in the preparations for what we are convinced will be a successful Beijing Conference.

We are part of the region of Southern Africa and the continent of Africa. As members of the Southern African Development Community and the OAU, and an equal partner with other member states, we will play our role in the struggles of these organisations to build a continent and a region that will help to create for themselves and all humanity a common world of peace and prosperity.

Ours must surely become a continent free of such tragedies as those that have afflicted our own country, Rwanda, Somalia, Angola, Mozambique, Sudan and Liberia. Happily, the OAU is actively addressing this issue of peace and stability on our continent.

We are greatly encouraged that the countries of our region, faced with a crisis in Lesotho, acted together speedily and, with the co-operation of the government and people of that country, succeeded to demonstrate that together we have the will to defend democracy, peace and national reconciliation.

Furthermore, as members of the Non-Aligned Movement and the Group of 77, we are committed especially to the promotion of South-South co-operation and the strengthening of the voice of the poor and disadvantaged in the ordering of world affairs.

We would like to take this opportunity to express our appreciation to the members of the General Assembly for the speed and readiness with which they accepted the credentials of democratic South Africa, enabling us to participate in the work of the last General Assembly. We are pleased to note that this same spirit characterised the approach of other international organisations towards our new democracy, including the Commonwealth and the European Union.

We would like to close by congratulating you, Mr President, on your election to your high post and express our confidence that you will guide the work of the Assembly with the wisdom and sense of purpose for which we admire you.

The millions across our globe who stand expectant at the gates of hope look to this organisation to bring them peace, to bring them life, to bring them a life worth living. We pray that the new South Africa which you helped to bring into being and which you have so warmly welcomed among the community of nations will, in its own and in the wider interest, make its own contribution, however small, to the realisation of those hopes.

Our common humanity and the urgency of the knock on the door of this great edifice demand that we must attempt even the impossible.

United Nations 1995

Statement at the Special Commemorative Meeting of the General Assembly
on the occasion of the 50th Anniversary of the United Nations,
New York, 23 October 1995.

When distinguished leaders came together, half a century ago, to consign to the past a war that had pitted humanity against itself, the ruins and the smoke from the dying fires were the monument to what should not have been.

Fifty years after the formation of the United Nations, we meet to affirm our commitment to the founding ideal and the common desire to better the life of all human beings.

What challenges us, who define ourselves as statespersons, is the clarion call to dare to think that what we are about is people – the proverbial man and woman in the street. These, the poor, the hungry, the victims of petty tyrants, the objectives of policy, demand change.

What challenges us is to ensure that none should enjoy lesser rights, and none tormented because they are born different, hold contrary political views or pray to God in a different manner.

We come from Africa and South Africa on this historic occasion to pay tribute to that founding ideal, and to thank the United Nations for challenging, with us, a system that defined fellow humans as lesser beings.

The youth at whom we have directed most of our awareness campaign on this golden jubilee should marvel at the nobility of our intentions. They are also bound to wonder why it should be that poverty still pervades the greater part of the globe; that wars continue to rage; and that many in positions of power and privilege pursue cold-hearted philosophies which terrifyingly proclaim: I am not your brother's keeper! For no one, in the North or the South, can escape the cold fact that we are a single humanity.

At the end of the Cold War, the poor had hoped that all humanity would earn a peace dividend, enabling this organisation to address an expectation it was born to address. And they challenge us today to ensure their security not only in peace, but also in prosperity. The changed world circumstances permit of neither the continued maldistribution of resources, nor the related maldistribution of decision-making power within this organisation itself.

Indeed, the United Nations has to reassess its role, redefine its profile and reshape its structures. It should truly reflect the diversity of our universe and ensure equity among the nations in the exercise of power within the system of international relations, in general, and the Security Council, in particular. We raise this matter to make the fundamental point that the agenda of the next century, and the programme of action to promote it, can only be true to the purposes of this organisation if they are set by all of us. We must, without delay, constitute a new leadership for the new age, and bring sunshine into the hearts of billions, including women, the disabled and children!

Circumstances may tempt us to bend to the pressures of *realpolitik*. However, like the founders, we are faced with the task of ensuring the convergence of word and deed. Unlike them, the obstacles we face are fewer and the conditions more auspicious. As the United Nations matures into the new millennium, it is called upon to facilitate the birth of a new world order of peace, democracy and prosperity for all. Thus we can honour the memory of those who perished in pursuit of the founding ideal; and protect future generations from the pestilences of war, hunger, disease, ignorance and environmental degradation.

The time is now!

United Nations 1998

Address to the 53rd Session of the General Assembly
of the United Nations, New York,
21 September 1998.

May I take this opportunity as President of the Republic of South
Africa and as Chairperson of the Non-Aligned Movement to extend
to you [Didier Opertti Badan] our sincere congratulations on your
election to the high post of President of the General Assembly.

You will be presiding over this august Assembly of the nations of
the world at a time when its deliberations and decisions will be of
the greatest consequence to the continuous striving of humanity at
last to achieve global peace and prosperity.

The Non-Aligned Movement, as well as my own country, which
is a proud member of that Movement, invest great trust in this organisation that it will discharge its responsibilities to all nations especially
at this critical period of its existence.

Quite appropriately, this 53rd General Assembly will be remembered through the ages as the moment at which we marked and
celebrated the 50th Anniversary of the adoption of the Universal
Declaration of Human Rights.

Born in the aftermath of the defeat of the Nazi and fascist crime
against humanity, this Declaration held high the hope that all our
societies would, in future, be built on the foundations of the glorious
vision spelt out in each of its clauses.

For those who had to fight for their emancipation, such as ourselves who, with your help, had to free ourselves from the criminal
apartheid system, the Universal Declaration of Human Rights served
as the vindication of the justice of our cause. At the same time, it
constituted a challenge to us that our freedom, once achieved, should
be dedicated to the implementation of the perspectives contained in
the Declaration.

Today, we celebrate the fact that this historic document has
survived a turbulent five decades, which have seen some of the most

extraordinary developments in the evolution of human society. These include the collapse of the colonial system, the passing of a bipolar world, breathtaking advances in science and technology, and the entrenchment of the complex process of globalisation.

And yet, at the end of it all, the human beings who are the subject of the Universal Declaration of Human Rights continue to be afflicted by wars and violent conflicts. They have, as yet, not attained their freedom from fear of death that would be brought about by the use of weapons of mass destruction as well as conventional arms. Many are still unable to exercise the fundamental and inalienable democratic rights that would enable them to participate in the determination of the destiny of their countries, nations, families and children and to protect themselves from tyranny and dictatorship.

The very right to be human is denied every day to hundreds of millions of people as a result of poverty, the unavailability of basic necessities such as food, jobs, water and shelter, education, health care and a healthy environment.

The failure to achieve the vision contained in the Universal Declaration of Human Rights finds dramatic expression in the contrast between wealth and poverty which characterises the divide between the countries of the North and the countries of the South and within individual countries in all hemispheres. It is made especially poignant and challenging by the fact that this coexistence of wealth and poverty, the perpetuation of the practice of the resolution of inter- and intra-state conflicts by war and the denial of the democratic rights of many across the world, all result from the acts of commission and omission particularly by those who occupy positions of leadership in politics, in the economy and in other spheres of human activity.

What I am trying to say is that all these social ills which constitute an offence against the Universal Declaration of Human Rights are not a pre-ordained result of the forces of nature or the product of a curse of the deities. They are the consequence of decisions which men and women take or refuse to take, all of whom will not hesitate to pledge their devoted support for the vision conveyed in the Universal Declaration of Human Rights.

This Declaration was proclaimed as universal precisely because the founders of this organisation and the nations of the world who joined hands to fight the scourge of fascism, including many who still had to achieve their own emancipation, understood this clearly that our human world was an interdependent whole. Necessarily, the values of happiness, justice, human dignity, peace and prosperity have a universal application because each people and every individual is entitled to them. Similarly, no people can truly say it is blessed with happiness, peace and prosperity where others, as human as itself, continue to be afflicted with misery, armed conflict and terrorism and deprivation.

Thus can we say that the challenge posed by the next 50 years of the Universal Declaration of Human Rights, by the next century whose character it must help to fashion, consists in whether humanity, and especially those who will occupy positions of leadership, will have the courage to ensure that, at last, we build a human world consistent with the provisions of that historic Declaration and other human rights instruments that have been adopted since 1948.

Immediately, a whole range of areas of conflict confronts us, in Africa, Europe and Asia. All of us are familiar with these, which range from the Democratic Republic of Congo, Angola and Sudan on my own continent, to the Balkans in Europe and Afghanistan, Tajikistan and Sri Lanka in Asia.

Clearly, this organisation and especially the Security Council, acting together with people of goodwill in the countries and areas concerned, has a responsibility to act decisively to contribute to the termination of these destructive conflicts. Continuously, we have to fight to defeat the primitive tendency towards the glorification of arms, the adulation of force, born of the illusion that injustice can be perpetuated by the capacity to kill, or that disputes are necessarily best resolved by resort to violent means.

As Africans, we are grateful to the Secretary-General for the contribution he has made to help us find the way towards ending violent strife on our continent. We have taken heed of his report, which will reinforce our efforts to banish war from our shores.

The very first resolution of the General Assembly, adopted in January 1946, sought to address the challenge of 'the elimination from national armaments of atomic weapons and all other major weapons adaptable to mass destruction'. We must face the fact that after countless initiatives and resolutions, we still do not have concrete and generally accepted proposals supported by a clear commitment by the nuclear-weapons states to the speedy, final and total elimination of nuclear weapons and nuclear weapons capabilities.

We take this opportunity to salute our sister Republic of Brazil for its decision to accede to the Nuclear Non-Proliferation Treaty, and urge all others that have not done so to follow this excellent example.

In an honest attempt to contribute to the definition of the systematic and progressive steps required to eliminate these weapons and the threat of annihilation which they pose, South Africa together with Brazil, Egypt, Ireland, Mexico, New Zealand, Slovenia and Sweden will be submitting a draft resolution to the First Committee for consideration by this Assembly. This is appropriately titled: 'Towards a Nuclear Weapon Free World: The Need for a New Agenda'. I call on all members of the United Nations seriously to consider this important resolution and to give it their support.

We must ask the question, which might sound naive to those who have elaborated sophisticated arguments to justify their refusal to eliminate these terrible and terrifying weapons of mass destruction – why do they need them anyway? In reality, no rational answer can be advanced to explain in a satisfactory manner what, in the end, is the consequence of Cold War inertia and an attachment to the use of the threat of brute force to assert the primacy of some states over others.

Urgent steps are also required to arrive at a just and permanent peace in the Middle East, on the basis of the realisation of the legitimate aspirations of the people of Palestine and respect for the independence and security of all the states of this important region.

We also look forward to the resolution of the outstanding issues of Western Sahara and East Timor, convinced that it is possible to take these matters off the world agenda on the basis of settlements that meet the interests of all the peoples concerned.

Similarly, we would like to salute the bold steps taken by the Government of the Federal Republic of Nigeria, this supremely important country of Africa, to enable it to return to democratic rule and a system of governance directed at serving the interests of all its people.

Together, we are also faced with the scourges of drug abuse and the illicit traffic in narcotics, organised transnational crime and international terrorism. We strongly support the measures adopted or being discussed by the United Nations to deal with these challenges and commit our country and government to co-operate fully in all regional and international initiatives to ensure that the peoples of the world, including our own, are spared the destructive impact of these crimes.

The world is gripped by an economic crisis which, as President Clinton said in this city only a week ago, has plunged 'millions into sudden poverty and disrupt[ed] and disorient[ed] the lives of ordinary people' and brought 'deep, personal disappointments [to] tens of millions of people around the world.'

'Recent press reports', President Clinton went on, 'have described an entire generation working its way into the middle class over 25 years, then being plummeted into poverty within a matter of months. The stories are heartbreaking – doctors and nurses forced to live in the lobby of a closed hospital; middle class families who owned their own homes, sent their children to college, traveled abroad, now living by selling their possessions.'

He said 'fast-moving currents [in the world economy] have brought or aggravated problems in Russia and Asia. They threaten emerging economies from Latin America to South Africa', and he spoke of 'sacrific[ing] lives in the name of economic theory'.

President Clinton further recognised that, in his words, 'with a quarter of the world's population in declining growth we [the United States] cannot forever be an oasis of prosperity. Growth at home [in the US] depends upon growth abroad.'

I have quoted the President of the United States at this length both because he is correct and because he is the leader of the most powerful country in the world.

Accordingly, we would like to believe that with the problem facing all humanity, and especially the poor, having thus been recognised, courage will not desert the powerful when it comes to determining the correct course to be taken, and following this course, to address the challenge that has been identified.

The tragedy President Clinton describes goes far beyond the sudden impoverishment of the middle class to which he correctly refers. Poverty has been and is the condition of the daily existence of even larger numbers of ordinary working people.

Paradoxically, the challenge of poverty across the globe has been brought into sharp focus by the fact of the destructive 'fast movements of currents' of wealth from one part of the world to the other. Put starkly, we have a situation in which the further accumulation of wealth, rather than contributing to the improvement of the quality of life of all humanity, is generating poverty at a frighteningly accelerated pace.

The imperative to act on this urgent, life and death matter can no longer be ignored. The central challenge to ensure that the countries of the South gain access to the productive resources that have accumulated within the world economy should not be avoided by seeking to apportion as much blame as possible to the poor.

Clearly, all relevant matters will have to be addressed, including such issues as greater inflows of long-term capital, terms of trade, debt cancellation, technology transfers, human resource development, emancipation of women and development of the youth, the elimination of poverty, the HIV/Aids epidemic, environmental protection and the strengthening of financial and other institutions relevant to sustained economic growth and development.

Fortunately, the matter is no longer in dispute that serious work will also have to be done to restructure the multilateral financial and economic institutions so that they address the problems of the modern world economy and become responsive to the urgent needs of the poor of the world. Similarly, this very organisation, including its important Security Council, must itself go through its own process of reformation so that it serves the interests of the peoples of the world, in keeping with the purposes for which it was established.

The issues we have mentioned were discussed in a comprehensive manner at the Twelfth Summit Meeting of the Non-Aligned Movement held in the city of Durban, South Africa, earlier this month. I am privileged to commend the decisions of this important meeting to the General Assembly and the United Nations as a whole, including the Durban Declaration, which the Summit adopted unanimously. I am certain that the decisions adopted by the Non-Aligned Movement will greatly assist this organisation in its work and further enhance the contribution of the countries of the South to the solution of the problems that face the nations of the world, both rich and poor.

This is probably the last time I will have the honour to stand at this podium to address the General Assembly. Born as the First World War came to a close and departing from public life as the world marks half-a-century of the Universal Declaration of Human Rights, I have reached that part of the long walk when the opportunity is granted, as it should be to all men and women, to retire to some rest and tranquillity in the village of my birth.

As I sit in Qunu and grow as ancient as its hills, I will continue to entertain the hope that there has emerged a cadre of leaders in my own country and region, on my continent and in the world, which will not allow that any should be denied their freedom as we were; that any should be turned into refugees as we were; that any should be condemned to go hungry as we were; that any should be stripped of their human dignity as we were. I will continue to hope that Africa's Renaissance will strike deep roots and blossom forever, without regard to the changing seasons.

Were all these hopes to translate into a realisable dream and not a nightmare to torment the soul of the aged, then will I, indeed, have peace and tranquillity. Then would history and the billions throughout the world proclaim that it was right that we dreamt and that we toiled to give life to a workable dream.

African Unity

Statement at the Organisation for African Unity Meeting
of Heads of State and Government, Tunis,
13–15 June 1994.

In the distant days of antiquity, a Roman sentenced this African city to death: 'Carthage must be destroyed (*Carthago delenda est*).'

And Carthage was destroyed. Today we wander among its ruins; only our imagination and historical records enable us to experience its magnificence. Only our African being makes it possible for us to hear the piteous cries of the victims of the vengeance of the Roman Empire. And yet we can say this, that all human civilisation rests on foundations such as the ruins of the African city of Carthage. These architectural remains, like the pyramids of Egypt, the sculptures of the ancients kingdoms of Ghana and Mali and Benin, like the temples of Ethiopia, the Zimbabwe ruins and the rock paintings of the Kgalagadi and Namib deserts, all speak of Africa's contribution to the formation of the condition of civilisation.

But in the end, Carthage was destroyed. During the long interregnum, the children of Africa were carted away as slaves. Our lands became the property of other nations, our resources a source of enrichment for other peoples and our kings and queens mere servants of foreign powers. In the end, we were held out as the outstanding example of the beneficiaries of charity, because we became the permanent victims of famine, of destructive conflicts and of the pestilence of the natural world. On our knees because history, society and nature had defeated us, we could be nothing but beggars. What the Romans had sought with the destruction of Carthage had been achieved.

But the ancient pride of the peoples of our continent asserted itself and gave us hope in the form of giants such as Queen Regent Labotsibeni of Swaziland, Mohammed V of Morocco, Gamal Abdel Nasser of Egypt, Kwame Nkrumah of Ghana, Murtala Mohammed of Nigeria, Patrice Lumumba of Zaire, Amilcar Cabral of Guinea

533

Bissau, Agostinho Neto of Angola, Eduardo Mondlane and Samora Machel of Mozambique, Seretse Khama of Botswana, WEB Du Bois and Martin Luther King of America, Marcus Garvey of Jamaica, Albert Luthuli and Oliver Tambo of South Africa. By their deeds, by the struggles they led, these and many other patriots said to us that neither Carthage nor Africa had been destroyed. They conveyed the message that the long interregnum of humiliation was over. It is in their honour that we stand here today. It is a tribute to their heroism that, today, we are able to address this august gathering.

The titanic effort that has brought liberation to South Africa, and ensured the total liberation of Africa, constitutes an act of redemption for the black people of the world. It is a gift of emancipation also to those who, because they were white, imposed on themselves the heavy burden of assuming the mantle of rulers of all humanity. It says to all who will listen and understand that, by ending the apartheid barbarity that was the offspring of European colonisation, Africa has, once more, contributed to the advance of human civilisation and further expanded the frontiers of liberty everywhere.

We are here today not to thank you, dear brothers and sisters, because such thanks would be misplaced among fellow combatants. We are here to salute and congratulate you for a most magnificent and historical victory over an inhuman system whose very name was tyranny, injustice and bigotry.

When the history of our struggle is written, it will tell a glorious tale of African solidarity, of Africans' adherence to principles. It will tell a moving story of the sacrifices that the peoples of our continent made, to ensure that that intolerable insult to human dignity, the apartheid crime against humanity, became a thing of the past. It will speak of the contributions to freedom — whose value is as measureless as the gold beneath the soil of our country — the contribution which all of Africa made, from the shores of the Mediterranean Sea in the north, to the confluence of the Indian and Atlantic Oceans in the south.

Africa shed her blood and surrendered the lives of her children so that all her children could be free. She gave of her limited wealth and resources so that all of Africa should be liberated. She opened her heart of hospitality and her head so full of wise counsel, so that we should emerge victorious. A million times, she put her hand to the plough that has now dug up the encrusted burden of oppression accumulated for centuries.

The total liberation of Africa from foreign and white minority rule has now been achieved. Our colleagues who have served with distinction on the OAU liberation committee have already carried out the historical task of winding up this institution, which we shall always remember as a frontline fighter for the emancipation of the people of our continent.

Finally, at this summit meeting in Tunis, we shall remove from our agenda the consideration of the question of Apartheid South Africa. Where South Africa appears on the agenda again, let it be because we want to discuss what its contribution shall be to the making of the new African Renaissance. Let it be because we want to discuss what materials it will supply for the rebuilding of the African city of Carthage.

One epoch with its historic tasks has come to an end. Surely, another must commence with its own challenges. Africa cries out for a new birth; Carthage awaits the restoration of its glory. If freedom was the crown which the fighters of liberation sought to place on the head of mother Africa, let the upliftment, the happiness, prosperity and comfort of her children be the jewel of the crown.

There can be no dispute among us that we must bend every effort to rebuild the African economies. You, your excellencies, have discussed this matter many times and elaborated the ideas whose implementation would lead us to success. The fundamentals of what needs to be done are known to all of us. Not least among these are the need to address the reality that Africa continues to be a net exporter of capital and suffers from deteriorating terms of trade. Our capacity to be self-reliant, to find the internal resources to generate sustained development, remains very limited.

Quite correctly, we have also spent time discussing the equally complex questions that bear on the nature and quality of governance. These, too, are central to our capacity to produce the better life which our people demand and deserve. In this regard, we surely must face the matter squarely that where there is something wrong in the manner in which we govern ourselves, it must be said that the fault is not in our stars, but in ourselves that we are ill-governed.

Tribute is due to the great thinkers of our continent who have been and are trying to move all of us to understand the intimate interconnection between the great issues of our day – of peace, stability, democracy, human rights, co-operation and development. Even as we speak, Rwanda stands out as a stern and severe rebuke to all of us for having failed to address these interrelated matters. As a result of that, a terrible slaughter of the innocent is taking place in front of our very eyes. Thus do we give reason to the peoples of the world to say of Africa that she will never know stability and peace, that she will never experience development and growth, that her children will forever be condemned to poverty and dehumanisation and that we shall for ever be knocking on somebody's door pleading for a slice of bread.

We know it is a matter of fact that we have it in ourselves as Africans to change all this. We must, in action, assert our will to do so. We must, in action, say that there is no obstacle big enough to stop us from bringing about a new African Renaissance.

We are happy to commit South Africa to the achievement of these goals. We have entered this eminent African organisation and rejoined the African community of nations inspired by the desire to join hands with all the countries of our continent as equal partners.

It will never happen again that our country should seek to dominate another through force of arms, economic might or subversion. We are determined to remain true to the vision which you held out for South Africa as you joined the offensive to destroy the system of apartheid. The vision you shared with us was one of a nonracial society, whose very being would assert the ancient African values of respect for every person and commitment to the elevation of human dignity, regardless of colour or race.

What we all aimed for was a South Africa which would succeed in banishing the ethnic and national conflicts which continue to plague our continent. What we, together, hoped to see, was a new South Africa freed of conflict among its people and the violence that has taken such a heavy toll, freed of the threat of the civil strife that has turned millions of people into refugees both inside and outside our countries. We all prayed and sacrificed to bring about a South Africa that we could hold out as a true example of the democracy, equality and justice for all, which the apartheid system was constructed and intended to deny.

The vision you shared with us was one in which we would use the resources of our country to create a society in which all our people would be emancipated from the scourges of poverty, disease, ignorance and backwardness. The objective we all pursued was the creation of a South Africa that would be a good neighbour and an equal partner with all the countries of our continent, one which would use its abilities and potentialities to help advance the common struggle to secure Africa's rightful place within the world economic and political system.

Thus must we build on the common victory of the total emancipation of Africa to obtain new successes for our continent as a whole. We are ready to contribute what we can to help end the genocide that is taking place in Rwanda and bring peace to that troubled sister country. We also join the distinguished heads of state and government and leaders of delegations in urging a speedy implementation of the OAU and UN decisions aimed at resolving the question of Western Sahara. We extend our best wishes to the leaders and people of Angola in the fervent hope that the process of negotiations in which they are engaged will, as a matter of urgency, bring about the permanent and just peace which the people of that country so richly deserve. Equally, we would like to express our deep-felt wish that the necessary measures will be taken by all concerned to guarantee the success of the peace processes in Mozambique and Liberia, to end the war in the Sudan and protect democracy and stability in Lesotho. We also appeal to the world community to respond in a sensitive and generous manner to the famine that threatens the peoples of East Africa.

Our delegation is also happy to announce that we have had the honour to pay the subscription that the OAU has levied for South Africa. In addition, and as a token of the commitment of the people of our country to support Africa's peace efforts, we are glad to inform the Assembly that we have also made an additional contribution of R1 million to the OAU fund for peace.

We congratulate you [Zine El Abidine Ben Ali] on your election as the current chairman of the OAU and thank you, your government and people for the extraordinary welcome you have extended to us. We are indeed glad to be here because Tunisia was among the first countries on our continent to respond to our appeal for help when we were obliged to take up arms to fight for our liberation. We thank our brother, President Hosni Mubarak, for the outstanding work he did during his chairpersonship, including the direction of the efforts of the OAU as it helped us to deal with political violence in our country and ensure the holding of free and fair elections. We salute too, our Secretary-General, HE Salim Ahmed Salim, the OAU Secretariat, the OAU Head of Mission to South Africa, Ambassador Joe Legwaila, the heads of state and government and the people of our continent who helped us successfully to walk our last mile of the difficult road to freedom.

To you all, we would like to say that your sacrifices and your efforts have not been in vain. Freedom for Africa is your reward. Your actions entitled you to be saluted as the heroes and heroines of our time. On your shoulders rests the responsibility to restore to our continent its dignity. We are certain that you will prevail over the currents that originate from the past, and ensure that the interregnum of humiliation symbolised by, among others, the destruction of Carthage, is indeed consigned to the past, never to return.

God bless Africa.

African Peace

Speech on accepting the Africa Peace Award,
Durban, 18 March 1995.

Last weekend at the United Nations Social Summit, leaders of Southern African states had the opportunity to consult on matters regional. Even in those exalted surroundings of global discourse, the stark reality was obvious to us that charity should begin at home.

The consultation was made urgent by our concern over the situation in the region. On the one hand, the fact that there is relative peace and stability is heartening. But we are all too aware that peace is more than just the absence of war. The dark clouds still hovering above our landscape, particularly in Lesotho and Angola, are matters of serious concern. Thus we sought to examine how we could further co-ordinate our efforts to bring about lasting peace.

We were due to have a summit of these leaders today in Harare to take this discussion forward. But it had to be postponed due to circumstances beyond our control.

I have given this background because I think these matters are at the heart of our august gathering today. One could go further to refer to political conflict in other parts of Africa; or even the deaths, though on a much smaller scale, that continue to plague this province of KwaZulu-Natal.

This is a reminder to us all, closeted in these beautiful surroundings, that we shouldn't for a moment forget the mothers and fathers, the children and grandchildren who yearn for our urgent intervention to bring them more than just a respite from war. They deserve lasting peace and lasting security. Only in this way shall we deserve the accolades often heaped on us as leaders.

For me, this occasion is laden with emotion. Certainly when any award is granted, it does evoke strong feeling. But that feeling is multiplied many-fold when the award is indigenous and carries the mantle of Mother Africa.

I therefore wish, from the bottom of my heart, to thank the

trustees and management of the African Centre for the Constructive Resolution of Disputes (Accord) for the honour bestowed on me. I wish particularly to express my gratitude to the distinguished foreign dignitaries who have travelled long distances to share this moment with us.

The principles underpinning Accord's operations are the very ideals for which humanity has striven for centuries: peaceful resolution of conflict, human rights and good governance. Weaving all these ideals together is the vexing issue of security. For, it is not merely good logic but the reality of life that, in the end, society's freedom from hunger, ignorance and disease is more often than not the dividing line between war and peace. The pursuit of the collective wellbeing of humanity, to ensure that all persons live life to the full, is an ideal whose time has come.

Humanity is suing for a new world order, premised, above everything else, on this objective. The task is daunting and the obstacles unlimited. But that quest has so captured the imagination of peoples that it can no longer be concealed behind fancy rhetoric.

Africa deserves all these rights. Its children deserve as much of a regular diet of protein as any other. They have the right to computers and instruments of modern communications. Like children elsewhere, they are born to play with gay abandon, confident about a bright future.

Certainly, colonialism and the selfish ordering of world affairs – past and present – have undermined Africa's development. And it is only just that Africa should demand her fair share of world resources; that we should challenge the untenable global division of power and wealth. But Africa has long traversed past a mindset that seeks to heap all blame on the past and on others. The era of renaissance we are entering is, and should be, based on our own efforts as Africans to change Africa's conditions for the better. If Africa's children, like all other children, should shelter a light of hope in their hearts about what life can offer, then we, as their parents and leaders, deserve to be judged by the same standards as anyone else.

In this regard, we face the urgent task of deepening the culture of human rights on the continent. We are called upon to ensure that our social structures reflect the will of the people. Our approach to issues of political power should proceed from the premise that it is an expression of popular will, and not a mysterious force wielded by a chosen few. This applies to all African states. It is even more pertinent to those states which, by the sheer size of their population and the attention accorded them by world media, are seen as standard-bearers of Africa's political culture and mores.

From this flow many challenges. For instance, how do we ensure that civil society in its various forms becomes an active participant in formulation and implementation of policy? How do we, individually and collectively, utilise rationally and to maximum effect the resources the continent possesses? How do we eliminate the scourge of political and religious intolerance?

These, we are aware, are questions that Africa has firmly and boldly put on the agenda. Our confidence in the continent as a whole, our challenge to the malaise of Afro-pessimism that seems to grip developed countries from time to time, is that Africa is set on a course to ensure thoroughgoing democracy, good governance, peace and all-round security for its peoples.

We dare say to the world: recognise the historical millstone that weighs around our necks; acknowledge and assist us to deal with the depths from which we have to launch our revival; but do not judge us by lower human standards.

The continent's challenge is one that equally faces South Africa. For, behind the glitter of city lights, the halo of a relatively advanced technology and the smoothness of paved roads, lies the reality of a rate of illiteracy that is among the highest on the continent, poverty, homelessness, landlessness and malnutrition that beset millions.

As such, if we appreciate the efforts of Africa's leaders to re-order the continent's affairs for the better, it is because they underpin our own humble endeavours. We are fully conscious that our programme to build a better life for all our people will benefit from a continent and sub-continent redefining themselves, as much as it will contribute to that effort.

We can only succeed if we work together, as we worked together to succeed against apartheid. And for the enormous sacrifices that Africa endured to complete her emancipation, we in South Africa shall forever be proud and grateful. Never again shall South Africa be the fountainhead of conflict in the region and further afield. Never again shall our country be the source of armaments used to suppress communities and to wage aggressive wars against neighbours. Never again shall we spend our people's resources to develop weapons of mass destruction.

Democratic South Africa is committed to full equality in our relations with our neighbours and all other nations. In promoting peace and preventing conflict, South Africa will work hand-in-hand with our neighbours and through multilateral forums such as the SADC and the OAU. In this regard, we welcome and are part of the OAU initiative for an early-warning mechanism and the shift from conflict management to conflict prevention.

However, we do recognise that while governments have an important role to play to foster a culture of peace and tolerance, it is crucial that civil society takes an active part in these efforts. It is for this reason that we appreciate the Accord initiative.

Perhaps the central message of this occasion is that we should all help develop a network of all such initiatives on the continent. Through such a continental network, we can strengthen Africa's monitoring capacity, research on how to prevent and eliminate conflict, and impart the skills of mediation. This would draw on work of this kind that is already being done in many parts of Africa by research centres, universities and other institutions. As such, the continent could develop creative and effective peace and human rights instruments, characterised by co-operation between governments and civil society.

It is with this sentiment that I humbly accept the Africa Peace Award. May peace and prosperity reign on the African continent.

Solidarity of Peace-Loving Nations

Speech by Nelson Mandela at the award of a National Order to
Prince Bandar bin Sultan (bin Abdul Aziz al Saud),
Saudi Arabian Ambassador to the US, and to Jakes Gerwel, Cape Town,
11 May 1999.

We are very happy to welcome so many of you here this afternoon to join us in this award ceremony. It is not often that we convene such a special ceremony for the award of national orders. But what we are celebrating has special significance.

Not only are we honouring rare and exceptional achievement by two accomplished individuals. We are also celebrating the vindication of an approach to solving problems that is based on the common humanity of all people everywhere. We take joy in the strengthening of our hopes that the peaceful resolution of conflict can become the normal approach.

We are also, thankfully, recording an event that confirms the efficacy and enhances the authority of the United Nations as the world body responsible for collective action in pursuit of world peace.

These may sound large claims to be making, especially if they appear to be the achievements merely of two individuals. There is no doubt that but for the efforts and the qualities of the two persons we are honouring as best we can, we would not today be in a situation in which two Libyan men would be awaiting trial in a Scottish Court in the Netherlands, with the hope of a fair hearing; in which the families of victims of the Lockerbie disaster could take some comfort from the fact that the judicial process is under way; and in which the Libyan people would be freed from the suffering inflicted on them by years of sanctions and the insecurity engendered by the memory of armed attack on their capital.

It is right that we should honour the two envoys. Their exceptional achievement required an exceptional combination of skills and virtues: discretion, modesty, patience, a commitment to justice, and an intellectual and moral depth that both extends trust and engenders it in a situation marked by years of conflict and tension. But we also know that what they did was made difficult but at the same time possible by the international environment within which they worked. That environment is defined on the one hand by institutions and norms that promote justice and peace, and on the other by entrenched and long-standing divisions.

If we praise their discretion, it is in the knowledge that this was an issue engaging the most powerful interests and bringing into play emotions and attitudes that have been divisively deployed in world affairs. Intense international media attention constantly solicited them to occupy a public place on the world stage. 'Lockerbie' and 'Libya' had become landmarks in the media landscape of a world divided between good and evil, the reasonable and the irrational, saints and demons.

Indeed, should we not as an international community now step back, in the wake of the resolution of the Lockerbie issue, to ask ourselves how well we, and the means of communication which we have created, are serving world peace in the portrayal of others, in particular religions of the world different to those we may share in?

Should we perhaps ask whether the portrayal in much of the world's media of Islam in particular may not be assisting in the creation of new generic divides in the post-Cold War world?

As we witness the inhuman acts of ethnic cleansing in Yugoslavia, we may be reminded of how the way we speak about one another can influence behaviour. And as we watch the destructive bombing of the capital of a sovereign country may we not ask whether the communications media are not now lending themselves to the prolongation of a conflict whose resolution should urgently be sought in negotiations and through the United Nations?

We inhibit the peaceful and negotiated resolution of conflicts not only by the extent to which we demonise one another. We do so also by the degree to which we separate, on the one hand, the processes of politics and international affairs and on the other hand, the moral relations between ourselves as human beings.

Our envoys succeeded because they acted upon certain fundamental moral premises: that men and women must be presumed to be of good intention unless proven otherwise; that there is in all of us a common humanity guided by the same fears and hopes, the same sensibilities and aspirations. That being so, talking to one another and discussion must be the prelude to the resolution of conflicts.

South Africa and her people suffered for generations because those with power refused to talk on this basis to those whom they oppressed.

When we dehumanise and demonise our opponents we abandon the possibility of peacefully resolving our differences, and seek to justify violence against them.

In the achievement of our two envoys, African and Arab, is embodied also the fact that peoples who were prevented by superior force from determining their own destiny, have reclaimed that dignity, and are once again exerting a profound influence upon world affairs and the course of human history. It is a significant contribution to the renaissance of the inter-linked African continent and Arab world.

In particular, it accords with the perspective of those who, having achieved their liberation with the collective support of others, are all the firmer in their conviction that the challenges facing the world require collective solutions and a consistently multilateral approach. What we are recognising today includes the fact that what was done was done in loyal and disciplined service of the United Nations Secretary-General.

As we honour two individuals for their accomplishment, we also acknowledge three heads of state or government who were prepared to take that extra step to resolve a matter that has occupied the world for far too long, even though the common sense of compromise was always clearly available.

Current developments on our continent and elsewhere in the world may often seem discouraging. But the actions of these statesmen in this matter signal the hope that the leaders who take us into the next millennium will be men and women who put the well-being of humankind in its entirety above sectarian and narrow national considerations.

Our tribute to them must be coupled to a salute to the Secretary-General of our world body. He has demonstrated in his comparatively short period in office a remarkable ability to mobilise the goodwill and capacity of others in peace-making efforts. In this demonstration that we are people through other people, he has brought his African heritage to the centre of international affairs.

This is a day to celebrate the award of South African national orders. Let us celebrate, through these orders, our unity as a nation at peace with itself and the international solidarity of peace-loving nations.

CONTRIBUTORS

Kofi A Annan is Secretary-General of the United Nations.

Kader Asmal, Member of Parliament, is Minister of Education for the Republic of South Africa.

David Chidester, Chair of Religious Studies at the University of Cape Town, is a research fellow in the Social Cohesion and Integration Research Programme of the Human Sciences Research Council.

William J Clinton is the 42nd President of the United States.

Bill Cosby is a comedian, actor, author, and patron of a host of charitable, social service, and civil rights initiatives.

GJ Gerwel, Director-General in the Office of the President during Nelson Mandela's administration, is Chancellor of Rhodes University and Chairperson of the Board of the Human Sciences Research Council.

Adrian Hadland is a chief research specialist in the Social Cohesion and Integration Research Programme of the Human Sciences Research Council and author of a biography of Nelson Mandela to be published in 2003.

Wilmot James is Executive Director of the Social Cohesion and Integration Research Programme of the Human Sciences Research Council and Trustee of the Ford Foundation of New York.

James A Joseph, former US Ambassador to South Africa, is Professor of the Practice of Public Policy Studies and Executive Director of the United States-Southern African Center for Leadership and Public Values at Duke University.

Ahmed Kathrada, who was imprisoned on Robben Island with Nelson Mandela, is Chairperson of the Board of the Robben Island Museum.

Graça Machel, former Education Minister of Mozambique, is Chancellor of the University of Cape Town and the United Nations

University of Peace, member of many international boards, and head of the Global Leadership Initiative, which is part of the Global Movement for Children. She is the wife of Nelson Mandela.

Miriam Makeba, singer and recording artist, is the cultural ambassador for the Republic of South Africa.

Fintan O'Toole is a writer, critic and columnist with *The Irish Times*.

Cyril Ramaphosa, former Secretary-General of the African National Congress, chief negotiator for the ANC, and chairperson of the Constitutional Assembly, is Chairperson of Millennium Consolidated Investments.

Mamphela Ramphele, former Vice-Chancellor of the University of Cape Town, is a Managing Director at the World Bank, Washington, DC, with special responsibility for Human Development.

Albie Sachs is a Justice on the Constitutional Court of the Republic of South Africa.

Olive Shisana, Director-General of the Department of Health during President Mandela's administration, is Executive Director of the Social Aspects of HIV/Aids and Health Research Programme of the Human Sciences Research Council.

F van Zyl Slabbert, former leader of the parliamentary opposition in apartheid South Africa, is a businessman, lecturer, political consultant, and Director of Khula Consulting.

Desmond Tutu, Archbishop Emeritus, served as Chairperson of South Africa's Truth and Reconciliation Commission.

INDEX

549